Canadian Families

Third Edition

diversity
conflict
and change

Nancy Mandell
York University

Ann Duffy
Brock University

THOMSON

NELSON

Australia   Canada   Mexico   Singapore   Spain   United Kingdom   United States

THOMSON

NELSON

Canadian Families: Diversity, Conflict and Change
Third Edition
by Nancy Mandell and Ann Duffy

Editorial Director and Publisher:
Evelyn Veitch

Executive Editor:
Joanna Cotton

Acquisitions Editor:
Cara Yarzab

Marketing Manager:
Lenore Taylor

Developmental Editor:
Glen Herbert

Permissions Coordinator:
Nicola Winstanley

Production Editor:
Julie van Veen

Copy Editor and Proofreader:
Erin Moore

Indexer:
Jin Tan

Senior Production Coordinator:
Hedy Sellers

Creative Director:
Angela Cluer

Interior Design:
Aaron Benson

Cover Design and Interior Modifications:
Peter Papayanakis

Cover Image
©Ted Mahieu/Corbis/Magma

Compositor:
Alicja Jamorski

Printer:
Transcontinental

National Library of Canada Cataloguing in Publication

Canadian families: diversity, conflict and change/[edited by] Nancy Mandell, Ann Duffy.— 3rd ed.

Includes bibliographical references and index.
ISBN-13: 978-0-17-622488-2
ISBN-10: 0-17-622488-2

1. Family—Canada.   I. Mandell, Nancy   II. Duffy, Ann

HQ560.C3584 2004   306.85'0971
C2004-900454-9

Dedication

To our mothers,
Margaret Louise Pennal
and
Elizabeth Matilda Kaiser

Contents

3 Making Sense of the Cultural Activities of Canadian Youth   64

Brian Wilson and Shannon Jette

4 Family Lives of Native Peoples, Immigrants, and Visible Minorities   87

Julianne Momirov and Kenise Murphy Kilbride

7   Lesbian and Gay Parents   176

Katherine Arnup

8   Divorce: Options Available, Constraints Forced, Pathways Taken   210

Carolyne A. Gorlick

Meg Luxton and June Corman

PREFACE

Since we last updated this edited collection, Canadian families have continued to change in complicated and challenging ways. Globalization reshapes the economic and social conditions within which we work, play, and form intimate relations. Rising income gaps between the economically secure and insecure mean that families interact with the public in profoundly different ways. Fragmentation of employment and the increase in part-time and insecure jobs leave many families worried about financial matters and scrambling to provide the necessities of life. In contrast, few financially well-off Canadian families occupy a privileged position within the social structure. All families wrestle with the social and cultural effects initiated by challenges from the dis/abled, post-colonial, feminist, gay, and racial/ethnic movements.

In this dynamic context, new ways for interrogating the personal and political context of Canadians' lives demand sociological attention. *Canadian Families: Diversity, Conflict and Change*, Third Edition, is intended to be a contribution to the growing debate on the direction and nature of change in family practices and policies. Each of the 12 chapters, written specifically for this collection, asks us to rethink traditional assumptions by including current empirical data and contemporary theoretical debates. Authors consider the appearance and significance of gendered and racialized encounters within and outside families that shape members' understandings of family life. Discourses of ethnicity, intimacy, and sexuality contour individual experiences of adolescence, parenting, love, and romance. Considerations of same-sex marriages, poverty, divorce, youth culture, and aging present contemporary and historically-based accounts of the diverse ethnic and cultural forces affecting the many distinct ways people create family units.

In this text, we seek to present material in a clear and organized manner using accessible and jargon-free language. Students are encouraged to critically examine their own assumptions. While undergraduates will find the material easy to read and comprehend, they will also be confronted with challenging and refreshing points of view. Their lives are reflected in the narrative accounts of minority families, lesbian and gay-male families, aging families, single-parent families, and poor families. Learning objectives, chapter summaries, and boxed inserts highlight important points. Critical thinking questions, websites, suggested further reading, and a glossary are included to stimulate both individual reflection and classroom debate.

To this third edition, we welcome our new contributors, who bring excellent contemporary debates on emergent family topics. A core of outstanding contributors has been with us since the first edition. Over the years, their research has continued to enliven debates in a wide range of topics. All of our contributors incorporate struggles around gender, race, economics, sexuality, dis/ability, and violence into their analysis. We remain inspired by and appreciative of the strong theoretical and analytic perspectives of our colleagues. Their efforts enrich and broaden our understandings of the everyday workings of Canadian families.

ACKNOWLEDGMENTS

We extend our sincere gratitude to all those who have helped us produce this third edition. We are very grateful for the support from the excellent team at Thomson Nelson including Glen Herbert, Joanna Cotton, Cara Yarzab, Julie van Veen, and Erin Moore, all of whom intervened at critical moments. We particularly want to acknowledge the enormous contribution of Julianne Momirov, who worked with Nancy Mandell, Ann Duffy, and Kenise Murphy Kilbride in revising and incorporating changes into their chapters. Without Julianne's help, Nancy and Ann would not have been able to produce this third edition in a timely fashion. We cannot thank her enough for pitching in at the last minute in such an effective, sophisticated, and efficient fashion. We continue to love and cherish the men and women in our lives: Lionel, Jeremy, Ben, Adam, Dusky, Hermana, and Mayra. Their presence sustains and enriches us.

Readers wishing further information on data provided through the cooperation of Statistics Canada may obtain copies of relevant publications by mail from Publications Sales, Statistics Canada, Ottawa, Ontario, Canada K1A 0T6, or by calling 1-613-951-7277 or toll-free 1-800-267-6677. Readers may also send their order by fax to 1-613-951-1584.

CONTRIBUTORS

Katherine Arnup
Carleton University

Katherine Arnup is the director of the Institute of Interdisciplinary Studies at Carleton University. A social historian of motherhood and the family, she is the author of *Education for Motherhood: Advice for Mothers in Twentieth Century Canada* (University of Toronto Press, 1994) and the editor of *Lesbian Parenting: Living with Pride and Prejudice* (Gynergy Books, 1995; 1997). She has written numerous articles on lesbian and gay parenting issues.

Dorothy E. Chunn
Simon Fraser University

Dorothy E. Chunn is professor of criminology and codirector of the Feminist Institute for Studies on Law and Society at Simon Fraser University. Among her recent publications are several coedited collections: *Law as a Gendering Practice* (with Dany Lacombe); *Regulating Lives: Historical Essays on the State, Society, the Individual and the Law* (with John McLaren and Robert Menzies); and *Contesting Canadian Citizenship: Historical Readings* (with Robert Adamoski and Robert Menzies). Current research projects focus on feminism, law, and social change in Canada since the 1960s; poor women's experiences of health and housing; and the reform of Canadian child custody law.

June Corman
Brock University

June Corman is a professor in and past chair of the Department of Sociology and has taught in and is past director of the Women's Studies Program at Brock University. She has just finished a term as editor of *Atlantis: A Women's Studies Journal*. Her research interests include the areas of work, family, community, and unemployment. She recently coauthored (with Meg Luxton) a multi-year study of working-class families entitled *Getting By in Hard Times: Gendered Labour at Home and On the Job*. Her most recent research grant focuses on the work, family, and community lives of rural women teachers during the Great Depression in Saskatchewan.

Deborah Davidson
York University

Deborah Davidson is completing her Ph.D. in sociology at York University. While her dissertation work examines the formation of prenatal bereavement protocols in Toronto between 1940 and 2000, her scholarly interests are more widely defined. Her research into the effects of the prenatal drug diethylstilbestrol (DES) on mother–daughter relationships has been published as a book chapter by Palgrave Press (*Gender, Identity and Reproduction*, S. Earle and G. Letherby, eds. 2003). Her research interests also lie in the areas of sexuality and pedagogy.

Ann Duffy
Brock University

Ann Duffy is a professor in the Department of Sociology and the Centre for Labour Studies at Brock University. She also teaches at the Women's Studies Centre. Professor Duffy is a coauthor of the award-winning *Sociology: A Down-to-Earth Approach* (Canadian edition). She has authored and coauthored a variety of books, chapters, and scholarly articles. Most of these publications concern some aspect of women, violence, employment, and aging. In addition, she has coedited several texts that have become popular resources in the sociology of the family, Canadian society, and work. She is currently working with Norene Pupo on a major research grant that explores the changing structure of employment in the new economy. Also, she is coauthoring a book with Nancy Mandell and Susan Wilson on the lives of mid-life women in Canada.

Carolyne A. Gorlick
King's University College, The University of Western Ontario

Carolyne Gorlick is an associate professor in the Faculty of Social Work at King's University College, The University of Western Ontario. She is currently teaching social policy (legal, social welfare, education, and employment) as well as social activism and advocacy. Recent research has involved a national study of welfare to work programmes in Canada as experienced by low-income programme participants, programme providers, employers, community representatives, and senior policymakers. Preliminary publications include *National Welfare to Work Inventory Vols. 1 and 2, National Welfare to Work Programs: From New Mandates to Existing Bureaucracies to Individual and Program Accountability* with Guy Brethour, and a final report: *Welfare to Work in Canada: Policy Intentions and Program Realities*. As well, she has published a chapter on "Drug Testing: Employability and Welfare" with Rick Csiernik in *Responding to the Oppression of Addiction, Canadian Social Work Perspectives*, Csiernik and Rowe, eds. 2003.

Lesley D. Harman
King's University College, The University of Western Ontario

Lesley D. Harman is professor of sociology at King's University College, The University of Western Ontario. She is the author of *The Modern Stranger: On Language and Membership*; *When a Hostel Becomes Home: Experiences of Women*; and *The River, My Soul: Women of the Thousand Islands*, as well as numerous book chapters and articles on gender, deviance, social theory, aging, poverty, and women and deviance. She is currently finishing her third community study, an ethnography of therapeutic touch practitioners in Canada.

Shannon Jette
University of British Columbia

Shannon Jette is a master's student in the area of leisure and sport management within the School of Human Kinetics at the University of British Columbia. Her primary research interests concern youth, culture, mass media, and gender, and her proposed thesis research will investigate young females' interpretations of smoking in popular film.

Debra Langan
York University

Debra Langan is an assistant professor of sociology, York University. She is a SCOTL Teaching Award nominee, and recipient of the 2001 John O'Neill Award for Teaching Excellence. Her publication, *Talking About Violence Against Women: Deconstructing Uncontested Discourses* (2001), analyzes how ideologies are perpetuated and/or challenged in interpersonal interactions. Her analyses guide participatory research/teaching with students, enhancing critical consciousness and practice. Substantive interests include gender, methodology, and critical criminology. Earlier work involved Alberta Correctional Services and community protocol development in Ontario concerning violence against women.

Meg Luxton
York University

Meg Luxton is a professor of social science and women's studies at Atkinson College and past graduate director of the School of Women's Studies, York University. She is currently editor of *Atlantis: A Women's Studies Journal*. In 2002, the Canadian Sociology and Anthropology Association awarded her the Distinguished Scholar Award and recognized her coauthored book (with June Corman) as runner-up for the John Porter Book Prize. Her recent publications include book chapters and articles on unpaid work, work–family contradictions, caregiving, and aging. She is currently completing a book on caregiving practices and dilemmas in Canada.

Nancy Mandell
York University

Nancy Mandell teaches in sociology and women's studies at York University. Her most recent research includes postmodern research methods, especially academic–community research partnerships; a coauthored study with Ann Duffy and Sue Wilson entitled *Canadian Women at Mid-Life* that examines the work, community, family, and intimate relationships of mid-life women and their involvement with the women's movement; and a series of coauthored book chapters and articles with Robert Sweet on gendered social capital and parental involvement in children's schooling, especially homework.

Anne Martin-Matthews
University of British Columbia

Anne Martin-Matthews is a professor of family studies in the School of Social Work and Family Studies at the University of British Columbia, and interim scientific director of the National Institute of Aging of the Canadian Institutes of Health Research (CIHR). Her publications include *Widowhood in Later Life*, an edited joint volume (with Ellen M. Gee) of *Canadian Public Policy* and the *Canadian Journal on Aging* on "Bridging Research and Policy on Aging," and articles on social support, work–home life balance, and aging in rural environments. Her current research examines men's filial care roles and the nature of home care work. She has served on the executive of the Canadian Association on Gerontology, the Research Committee on Aging of the International Sociological Association, B.C.'s Michael Smith Foundation for Health Research, and on the editorial boards of the *Canadian Journal on Aging* (as editor-in-chief) and *Journal of Aging Studies*.

Julianne Momirov
McMaster University

Julianne Momirov has a background in history, politics, and sociology. She has taught in the sociology departments of Brock University in St. Catharines, Ontario, and University College of the Cariboo in Kamloops, B.C. Her research interests involve matters of race and ethnicity, gender, and identity.

Kenise Murphy Kilbride
Ryerson University

Kenise Murphy Kilbride is professor emerita in the School of Early Childhood Education at Ryerson University in Toronto, and Senior Fellow at Joint Centre of Excellence for Research on Immigration and Settlement (CERIS). She is coeditor (with Dr. Paul Anisef) of *Managing Two Worlds: Immigrant Youth in Ontario* (2003), editor of *"Include Me Too!" Human Diversity in Early Childhood* (1997), and coeditor of *Children at the Centre* (1996). With Dr. Mehrunissa Ali of Ryerson, she recently conducted a study for Human Resources Development Canada of the needs of new immigrant parents of young children, and produced a video (2003) and handbook (2004), *Forging New Links, Planting New Roots: Canadian Resources for Immigrant Parents of Young Children*.

Brian Wilson
University of British Columbia

Brian Wilson is an assistant professor in the School of Human Kinetics at the University of British Columbia. His research interests include youth culture, media constructions of race and gender, audience studies, social movements, and the sociology of sport and leisure generally. His published work appears in such journals as the *Canadian Journal of Sociology*, the *Canadian Journal of Communication*, the *Sociology of Sport Journal*, the *International Review for the Sociology of Sport*, and the *Journal of Sport and Social Issues*.

Part 1

Canadian Families in Social Context

Chapter 1

Explaining Family Lives

Nancy Mandell and Ann Duffy

LEARNING OBJECTIVES

In this chapter, you will learn that:

1. definitions of family life have reflected both significant social changes and important power struggles in society;

2. the contemporary family is a multi-defined unit;

3. both modernist and postmodernist theories explain family change;

4. societal forces affect change and consider their implications for family life in Canada.

INTRODUCTION

Forty years ago, social scientists could start their discussions of the "**family**" with a nice, neat definition: "The family is a social group characterized by common residence, economic cooperation, and **reproduction**. It includes adults of both sexes, at least two of whom maintain a socially approved sexual relationship, and one or more children, own or adopted, of the sexually cohabiting adults" (Stephens, 1963, p. 1). This was considered a generous definition since it held a place for the diverse family forms—**polygamy**, polyandry, and so on—revealed by anthropology. According to this approach, there could be multiple wives and/or multiple husbands and it encompassed children who were not the biological product of the adult sexual unions.

Today, not a half-century later, such an approach appears hopelessly inaccurate and inappropriate. It fails to address a complex variety of family forms embraced in Canadian society. Indeed, if we restricted our notion of "family" to the traditional mom, dad (married or common-law), and their kids (who are living at home), only 44 percent of all families in Canada would be included (Statistics Canada, 2003a, p. 11). Clearly, any traditional definition leaves many people out. Are the 7 percent of Canadian couples who have decided to be voluntarily childless couples still a family (Stobert and Kemeny,

2003)? Are a gay or lesbian couple with or without children a family (Sullivan, 1999)? Is a single man and his foster children a family? Are a group of friends who make a long-term commitment to share their lives a family (Watters, 2003)? At what point do two adults who decide to share an emotional, sexual, economic relationship in a common residence (the 16 percent of all Canadian couples who are living common-law—of which 46 percent include children) become a family (Statistics Canada, 2003a, p. 11)? If economic, educational, familial, or other considerations mean that an intimate couple must live apart from one another, does this mean they are not a family while the common-law couple who are able to share a residence are (Milan and Peters, 2003)? Is the family friend, that the kids all call "auntie," but who is not a biological relative really a member of the family? Are grandparents who have assumed parenting responsibilities for their grandchildren a family (Milan and Hamm, 2003)? To which family does the Filipino woman belong who works as a nanny to children in Toronto in order to support her own, rarely seen, biological children back home? The questions are seemingly endless and each speaks to fundamental issues in contemporary Canadian society.

The term "family" is not simply a concept used by social scientists; it is a minefield of contested values and power relationships (Silva and Smart, 1999). In this regard, it is not surprising that "family" has been at the centre of the contemporary women's and **lesbigay** movements and has played a prominent part in social movements to improve the lot of poor, immigrant, and visible minority Canadians. Defining a certain social arrangement socially and legally accepted as a "family" has direct implications not only for the participants but also for their relationship to numerous other societal institutions. For example, the social and legal acceptance of lesbian or gay families means that partners are eligible for the numerous rights and benefits taken for granted by heterosexual couples. Partners can share employment benefits, they can apply to adopt and foster children, they are the first to be called upon in the event of medical emergency, and they have legal rights in the event of death or disability.

As discussed in the chapter on poverty (Chapter 9), the woman (or man) receiving welfare benefits has a similar vested interest in the meanings attached to family. If a man or woman is assumed to have entered into a relationship with a welfare recipient simply by token of "spending the night" with that individual, then they may no longer be eligible for state assistance. This "man in the house" rule is, at base, about definitions of family relations and has enormous implications for the lives of men and women living on welfare. While the government has a clear vested interest in arguing that the presence of an opposite-sex adult in the home implies, in some sense, membership in the family, the welfare recipient would advocate a definition of family relations that is less restrictive.

The meaning of "family" has been similarly central to the burgeoning numbers of single-parent, mother-headed families. The issues range from "whether

BOX 1.1   SOCIAL RESEARCHERS AND CHANGING DEFINITIONS OF FAMILY

Needless to say, social researchers must start with some definition of the family in order to collect information. For example, a recent Statistics Canada study on family wealth explained the
term "family" "refers to economic families and unattached individuals. An economic family is a
group of persons sharing a common dwelling and related by blood, **marriage**, common law, or
adoption. An unattached individual lives alone or with unrelated persons." Subsequent tables
listed unattached individuals under family (Chawla and Pold, 2003, p. 6). Note also that,
according to this definition, sharing a common dwelling is a crucial criterion along with some biological or legal relationship. This distinction suggests, for example, that at some point the couple
that commutes between two cities may spend sufficient time apart to be redefined as not a
family.

Compare this conceptualization of the family with the revisions made in Statistics Canada's
2001 **Census definition of the family**:

- Two persons living in a same-sex common-law relationship, along with either
  partner's children, are now considered a census family.

- Children in a census family may now have been previously married. In previous censuses they had to be "never-married."

- A grandchild living in a three-generation household where the parent has never
  married is now considered a child in the census family of his or her parent. In previous censuses, the census family consisted of the two older generations and the
  child was considered a non-census family person.

- A grandchild of another household member, where the middle generation is not
  present, will now be considered a child in the census family of his or her grandparent. In previous censuses, the grandchild was considered a non-census family
  person (Statistics Canada, 2003b, p. 27).

In short, from even this short review it is clear that research definitions are a work in
progress, required to respond to changes in the social environment. Despite such improvements, research definitions may remain inconsistent with commonsense understandings of
family boundaries.

the single-parent home is seen as a 'proper' family" to "what are the financial
responsibilities of the ex-**spouse** to support this family." To the degree to which
the government supports the legal provision of support for mothers and their
children and strenuously enforces punishments on dead-beat dads, it is com-
menting on public acceptance of the legitimacy and rights of these families.

The explosion in divorce rates and the growth in single-parent and
common-law "families" have also triggered a great deal of personal as well as
societal debate about family membership. In the event of divorce and remarriage, there are clearly issues in **blended families** about who belongs and who
does not. The paternal grandmother of children of a divorced mother (who
now has remarried and acquired a new set of in-laws) may find that she has
"disappeared" from the family—not invited to family events, not included in

the lives of her grandchildren. Under law—premised on certain notions of family and family rights—she has little in the way of legal recourse. Her personal plight is the result of social and legal definitions of the family.

The dramatic growth in reproductive technology has added a further twist to the struggle over definition (Eichler, 1997). Some of these issues were already excavated in the debates surrounding the rights of biological and adoptive parents and adopted children. Some biological parents of children who have been adopted have argued that "open adoption"—wherein biological parents can participate in some way in the rearing of their children—is preferable and some adoptive children have argued for their rights to know their biological parents. Conversely, others—both biological parents and their adopted children as well as adoptive parents—have argued for their right to privacy and the rights of adoptive parents to completely assume the rights and roles of parents. Somewhat similar issues can arise around the new reproductive technology. If "family" is assumed to be fundamentally about biology, does the child of a sperm donor or ovum donor or womb-loaner have the right to know and form a relationship with the individual whose genetic code they share or who provided them with their earliest sustenance? Conversely, does the donor have any financial or legal obligations to his or her biological child? These, of course, are not hypothetical concerns since they have led to a variety of litigations. If a woman contracts to be inseminated by the husband of a childless couple and to allow them to adopt the resultant infant, is she allowed to change her mind and keep the child and should the biological father be held socially and financially responsible? If, unknown to the biological father, his child is adopted by a couple who then raises the child for a number of years, is the father, once he learns of the situation, allowed to demand custody of the child and take him/her from the only social family they have known? Each question hinges on the meaning our society and institutions, notably the courts, attach to family and family relations.

These definitions have potential implications for virtually every Canadian. As noted in Martin-Matthews' chapter on aging (Chapter 11), the state's definition of family means that the government may ultimately turn to family members to assume social, legal, and financial responsibility for other family members. Although, until now, rarely applied, the law allows a financially deprived senior to demand financial support from his/her adult children. In addition, in some regions, parents of children are held civilly responsible for the acts of vandalism, trespass, and so on perpetrated by their children. Clearly, how the state defines who is a member of a family and what the implications of that membership are has potentially momentous implications.

Given these few examples, it is understandable that efforts to designate a definition of family have long been a power struggle—with some groups lobbying for acceptance as families while others lobby to restrict the familial rights of others. However, the promotion of certain definitions of the family is not only about personal, legal, and economic rights; for example, who gets to see whom and who has to support which children. "Family" also is deeply embedded in the most fundamental beliefs and values in our society. It is a "master symbol"—"a symbol that justif[ies] the institutional arrangement of the [social] order.... By lending meaning to the enactment of given roles, these master symbols sanction the person in re-acting the roles. When internalized they form unquestioned categories which channel and delimit new experiences; they promote and constrain activities" (Gerth and Mills, 1953). Certainly, for the women's movement and its opponents, the meaning attached to "the family" has long been a battleground for a struggle over fundamental values (Thorne with Yalom, 1982). Opponents of the women's movement evoked the traditional **patriarchal family**—the "proper" family in which father was the head of the ship and responsible for the economic support of the family and mother was the first mate and responsible for the caring and emotional well-being within the family. The "family" in this sense was presented as the apogee of domestic bliss and as a refuge for all from the demands and distractions of society. Much of the early feminist literature was clearly directed at challenging this master symbol and dismantling this mythical family—presenting it instead as stifling, claustrophobic, sometimes violent, and basically inimical to the full development of women and their children. Feminist academics pointed out that even scholarly definitions of family were rife with political agendas—rendering invisible some forms of family (same-sex families) while legitimating a narrow range of "normal" families (Eichler, 1997). These struggles over the family and its meaning, of course, continue today.

In some respect the word "family" has been imbued with many of the dreams and fears concerning private life and personal relationships. Public opinion polls consistently reveal that the clear majority of Canadians view their "families" as a source of great joy, happiness, and love (Milan, 2000, p. 5). Yet, rates of divorce and family violence along with research on stress in the family would suggest that this happiness is, at least, difficult to achieve. Nonetheless, it is not surprising to find politicians embracing the family as a master symbol, not only rationalizing their policies in terms of the well-being of "the family" but frequently posing with their "loving" family—husband/wife, loving children, and family dog/cat—to convey a powerful image of sobriety, traditionalism, and "normalcy."

The symbolic value of "the family" is, in part, the reason religious leaders have recently leapt energetically into the debate about gay marriage. The **traditional family** has been a core image of established religion; in some sense, by attending church (however infrequently), members of the congregation could be seen by the community as embracing a very traditional approach to sexuality, personal mores, and private dreams. Expanding the religiously legitimate meaning of "family" so that single mothers and fathers, lesbians,

common-law couples, groups of friends, and so on can freely lay claim to equal status as a "family" can be seen as an important step away from traditional beliefs and values and towards a more anarchic and secular society.

Given this heated and lengthy debate about what "family" means, it is not surprising that in recent years feminist analysts have moved increasingly away from attempting to categorize "the family" and have accepted that, first, there are diverse patterns of family life and, second, people continue to define important aspects of their lives as "family life." Since families still count in many people's lives, the emphasis has shifted to considering what people mean when they are "doing family life." Following the logic that "what a family is appears intrinsically related to what it does," the emphasis is on examining the process of family life and providing support for the diverse ways in which families go about sharing "resources, caring, responsibilities and obligations" (Silva and Smart, 1999).

From the preceding brief review of the ongoing struggle over the basic meanings attached to "family," it is clear that this concept is central to many sociological considerations—the roles of women and men, the boundaries of deviance, the nature of social change, and so on. It is not simply one of the important institutional structures in society; it and the economy are the key structures. In this context, it is not surprising to find considerable sociological theorizing devoted to exploring and explaining family life.

STUDYING FAMILIES: THEORETICAL PERSPECTIVES

At the turn of the century, sociology was dominated by theories of modernization that described the overall movement from traditional to modern social systems. Family sociologists exploring the implications of the Industrial Revolution on family life attempted to explain how large-scale social and economic changes had given rise to what was called the "modern" family. Industrialization and urbanization were seen as radically transforming the family from an extended, authoritarian, stable rural form into a nuclear, more egalitarian and relatively isolated and unstable type.

Modernization Theorists

Both radical theorists like Marx and Engels, and conservatives like Durkheim, Tonnies, and Maine, were nostalgic for the past and viewed the city with distaste (Nisbet, 1966). Cities were seen as chaotic, alienating, and potentially dangerous places making urban families disorganized, competitive, and unpredictable. The world of work became increasingly contrasted with the world of home. Work was seen as hostile, harsh, and precarious, whereas home took on the idealized image as a place providing safety, security, and protection. What could no longer be obtained from the extended family, community, or village relationships were meaningful emotional attachments with others. In the modernist story, the family turned in and became increasingly identified as an emotional haven. Family relationships were transformed into private, exclusive attachments between married partners, and between parents, especially mothers, and their children.

Some influential modernization theorists viewed social and economic change as propelling changes in family structure, ideology, and behaviour. For others, changes in industrialization and the family were seen as parallel processes. In this latter view, modernization was seen as having brought about value changes in ideologies partly independent of economic changes advanced by industrialization and equally as important in precipitating family change. Both perspectives took account of changing social and personal ideologies of economic progress, the **conjugal family**, and egalitarianism (Goode, 1963).

While theorists quibble over the nature and direction of change, all agree that ideological change characterizes modern life. The ideology of the conjugal family asserts the worth of the individual over lineage and the significance of personal welfare over family continuity. The ideology of economic progress stresses societal industrial growth and change and its regulation of the issue of tradition and custom. The ideology of egalitarianism between the sexes emphasizes the uniqueness of each individual within the family with less importance given to sex status and seniority, thus reducing age and status inequalities within families.

Structural Theories of Family Change

Two types of modern family change theories predominate: **materialist** and structural **functionalist**. Both are structural, determinist theories preoccupied with detailing the effects of modern social and economic change on family structure and function.

Materialism   Karl Marx offered a penetrating critique of the ways midnineteenth century family life altered as a result of the spread of capitalism. In particular, he produced a scathing analysis of the inherent exploitation built into capitalist economies. According to Marx, with the growth of the industrial economy, small landowners and businesses were lost and men became wage earners in factories, dependent on owners for their survival. Rather than producing what they consumed, mechanization and industrial production meant that families, especially urban ones, found it cheaper and easier to buy products in the marketplace. Food, clothing, and housing—all the essentials needed for survival—were commodified and only available for sale. Unable to barter or trade services for products, families became dependent on wages to purchase essentials.

According to Marx and his co-writer Friedrich Engels, social change is determined by change in the ways individuals ensure satisfaction of their basic survival needs. In other words, the mode of **production** in material life determines the social, political, and intellectual life processes of a society. Being dependent on owners, what Marx called the bourgeoisie, made the workers, or proletariat, open for economic exploitation. Capitalism thrives by paying workers a wage less than the value of what they produce, thus allowing the owner to sell their products at a profit, most of which is then reinvested in the businesses. Labourers became dependent on business and factory owners for wages; women, and children, the lowest on the earning ladder, became dependent on male wage earners for survival. The poorest and most unfortunate men, women, and children worked as marginal labourers in mills, factories, and mines under exploitative conditions for subsistence wages. Even though they often worked for wages, for the most part, married women were defined by their domestic roles as private, subservient domestic labourers subject to male control and authority within the home.

In his seminal piece *The Origin of the Family, Private Property and the State*, Engels studied the family as an economic unit, arguing that family change is shaped by material change. Power accrues to those who provide for life's necessities—food, clothing, and shelter—that in an industrializing society happens to be male wage earners. Material conditions determine male domination. In short, capitalism causes women's oppression. Gender inequality, born of women's economic dependence on men, asserts the superiority of men over women in all spheres of life. As subordinates, women perform necessary but unpaid domestic labour in the home. Through their material activities, their social, biological, and cultural reproductive work, women become domestic servants of men. Or put more positively, women become skilled in domesticity, childrearing, homemaking, nurturing, and emotionally caring for family members. Within marriage, patriarchal ideology is played out in marital relationships in which the role of wives is to serve, please, and satisfy the wishes and needs of husbands. As the subordinate domestic specialists, women are expected to organize their time, resources, and energy around the agendas of husbands and children, putting their own needs and desires last. The conjugal, nuclear family becomes a private form isolated from the social control of neighbours and extended family. In extreme cases of sexual inequality, the marriage licence becomes a hitting licence for men.

Following Marx, contemporary materialists see capitalism as gendering relationships in its organization of work and home. Production and reproduction are classed and gendered activities structured and shaped by the ways in which men, women, and children satisfy their economic or material needs. Contemporary theorists examine the ways in which global capitalism spreads class exploitation internationally. Materialist feminists see the end of women's oppression as arising through women's engagement in paid labour, which ends women's economic dependence on male wages. What many theorists neglected to consider was the role of ideology as a system of social, cultural, and economic ruling representations spread in the form of images, myths, ideas, and concepts (Althusser, 1971). Gender inequality represents one such type of ideology that seems to exist independent of the economic system. Patriarchal ideas are fostered through the practices of social structures such as churches, political parties, schools, and the media, all of whom transmit ideas in such a way as to make individuals feel they are freely choosing to subscribe to unequal gendered behaviour rather than having these ideas unfairly thrust upon them.

Structural Functionalism Structural functionalists present a more positive view of the effects of modernization and industrialization on the family. This perspective sees social institutions as existing in harmony with one another. Change in one institution, such as the family, polity, economy, or education system, invariably leads to change in another institution. Within institutions, individuals take up scripted roles in order to fulfill the purpose and goals of particular institutions. Within the family, for example, husband-father, wife-mother, and children are bound together by interaction and interdependence. Stability, sound functioning, harmonious relationships, and social order are maintained when institutions, and its individuals, co-exist in a state of equilibrium (Parsons, 1955).

Talcott Parsons (1955) applied the structural functionalist perspective to the study of the modern family. According to Parsons, with industrialization, the family ceased being an economic unit of production, so family members sought employment in the labour market. Modern, urban families became more isolated, specialized, flexible, and mobile units designed to meet the needs of a changing society. The family adapted to changing occupational demands and requirements of geographical and social mobility. Family functions became narrower and activities more concentrated around **socialization** of children, transmission of **social capital** to reproduce class positions, emotional gratification through the development of intimacy and affection, and self-actualization through involvement in close, personal relationships.

One way in which families accomplished their new, specialized functions was to develop more specialized family roles for men, women, and children. Two family functions took precedence: socialization of children and the maintenance and stabilization of adult personalities. To fulfill these functions, the family developed role specialization. Family activities concentrated on emotional gratification and socialization of children became the purview of women with mothers developing more intense emotional relationships with children due to the absence of fathers on the job market. Husbands took on public roles as breadwinners who maintained and exerted patriarchal authority through their positions as "heads of households." In this new sexual division of labour, women became the affective or "love" experts while men became the instrumental or "work" experts. Family harmony was maintained when specialized family functions were undertaken as a set of reciprocal, but essentially equal, tasks.

Parsons and other structural functionalists embraced modern families as units increasing individualism and specialization, thus ultimately leading to increased freedom for individuals and for families. Theorists see a functional fit between the desire of individuals to maximize their needs for equality and individualism and the structure of conjugal family as best equipped to fulfill these needs. The ideology of the nuclear family emphasizes the relationship of husbands, wives, and children, de-emphasizes obligatory relationships with extended kin systems, and asserts the equality of individuals over sex, kinship, caste, and class barriers (Nisbet, 1966). Freedom of choice reigned over binding kin obligations thus freeing individuals to make work and family choices enabling them to be mobile. Conjugal families are seen as maximizing possibilities for individuals to achieve equality, individuality, and achievement by advocating free choice in mate selection, emphasizing individual welfare as opposed to family continuity, encouraging **neolocal** residence patterns where husbands and wives establish independent households, and favouring bilineal descent systems rather then either **patrilineal** or **matrilineal** patterns.

Structural functionalism dominates American, but not Canadian or European, sociology of the family. In Canada, it has precipitated a number of critiques of modernization theories, especially those that focus on the interdependence of social institutions. Historical analyses of modern families have challenged the notion that the nuclear family is the product of economic development and technological change. Historians assert that modernization of the family can best be understood as resulting from a change in family values and orientations coupled with a change in the family's involvement with work and community (Laslett, 1965). Family reconstitution critiques argue that the notion that families changed with industrialization from a nuclear to an extended form was simply not supported by historical work in many parts of Europe. Moreover, critics point to a difference between nuclear and conjugal families. While nuclear has a structural meaning including a family system based on households composed of couples and their dependent children, conjugal has a cultural meaning, namely that the central focus of family life remains the bond of the couple and their relationship with their co-resident children. Families of the past were typically nuclear but not conjugal. A final criticism precipitated by a critique of structural functionalism has to do with the analytic focus of theorists. Rather than describing the family solely in terms of its structure or size, some argued that we must take account of the emotional dynamics of the family and discuss these changes in relation to larger social, economic, political, and cultural activities in society (Lasch, 1977).

Postmodern Theories

The failure of modernization theories to provide satisfactory analyses of social change led to a critique of modernity and the emergence of what have come to be known as "postmodern" social theories (Lyotard, 1984). **Postmodernism** refers to the massive questioning of the basic assumptions of modern thought such as reason, progress, and nature. Political cynicism, social upheaval, and economic dissatisfaction fuelled a growing intellectual movement in the 1960s that recognized global societies were rapidly moving into a postmodern world where the major tenets, key assumptions, and theoretical propositions underlying modernist views no longer helped analyze social change. The postmodern refers, above all, not to the demise but to the exhaustion of modernity (Lyon, 1999, p. 9). Postmodern theories suggest new methods of analyzing social change that are grounded in the historical, take account of the social and the political contexts within which action emerges, highlight the potential of local sites as points of resistance, and favour multiple and provisional explanations.

Critical of modernist theories, postmodernists suggest a set of guiding propositions to interrogate emergent postmodern conditions: a refusal to accept what we call "natural" and an incredulity toward **metanarratives**, those grand stories or explanations about the world that make sense of the world according to one overarching truth. For postmodern sociologists, rather than seeing family as a natural, fixed, and unchanging unit, families are viewed as fluid, multiple, and malleable. Rather than seeing Marxism or structural functionalism as adequate explanations of family change, postmodernists remain skeptical of what they see as master narratives (Marshall, 1992). Postmodernism deconstructs traditional family ideals and ideas including such modernist staples as the myth of family consensus, the myth of undifferentiated family experience, the myth of separate gender worlds, the myth of family as haven, the myth of family as fulfillment, and the myth of families as stable and harmonious units.

Foucault is often cited as an interpretive social theorist whose analysis of power helps us understand family relations. For Foucault, power is not something that hangs over family members, or is wielded exclusively by certain family members and not others. Rather, power exists in and finds expression through everyday family practices. Power, the postmodernists say, is constitutive of social relations. Power is not only oppressive but can also be constitutive of pleasure, thus explaining women's active involvement in power relations that subordinate them. Sandra Harding (1986) suggests that the study of gender relations involves three elements: structure, culture, and agency. Applied to the study of family, this framework directs our attention to a consideration of family structures (the sociosexual division of labour within families), family cultures (symbolism), and family agency (family identities).

In becoming postmodern, family sociologists embrace what is called the "cultural turn," the shift from studying family structures to studying agency and culture. The family as conceived by modernists consists of individuals who are portrayed by postmodernists as being too rational, too knowing, too fixed, and too stable. Family life, postmodernists argue, is rather unstable and families are composed of many different, often irrational, types of people. Families are "works in progress" whose character and composition shift over a lifetime. Instead of emphasizing structures such as industrialization, patriarchy, and material conditions, postmodernists suggest we emphasize the processes by which different and varied families are produced and how family members, through their own agency and actions, take up certain family identifications and not others. Instead of asking how social structures and institutions determine family life, postmodern family sociologists ask, "What are the ways in which family actors, in their daily lives, reproduce and/or challenge the social and cultural relations which shape their experiences?" (Charles, 2002).

WHAT DO CONTEMPORARY FAMILIES LOOK LIKE?

What is it like to be in a family in Canada in the twenty-first century? Official Canadian sources, such as Statistics Canada, regularly produce data from which we can track trends in personal relationships and domestic life. These trends suggest that family and domestic life has been in a state of flux in recent decades, lending support to the notion that the traditional family is in decline. The rise in intimate diversity challenges the **ideological hegemony** of the nuclear family. Canadians support this growing diversity in intimate formations. Despite what some insist, marriage remains popular and intimate relationships with partners, children, and parents remain important for Canadians. Families stay in touch and sometimes even share households across generations. As the population ages, grandparents have the potential to be very influential in the lives of their grandchildren (Milan and Hamm, 2003). Here we track some of the most significant trends[1] in contemporary family life.

Families are Diverse   In the past 30 years, Canadians have embraced the notion of diversity in intimate relationships. A wide variety of domestic, social, and

BOX 1.2   WHAT MAKES *BLADE RUNNER* A POSTMODERN MOVIE?

Set in Los Angeles, AD 2019, a group of "replicants," bio-engineered near people who normally reside "off-world," have returned to confront their makers, the high-tech Tyrell Corporation. They object to their four-year lifespan and want to be extended to full human status. Deckard, the "blade runner," tracks escaped replicants and "retires" them through elimination. Blade Runner has a number of themes that makes the movie postmodern. Reality is debated and uncertain. Replicants want to be "real" people but proof of reality is a photographic image, a constructed identity. Late modernity is seen as collapsing, disintegrating, and giving way to a postmodern world organized around knowledge and technical, information systems. Production is international. Gender, class, and ethnic identities are global. Replicants exist in a world in which boundaries of time and space have been replaced by virtual spaces. In the consumer society, public image dominates and individual privacy disappears. What is human, what are bodies, and what is identity are thrown into question in a world in which virtual reality, genetic engineering, and cosmetic surgery reshape humans in strange but subtle ways (Lyon, 1999, pp. 1–4).

emotional relationships offer Canadians a range of possibilities in creating intimate relationships. This diversity includes same-sex partnerships; **serial monogamy**; separation, divorce, and remarriage/recohabitation; solitary living; the growth of cross-household relationships; the significance of adult friendship networks; and the emergence of "families of choice" that may include friends, lovers, and ex-lovers. Household formation is now more interesting than in previous decades. Young people remain in parental homes for longer periods of time; non-familial households are increasing as people share accommodation with friend, lovers, acquaintances, and strangers. As more Canadians live alone, solitary living is recognized as a distinct household type.

Of the 8.4 million families in Canada:

- 41 percent are married couples with children.
- 30 percent are married couples without children.
- 6 percent are common-law couples with children.
- 7 percent are common-law couples without children.
- 16 percent are **lone-parent families** (81 percent of which are female).

Marriage Remains Resilient   In the 1960s, a number of new patterns emerged that altered our ideas about marriage, including a decrease in the number of marriages, a sharp rise in the number of marriages ending in divorce, and a rise in non-marital **cohabitation**. Rather than indicating an overall movement away from marriage, trends indicate a commitment to the ideals of marriage but a shift in the way marriage is constructed. Marriage is still popular but more couples live together without "tying the knot," often until their first child is born.

- Over 84 percent of all women will marry or live common-law once in their lives.
- 94 percent of women between the ages of 30 and 39 will live as part of a couple.
- One-third of all marriages involve at least one person who has been married before (Statistics Canada, 2002b).

Divorce Continues   The resilience of marriage is also reflected in the divorce statistics. Even when the divorce rate settled into the low teens in the early 1980s, this still meant that 66 percent of marriages could be expected to endure. Furthermore, the rise in divorce rates coincided with a rise in remarriage rates, suggesting people's resilience in embracing the idea of marriage even when individual marriages end.

- 31 to 36 percent of all marriages end in divorce.
- About 50 percent of these do not involve dependent children.

- About 70 percent of divorced men and 58 percent of divorced women remarry—excluding Quebec, where couples are more likely to form common-law unions (Ambert, 2002).

Divorce is costly, especially for women, who tend to earn less than men and who can lose a major source of financial support upon separation. A study of married people who became separated between 1987 and 1993 showed that women who were lone parents remained 21 percent below their pre-separation family incomes five years after separation. By contrast, men who were lone parents reported a 5 percent gain in income after five years (Ambert, 2002).

Premarital Cohabitation is Popular   Premarital cohabitation has grown in popularity. Rather than replacing marriage, cohabitation is considered by many to be a stage before marriage, albeit one perceived as entailing fewer legal, economic, and emotional responsibilities (Ambert, 2003). Cohabitation is seen as an easier relationship to enter into and an easier one to leave, which may account for the high rate of dissolution (Ambert, 2002). Cohabitants have similar rights and legal obligations to those of married couples, including property rights and eligibility and entitlements to health insurance, pension plans, and inheritance.

- 16 percent of all Canadian couples are common-law.
- 14 percent of Canada's 8.4 million families are common-law.
- 8 percent of everyone, or approximately 1 828 770 Canadians, over the age of 15 lives common-law.
- More than 53 percent of women between the ages of 20 and 29 and 40 percent of women between the ages of 30 and 39 choose common-law as their first union.
- For people in their thirties, 60 percent of those who first experienced a common-law union and about 30 percent of those who married directly are expected to separate, only to go on and establish new unions (Statistics Canada, 2003b).

Blended Families are Common   Stepfamilies have always been common in Canada. At the turn of the century, they were formed mostly due to the death of a spouse. Today they are most often formed when a mother or father remarries or cohabits after separation or divorce. Stepfamilies or blended families pose new challenges for both the adults and the children, who must figure out how to get along with half sisters and brothers along with a new stepparent.

- About 10 percent of all children under 12 years of age live in a stepfamily.
- In 2001, about 12 percent of all families (503 100 families) were stepfamilies.
- Of these, five out of 10 stepfamilies contained only the female spouse's children and one out of 10 contained only the male spouse's children.

Figure 1.1   A MAJORITY OF YOUNG CANADIANS CHOOSE COMMON-LAW AS A FIRST UNION

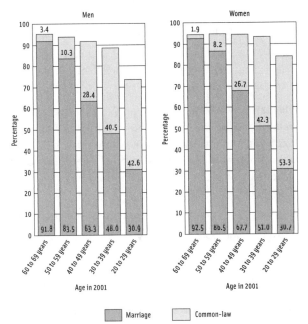

Source: From the Statistics Canada publication "The Daily," Catalogue 11-001, July 11, 2002, available at: http://www.statcan.ca/Daily/English/020711/d020711a.htm

- The other 40 percent of stepfamilies are "blended"; in most cases, they were formed after the birth of a child to the couple in addition to the children born from a previous union (Statistics Canada, 2002b, p. 9).

Some Families are Same-Sex   At the time of writing, discussions are taking place at the Canadian federal level concerning the legalization of same-sex marriages. Ontario and British Columbia have legalized same-sex marriage. Canadians support these changes. Fifty-three percent of Canadians favour gay and lesbian couples marrying while 40 percent remain opposed (Department of Justice, 2002, p. 6).

Since 1999, the Supreme Courts of Ontario, Quebec, and British Columbia have declared that **same-sex couples** are entitled to receive the same legal and economic benefits as other couples. The definition of "spouse" has been changed to include any two persons who have lived together in a "marriage-like" relationship for at least two years. In 2000, the federal government extended benefits and obligations to common-law couples, be they of opposite sexes or the same sex. In many provinces, same-sex couples can now adopt children (Ambert, 2003).

- A total of 34 200 same-sex common-law couples were counted in Canada in 2001.

- These represented 0.5 percent of all couples in 2001.

- 15 percent of households headed by lesbian couples have children.

- 3 percent of households headed by gay males have children.

- The majority of same-sex couples (88 percent of male couples and 77 percent of female couples) have no other people living in the household (Statistics Canada, 2002c).

Couples are Marrying Later   Over the past decade, Canadians got married progressively later in life. Canadians are taking time to finish their education, pay off their debts, get a job, and establish a home before marriage. Nearly one-quarter of women getting married for the first time were doing so after the age of 30. Later marriages are even more popular for men (www.vifamily.ca/library/profiling2/partil8.html).

- In 1997, the average age at marriage for women was 30.9 years of age.

- For men, the average was 33.5 years of age.

Most Lone-Parent Families are Headed by Females   Lone parents may be married, divorced, widowed, separated, or never married. Demographers estimate that just over one-third of Canadian women and one-quarter of men will be lone parents at some point in their lives. Usually lone parenthood is a single state. Most single-parent families are still headed by women. The economic circumstances of lone mothers differ greatly from those of lone fathers. Female lone parents earn less than men, work at low-end jobs, and face the problem of finding affordable childcare. Becoming a father in the past almost always meant beginning a family with a wife who had no children. Today, men may begin parenting as stepfathers (Dubeau, 2002).

- 16 percent of all Canadian families are lone-parent.

- 16 percent of all lone-parent families are headed by male parents.

- 81 percent of lone-parent families are headed by female parents.

Families are Smaller   Reproductive trends also began to shift in the last 30 years. People are having fewer children. While many couples have two children, increasingly couples are having only one child. This means that 43 percent of children are the oldest or only child in a family while 39 percent have an older brother or sister and 18 percent have two or more siblings. Moreover, people are having children later in life, in particular delaying the birth of the first child until women are in their late 20s or early 30s. One-parent households are common. Increasing numbers of people are living alone and more women are not having any children. Reasons for not having children are diverse: medical conditions preclude the possibility; not having the right partner; living with a partner who does not want children; having a career that is too fulfilling or demanding to allow time for childcare; simply not liking children; religious or environmental reasons (Stobert and Kemeny, 2003, p. 8).

- The fertility rate dropped from 3.5 children in 1921 to 1.5 in 1999.
- 7 percent of women and 8 percent of men aged 20 to 34 do not intend to have any children In 2001, the average household size fell to 2.6 persons.
- 13 percent of the Canadian population over the age of 15 lives alone.

Children are Expensive! The typical middle-income couple with one child counts on two paycheques and spends about 15 percent of everything they earn to feed, clothe, house, educate, and care for their child.

- It costs about $154 000 to raise a child to age 18.

Grandparents Do Not Share Households with Their Grandchildren Becoming a grandparent is a mid-life event that the majority of older Canadians experience. Grandparents provide grandchildren with material resources, family traditions, history, and social values, and they act as role models and confidants (Rosenthal and Gladstone, 2000).

The 2001 Census counted more than 474 400 grandparents who **shared households** with their grandchildren. Usually, grandparents live in separate households from their adult children and grandchildren. According to the 2001 Census, nearly 4 percent of Canadians live in **multigenerational households**, that is, households with at least three generations including grandparents, parents, and grandchildren. Historically, historians called this multigenerational arrangement an extended family. Grandparents who live without a middle generation are called **skip-generations**. Sixty-seven percent of skip-generation grandparents are women, 57 percent are married, and 46 percent are retired. In addition to assuming responsibility for raising a grandchild, some 35 percent of grandparents in shared households are also the primary financial providers (Milan and Hamm, 2003).

- Less than 3 percent of people Canadian-born lived in multigenerational households in 2001.
- 7 percent of those born outside of Canada lived in multigenerational households in 2001.
- 3.3 percent of grandchildren share a home with at least one grandparent.
- More than 1 in 10 grandparents in shared households live without a middle generation.

Families Earn Average Wages The majority of Canadian families earn what we call average incomes. In 1996, it took about a year and a half or 75.4 weeks on the job at an average wage for a family to earn enough to cover the typical annual expenditures, such as food, shelter, clothing, taxes, life insurance, gifts, health and personal care, interest on loans, union dues, recreation, cigarettes, alcohol, and lottery tickets (www.vifamily.ca/library/profiling2/partii49.html).

- In 2001, two-parent families with two earners and children earned an average of $81 179.

- In 2001, two-parent families with one earner and children earned an average of $53 364.

- Lone-parent families headed by females earned an average of $34 357.

- In 2001, almost 16 percent of children under the age of 18 lived in low-income families (Statistics Canada, 2003b).

Most Husbands and Wives are Employed   Most children grow up in families where both the husband and wife are employed at least part of the week. A century ago, the traditional family of a male breadwinner and a stay-at-home mother predominated. This profound change has economic, social, and psychological implications for how Canadians think and behave in families.

- 7 out of 10 couples count on two wages.

- 94 percent of married men are employed.

- 77 percent of married women are employed.

- 69 percent of wives with pre-schoolers are employed.

Families are Pseudo-Egalitarian   While both spouses share in the responsibilities for paid and unpaid work, husbands remain the main source of income from paid employment and wives retain major responsibilities for child and family care. Canadian family members spend 20 billion hours doing housework each year with women doing two-thirds of this unpaid housework. Husbands work the longest hours at paid work, are most likely to work overtime, and earn more per week than their wives do. Female-headed single families report the highest levels of stress when compared to wives without children (Sauve, 2002).

- Men work longer hours at paid jobs.

- Employed wives with children are working 40 or more hours.

- Families with children report more stress.

Teenagers Work Part-Time

- Nearly half of all teenagers between the ages of 15 and 19 were living with their parents in 1995 and had jobs. Almost eight out of ten older teens, aged 18–19, worked for average annual earnings of $5582. Juggling school and part-time jobs provide increased purchasing power along with increased stress. In some lone-parent families, teenagers are sometimes the only source of money (www.vifamily.ca/library/profiling2/partii45.html).

- Teens earned more than $4 billion in 1995.

Paid and Unpaid Work = Stress for Family Members More Canadians report feeling time-stressed. One in four men and women in their prime child-bearing and childrearing years are severely time-stressed. The people most likely to be crunched for time are between the ages of 25 and 44. More than half are worried they do not spend enough time with their family and friends. Employed mothers with pre-school aged children are most likely to be time-stressed but even full-time employed men report time-stress. Time-stressed parents often cope by purchasing services from others to buy time for themselves such as domestic services, restaurant meals, babysitters, and daycare (www.vifamily.ca/library/profiling2/partii66.html).

- Work and family conflicts cost employers $2.7 billion per year due to absences from work.

- 85 percent of employed married mothers and 79 percent of employed married fathers find the weekdays too short to do everything they set out to accomplish.

- Families spent an average of $2114 for childcare, $1122 for domestic services, and $1181 for restaurant and take-out meals each year.

Families are Aging The aging of the population will affect family structure and family ties. Smaller families will be supporting larger numbers of aged family members, most of whom will be women. New forms of family caregiving will emerge to look after the growing numbers of elderly (Martin-Matthews, 2001).

- By 2011, approximately 14 percent of the Canadian population, or five million people, will be aged 65 and older.

- Women live an average of seven years longer than men.

Families Stay in Touch Adults keep in close touch with their families. Daughters are more likely than sons to be in frequent touch with their mother, that is, at least once a week. This is not surprising since women's traditional family role has been to play the main caregiver and kin keeper of the family and women generally feel more "responsible" for keeping open the lines of communication.

- Almost 7 in 10 adults aged 25 to 54 phone, write, or visit their mother at least once a week.

- 6 in 10 communicate with their father that often.

- 8 percent have contact less than once a month with their mother and 13 percent have contact less than once a month with their father.

THE FUTURES OF CANADIAN FAMILIES

Will Canadians move towards a postmodern *Blade Runner* world? Is it feasible or desirable to return to the *Happy Days* families of the 1950s? Some speculation on future directions in family life is possible, since there are a number of perceptible shifts in Canadian society already in motion and likely to impact on families. Among the most notable is the aging of the population. Our society will be made up of increasing numbers of not only senior (over 65 years old) but also aged Canadians (over 85 years old). As explained in Chapter 11 on aging, this global phenomenon is the result not only of improvements in medical interventions, improved nutrition and so on but also the decreased numbers of children being born to Canadian families.

This shift in the age pyramid has clear implications for the increased burden of caregiving in many families as adult children and grandchildren respond to the increasing dependency and needs of their aging family members. Much of this burden, given past experience, is likely to fall on women's shoulders and, as a result, many women's experience of family life is likely to be increasingly conditioned by responsibilities for aging relations, ranging from providing in-home 24-hour care to occasionally visiting relations in seniors' residences (Townsend-Batten, 2002). The ultimate fallout from these shifts—perhaps more stressed-out mothers who juggle paid work, family responsibilities along with care for aging relations, less parental time for children and adolescents who already are sharing their parents with increasing time pressures from paid work and so on—remains to be seen.

Another very likely shift in Canadian families is the increased presence of immigrant families in Canada. As Canadians age, many will retire from the paid labour force and become reliant (at least, in part) on government-funded support systems, including an increasingly pressed medical system. If government systems are to sustain themselves and economic enterprises are to have sufficient employees, it will be necessary to maintain healthy rates of immigration into the country. Certainly, this logic reflects current realities. From 1986 to 1996 immigrants accounted for about half of the population growth in Canada and by 1996 almost one-fifth (over 17 percent) of Canadians were foreign-born—"the largest proportion in more than 50 years" (Boyd and Vickers, 2000, p. 9).

Not surprisingly, particularly given the family reunification aspects of Canadian immigration policy and legislation, many immigrants either arrive as families or reunite as families once one or more members have established themselves here. Indeed, policy analysts believe that by strengthening the immigrant family unit, newcomers, especially those who do not speak English or French, will find it easier to adjust to Canada (Thomas, 2001). Immigrant families, in turn, help to transplant many of the beliefs and values from the country of origin and help to sustain the distinctive communities—Chinese, Russian, Caribbean and so on—that dot the Canadian landscape.

Further, many of these immigrant families offer a different model of family living. For example, immigrants, especially those from Asian countries, are twice as likely to live in multigenerational families. In 2001, 7 percent of those born outside Canada lived in households containing grandparents, parents, and children. While these families may be particularly helpful in providing support to new immigrants, they may also set the family up for a clash of values as members of the older generation must come to terms on a daily basis with the Western values of their grandchildren (Milan and Hamm, 2003).

At the same time as many immigrant families may appear on the Canadian scene and embody a very traditional approach to family life, it is likely that many younger Canadians will continue to move towards a more individualistic lifestyle—spending a considerable part of their youth living on their own or continuing to live with their parents, opting for common-law rather than legally sanctioned personal relationships, pursing personal jobs or careers along with their family responsibilities, and accepting divorce as an important response to problems in intimate relationships. For example, from 1951 to 2001 the percentage of Canadians 15 and older living alone almost quintupled from 2.6 percent to 12.3 percent (Clark, 2002). While in many instances these solo individuals are seniors, there are increasing numbers of young men and women living alone or continuing to live in their parents' home. From 1981 to 2001 the percentage of 20 to 29-year-olds living with their parents increased from 27 percent to 41 percent (Statistics Canada, 2003a).

It should be emphasized that this "individualism" does not suggest a rejection of marriage and children as an important adult goal. Marriage is being postponed but not rejected and as much as divorce is embraced, so too is remarriage. In many respects the changes can be traced back to changes necessitated by the economic system rather than a rejection of family life. As seen in Chapter 12, Luxton and Corman note women's participation in the paid labour force was frequently inspired by the lack of wage increases for male workers and the increased availability of service sector employment for women. Families mobilized women (and teens) into paid employment in part because they needed to and in part because they could. At the same time, the rapidly expanding consumer economy, which now markets almost all of the traditional comforts of home, made it possible for women to reduce their labours in the home and for others to purchase replacements for the labours of wives and mothers (Ehrenreich, 1984). None of these trends is likely to be stalled in the foreseeable future, particularly since the popular neo-liberal political agenda—aimed at dramatically reducing or eliminating governmental responsibilities—is openly endorsing an "each person for him/herself" approach (Crompton, 2002).

While some analysts lament the loss of a traditional family—with its presumed warmth, interpersonal closeness, and parental altruism—it should be remembered not only that this rosy picture was often not accurate but also that the alternatives that are emerging may have their benefits. For example, postponing marriage and childrearing, experimenting with common-law relationships, and experiencing an independent lifestyle may be a much more preferable antecedent to becoming a parent and intimate partner. More mature partners and parents may be an important advance over current arrangements. In particular, more seasoned and personally independent partners may be less likely to succumb to destructive patterns of abuse and violence.

It is also likely that in the future family life will continue to be complexly interwoven with changes in the economy. We have seen that in recent years more and more family members have been drawn into paid employment and family members are spending increasing periods of their lives in preparation for paid employment (education) as well as actually working for pay. For example, by 2001, 70 percent of all women with children less than 16 years old had paid employment, in contrast to 39 percent in 1976 (Statistics Canada, 2002a). Many of the tensions currently noted in family life—the work–family conflict for women, the time pressures, the struggle over the gendered division of domestic work, the prolonged dependency of adult children—can be seen to be rooted in this increasingly intense and interwoven relationship between the world of work and family life (Silver, 2000; Kemeny, 2002; Fast et al., 2001).

Equally important, future changes in the economic order—periods of recession with attendant unemployment and underemployment—will directly impact on the quality and nature of family life. For example, considerable research documents that decisions to marry and/or have children are influenced by the health of the economy and the prospects for secure employment (Belanger and Ouellet, 2001; Orrange, 2003). Given the nature of current economic changes—the technological shifts in paid employment, the expansion of insecure forms of paid work (contract work and self-employment), the growth of a highly competitive global workforce, to name a few—it is likely that in the immediate future families will continue to experience upheaval and dislocation. In this context, it is also likely that many families, along with organized labour and other public groups, will actively seek to resist this increased intrusion of the economy into familial relations and will strive to arrive at more manageable arrangements (such as home-based work, extended familial or parental leave, reduced work time) (Marshall, 2003; Hayden, 1999).

Finally, it is likely that the future quality of many families' lives will be impacted by the growing social inequality gap. Research indicates that in Canada (as well as the United States and elsewhere around the globe) the rich are getting richer and the poor are getting (relatively) poorer. As one analyst comments, "between 1984 and 1999, wealth distribution [in Canada] became more unequal. Some groups, such as young couples with children and recent immigrants, have suffered substantial declines. The growing proportion of young couples with children who have zero or negative wealth suggests that a non-negligible fraction of today's young families may be vulnerable to negative shocks" (Morissette, Zhang, and Drolet, 2002, p. 19). Similarly, another report concludes, "Incomes of families at the bottom half of the income distribution showed little or no improvement through the 1990s. On the other hand, the 10 percent of Canadian families with the highest incomes experienced substantial gains" (Statistics Canada, 2003b, p. 5). Currently, the wealthiest 10 percent of Canadian families is earning on average $185 070 yearly (up from $161 460 in 1990) while the poorest 10 percent average $10 341 (up from $10 260 in 1990).

This pattern of growing disparity is important on several grounds. First, it clearly speaks to the quality of life amongst those families who will be so firmly shut out from the enormous range of opportunities enjoyed by more advantaged Canadians. Secondly and perhaps more importantly, it suggests the growth of a society in which the gap between the family lives of the haves and the have-nots starts to mirror that of earlier centuries. If Canada, along with countries around the globe, continues to ignore this pattern of growing social inequality, fundamental social values—progress, equality, opportunity—will be called ever more into question.

CONCLUSION

This chapter is intended to introduce you to some of the issues that surround the contemporary Canadian family. As noted in the introduction, there is not even consensus amongst analysts and scholars regarding a reasonable definition of the family. In part this conceptual debate reflects changes in the experience of family life and in part it is the result of growing awareness of the diversity of families. Within this argument over what "the family" is, it remains clear that "family" is a heavily laden term with dramatic implications far beyond the couple and their household. "Family" can be understood as a "master symbol" that is currently at the centre of struggles between those who wish to challenge the restrictions of that symbol and those who wish to retain traditional beliefs and values.

Given the centrality of "family" to these heated debates, it is not surprising to find "family" as a popular topic amongst sociological theorists. Here we review several of the leading contemporary theoretical positions and consider their broader implications. Next, some of the outstanding features of contemporary Canadian families are identified. These "facts" serve to challenge many of the popular myths surrounding family life.

In the final section, questions are posed regarding the future of the Canadian family. While it appears inevitable that "family" will continue to exist, it also seems likely that a number of important societal elements—the aging of the general population, increased numbers of immigrant families, continued upheavals in the economy, and patterns of employment and growing social inequality—will demand new forms of family living. Each one of these elements will be discussed in more detail in the chapters that follow.

Summary

- Definitions of family are widening.
- Economics and culture shape family forms.
- Traditional families are declining.
- Many first unions are now common-law.
- Same-sex marriage is accepted.
- Most families have two earners.
- Lone-parent families are increasing.
- There is a growing gap between rich and poor families.

Note

1. All of the statistics on contemporary families are from The Vanier Institute of the Family website, which relies on Statistics Canada information.

Critical Thinking Questions

1. Why has arriving at a generally accepted definition of "the family" been so difficult and what does this difficulty reveal about our society?
2. In what ways do material and structural forces shape family life?
3. What are traditional family roles? What are modern family roles? How are the roles of men and women influenced by gender and popular culture?
4. Compare and contrast modernist theories of family change with post-modern perspectives.
5. Consider some of the future influences on the family and identify how they might impact on your future personal experience of family life.

Websites

Vanier Institute of the Family
http://www.vifamily.ca
> The Vanier Institute of the Family website contains the most up-to-date statistics and analysis of Canadian families.

Statistics Canada
http://www.statcan.ca
> Statistics Canada provides the most recent Canadian information on all aspects of marriage including marital status, common-law status, families, dwellings, and households.

Natural Resources Canada
http://atlas.gc.ca/site/english/maps/peopleandsociety/families/familystructure

> Natural Resources Canada's website provides maps of Canada indicating the distributions of various elements. These particular maps indicate the concentration of family types across Canada and within specific regions.

Suggested Reading

Anne-Marie Ambert. 2003. *Same-Sex Couples and Same-Sex Parent Families: Relationships, Parenting, and Issues of Marriage.* Ottawa: The Vanier Institute of the Family.

> This occasional paper provides up-to-date information on the numbers of same-sex couple relationships in Canada, their legal status, their intimate relationships, fidelity, conflict, couples raising children, and the consequences of same-sex parenting for children.

Pamela Paul. 2002. *The Starter Marriage and the Future of Matrimony.* New York: Villard.

> Based on 60 interviews with American men and women who had starter marriages, the author explores the social and cultural consequences of this emerging marriage pattern. Students will find this description of early and short-lived marriages useful, accessible, and timely.

Michael Peplar. 2002. *Family Matters: A History of Ideas about Family since 1945.* London: Pearson Education.

> Drawing on a combination of first-person narrative accounts, popular cultural representations, official discourse and policy, and academic research, the author provides a comprehensive review of public debates since 1945 about the meaning and function of family.

Ethan Watters. 2003. *Urban Tribes: A Generation Redefines Friendship, Family and Commitment.* New York: Bloomsbury.

> Basing his book on personal experience as well as interviews, Watters explores the world of 30-somethings who have not married. He argues that, based on his research, these individuals have banded together as tightly knit groups of friends in urban centres across America. Although they have not yet married, they have created a kind of extended family that provides support and rituals, i.e., urban tribes. While Watters anticipates that most of his generation will eventually marry, he argues that they will do so on the basis of greater personal development and a more solid social support system.

References

Althusser, Louis. 1971. "Ideology and Ideological State Apparatuses." In *Lenin and Philosophy and Other Essays.* London: New Left Books. Pp. 17–33.

Ambert, Anne-Marie. 2003. *Same-Sex Couples and Same-Sex Parent Families: Relationships, Parenting, and Issues of Marriage.* Ottawa: The Vanier Institute of the Family.

———. 2002. *Divorce: Facts, Causes, and Consequences,* 2nd ed. Ottawa: Vanier Institute of the Family.

Belanger, Alain, and Genevieve Ouellet. 2001. "A Comparative Study of Recent Trends in Canadian and American Fertility, 1980–1999." *Report on the Demographic Situation in Canada.* 91-209-XPE. Ottawa: Minister of Industry.

Boyd, Monica, and Michael Vickers. 2000. "100 years of Immigration in Canada." *Canadian Social Trends* 58 (Autumn): 2–12.

Charles, Nickie. 2002. *Gender in Modern Britain.* London: Oxford University Press.

Chawla, Raj, and Henry Pold. 2003. "Family Wealth Across the Generations." *Perspectives on Labour and Income* 15 (4) (Winter): 5–15.

Clark, Warren. 2002. "Time Alone." *Canadian Social Trends* 66 (Autumn): 2–6.

Crompton, Rosemary. 2002. "Employment, Flexible Working and the Family." *British Journal of Sociology* 53 (4)(December): 437–49.

Department of Justice. 2002. *Marriage and Legal Recognition of Same-Sex Unions.* Ottawa.

Dubeau, Diane. 2002. *The Involved Father.* Ottawa: The Vanier Institute of the Family.

Ehrenreich, B. 1984. *The Hearts of Men: American Dreams and the Flight from Commitment.* Garden City, NY: Anchor/Doubleday.

Eichler, Margrit. 1997. *Family Shifts: Families, Policies and Gender Equality.* Toronto: Oxford University Press.

Fast, J., J. Frederick, N. Zukewich, and S. Franke. 2001. "The Time of Our Lives…" *Canadian Social Trends* 63 (Winter): 20–23.

Gerth, Hans, and C. Wright Mills. 1953. *Character and Social Structure: The Psychology of Institutions.* New York: Harcourt Brace Jovanovich, Inc.

Goode, William. 1963. *World Revolution and Family Patterns.* New York: The Free Press.

Harding, Sandra. 1986. *The Science Question in Feminism.* Milton Keynes: Open University Press.

Hayden, Anders. 1999. *Sharing the Work, Sparing the Planet: Work Time, Consumption and Ecology.* Toronto: Between the Lines.

Kemeny, Anna. 2002. "Driven to Excel: A Portrait of Canada's Workaholics." *Canadian Social Trends* 64 (Spring): 2–7.

Lasch, Christopher. 1977. *Haven in a Heartless World: The Family Besieged.* New York: Basic Books.

Laslett, Peter. 1965. *The World We Have Lost: England Before the Industrial Revolution.* New York: Charles Scribners Sons.

Lyon, David. 1999. *Postmodernity*, 2nd ed. Minneapolis: University of Minnesota Press.

Lyotard, Jean-Francois. 1984. *The Postmodern Condition: A Report on Knowledge*. Minneapolis: University of Minnesota Press.

Marshall, Brenda K. 1992. *Teaching the Postmodern: Fiction and Theory*. London: Routledge.

Marshall, Katherine. 2003. "Parental Leave: More Time Off for Baby." *Canadian Social Trends* 71 (Winter): 13–18.

Martin-Matthews, Anne. 2001. *The Ties that Bind Aging Families*. Ottawa: The Vanier Institute of the Family.

Milan, A. 2000. "One Hundred Years of Families." *Canadian Social Trends* 56 (Spring): 2–12.

Milan, Anne, and Brian Hamm. 2003. "Across the Generations: Grandparents and Grandchildren." *Canadian Social Trends* 71 (Winter): 2–7.

Milan, Anne, and Alice Peters. 2003. "Couples Living Apart." *Canadian Social Trends* 69 (Summer): 2–6.

Morisette, Rene, Xuelin Zhang, and Marie Drolet. 2002. "Wealth Inequality." *Perspectives on Labour and Income* 14 (Spring): 15-22.

Nisbet, Robert. 1966. *The Sociological Tradition*. New York: Basic Books.

Orrange, Robert M. 2003. "The Emerging Mutable Self: Gender Dynamics and Creative Adaptations in Defining Work, Family, and the Future." *Social Forces* 82 (1)(September): 1–35.

Parsons, Talcott. 1955. "The American Family: Its Relation to Personality and to Social Structure." In Talcott Parsons and Robert F. Bales, eds., *Family, Socialization and Interaction Process*, pp. 3–33. New York: The Free Press.

Rosenthal, Carolyn J., and James Gladstone. 2000. *Grandparenthood in Canada*. Ottawa: The Vanier Institute of the Family.

Sauve, Roger. 2002. *Connections: Tracking the Links Between Jobs and Family: Job, Family and Stress Among Husbands, Wives and Lone-parents 15-64 from 1990 to 2000*. Ottawa: The Vanier Institute of the Family.

Silva, Elizabeth B., and Carol Smart. 1999. "The 'New' Practices and Politics of Family Life." In E.B. Silva and C. Smart, eds. *The New Family?* London: Sage Publications. Pp. 1–12.

Silver, Cynthia. 2000. "Being There: The Time Dual-Earner Couples Spend with Their Children." *Canadian Social Trends* 57 (Summer): 26–29.

Statistics Canada. 2003a. "Update on Families." *Canadian Social Trends* 69 (Summer): 11–13.

———. 2003b. "2001 Census: Analysis Series—Income of Canadian Families." 96F0030IX2001014. Ottawa: Minister of Industry.

———. 2002a. "Work Chapter Updates." *Women in Canada* 89F0133XIE. Ottawa: Minister of Industry.

————. 2002b. *Changing conjugal life in Canada*. Catalogue no. 89-576-XIE.

————. 2002c. Profile of Canadian families and households. Catalogue no. 96F0030XIE2001003.

Stephens, William N. 1963. *The Canadian Family in Cross-Cultural Perspective*. Holt, Rinehart and Winston: New York.

Stobert, Susan, and Anna Kemeny. 2003. "Childfree by Choice." *Canadian Social Trends* 69 (Summer): 7–10.

Sullivan, Richard, ed. 1999. *Queer Families, Common Agendas: Gay People, Lesbians, and Family Values*. New York: Harrington Park Press.

Thomas, Derrick. 2001. "Evolving Family Living Arrangements of Canada's Immigrants." *Canadian Social Trends* 61 (Summer): 16–22.

Thorne, B. and M. Yalom. 1982. *Rethinking the Family: Some Feminist Questions*. New York: Longmans.

Townsend-Batten, Barbara. 2002. "Staying in Touch: Contact Between Adults and Their Parents." *Canadian Social Trends* 64 (Spring): 9–12.

Watters, Ethan. 2003. *Urban Tribes: A Generation Redefines Friendship, Family and Commitment*. New York: Bloomsbury.

Chapter 2

Family Histories

Nancy Mandell and Julianne Momirov

LEARNING OBJECTIVES

In this chapter, you will learn that:

1. there are multiple perspectives, some of which are better known than others, from which Canada's history can be constructed;

2. gender, race, and class shape family histories;

3. historical accounts tend to idealize the past;

4. the social positions of family members vary according to the economic, cultural, and social context within which they live;

5. gendered assumptions about wage and domestic labour shape family life.

INTRODUCTION

In this chapter, we sketch the histories of Canadian families. Our purpose is threefold: to stress the multiplicity and diversity of our family histories; to assess the classed, raced, gendered, and sexed nature of family structures; and to devote our attention to our early Canadian history. The rest of this book concentrates on contemporary roles, relationships, and issues.

HUNTING AND GATHERING

Many Aboriginal peoples claim North America as their original home. Some tell stories of how the mother of human beings fell through a hole in the sky and landed on the back of a tortoise covered with earth.[1] Others tell how humans had to make their way through a hollow log to reach the earth[2] (Dickason, 2002, p. 4). Academics claim that humans first entered Canada about 300 000 years ago, probably by boat (Dickason, 2002, p. 6). About 10 000 years ago, the first peoples moved into the far north of what is now the Yukon. Information gathered during the establishment in 1999 of the new Canadian territory of

Nunavut[3] indicates that from pre-contact times, the Inuit have occupied virtually all of the land north of the tree line and used most of the northern ocean
(Bryan, 1986; Elliott, 1983; Price; 1979; Stout, 1997).

Canada's Aboriginal peoples are ethnically diverse. Some Southern
Ontario tribes were sedentary while others took up a migratory, buffalo-oriented
life on the prairies (Ponting, 1986). Some groups were affluent, acquiring
surplus supplies of food, while others were impoverished (Ray, 1996, p. 84).
Some were **matrilocal** while others were **patrilocal**. All Aboriginal groups
successfully adapted to their environment, developing distinct economies,
oral cultures, art forms, and philosophies (Bryan, 1986).

For 99 percent of human history, hunting and gathering was the principal
means of subsistence.[4] Today, hunters and gatherers, including Canadian Inuit
and Indians, constitute about 0.01 percent of the world's popuation (Nett,
1988, p. 40). In the past, Canadian hunters and gatherers moved with the sea-
sons following available food supplies. Groups between six and 30 people (one
to five families) hunted and trapped wild game—caribou, moose, beaver, bear,
hare, porcupine, and waterfowl—fished, hunted small animals, and gathered
wild berries and vegetation (Leacock, 1991). They travelled light, lived frugally,
and seldom recorded their accomplishments (Bryan, 1986). Hunting and gathering groups developed shared economies and leadership based on residence,
gender, age, and ability. Life expectancy was short (Druke, 1986).

Hunting and gathering families retained distinct structures and organizational forms. For First Nations groups, family represented the basic unit of the
community. They based their social, political, and economic systems on kinship
networks, which were interdependent and extensive (Comacchio, 1999, p. 16).
Intragroup marriage led to large, **extended families** with multiple obligations.
Many families were **matrilineal**, wherein mothers, daughters, and sisters
worked together. Hierarchies of status, gender, and authority existed but family
members understood that their survival depended on trusting and relying on
the work of each other. Native men considered the work of women to be as
important as, and equal to, that of males (Anderson, 2000).

Coexistent with gender respect, within families a gendered division of
labour existed. Women and men lived in separate but reciprocal spheres, each
responsible for certain tasks (Leacock, 1991). Both genders had freedom to
contravene the stereotypical division of labour if they displayed a particular
talent (Anderson, 2000, p. 59). Men cut and hauled wood, hunted large
game, fished, and participated in warfare, councils, religion, politics, building,
and manufacturing implements for hunting and fishing. Among the
Iroquoian- and Algonquian-speaking people, men were associated with
forests, while among groups involved in horticulture, men were associated
with clearing the fields (Druke, 1986). Men made wooden devices such as
toboggans, sleds, snowshoe frames, and spoons. Men butchered animals and
skinned them for pelts, and repaired lanterns, canoes, fish nets, and clothes.

Women and children did most of the agricultural work and gathering of fruits, vegetable foods, and firewood (Druke, 1986). Women's foraging took place close to home, with children in tow. Men's hunting and fishing was intermittently successful, often taking them far from home for long periods of time. Groups depended on women's fishing, hunting of small animals, and gathering of roots, herbs, fruits, berries, insects, birds, and eggs, all of which supplied the band's basic caloric and protein requirements (Leacock, 1991). Although women had considerable freedom, they were restricted from making war, hunting large animals, and ruling the tribe. Group respect for women's essential work allowed women autonomy and control over their work and their sexuality, and allowed them to exercise some authority in local politics (Bourgeault, 1988; Bradbury, 1996; Van Kirk, 1992). Women had authority over property, including land and lodging (Anderson, 2000, pp. 60–61). In Iroquois culture, stored food was considered wealth and was completely controlled by women (Anderson, 2000, p. 60).

In addition to controlling food preparation, women managed the household, reared children, made clothing, repaired household items, and developed domestic equipment such as wooden utensils, basketry, pottery, and the mortar and pestle. Native women knew medicinal herbs, midwifery, and some surgery. Women's fertility was often depressed and the reasons include their nomadic lifestyle, irregular diet, taboos restricting sexual relations (Van Kirk, 1992); their knowledge of birth control and abortifacients (McLaren, 1977); and the fact that they were pregnant or nursing most of their brief lives (Price, 1979).

Hunting cultures survived in Canada well into the 1800s and were described by colonizing Europeans as among the most highly developed in the world. When, in the mid-1800s, the first major wave of white immigration settled the Canadian West, they found about 30 bands in Quebec and Labrador, and a Native population of 150 000 peoples harvesting herds of millions of buffalo in the West.

HORTICULTURE AND AGRICULTURE

Agriculture is a recent phase in Canadian history. For most of our past, hunting predominated and was supplemented by other food sources, such as fish in coastal British Columbia, agriculture in Southern Ontario and in the St. Lawrence River valley, shellfish on Prince Edward Island, and wild rice around the Great Lakes.[5]

By the 1500s, there were two cultures in Ontario: hunter-gatherer bands in the north, and horticultural, tribally organized Native people in the south. Permanent Iroquois settlements appeared in the St. Lawrence River valley and the Great Lakes region, while those speakers of the Algonquian language family remained hunter-gatherers, inhabiting what is now Quebec and the forests bordering the Atlantic (Morrison and Wilson, 1986; Price, 1979).

Plant-gathering, shellfish-gathering, and fishing societies are largely sedentary communities. Societies that domesticated plants were provided with a more reliable food supply, allowing communities to become sedentary. Staying in one place allows groups to increase their population and to develop more complex social and political arrangements (Nett, 1988). The Maritime Mi'kmaq were a maritime group with extended family living in villages stretched along the Atlantic coast (Miller, 1986).

Women took on most of the responsibility for agriculture, just as they were more likely to be the ones gathering plants in tribal societies. The **communal family** was the primary unit of production. Married women worked cooperatively with their mothers and sisters planting corn, beans, and squash. The increased protein provided by crops led to a steady supply of nutrients and eventually to population expansion. Gradually, large villages with rows of multifamily longhouses were built (Druke, 1986).

In agricultural societies, the **nuclear family** functioned as an integral part of each band. Intricate ties of blood and ceremonial kinship organized rights and obligations in all aspects of life, such as naming a child at birth, residence, labour, trade, gender relations, political and cultural leadership, diplomacy and war, marriage and divorce, and death and inheritance (Comacchio 1999, p. 16).

THE EUROPEAN CONQUEST: 1500s–1700s

With the establishment of English and French settlements, Europeans began a long process of cultural genocide, of what Ponting (1986) calls "the deliberate extinction of Indians as Indians." Even though Aboriginal peoples resisted, European colonizers drained resources from Native lands and transferred wealth back to England and France; in the process, they destroyed numerous Native cultures (Bolaria and Li, 1988).

In the early 1400s and 1500s, fur trading led to the establishment of trading posts and the provision to Natives of a stable food supply in exchange for furs. Over time, Natives became economically dependent on the Europeans when alcohol was introduced to them; when European goods replaced their traditional goods; when new tools such as guns, knives, and axes became their work implements; and when their labour fell largely under European control (Bourgeault, 1988). Europeans were not interested in obtaining what Native women produced (Anderson, 2000, p. 62).

When English and French explorers entered Canada in the 1400s and 1500s, Native people were thriving (Druke, 1986). Europeans brought disease, destruction, and defeat. Smallpox and other infectious illnesses decimated populations, as did the warfare central to the fur trade (Druke, 1986). Native warfare over the immensely profitable fur trade led to disease and famine. The Huron population was reduced from between 60 000 and 80 000 in the late

1500s to 24 000 in 1640, and finally to a mere 1500 in 1651. Europeans fostered Native warfare by pitting one tribe against another and participated in vile acts such as serving poisoned food to the Mi'kmaq peoples at a feast in 1812; trading contaminated cloth in 1745; and employing Mohawks, Algonquians, and soldiers to track and kill Mi'kmaqs (Miller, 1986).

Fur trading was what some call the first stage of economic globalization (Walters, 1995). It was organized around European production and circulation of fur as an important commodity in the world market. In order to gurantee profit, colonizers precipitated change in Native societies and in their lifestyles that resulted in the depletion of their populations. Indian society transformed from one based on subsistence to one producing goods for exchange to fur traders (Bourgeault, 1988). Diets were affected, traditional food stores became inadequate and nutritionally deficient, miscellaneous accidents and injuries increased, and life expectancy dropped dramatically (Miller, 1986). Some tribes had to become specialists in trapping and reduce their time spent and reliance on traditional subsistence practices. By the time Champlain landed in 1603 in the once-prospering villages of what eventually became Montreal and Quebec, the sites had been abandoned.

NATIVE SENSE OF FAMILY

From the 1500s to the 1700s in Canada, mostly white men and Native people engaged in fur trading, hunting, gathering, horticulture, and agriculture. From the paternalistic accounts written by white settlers, or colonizers, about Natives, we learn of the clash of two cultures. With the beginning of the Christian conversion of Natives, which began around 1632, cultural clashes were exacerbated. Jesuit priests in Quebec, for example, were forced to confront vast differences between European and Native family lifestyles. Native spouses were described as enjoying easy relations, as "women know what they are to do and the men also; and One never meddles with the work of the other" (Leacock, 1991, p. 13). Many Native family relationships and practices baffled Europeans: personal autonomy; lack of hierarchy; spousal interdependence; abundant love for their children; abhorrence of inflicting corporal punishment, fear, or humiliation on children; easy divorce by consent; flexible residential choice; polygamy; and sexual freedom after marriage for both women and men.

In contrast, European marriages of the 1600s adhered to patriarchal norms of family life, as men's superiority was enshrined in law and religion. Wives, especially bourgeois ones, were enjoined to be obedient, pious, and dependent decision-makers in deference to their husbands. Frequently, husbands were physically abusive and enjoyed the legal right to beat their wives and children. Divorce was virtually unobtainable. Husbands' adultery was sanctioned, whereas that of wives was severely punished (Zinn and Eitzen, 1993).

Inevitably, Native women clashed with Catholic priests. Used to consultative and co-operative decision-making, Native women found European demands for unquestioned obedience to men ludicrous and demeaning. Most Native people never accepted European ideas of unequal spousal relationships, premarital chastity, marital fidelity, **monogamy**, male courtship, and male dominance.

Despite their resistance to European and Christian mores, Native women played such a vital role in fur trading that interracial unions were sanctioned by an indigenous rite known as customary marriages with *les femmes du pays* (country wives). Women's skills in hunting, gathering, skinning animals, and preserving furs, their abilities in trade and diplomacy, and their knowledge of several Native languages made their services invaluable to their voyageur husbands (Jamieson, 1986). Many European traders survived harsh Canadian winters by supplementing their unreliable meat diets with the small game, berries, and wild rice their Native wives provided (Van Kirk, 1992). Children provided another important outcome of alliances between Native women and European fur traders. "Much of the labour force of the fur trade companies consisted of the children of these marriages, the first generation of the Métis people instrumental in the creation of Manitoba in 1870" (Comacchio, 1999, p. 17).

For most of the 1700s, Native people were treated with the cautious respect accorded allies in war and partners in trade (Jamieson, 1986). However, after 1812, Native people were no longer regarded as useful allies. Once agriculture replaced the fur trade as the basis of the economy, customary marriages were rejected and European settlers increasingly adhered to French and British class and ethnic codes of behaviour. Métis, or mixed-blood, daughters became fashionable as wives of those establishing and working with the trading posts that were being settled across the north and west of Canada. By the early 1800s, the North West Company, an agent of British imperial interests, outlawed marriages with full-blooded Native women. Missionaries who arrived with the Hudson's Bay Company in the 1820s, company officials, and government representatives denounced interracial marriages in an effort to prescribe strict racial segregation and to eschew efforts at assimilation characteristic of the earlier French regime (Jamieson, 1986). White women, heretofore unknown in the fur trading era, began slowly to settle in trading posts.

As the agrarian frontier developed in the mid-1800s, Native and Métis women's status declined precipitously. They moved from being wives to being domestics; today, their essential role in opening the Canadian West and the fur trade is largely forgotten (Anderson, 1987; Van Kirk, 1992). By the 1830s, 20 percent of the contracted servants were Métis, and by the 1850s, 50 percent of the Métis were employed as seasonal labourers in transportation or general labourers around the posts (Frideres, 1998).

The Canadian state implemented an **ethnocentric** ideology of "civilizing" Indians, a policy that replaced previous military and economic alliances with racist employment and marriage regulations (Jamieson, 1986).

BOX 2.1   RECOVERING A MOHAWK IDENTITY

When I began researching my family tree, I had not planned to take such a significant part in the process. I had not expected it to get so personal. But in learning about my family history, I started remembering things I had long forgotten. In learning about my ancestors, I saw the other parts of who I am. I saw myself as carrying on a part of them, and in doing so, honouring both their spirits and my own.

As a person of mixed heritage, honouring the spirit has not been easy. My journey begins with two white women—my mother and my paternal grandmother—who have supported and encouraged my exploration of my Native identity. My Native family, on the other hand, have passed on to me messages of shame and denial throughout my whole life. Today, I only see irony in this treatment of my heritage. Five hundred, one hundred, fifty years ago the white community discouraged Nativeness—it continues even today. In seeking out the lives of my ancestors, I begin my journey of recovering a Mohawk identity. Living in a non-Native society has made embracing Native traditions and values feel like coming home. My challenge now is to feel at home with the spirit, in the truest, most honest sense, balancing myself in the worlds in which I am a part. I was not raised in an environment of Native heritage; I only know the effects of it. I only know that I cannot ignore the beating force of its strength within me.

Source: Taken from Laura Schwager, "The Drum Keeps Beating: Recovering a Mohawk Identity." In Kim Anderson and Bonita Lawrence, eds., *Strong Women Stories: Native Vision and Community Survival.* Toronto: Sumach Press, 2003, pp. 37–38.

By forcing Natives to shed their languages, customs, religious beliefs, and traditional structures, the government hoped to assimilate Native peoples. A series of acts, culminating with the Indian Act of 1876, offered Natives enfranchisement, forcibly Christianized them through residential schools, and separated them from their children as ways of encouraging assimilation (Ponting, 1986). (See Chapter 4 for a discussion of recent Native life.)

PRE-INDUSTRIAL FAMILIES: 1600s–1700s

In the 1600s, marriage and family patterns varied in the new settlements of what is now Ontario, Quebec, and the Maritimes. New France (Quebec) was populated by male soldiers, sailors, merchants, indentured labourers, interpreters, and of course, Native people (Dumont et al., 1987). In 1617, the first French family arrived in Quebec and was the only family to own a house there until 1634. When official settlement began, the French-Canadian rang system provided uniformly sized river lots for peasant-status settlers. Immigrants centred their family and community life around the Church parish. In the 1600s and 1700s, **romantic love** was not the basis for marriage but rather marriage was a family and kinship matter arranged, by contract, with dowries. If families disapproved of the marriage, they could either disinherit couples or withhold dowries (Krull, 1996, p. 374). In the middle-class families of merchants, administrators, and seigneurs, children tended to marry with parental consent, in religious ceremonies, someone they knew in the community. Rural families were equally patriarchal with fathers exercising legal, religious, and civil authortiy. Farmers and peasants favoured hardworking, healthy spouses who could contribute long and successfully to the family enterprise (Landry and Legare, 1987).

New France profited from the heroic and enterprising activities of women. The "King's Daughters," **les filles du roi**, consisted of nearly 800 women whose transportation to and keep in the colony were paid for by the king of France. Originating from the Paris Hôpital-Général, an institution that housed disadvantaged, poor, sick, insane, and abandoned women and children, these women were recruited between 1663 and 1673 and sent to New France as brides for male settlers (Landry, 1992). The other notable group of emigrating women were called the *religieuses*. The first *religieuses* to arrive were extremely well born, highly dedicated religious figures with generous dowries. The Ursulines and Hospitallers, who landed in Quebec in 1639, were nuns who undertook missionary work that gave them an active role in the colony, supplying money, publicity, skills, and settlers. These women conducted schools, recruited settlers, and raised money for hospitals and charities, thus playing an important role in supplying leadership, funding, publicity, recruits, and social services for the colony (Noel, 1991). In 1663, Montreal had a school for girls but not boys, indicating that for a short historical time, Montreal women surpassed men in literacy skills.

In the early settlement period, **gender roles** for women were surprisingly flexible, a result perhaps of their complex, enterprepreneurial tasks in the emerging fur trading and military economy. Harsh conditions demanded the labour and ingenuity of both sexes. While legally, men had authority over their wives and were responsible for their misdemeanours, in fact men did not always exercise control in economic and domestic life (Noel, 1991).

In the pre-industrial economy, many families barely eked out a living. Death left women widowed and children orphaned. Female-headed households were mostly poor (Bradbury, 1992). Financial security was most likely found in families with access to male earnings, who lived either in towns, on French Canadian seigneurial manors, or on Southern Ontario estates. In all social classes, public life was not differentiated from private life. On farms, women were often responsible for the stables, the henhouses, and the vegetables gardens; for preparing food; for making clothes; for tending the sick; for keeping farm accounts and managing purchases and sales. Men and women worked the fields together except when men went off logging and women performed the farm work themselves. In the towns, both men and women were tavern owners, storekeepers, grocers, moneylenders, peddlers, and bonesetters (Noel, 1991). In towns, women took in boarders, sewing or washing clothes, and minding children. Women worked alongside men, operating businesses and supervising apprentices. They worked for wages as maids, laundresses, publicans, prostitutes, and nurses. They engaged in fur trading, shipping and selling imported goods. Still others began commercial enterprises.

In both agricultural and commercial enterprises, women's work was recognized as being as indispensable as that of men. Spousal interdependence made marriage an economic necessity for both men and women. While in Europe, women were slowly losing their status in guilds and professions, in New France wives tended to be equal partners to their husbands. Rules governing inheritance and marriage protected women's rights and property. Widows acquired the right to manage the family's assets until their children reached age 25; in this way, by 1663, women held the majority of seigneurial land (Dumont et al., 1987). In contrast, in English Canada, common law dictated that men held all power and property in families. Upon marriage, women lost all legal status, could not control property, start businesses, initiate legal actions, or administrate family assets without their husbands' approval.

North America in the 1600s and 1700s was often a colonial battlefield. Both the British and French maintained military bases from which to fight for territorial control over the highly lucrative fur trade. The French war machine employed one-quarter of the Quebec population by the late 1600s. War altered Canadian society. After the defeat of the French on the Plains of Abraham in 1759, Canada was handed over to the British in 1763 under the Treaty of Paris. Quebec City was bombarded and besieged, and hundreds of farms were burned and destroyed (Dumont et al., 1987). With British rule came waves of English and Scottish immigration along with the United Empire Loyalists fleeing the 1776 American Revolution. Many Irish Protestants and Catholics emigrated. Initially, most British immigrants stayed on the Atlantic coast, so that, during the 1600s, Atlantic coast populations increased 25 times more rapidly than did the population of New France.

By the 1700s, most Canadian families lived in rural settings clustered in Quebec, Ontario, and the Maritimes. Generally, the 1700s were economically prosperous. Families continued to produce most of the articles needed, land was available, and harvests were plentiful (Dumont et al., 1987). With agricultural settlements, populations stabilized and women's family positions became more traditional. Marriageable girls were more readily available, seigneuries filled up, social classes became more readily distinguishable, and women began to be relegated to the domestic sphere of the family. Alongside prosperous settlers were the poor, of whom two-thirds were women. So numerous were their numbers that Montreal opened a shelter for the destitute in the late 1600s. Women had difficulty earning a living as their salaries were half those earned by men. Most of the lucrative professional jobs were closed to women who lacked specialized training and education (Bradbury, 1992).

In the 1700s, men and women continued to rely on one another to keep their **family-based economy**—domestic, economic and social activities—

functioning. Yet, spousal interdependence did not translate into spousal equality. Children also performed necessary economic functions although, following the roles of their parents, girls performed different tasks than boys. Schooling took place largely through religious communities and girls received access through convents, more so than did boys. Still, education was generally not widespread and did not extend much past teaching basic literacy skills. Upper-class boys in Ontario, Quebec, and the Maritimes received formal instruction, more sophisticated teaching, and more specialized and professional training than did girls. Working-class boys of age 9 or 10 apprenticed in jobs as carpenters, coopers, blacksmiths, accountants, doctors, and lawyers. Working-class girls filled domestic contracts around age 10, which lasted until they were married or financially self-sufficient. Apprenticeship as a seamstress began at age 19 and lasted one year. Young adults married when their parents could spare their labour (Conrad, 1991).

Family and work lives were often violent for women and children. Women had little protection against sexual harassment and those who retaliated in self-defence were harshly punished. Marie-Josephte Corriveau is legendary in Quebec. At her trial in 1783, she admitted to killing her abusive husband with an axe while he slept. British authorities hanged her and left her body hanging for public display for more than a month (Dumont et al., 1987, p. 98).

CANADIAN SLAVERY

Slavery was a constituent feature of pioneer life in colonial society (Calliste, 1996b). From the late 1600s until the early 1800s, black slaves were held in Quebec, Nova Scotia, New Brunswick, and Ontario. The majority of slaves were Native people, either Pawnees or members of closely related tribes (Winks, 1971, p. 17). The first written record of a person of African descent in Nova Scotia is from 1605, when Matthew da Costa arrived with the Champlain expedition (Williams, 1983). The first known black slave arrived in Canada in 1628 as a boy of 7 or 8; he was brought from Madagascar and sold to a Quebec resident (Walker, 1980, p. 19).

Through a series of French laws, slavery was given legal foundation in New France. The 1685 Code Noir, which regulated the practice of slavery in the West Indies, was assumed to have legal application in France's North American colony. The code was actually designed to protect owners, not slaves, from slaves' violence and escape (Thomson, 1979). By 1762, the colony recognized slavery as an acceptable institution. Whereas initially the fur trade had little need for slave labour, beginning in 1663 the demand for cheap labour escalated so much that colonists petitioned their governors for the right to import black slaves to supplement scarce labour (Winks, 1971). Both the necessity of slave labour in the development of Canada and slaves' resistance to their servitude was evident in the 1709 fining law instituted in New

France. Despite reports of "humane and familial treatment," slaves obviously did not find the terms so agreeable, as evidenced by their numerous attempts to escape (Winks, 1971, p. 14). Those assisting slaves to escape were fined, and colonial newspapers were full of notices regarding runaways. Despite these punishments, free blacks sheltered runaways, petitioned governments to abolish slavery, and frequently brought cases to court when they believed that blacks, especially children, were being mistreated or illegally detained.

In 1749, when the English settled in Halifax, they evidently brought slaves with them (Williams, 1983). The first recorded slave sales in Halifax occurred in 1752. In 1767, Nova Scotia, which then included New Brunswick, had a population of 3022, of which 104 were slaves living mostly in Halifax (Walker, 1980). By the time of the British conquest of New France in 1759, local records revealed 3604 slaves, of whom 1132 were black and the rest were Pawnee. Half of the blacks lived in or near Montreal, working mostly as domestic servants. Few worked in the fields or mines. Many were held at the French fortress of Louisbourg (Walker, 1980; Winks, 1971). The exploitation of black labour in commercial enterprises and on farms was essential to Canada's economic development. Free blacks received about one-quarter the prevailing wage rate for whites for day work and were especially vulnerable to exploitation because they were desperate for work (Walker, 1980). Slave women worked mostly as domestics. In 1744, 5 percent of all female servants in Quebec City were black slaves and 10 percent were Native people (Dumont et al., 1987, p. 97).

The treatment of black slaves ranged from paternalistic to outright exploitative. Some authors suggest that slavery in New France was benevolent, compared with slavery in the United States (Thomson, 1979; Walker, 1980; Winks, 1971). The family life of slaves was severely restricted by their legal status. Slaves could marry only with their owner's permission. Children became the property of the mother's owner; so female slaves were prized for their reproductive capacity. Some writers suggest gender roles among slaves were not as differentiated as those of white people, as males and females often performed the same types of work (Calliste, 1996a, p. 248).

Canadian blacks were socially, economically, and legally excluded. They were without rights, could not vote, could not associate with white people as equals, could not marry interracially, were not welcome in white churches, and were segregated in black schools (Thomson, 1979). Social Darwinism described blacks as fun-loving, imitative, and "naturally" obsequious, thus academically instituting a racist theory of social inequality that many aca-demics and journalists supported (Thomson, 1979). Given these policies, it is not surprising that blacks were thought of as unlikely to assimilate and unsuited to the northern climate.

The arrival of Loyalists in 1783, following the American Revolution, brought another 2000 or more blacks into Canada. About 1232 arrived in

Nova Scotia, 300 in Lower Canada, and about 500 in Upper Canada. Loyalist-owned slaves were also found in Prince Edward Island, Cape Breton Island, and Newfoundland. The end of 1783 found blacks in virtually every white settlement in Canada (Clairmont and Magill, 1974, p. 40). With the Loyalist influx, black slaves supplanted Pawnee slaves, even in Quebec (Winks, 1971).

Britain freed many American **black Loyalists**, offering them free land and free provisions while they prepared their farms for harvest (Clairmont and Magill, 1974, p. 41). However, only about a third of black Loyalists in Nova Scotia and New Brunswick received any land at all, and their farms were considerably smaller and usually in less fertile or more remote regions than those of white Loyalists. Usually, blacks failed to receive any provisions and found that they were economically dependent. Groups of Loyalists, black and white, were settled together. Three separate black settlements were created in Nova Scotia. The largest one, Birchtown, consisted of 649 male family heads; the one at Preston contained 100 families (Walker, 1980; Winks, 1971).

Most white and black Loyalists arriving in Nova Scotia in the late 1700s were wretchedly destitute. Blacks were even more deprived. They were disproportionately represented in sharecropping, domestic service, and indentured occupations. A number of free blacks were forced to sell themselves, or their children, into slavery or long-term indenture. Conditions were so desperate that, when an agent of the Sierra Leone Company came recruiting among Nova Scotia blacks in 1792, offering free land and full equality, about 1200 accepted his company's offer and sailed to the British colony in West Africa. Additional migration took place in 1800 to Sierra Leone, and in 1821 to Trinidad, leaving 2500 blacks in North America, more slaves than free (Clairmont and Magill, 1974, p. 42).

By 1815, another 2000 free blacks arrived in Nova Scotia, having been offered freedom by the British during the War of 1812. Those hardworking refugee blacks came in search of a new life, bringing with them numerous skills. They built homes, petitioned for schools and churches, and used their skills to farm and do other jobs (Williams, 1983). They settled on small lots of rocky soil and scrubby forest, politically free but physically starving. Their condition of subsistence poverty, begun in the early 1800s, continues today. A number of blacks moved to Victoria, British Columbia, in 1859 from California. They worked on farms, in shops, and on wharves; owned farms; became teachers and businessmen; and achieved community success, as they had in other parts of Canada.

Slavery as a system was accepted and supported by many prominent and respectable Canadians for about a hundred years, from the early 1700s, when it was first authorized, until 1834, when it was abolished throughout the British Empire. Ontario was the first British territory to legislate against slavery, in 1793. The abolition bill faced severe opposition from large landowners concerned about the scarcity of cheap labour. The heroes of

Canadian abolition were the judges who, by judicial legislation, moved against an institution that retained sufficient public support in Nova Scotia, New Brunswick, and Lower Canada to prevent popularly elected assemblies from

BOX 2.2   BLACK CANADIANS

Writers have only recently admitted that the recording of Canadian history is often racist, erasing the history of black Canadians. Adrienne Shadd (1987) relates the history of blacks in Canada, a history too seldom taught in schools. Blacks, first brought as slaves in the 1600s and 1700s, were among the earliest to settle on Canadian soil. Ten percent of the Loyalists who migrated to Canada after the American Revolution were black. Their descendants, particularly in the Maritimes, have been living in quasi-segregated communities for over 200 years. Between 1815 and 1860, blacks were one of the largest groups to enter Canada, when between 40 000 and 60 000 fugitive slaves and free people "of colour" sought refuge in Ontario (Shadd, 1987, p. 4).

These settlers enriched the culture of the country, yet their many contributions are often neglected. Founder of the Queen Victoria Benevolent Society in 1840, the first organization to offer aid to black women, indigents, and fugitive slaves, was Mrs. Wilson Abbot. Founder of the Anti-Slavery Society and the first newspaperwoman in Canada was Mary Ann Shadd, who edited a paper for fugitives between 1853 and 1859 in Toronto, and later in Chatham, Ontario. In 1883, Elizabeth Shadd Shreve, a black preacher, established the Women's Home Missionary Society in Ontario. Joe Fortes, a Barbadian-born sailor, came to British Columbia in 1885 and, as a life-guard, taught three generations of people to swim at English Bay. The term "the real McCoy" was coined after the inventions of a black man, Elijah McCoy, born in Harrow, Ontario, in 1840 (Whitla, 1995, pp. 321–49; Shadd, 1987, p. 3).

As Violet Blackman tells us, the lives of black Canadians continued to be difficult far into the twentieth century. In Toronto, immigration was restrictive, work was scarce, and societal discrimination was rampant. Yet, individuals prevailed and succeeded:

> You couldn't get any position, regardless who you were and how edu-cated you were, other than housework, because even if the employer would employ you, those that you had to work with would not work with you.

> It was a man here—Donald Moore. He saw the conditions, he formed a committee, and we used to go to different churches and hold different ral-lies. It was the '30s. Later, with this committee, he went to Ottawa with a brief and presented it—of allowing the coloured people from the different islands to come in. Then, after that, the government permit that so many could come in each year from different islands. But you had to come in as a domestic: you had to go and serve a year with some lady up in Rosedale or up in the upper section, and then when you're satisfactory—took a year—you get your landing, and you're free to go and do anything that you want to do. That was how coloured people start coming into this country.

Source: Based on Dionne Brand. 1991. *No Burden to Carry: Narratives of Black Working Women in Ontario, 1920s to 1950s.* Toronto: Women's Press, pp. 37–38.

abolishing slavery (Winks, 1971, p. 110). By 1800, the chief justices of Lower Canada and the Maritimes felt slavery was illegal and refused to use state power to retrieve runaways, instead insisting that owners produce the almost unobtainable proof of ownership. Any slave who quit could do so without fearing a return to enslavement by the courts or state officials (Walker, 1980).

THE SHIFT TO INDUSTRIALIZATION

At the beginning of the 1800s, Canada was still a sparsely populated colony whose pre-industrial economy was small-scale, labour-intensive, and focused primarily on farming, fishing, lumbering, and some fur trading (Wilson, 1991, p. 14). Daily life was centred on the land, production was based in the **household**, age and gender roles were fixed by custom, and few people lacked useful work (Gaffield, 1990). Wage labour and an emerging capitalist economy co-existed with domestic production often because early industry was based on expanding family businesses (Comacchio 1999, p. 18). Handicrafts and homemade goods could be found alongside goods manufactured in small factories.

As the century progressed, two major economic changes occurred. Small-scale subsistence farming was gradually replaced with large-scale, high-volume commercial agriculture; and employment based at or near the home was replaced by work at central locations like shops and factories (Zinn and Eitzen, 1993). The Canadian economy was slowly transformed from one based on agriculture to one based on cash and determined by industrial capital. Factories increased from 2.4 million in 1851 to 5.4 million in 1901, cities like Montreal, Quebec, and Hamilton grew rapidly, and immigration exploded (Katz, 1975). Profound social and economic transformation was taking place.

With the advent of commercial and industrial enterprise in the nineteenth century, work and family life became increasingly separate. Men and women no longer worked side-by-side in family businesses; the land could no longer support all members of a family, so people migrated to cities in search of work for wages, often in one of the new factories being established. "Wage labour became part of the life-course of unmarried young people, allowing them to contribute to the family economy, and eventually to leave their parents' homes and set up on their own" (Comacchio, 1999, p. 18). New immigrants also followed this model. An urban, industrialized working class developed.

Along with the growth of wage labour, the ideology of separate spheres emerged. Femininity became associated with women's domestic and child-rearing work in the home while masculinity was associated with men's roles in the world of paid work. For middle-class families, the ideology often seemed to match the reality. Middle-class women were engaged in all kinds of unpaid work outside their homes (albeit unpaid) as they organized and conducted charity and church work. These privileged women were frequently face-to-face with the social ills and dislocations resulting from the changes in society (Comacchio, 1999, pp. 20–21).

For working-class families, the notion of a "**family wage**," a wage adequate for a male worker to support himself, a dependent wife, and children, remained elusive. Most working-class men rarely earned enough money to support all their dependants. Moreover, industrial accidents, sudden layoffs, and illnesses meant that working-class jobs were mostly irregular, seasonal, and unhealthy. In order to stay above the poverty line, family members pooled their resources. Children's wages were turned over to parents, and often children dropped out of school to work to supplement their parents' earnings (Palmer, 1983).

It was considered demeaning for married women to labour for wages, compromising the husband's authority as household head and potentially dangerous for children's moral and cognitive development (Wilson, 1991). Only about 5 percent of married women took up labour, and then only because of dire economic necessity, brought about through desertion or widowhood. When extra money was required, wives took in washing or sewing, cleaned

BOX 2.3   THE EMERGENCE OF THE "MODERN" WOMAN

Large numbers of young women moved to cities during the mid-nineteenth century to work for wages. Some women were inventive, adhering to traditional ideas about women's "proper" roles as wives and mothers while earning money. The story of middle-class Halifax resident Annie Hamilton illustrates prevailing domestic ideology. Annie took herself and her children to stay with relatives in the country whenever her husband's business was not doing well. In this way, Annie's husband did not have to support her and their children, and could redirect his funds into the business. In another Halifax case, Maria Morris Miller, whose father died when she was only 3, began her own drawing school and worked as an artist when she was 23. She married and had five children but lived apart from her husband for most of the year. Thanks to her ability to produce an income, Maria was able to assist her mother and gain a certain amount of independence when her married life did not turn out to be what she expected (Guildford, 1997). Both Maria and Annie perpetuated their middle-class status by finding creative ways to earn money.

The appearance of women in the public sphere alarmed many people who fretted that these young women might not be willing to retreat into the domestic realm after experiencing independence. They also worried that these young women would fall prey to all kinds of licentious and immoral temptations, as they lacked supervision. The emergence of new forms of entertainment, such as dance halls, vaudeville, and amusement parks, raised more concerns among staid Torontonians (Strange, 1997). After World War I, the "modern" women appeared on the scene. The "flapper" terrified many with her short hair, boyish figure, and short skirt. She was able to vote and to pursue an education. She worked outside the home in the company of men. She seemed to have abandoned "womanliness" and it was believed that she was rejecting home and family. Many concerned Canadians thought she might very well bring about the demise of middle-class domestic ideals.

Source: Based on Cynthia R. Comacchio. 1999. *The Infinite Bonds of Family: Domesticity in Canada, 1850-1940*. Toronto: University of Toronto Press, p. 73.

homes for other people, grew vegetables, kept animals such as cows for their milk, and bartered goods (Bradbury, 1996; Comacchio, 1999). Situated in the home, women's economic contributions remained invisible. When they worked for wages, all classes of women were concentrated in gender-specific occupations in textile and garment industries, in shoe factories, in the tobacco industry, in domestic service, and in teaching (Bullen, 1992). Few women laboured at middle-class jobs as innkeepers, grocers, clerks, or tax collectors (Bloomfield and Bloomfield, 1991; Katz, 1975). The exception was found in the Ontario town of Paris, where the Penman knitting company employed mostly women. In Paris, women were less likely to marry, more likely to work their entire lives, and more likely to establish their own homes. Their family lives were unique compared to the rest of the province (Parr, 1990).

Testimony to the 1889 Royal Commission on the Relations of Labour and Capital revealed that women and children were economically exploited, often brutalized, and frequently dismissed without cause. Jobs did not necessarily offer security or protection (Bullen, 1992; Katz, 1975; Parr, 1990). Employers used the ideology of separate spheres, which glorified women as home-makers, as their justification for paying women one-third less than men. Their income was seen as supplemental to that of their husbands. Although some legislation passed in the 1880s gave certain rights over property and contracts to married women, for the most part women remained legally, professionally, and economically subordinate to men (Comacchio, 1999, p. 27).

The lack of stable, well-paying work plunged single, widowed, and deserted women into poverty. It was not until 1920 that four Canadian provinces introduced Mothers' Pensions as a way of providing "deserving" women and children with financial support. Rampant hostility towards the large number of recent immigrants coupled with a strong desire to preserve the Anglo-Celtic family led British Columbia legislation to exclude most racial minorities, particularly Asians, from receiving Mothers' Pensions (Little, 1998).

CHANGES IN WOMEN'S, MEN'S, AND CHILDREN'S ROLES

Industrialization brought about changes in functions and values attributed to the home and its members. Rather than operating as a mini-manufacturing workshop, an agent of religious indoctrination, or an apprenticeship training site, the family became more specialized in its functions concentrating on pro-creation, childrearing, consumption, and affection (Hareven, 1977, p. 198). With many family members migrating to jobs in the cities, fears heightened that the modern family was in "crisis." Middle-class, professional reformers from the fields of education, health, and social work developed rules, books, and doc-trines aimed to fix what they saw as the "pathological," "broken" homes of the working class, the source of all society's problems. These reformers called upon the Canadian government to intervene to take strict measures to ensure that families produced "normal" children who represented the future building blocks of the nation. Canadian nationalism was being built on the notion of the white, middle-class family. Thus, it was imperative to regulate and normalize family values. During this period, the Children's Aid Society (which emerged out of the Toronto Humane Society) began to turn its attention from saving children to regulating families. Schools were enlisted as moral regulators of children's lives, helping to mould children into "proper" Canadians. As cities developed new sites of leisure that offered adolescents opportunities for activities away from the supervision of parents and adults, moral regulation discourse achieved new urgency in the public agenda (Comacchio, 1999).

As economic production moved into the public sphere, consumption moved into the private sphere, becoming a chief function and defining element of family life. This shift characterized working classes, farm people, and those from the middle class. Rather than producing daily needs such as food and clothing, women bought them. As well as becoming consumption units, families also specialized in moulding personalities. One of the marks of the "modern" family is its emphasis on personality development and satisfaction of emotional needs (Comacchio 1999). Family as the source of intimate satisfaction created a new quality of family life by opening up a space within which individual and group self-actualization could occur. Critics then, and today, contend that such self-scrutiny degenerates into individualized narcissism when the family is asked to function as an encounter group (Lasch, 1977).

Structurally, household size and composition altered to accomplish the family's new industrial functions. Families gradually became smaller, as birth rates continued to decline, marriages were delayed, and the incidence of living alone increased. In 1871, Canadian households averaged 5.9 people (Darroch and Ornstein, 1984, p. 163). Husbands, wives, and children shared living quarters with dependent elderly relations. Fifty years later, households were smaller, more specialized, isolated, and urbanized.

In the wage-labouring economy, kin remained sources of social and economic family support. Working-class families lacked savings, pensions, social security, and social assistance. When widowed, women often discovered that their domestic talents of cooking and caring did not easily translate into marketable skills; nor were they welcomed into scarce jobs reserved for male heads of households (Bradbury, 1992). Thus, kin were forced to rely on one another to get through rough economic times, and work continued to be considered a family enterprise, even if it did not take place in the home.

If families could not help, those in need turned to social institutions. One social institution created to help families in need was The Toronto Boys' Homes. Parents placed boys in the home, not to give them up, but only to ease their responsibilities until their finances improved. Parents made monthly payments for their sons' maintenance, which gave parents the clout necessary to bend the managers' will to their own interpretation of the Home's function in their family lives. Although the Home managers often wanted to indenture the boys to farmers, parents had other ideas. Managers were helpless to stop them because they had no legal power to keep the boys from their parents (Posen, 1998).

Another social institution designed to help families was the poorhouse. Between 1877 and 1907, the majority of inmates in the Guelph poorhouse, called The Wellington County House of Industry, were men 55 years of age and over who could no longer work or for whom work was seasonal. Men entered the poorhouse when they were unable to work and left as jobs presented themselves. Few older women were to be found in the House of Industry since they were more likely to be taken in by their families. Unless they were infirm, women continued to provide valuable services and thus were assets to their families. Nevertheless, there were times when families simply could not afford to keep their elderly with them at home, even the women. Such was especially the case for those families with small children and limited resources. When a choice had to be made, it was the aged man or woman who had to be sacrificed (Stewart, 1998). With the establishment of the Old Age Pension in 1927, some families found greater incentive to take in elderly parents (Snell, 1998).

Lest we drift into romantic visions of multigenerational families all living happily under one roof, we should note that there is very little evidence of such families in Canada. Records for Brigus, Newfoundland, from 1920 to 1945 reveal that married and more affluent elderly people were more likely to live by themselves (McDaniel and Lewis, 1998). In the 1871 census, in those families where children and elderly parents lived in the same household, the children were frequently unmarried. Elderly men were more likely to live with their children than were elderly women because men married later and thus were older when childrearing ended. Children stayed in their parents' home longer when there was little land or work available (Dillon, 1998). These family living arrangements sometimes resulted from financial necessity but often resulted from notions of family obligations and values. At the turn of the twentieth century in Ontario, the average reported income of elderly people was not at the poverty level, suggesting money was not the only incentive for families to take in relatives to live with them (Montigny, 1998).

Families were resourceful and flexible units, strongly shaped by class, gender, economics, and age. For the middle-classes, the physical separation of the home from the workplace led to a new articulation of family privacy. The home was glorified as a domestic retreat, as a haven of intimacy against the harsh realities of the workplace (Lasch, 1977). Unlike working-class homes, middle-class homes were defined as non-work domains in which family members experienced personal intimacy unachievable, undesirable, and unsuitable in workplace environments (Smith, 1985).

The transformation of the household from a busy workplace and social centre to a private enclosure widened the division between men's and women's tasks. Husbands became responsible for breadwinning, and wives for homemaking and childrearing. Children existed as sentimental love objects, offering an opportunity for intimacy not experienced in other relationships. Parents were now expected to become "pals" with their children and to act as role models, rather than as authoritarian figures. This method of nurturing and solicitous childrearing was thought to be best suited to allowing children to mature into model citizens who would function in the best interests of the larger society (Comacchio, 1999, p. 77).

Family **ideology** emphasized strong feelings of affection as essential ingredients in marriage. The ideal marriage was based on mutual love, affection, attraction, and respect. Sentimental love replaced economic considerations in bringing couples together; individual self-development and personal happiness replaced property and lineage as criteria for choosing spouses. The role of parents as matchmakers virtually disappeared. In the 1920s, following World War I, new courtship patterns emerged. "Dating" was now in style. Rather than young men coming to "call" on young women in their homes, they all went out, often in groups, to movies, dances, and other spots. Dating was more relaxed and assumed there would be a certain multiplicity of partners. There may have been an increase in premarital sexual activity as well, but it is likely that any sexual relations outside of marriage continued to conform to certain traditional relationship lines (Comacchio, 1999, pp. 74–75). There were exceptions to this new marital pattern. Franco-Albertan women retained traditional patterns of courtship and marriage, especially between 1890 and 1940. Rural, largely Roman Catholic, young women had courtship experiences controlled by their parents. Courtship continued to entail young men visiting young women in their homes on Sundays. Chaperones accompanied couples, even if the chaperone was only a sibling. Short courtships preceded marriage, which tended to take place at young ages (Gagnon, 1998).

The burgeoning marital ideal stressed companionship, affection, and enjoyment. New companionship demands brought new marital strains. While both spouses were expected to contribute to mutual matrimonial bliss, wives were considered more responsible than husbands were for nourishing and maintaining the sentimental and romantic qualities of relationships. Women were thought to possess characteristics more attuned to childcare, emotional nurturing, and tension management—namely, gentleness, patience, sweetness, and a comforting demeanour (Smith, 1985).

For men, the gradual separation of the private and the public led to a new emphasis on masculinity as measured by the "breadwinner" role. Success in this role was measured by the size of a man's paycheque. For men, earning a "good" living, or family wage, meant that their wives did not have to work outside the home (Bernard, 1981). For instance, Cape Breton coal miners during the 1920s were considered to be "real" men if they maintained solidarity with fellow workers in opposing management (Penfold, 1996). Positive male attributes were those associated with successful workers: aggressiveness,

perseverance, toughness, and competitiveness were valued. These male qualities were in sharp contrast to the presumed female traits. The ideological **cult
of domesticity**, with its clear division of family roles and responsibilities, was
dominant until the 1970s.

Most of the changes that took place in family life were readily achievable
only for the middle classes. Nevertheless, working-class people came to aspire
to the same standards for themselves.

> Getting "something better" was contingent upon smaller families, a family wage, improved
> health, a comfortable house, and a less-wearing round of daily tasks. A developing agenda
> of public health and social welfare, and an economy increasingly focused on domesticity
> and household consumption, made the dream at least appear worth dreaming. By 1928 it
> was, for the first time, theoretically possible for the average male industrial worker to earn
> sufficient wages to provide for a family on his own—providing that he was employed the
> entire course of the year, that he had three or fewer children, and that no serious illness or
> accident befell his dependents (Comacchio, 1999, p. 77).

The family home became an important focus for these aspirations. While
middle-class families bought large, spacious houses, working-class families
bought small homes that could be expanded as needed and desired. Recreation
was becoming more private, particularly among members of the middle class,
who retreated to their backyards, eschewing the more traditional socializing on
the front stoop or the street with neighbours (Comacchio, 1999, pp. 78–80).

This new ideology of domesticity was built on women's homemaking
skills and legal dependence on men. Middle-class women were glorified for
their domestic pursuits, for their childbearing skills, and for their "natural
abilities" as emotional nurturers of their wage-labouring husbands. So constraining were these domestic demands that, by the beginning of the 1900s,
some Canadian writers were describing marriage as the legal death of women
(Dumont et al., 1987). Husbands were legally the uncontested heads of families; they controlled the family's resources. Wives' income, resources, and
legal rights were subject to their husbands' authority.

As women's roles altered, there followed a repositioning of children within
the family. New ideas about children grew alongside the cult of domesticity.
Children began to be defined as incomplete adults in need of special cognitive
and emotional protection and development; women, as mothers and teachers,
were designated to provide for their development. Class distinctions in childrearing appeared. Middle-class mothers were seen as economically unproduc-
tive but emotionally and morally superior in childrearing, while working-class
women were seen as economically productive wives but incompetent mothers
in need of scientific and school guidance (Smith, 1985).

A gradual combination of restrictive child-labour laws, compulsory education in 1871, and declining employment opportunities pushed children out
of the labour market. The 1891 Census records 13.8 percent of Canadian children between the ages of 11 and 14 were gainfully employed. By 1921, this

BOX 2.4   IMMIGRANT WOMEN'S LIVES

Responding to the Canadian government's offer of cheap land, pushed out of their own country by the scarcity of land in Roumania, the family of the little girl who would later become Mrs. Veronia Kokotailo crossed the ocean and travelled across the country to Alberta.

Shortly after establishing a "burdey" (a dugout, sod-covered hut), Veronia's father and grandfather went off to look for work to buy supplies, leaving the women and children behind. Veronia's mother (who hated living in the burdey) decided that a log house could be erected and set about building it herself, despite the fact that she had never done anything like that before. She displayed incredible ingenuity as, among other things, she erected a porch out of woven willow branches, plastered walls and roof with clay and sedge, and made her own chimney and clay oven. This home lasted for many years.

The men returned with some supplies for the winter. Veronia's mother had another baby. Even though Veronia was only about five years old at the time, she had to take care of her younger siblings and tend the fire. She also ran errands. When she got older, she worked in the fields with her father, replacing her mother, who was now taken up with the responsibilities that came with a larger family.

In the spring, Veronia's father left to seek employment again in order to buy what they needed for the winter and for growing crops. The food supply was already running short. When it ran out, Veronia's mother made soup from grass and wild mushrooms she found in the woods. She had no idea whether the mushrooms were poisonous but she felt she had to take the chance that they were edible. They had nothing to lose at that point.

When Veronia's mother had the chance to work for someone else, she took it, hoping that she could earn some money. Instead, after two weeks of back-breaking labour, she received a pail of potatoes.

The men and women of the family had to work side-by-side for years developing their acreage into a farm that could sustain them. All of them depended on each other's labour to survive. Yet, on top of that, the women shouldered the full responsibility for domestic work. The necessity of the women's labour did not grant them equality with the men, however. This is demonstrated by the fact that, when Veronia married Thomas Kokotailo in 1913 and they set up their own homestead, she knew better than he how to set up the binder machine. He, however, would not allow her to show him how it was done, despite the fact that he was struggling, taking offence that a mere woman would attempt to show him how to do what was clearly a man's work.

Because Veronia had been denied the opportunity to go to school due to the fact that her labour was needed at home, she did everything she could to ensure that her own eight children attended school. She earned money in numerous labour-intensive ways to put her eldest son through university and then he, in turn, helped his younger brothers to get their education.

The story of Veronia's family attests to the ongoing struggle and hardship that accompanied pioneer life in Canada. Even more, it demonstrates how pioneer life depended on the never-ending work of women.

Source: Based on Anne B. Woywitka. 1998. "A Roumanian Pioneer." In Franca Iacovetta, with Paula Draper and Robert Ventresca, eds. *A Nation of Immigrants: Women, Workers, and Communities in Canadian History, 1840s–1960s.* Toronto: University of Toronto Press.

number had declined to 3.2 percent. Middle-class parents relinquished their children's wages and subsidized their spending through allowances. By 1893, child labour had declined so dramatically that giving their children an allowance was a routine middle-class practice. Slowly, children, especially middle-class ones, became defined as economically useless but emotionally priceless (Penfold, 1996; Zelizer, 1985).

IMMIGRATION AND FAMILY LIVES

The Canadian West was settled by immigrants during the late 1800s and early 1900s. Government policy focused on attracting what it called the "ideal immigrant," one skilled in agriculture who belonged to a family of experienced farmers. While white British and American immigrants were preferred, Europeans were desirable as long as they were farmers with families (Iacovetta, Draper, and Ventresca, 1998, p. 116). Not suprisingly, immigrants often chose to settle in areas where they knew people from their village or homeland (Woywitka, 1998) and they often chose to farm land with which they were familiar. The Ukrainians settled in the wooded areas, which were considered to have poorer farming land, rather than settling in southern prairies in the good wheat-growing areas because in the Ukraine, wooded land was highly prized, owned only by the upper-class (Darlington, 1998).

As industrialization progressed and economic needs changed, Canada populated its cities and recruited the bulk of its working class through immigration. Immigrant families faced particular circumstances and thus responded with special family coping strategies and structures. For example, the Chinese workers who first arrived in Canada from China and San Francisco in the 1860s and 1870s were men. Women were specifically excluded on the grounds that Chinese men were merely temporary workers, and by a federal head tax, a substantial fee only the Chinese had to pay to enter the country. This tax was sufficiently burdensome to make it difficult for men to bring their wives or female relatives into the country. Racism and cruel treatment were also to blame for the low number of Chinese wives joining their husbands in Canada. Husbands feared the anti-Chinese sentiments of Canadians, manifested in acts such as stone-throwing and verbal taunts, so they decided to leave their families in their home villages in China. Some of these unfortunate men spent their entire lives in Canada without their families (Chan, 1998). The first Chinese women who came to Canada were merchants' wives, who were excluded from the head tax, prostitutes bought and sold by men, and "slave girls" or female servants imported to Canada to work as unpaid labourers. Slave girls performed domestic labour, freeing Chinese women to engage in piecework sewing and as general labourers or clerks, or in family-run businesses such as tailor shops, laundries, restaurants, and small grocery stores. Women's labour, both unpaid and poorly paid, enabled Chinese businesses to succeed (Adilman, 1984).

Another strategy used by immigrants was sojourning. Men would come to Canada with the plan of staying only long enough to earn sufficient money to send back home to their families to improve their quality of life. The fact that these men were working and earning money to support their families at home meant that they were still the family breadwinners. These sojourners usually relied on kinship networks to help them find work and a place to live, and to help them with finances. Bad luck and bad treatment could bring a sojourn to an untimely end or prolong it indefinitely. Such eventualities took a tragic psychic toll on the sojourner and caused him to be completely alienated from his family (Comacchio, 1999, p. 40).

Italian sojourners populated the mining, railway, and timbering camps. They were often viewed as not being "useful immigrants" (Harney, 1998, p. 210) and feared as foreigners who would "prey" on Canadian women. In fact, for Italian men, sojourning was a project in creating and maintaining home. They remained committed to their home villages and families and sent money back home. These commitments functioned as surveillance mechanisms, keeping the Italian men more or less on the "straight and narrow." Fearing that word of their misdeeds would get back to home and family, the Italian sojourners regulated their own behaviour. Some sojourners moved into cities to work and often moved in with families to enjoy the benefits of family life that were unavailable in the camps. Such a move often signalled an extended sojourn. Sojourns ended in a number of different ways, such as returning home to their families or bringing them to Canada to be reunited (Harney, 1998).

Family life was often solitary, arduous, and lonely for early immigrants. Families frequently lived in poor housing. "Light and ventilation were frequently inadequate, and existing windows were often sealed or covered to lower fuel costs" (Comacchio, 1999, p. 29). Poor housing often meant that inhabitants suffered ill health and early death. Tuberculosis was such a problem that it was called "the working-man's disease" (Comacchio, 1999, p. 29).

Early twentieth-century Greek and Japanese immigrants followed a pattern that subsequent groups experienced. First, young men immigrated to Canada seeking economic opportunity and fleeing political restrictions. They lived in boarding houses and married as soon as financially feasible. Their wives, often Greek and Japanese immigrants, found married life lonely and isolating, and missed the warmth and familiarity of their former communities (Ayukawa, 1995; Pizanias, 1996). Too often families found that discrimination restricted their work experiences. Chinese women were not accepted into the teaching or nursing professions as late as the 1940s, forcing women to remain in working-class positions in mostly Chinese-run businesses (Nipp, 1986; Yee, 1992). Canadian migrant miners in single-industry towns like Timmins were often forced to live as bachelors, unable to bring their wives or children to live with them. Companies built family accommodations usually only for their office and supervisory staff and did not extend medical and hospital benefits to the families of miners. The only hospital, built by the company, was reserved for employees (Forestell, 1998).

Government employment goals shaped immigration policies. South Asian men arrived in the mid-1800s after the imposition of the Chinese head tax temporarily limited immigration. Asian Indian men left behind their families as immigration laws banned Indian women from entering Canada until the 1917–19 Imperial War Conference agreement legislated their entry (Doman, 1984). Between 1900 and 1930, more than 170 000 British women came to Canada as domestics. In the 1920s, the Ontario government, encouraged by affluent women's groups, actively recruited English, Welsh, Irish, and Scottish girls by advertising "Sunny Ontario for British Girls" on posters across Britain (Barber, 1986). Black women from Africa and the West Indies worked largely on farms, in domestic service, and at home. Until the 1940s, 80 percent of black women worked as domestics, as mother's helpers, as housekeepers, as general helpers, and as laundresses. It was not until World War II that labour shortages forced employers to hire black women to work in areas that formerly employed only white females. When white females moved into essential war-industry jobs, black women took up their spaces in hospitals, restaurants, hotels, laundries, dry cleaners, and in non-essential companies making candy, tobacco, and soft drinks (Brand, 1991, p. 15).

Racist immigration policies affected family strategies. Girls from immigrant families started work and left home earlier. Immigrant families had consistently higher fertility rates, higher rates of child labour, and lower rates of non-kin living with them than did non-immigrants. Most working-class families, and especially those from visible minorities, rarely earned enough money to support their families, so the income-producing activities of women and children were essential. Low rates of pay, seasonal layoffs, and lack of trade unionization and social-security measures meant working-class and immigrant families had to organize themselves as economic units, closely coordinating their productive, reproductive, and domestic strategies. Unless the family was living substantially below the subsistence level, the family was better off having a wife engage in **domestic labour**, preparing food and engaging in income-generating schemes such as doing piecework at home or taking in boarders or laundry (Katz, 1975). Still, different groups evolved different strategies. Irish women tended to withdraw more completely from paid employment than did Germans. Italian mothers chose cannery and field work over factory employment because it permitted them to work alongside their children. Polish women preferred domestic work to factory work, whereas Jewish women avoided domestic work and sought industrial employment at home or in factories (Coontz, 1988; Draper and Karlinsky, 1986; Iacovetta and Valverde, 1992).

CONCLUSION

Family histories reveal the ways in which family strategies are shaped by structural forces and individual actions. Economic recessions, for example, may force young adults to remain at home for longer periods and to delay marriage and childbearing. Young adults are reshaping family roles and realigning family priorities to achieve equilibrium between wage and domestic demands. Government employment goals affect immigration policies. Ideologies of gender, race, economics, sexuality, dis/ability, and age contour political and cultural discourse. Our knowledge of history helps us interpret past and current trends. Understanding family histories places the actions of individuals within a social and economic context. Reading about the histories of particular groups reveals how the actions of individuals actually has a political, historical, and cultural explanation.

Summary

- For First Nations communities, family has been a fundamental unit of organization, structuring kinship relations, assigning roles and responsibilities, and shaping intimate relations.
- European colonization attempted to destroy Native culture.
- Public and private life were undifferentiated in the pre-industrial family-wage economy.
- Economics, culture, and politics have shaped family lives.
- The roles of women, men, and children have shifted over time.

Notes

1. This creation story comes from the Iroquois, or Haudenosaunee, peoples, hence the name "Turtle Island" for North America.
2. The Athapaskan Beaver tell this creation story.
3. As of April 1, 1999, Canada has a new northern territory; what was previously the Northwest Territories has been divided in two. The eastern two-thirds of the existing Northwest Territories is now known as Nunavut, meaning "our land" in the Inuktitut language of the Innu. The western region has yet to be named. Names being considered include "Northwest Territories," "Denendeh," meaning "home of the people" in the Athapaskan language of the Dene people, and "Nunakput," meaning "our land" in the western arctic Inuktitut dialect. The current Northwest Territories was once part of a larger area known as "Rupert's Land and the Northwest Territory." The province of Manitoba was separated from this territory in 1870, the Yukon Territory in 1898, and the provinces of

Alberta and Saskatchewan in 1905. In 1912, following the northward extension of Manitoba, Ontario, and Quebec, the current boundaries of the Northwest Territories were established (Stout, 1997).

4.   Anthropologists date the first occurrence of hunting-and-gathering societies involving the use of tools, language, cooking, and a sex-based division of labour to between 200 000 and 500 000 years ago. By 10 000 to 15 000 years ago, hunting-and-gathering societies were widespread. These arrangements were gradually replaced by horticultural-and-agricultural settlements about 12 000 years ago. Industrial society is only about 200 years old (Nett, 1988).

5.   The west coast was home to the most dense pre-agricultural fishing society in Canada, with an aboriginal population of about 50 000 extending along 2400 kilometres (Morrison and Wilson, 1986; Price, 1979).

Critical Thinking Questions

1.   In what ways have the family lives of Native peoples been affected by the economic, social, and cultural practices of colonizers?

2.   Outline how immigration policy and practice shaped the family lives of settlers. How and to what extent has official policy been discriminatory?

3.   The roles of women, men, and children have been altered throughout Canadian history. Outline the changes and trace the material, social, and cultural forces affecting these changes.

4.   In what ways have gender, race, and social class produced distinct and multiple family histories?

Websites

Early Canadiana Online
http://www.canadiana.org
Lots of good articles and scanned books providing information on life in the early days of this country.

Canadian Women's Internet Directory
http://directory.womenspace.ca
Many different categories of information on women, including Herstory.

Cool Women
http://www.coolwomen.ca
A site featuring the history of girls and women in Canada, including links to women's history.

Suggested Reading

Kim Anderson and Bonita Lawrence. 2003. *Strong Women Stories: Native Vision and Community Survival.* Toronto: Sumach Press.

This important edited collection highlights the voices and experiences of Native women. Their family and community commitments remain a strong thread tying together different generations.

Joanne Bailey. 2003. *Unquiet Lives: Marriage and Marriage Breakdown in England, 1660-1800.* Cambridge: Cambridge University Press.

Based on vivid court records and newspaper advertisements, this book is a pioneering account of the expectations and experiences of married life among the middle and labouring ranks in the eighteenth century. It challenges ideas about the gendered and oppositional lives of spouses.

Cynthia R. Comacchio. 1999. *The Infinite Bonds of Family: Domesticity in Canada, 1850–1940.* Toronto: University of Toronto Press.

An excellent historical portrait of Canadian family life, covering families of different classes, races, and ethnicities, in meticulous detail.

Micheline Dumont, Michele Jean, Marie Lavigne, and Jennifer Stoddart (The Clio Collective). 1987. *Quebec Women: A History.* Translation by Roger Gannon and Rosalind Gill. Toronto: Women's Press.

An in-depth account of the history of Quebec women from the earliest days of settlement to more recent times.

Valerie Korinek. 2000. *Roughing it in the Suburbs: Reading Chatelaine in the Fifties and Sixties.* Toronto: University of Toronto Press.

Canada's top-selling magazine offers us an indirect but excellent source of information about postwar food, health, and homemaking campaigns. Norms, ideals and assumptions about Canadian family life are revealed.

Marion Lynn, ed. 2004. *Voices: Essays on Canadian Families* (2nd ed.). Scarborough, ON: Thomson Nelson Canada.

An extensive and inclusive collection of narratives on many different ethnocultural groups in Canada.

References

Adilman, Tamura. 1984. "A Preliminary Sketch of Chinese Women and Work in British Columbia, 1858–1950." In Barbara Latham and Roberta Pazdro, eds., *Not Just Pin Money: Selected Essays on the History of Women's Work in British Columbia.* Victoria: Camosun College.

Anderson, Karen. 1987. "A Gendered World: Women, Men, and the Political Economy of the 17th-Century Hurons." In Heather Jon Maroney and Meg Luxton, eds., *Feminism and Political Economy: Women's Work, Women's Struggles.* Toronto: Methuen.

Anderson, Kim. 2000. *A Recognition of Being: Reconstructing Native Womanhood.* Toronto: Second Story Press.

Ayukawa, Midge. 1995. "Good Wives and Wise Mothers: Japanese Picture Brides in Early Twentieth-Century British Columbia." *B.C. Studies* 105/106 (Spring/Summer): 103–18.

Barber, Marilyn. 1986. "Sunny Ontario for British Girls, 1900–30." In Jean Burnet, ed., *Looking into My Sister's Eyes: An Exploration in Women's History.* Toronto: Multicultural History Society of Ontario.

Bernard, Jessie. 1981. "The Good Provider Role: Its Rise and Fall." *American Psychologist* vol. 36, no.1 (Jan): 1–12.

Bloomfield, Elizabeth, and G.T. Bloomfield. 1991. *Canadian Women in Workshops, Mills, and Factories: The Evidence of the 1871 Census Manuscripts.* Department of Geography, Research Report 11. Guelph: University of Guelph.

Bolaria, B. Singh, and Peter S. Li, eds. 1988. *Racial Oppression in Canada,* 2nd ed. Toronto: Garamond.

Bourgeault, Ron. 1988. "Race and Class under Mercantilism: Indigenous People in Nineteenth-Century Canada." In B. Singh Bolaria and Peter S. Li, eds., *Racial Oppression in Canada,* 2nd ed. Toronto: Garamond.

Bradbury, Bettina. 1992. "Gender at Work at Home: Family Decisions, the Labour Market, and Girls' Contributions to the Family Economy." In Bettina Bradbury, ed., *Canadian Family History: Selected Readings.* Toronto: Copp Clark Pitman.

———. 1996. "The Social and Economic Origins of Contemporary Families." In Maureen Baker, ed., *Families: Changing Trends in Canada,* 3rd ed. Toronto: McGraw-Hill Ryerson.

Brand, Dionne. 1991. *No Burden to Carry: Narratives of Black Working Women in Ontario, 1920s to 1950s.* Toronto: Women's Press.

Bryan, Alan Lyle. 1986. "The Prehistory of Canadian Indians." In R. Bruce Morrison and C. Roderick Wilson, eds., *Native Peoples: The Canadian Experience.* Toronto: McClelland & Stewart.

Bullen, John. 1992. "Hidden Workers: Child Labour and the Family Economy in Late Nineteenth-Century Urban Ontario." In Bettina Bradbury, ed., *Canadian Family History: Selected Readings.* Toronto: Copp Clark Pitman.

Calliste, Agnes. 1996a. "Black Families in Canada: Exploring the Interconnections of Race, Class, and Gender." In Marion Lynn, ed., *Voices: Essays on Canadian Families.* Toronto: Nelson Canada.

————. 1996b. "Race, Gender and Canadian Immigration Policy: Blacks from the Caribbean, 1900–1932." In Joy Parr and Mark Rosenfeld, eds., *Gender and History in Canada*. Toronto: Copp Clark.

Chan, Anthony. 1998. "Bachelor Workers." In Franca Iacovetta, with Paula Draper and Robert Ventresca, eds., *A Nation of Immigrants: Women, Workers, and Communities in Canadian History, 1840s–1960s*. Toronto: University of Toronto Press.

Clairmont, Donald, and Dennis Magill. 1974. *Africville: The Life and Death of a Canadian Black Community*. Toronto: McClelland & Stewart.

Comacchio, Cynthia R. 1999. *The Infinite Bonds of Family: Domesticity in Canada, 1850–1940*. Toronto: University of Toronto Press.

Conrad, Margaret. 1991. "Sundays Always Make Me Think of Home: Time and Place in Canadian Women's History." In Veronica Strong-Boag and Anita Clair Fellman, eds., *Rethinking Canada: The Promise of Women's History*, 2nd ed. Toronto: Copp Clark Pitman.

Coontz, Stephanie. 1988. *The Social Origins of Private Life*. London: Verso.

Darlington, James W. 1998. "The Ukrainian Impress on the Canadian West." In Franca Iacovetta, with Paula Draper and Robert Ventresca, eds., *A Nation of Immigrants: Women, Workers, and Communities in Canadian History, 1840s–1960s*. Toronto: University of Toronto Press.

Darroch, Gordon, and Michael Ornstein. 1984. "Family and Household in Nineteenth-Century Canada: Regional Patterns and Regional Economies." *Journal of Family History* 9/2: 158–77.

Dickason, Olive Patricia. 2002. *Canada's First Nations: A History of Founding Peoples from Earliest Times*, 3rd ed. Toronto: Oxford University Press.

Dillon, Lisa. 1998. "Parent-Child Co-Residence among the Elderly in 1871 Canada and 1880 United States: A Comparative Study." In Lori Chambers and Edgar-Andre Montigny, eds., *Family Matters: Papers in Post-Confederation Canadian Family History*. Toronto: Canadian Scholars' Press.

Doman, Mahinder. 1984. "A Note on Asian Indian Women in British Columbia, 1900–1935." In Barbara Latham and Roberta Pazdro, eds., *Not Just Pin Money: Selected Essays on the History of Women's Work in British Columbia*. Victoria: Camosun College.

Draper, Paula J., and Janice B. Karlinsky. 1986. "Abraham's Daughters: Women, Charity and Power in the Canadian Jewish Community." In Jean Burnet, ed., *Looking into My Sister's Eyes: An Exploration in Women's History*. Toronto: Multicultural History Society of Ontario.

Druke, Mary A. 1986. "Iroquois and Iroquoian in Canada." In R. Bruce Morrison and C. Roderick Wilson, eds., *Native Peoples: The Canadian Experience*. Toronto: McClelland & Stewart.

Dumont, Micheline, Michele Jean, Marie Lavigne, and Jennifer Stoddart (The Clio Collective). 1987. *Quebec Women: A History.* Trans. Roger Gannon and Rosalind Gill. Toronto: Women's Press.

Elliott, Jean, ed. 1983. *Two Nations, Many Cultures.* Toronto: Prentice-Hall.

Forestell, Nancy M. 1998. "Bachelors, Boarding-Houses, and Blind Pigs: Gender Construction in a Multi-Ethnic Mining Camp, 1909–1920." In Franca Iacovetta, with Paula Draper and Robert Ventresca, eds., *A Nation of Immigrants: Women, Workers, and Communities in Canadian History, 1840s–1960s.* Toronto: University of Toronto Press.

Frideres, James S. 1998. *Native Peoples in Canada: Contemporary Conflicts,* 5th ed. Toronto: Prentice-Hall.

Gaffield, Chad. 1990. "The Social and Economic Origins of Contemporary Families." In Maureen Baker, ed., *Families: Changing Trends in Canada,* 2nd ed. Toronto: McGraw-Hill Ryerson.

Gagnon, Anne. 1998. "The Courtship of Franco-Albertan Women, 1890–1940." In Lori Chambers and Edgar-Andre Montigny, eds., *Family Matters: Papers in Post-Confederation Canadian Family History.* Toronto: Canadian Scholars' Press.

Guildford, Janet. 1997. "'Whate'er the duty of the hour demands'": The Work of Middle-Class Women in Halifax, 1840–1880." *Social History* 30/59 (May): 1–20.

Hareven, Tamura. 1977. "Family Time and Industrial Time." *Daedalus* 106: 57–70.

Harney, Robert F. 1998. "Men Without Women: Italian Migrants in Canada, 1885–1930." In Franca Iacovetta, with Paula Draper and Robert Ventresca, eds., *A Nation of Immigrants: Women, Workers, and Communities in Canadian History, 1840s–1960s.* Toronto: University of Toronto Press.

Iacovetta, Franca, and Marianna Valverde, eds. 1992. *Gender Conflicts: New Essays in Women's History.* Toronto: Women's Press.

Iacovetta, Franca, with Paula Draper and Robert Ventresca, eds. 1998. *A Nation of Immigrants: Women, Workers, and Communities in Canadian History, 1840s–1960s.* Toronto: University of Toronto Press.

Jamieson, Kathleen. 1986. "Sex Discrimination and the Indian Act." In J. Rick Ponting, ed., *Arduous Journey: Canadian Indians and Decolonization.* Toronto: McClelland & Stewart.

Katz, Michael. 1975. *The People of Hamilton, Canada West: Family and Class in a Mid-Nineteenth-Century City.* Cambridge, MA: Harvard University Press.

Krull, Catherine D. 1996. "From the King's Daughters to the Quiet Revolution: A Historical Overview of Family Structures and the Role of Women in Quebec." In Marion Lynn, ed., *Voices: Essays on Canadian Families.* Toronto: Nelson Canada.

Landry, Yves. 1992. "Gender Imbalance, *Les Filles du Roi,* and Choice of Spouse in New France." In Bettina Bradbury, ed., *Canadian Family History.* Toronto: Copp Clark Pitman.

Landry, Yves, and Jacques Legare. 1987. "The Life Course of Seventeenth-Century Immigrants to Canada." In Tamara Harevan and Andrejs Plakans, eds., *Family History at the Crossroads*. Princeton, NJ: Princeton University Press.

Lasch, Christopher. 1977. *Haven in a Heartless World: The Family Besieged*. New York: Basic Books.

Leacock, Eleanor. 1991. "Montagnais Women and the Jesuit Program for Colonization." In Veronica Strong-Boag and Anita Clair Fellman, eds., *Rethinking Canada: The Promise of Women's History*, 2nd ed. Toronto: Copp Clark Pitman.

Little, Margaret Hillyard. 1998. "Claiming a Unique Place: The Introduction of Mothers' Pensions in B.C." In Lori Chambers and Edgar-Andre Montigny, eds., *Family Matters: Papers in Post-Confederation Canadian Family History*. Toronto: Canadian Scholars' Press.

McDaniel, Susan, and Robert Lewis. 1998. "Did They or Didn't They? Intergenerational Supports in Families Past: A Case Study of Brigus, Newfoundland, 1920–1945." In Lori Chambers and Edgar-Andre Montigny, eds., *Family Matters: Papers in Post-Confederation Canadian Family History*. Toronto: Canadian Scholars' Press.

McLaren, Angus. 1977. "Women's Work and Regulation of Family Size." *History Workshop Journal* 4 (Autumn): 70–73.

Miller, Virginia. 1986. "The Micmac: A Maritime Woodland Group." In R. Bruce Morrison and C. Roderick Wilson, eds., *Native Peoples: The Canadian Experience*. Toronto: McClelland & Stewart.

Montigny, Edgar-Andre. 1998. "The Economic Role of the Elderly within the Family: Evidence from Turn-of-the-Century Ontario." In Lori Chambers and Edgar-Andre Montigny, eds., *Family Matters: Papers in Post-Confederation Canadian Family History*. Toronto: Canadian Scholars' Press.

Morrison, R. Bruce, and C. Roderick Wilson, eds. 1986. *Native Peoples: The Canadian Experience*. Toronto: McClelland & Stewart.

Nett, Emily. 1988. *Canadian Families: Past and Present*. Toronto: Butterworths.

Nipp, Dora. 1986. "But Women Did Come: Working Chinese Women in the Inter-War Years." In Jean Burnet, ed., *Looking into My Sister's Eyes: An Exploration in Women's History*. Toronto: Multicultural History Society of Ontario.

Noel, Jan. 1991. "New France: Les Femmes Favorisées." In Veronica Strong-Boag and Anita Clair Fellman, eds., *Rethinking Canada: The Promise of Women's History*, 2nd ed. Toronto: Copp Clark Pitman.

Palmer, Bryan D. 1983. *Working Class Struggle: The Rise and Reconstitution of Canadian Labour, 1800–1980*. Toronto: Butterworths.

Parr, Joy. 1990. *The Gender of Breadwinners: Women, Men and Change in Two Industrial Towns, 1880–1950*. Toronto: University of Toronto Press.

Penfold, Steven. 1996. "'Have You No Manhood in You?': Gender and Class in the Cape Breton Coal Towns, 1920–26." In Joy Parr and Mark Rosenfeld, eds., *Gender and History in Canada*. Toronto: Copp Clark.

Pizanias, Caterina. 1996. "Greek Families in Canada: Fragile Truths, Fragmented Stories." In Marion Lynn, ed., *Voices: Essays on Canadian Families*. Toronto: Nelson Canada.

Ponting, Rick, ed. 1986. *Arduous Journey: Canadian Indians and Decolonization*. Toronto: McClelland & Stewart.

Posen, Sara. 1998. "Examining Policy from the 'Bottom up': The Relationship between Parents, Children and Managers at the Toronto Boys' Home, 1859–1920." In Lori Chambers and Edgar-Andre Montigny, eds., *Family Matters: Papers in Post-Confederation Canadian Family History*. Toronto: Canadian Scholars' Press.

Price, John A. 1979. *Indians of Canada: Cultural Dynamics*. Toronto: Prentice-Hall.

Queen, Stuart A., Robert W. Habenstein, and Jill S. Quadagno. 1985. *The Family in Various Cultures*, 5th ed. New York: Harper and Row.

Ray, Arthur J. 1996. "Periodic Shortages, Native Welfare, and the Hudson's Bay Company, 1670–1930." In Ken S. Coates and Robin Fisher, eds., *Out of the Background: Readings on Canadian Native History*, 2nd ed. Toronto: Copp Clark.

Shadd, Adrienne. 1987. "300 Years of Black Women in Canadian History: Circa 1700–1980." *Tiger Lily* 1/2: 4–13.

Smith, Dorothy E. 1985. "Women, Class and Family." In Varda Burstyn and Dorothy E. Smith, *Women, Class, Family and the State*. Toronto: Garamond.

Snell, James. 1998. "The Family and the Working-Class Elderly in the First Half of the Twentieth Century." In Lori Chambers and Edgar-Andre Montigny, eds., *Family Matters: Papers in Post-Confederation Canadian Family History*. Toronto: Canadian Scholars' Press.

Stewart, Stormie. 1998. "The Elderly Poor in Rural Ontario: Inmates of the Wellington County House of Industry, 1877–1907." In Lori Chambers and Edgar-Andre Montigny, eds., *Family Matters: Papers in Post-Confederation Canadian Family History*. Toronto: Canadian Scholars' Press.

Strange, Carolyn. 1997. "'Sin or Salvation?' Protecting Toronto's Working Girls." *The Beaver* 77/3 (June/July): 8–13.

Stout, Cameron. 1997. "Canada's Newest Territory in 1999." *Canadian Social Trends*. Ottawa: Catalogue no. 11-008-XPE, Statistics Canada (Spring).

Thomson, Colin A. 1979. *Blacks in Deep Snow: Black Pioneers in Canada*. Toronto: J.M. Dent.

Van Kirk, Sylvia. 1992. "The Custom of the Country: An Examination of Fur Trade Marriage Practices." In Bettina Bradbury, ed., *Canadian Family History*. Toronto: Copp Clark Pitman.

Walker, James W. 1980. *A History of Blacks in Canada: A Study Guide for Teachers and Students.* Hull, PQ: Minister of State for Multiculturalism and Supply and Services Canada.

Whitla, William. 1995. "A Chronology of Women in Canada." In Nancy Mandell, ed., *Feminist Issues: Race, Class and Sexuality.* Toronto: Prentice-Hall.

Williams, Savanah E. 1983. "Two Hundred Years in the Development of the Afro-Canadians in Nova Scotia, 1782–1982." In Jean Elliott, ed., *Two Nations, Many Cultures.* Toronto: Prentice-Hall.

Wilson, S.J. 1991. *Women, Families, and Work.* Toronto: McGraw-Hill Ryerson.

Winks, Robert W. 1971. *The Blacks in Canada: A History.* Montreal: McGill-Queen's University Press.

Woywitka, Anne B. 1998. "A Roumanian Pioneer." In Franca Iacovetta, with Paula Draper and Robert Ventresca, eds., *A Nation of Immigrants: Women, Workers, and Communities in Canadian History, 1840s–1960s.* Toronto: University of Toronto Press.

Yee, May. 1992. "Chinese Canadian Women: Our Common Struggle." In Gillian Creese and Veronica Strong-Boag, eds., *British Columbia Reconsidered: Essays on Women.* Vancouver: Press Gang.

Zelizer, Viviana. 1985. *Pricing the Priceless Child: The Changing Social Value of Children.* New York: Basic Books.

Zinn, Maxine, and D. Stanley Eitzen. 1993. *Diversity in Families,* 3rd ed. New York: HarperCollins.

Chapter 3

Making Sense of the Cultural Activities of Canadian Youth

Brian Wilson and Shannon Jette

LEARNING OBJECTIVES

In this chapter, you will learn that:

1. the history of the term "youth" helps to demonstrate the evolution of the rift between teen and parent generations;

2. cultural activity of youth has been interpreted by sociologists in various ways;

3. youth interpret the cultural activities they participate in in complex ways;

4. media and popular culture is central in the everyday lives of young people.

INTRODUCTION

The cultural activities of young people inspire both fascination and concern. Mass media reports often include stories about school bullying, drug abuse, teen pregnancy, race-related violence, and gang membership. Activities like skateboarding and snowboarding, formerly alternative leisure pursuits for youth, have entered mainstream culture through televised events like the "X-Games" (i.e., extreme sport games) and are often the focus of news segments that describe the lifestyles of highly committed participants. Marketers enamoured with the "teen demographic" devise ultra-appealing commercials and advertisements in hopes of wooing young consumers into buying sneakers, clothes, video games, soft drinks, and other items.

Those who study youth and **youth culture** have identified a number of problems with these portrayals and product positionings. Some researchers argue that youth are too often depicted in overly simplistic and deceiving ways in mass media reports. These critics suggest that young people are frequently portrayed as *either* menaces to society who need to be disciplined or incarcerated, or as troubled, unstable "at risk" adolescents who require serious help and protection—while the mundane, everyday activities and behaviours

64

of most youth are seldom acknowledged (Acland, 1995). Still other commentators suggest that youth are not given enough credit for their ability to critically interpret media and advertising (Rushkoff, 1996). These scholars assert that youth are too often viewed as passive, impressionable, and easily influenced by the "evils" associated with popular culture (e.g., violence in movies; ads for high-priced sneakers). Underlying many of these apprehensions is the worry that mass media and associated cultural influences are threatening the role of the family and community as primary socialization agents (Furlong and Cartmel, 1997).

Emerging from this myriad of concerns is a series of questions about youth, culture, and society. These include: what are the various meanings of the term "youth"?; what do young people do with their time beyond the spectacular and problematic activities that receive so much attention?; how can the leisure preferences and cultural involvements of young people be explained?; to what extent are youth passive "dupes" who uncritically accept the media messages they are exposed to?; to what extent are these same youth active and informed consumers of information and culture?; and how can an understanding of youth activity help us understand the contemporary Canadian family?

With the goal of engaging these topics and questions, we have organized this chapter into the following four sections. In the first section, we describe and consider the range of ways that the term "youth" has been defined and the cultural meanings that the concept has taken on. The second section is a discussion and overview of patterns of leisure activity that have been identified within large-scale research on youth in Canada. This is followed, in the third section, by an exploration of the range of ways that young people's activities have been interpreted and explained by scholars who study youth and culture. In the fourth section, a case study of the **rave** subculture in southern Ontario is presented and used as a departure point to help us describe and interrogate some of the theories of youth outlined in section three. The rave case is also used to illustrate our argument that youth are a complex and diverse group that negotiate, understand, and interpret the various cultural influences they encounter in different ways at different times. We conclude the chapter with a summary of key points and a reflective assessment of contemporary work on youth culture and its relationship to the family.

WHO ARE YOUTH?: A SOCIAL HISTORY OF THE TERM AND ITS MEANINGS

Although in contemporary Western society the term "youth" refers broadly to a transition stage between childhood and adulthood that is characterized by distinct physical, psychological, and social developments (c.f., Coleman, 1992), current understandings of "youth" are quite different from those of earlier generations. Authors like Tanner (1996), Tyyskä (2001), and Gillis (1974) describe how, prior to the Industrial Revolution in the early 1800s, conceptions of "youth" were akin to what we now think of as "young adulthood." Tanner (1996), in his work on youth and deviance in Canada, explains how in pre-industrial Europe, different age groups were far more integrated in work and leisure than in contemporary times, and how in medieval France especially, children as young as 7 years old worked alongside adults. Kline (1993) elaborates on this point:

> [during medieval times, the] objects that children handled were no different to the cultural objects that adults had, and children's lives were essentially no different from those of adults. The whole community shared work and leisure as well as games, songs, and tales (p. 46).

Thus, working-class children were expected to contribute to the maintenance of the household from almost the time they could walk. This adult status extended into non-work activities such that "children were present at, and participated in, all the great ceremonies and rituals of the life cycle—including death" (Tanner, 1996, p. 19).

The Industrial Revolution was a pivotal time in the development of the notion of "youth." Two key social changes occurred at this time that ultimately served to increase the transition period between childhood and adulthood. First, there was a general shift from an agrarian to an industrial lifestyle, with many families in both European and North American societies migrating from their homes in the countryside to burgeoning urban centres. Second, there was a shift from a tradition of home-based work and family businesses to factory work (Tanner, 1996). In these new circumstances, young people quickly became a threat to the employment of male industrial workers. Fearful of losing their jobs, these male workers began to lobby through their trade unions to restrict the employment of children. At approximately the same time, humanitarian groups, largely made up of members of the middle class, began to oppose the use of children in the mines and factories on the basis that the working conditions were too severe and that the young were being exploited. This combination of factors resulted in the passage of legislation in Canada from the 1880s onwards that restricted the use of child labour (Tanner, 1996; Tyyskä, 2001).

This legislation had a profound effect on the role of young people in Western society and the ways in which youth were perceived. Unemployed working-class youth who had been displaced from the factories and mines throughout the nineteenth century began to populate the streets of major North American and European cities. While many attempted to earn a living by selling newspapers or matches, some of the displaced youth began to steal in order to survive (Tanner, 1996). Members of the middle class, increasingly disturbed by the work and leisure activities of this newly formed youth group, successfully lobbied for compulsory education as a means of civilizing and controlling these "ruffians." Tyyskä (2001), for example, notes, "the first public schools were aimed not only at creating a literate population, but at raising a patriotic citizenry and instilling into 'idle youth' habits valuable in the workforce, such as obedience and punctuality" (p. 29).

This connection between delinquency and adolescence was not restricted to lower-class street youth. In fact, conventional thinking in psychology and psychiatry at the time was that rebellion was a *natural* part of adolescent development. G. Stanley Hall, an early twentieth-century psychologist, was at the leading edge of this work and was well known for his belief in an association between a young person's biological development and their inclinations toward deviant behaviour. Adams (1997), in her study of Canadian youth and societal perspectives on sexuality, acknowledges that while Hall's work linking biological changes with deviant behaviour during adolescence (i.e., puberty) still informs much work on youth today, these perspectives have led many to adopt the deceiving and problematic view that youth-related deviance was somehow "natural." As she explains:

> [Acknowledging that] Hall's conceptualization of adolescence as a stressful, instinct-driven, transitional stage between childhood and adulthood has yet to be completely overturned...[Hall's ideas] fit nicely into common-sense discussions of puberty as the grounds of the "youth problem", a perspective made evident in the 1940s and 1950s by some of the strategies used to regulate juvenile delinquency, strategies based on efforts to control adolescent sexuality (Adams, 1997, pp. 46–47).

A consequence of these concerns/panics about the behaviour of *all* youth was the development of federal controls and legislation, such as the Juvenile Delinquency Act of 1908, that were intended to prevent youth from being pulled into the delinquent lifestyle to which they were supposedly "predisposed." For example, in 1912, the city of Vancouver passed a curfew law that prohibited any person under the age of 16 from being out in public between the hours of 9 p.m. and 6 a.m. without the accompaniment of an adult. This was done in an effort to stop shouting and yelling on the streets and prevent the loitering of youth, especially young girls (*The Vancouver Sun*, June 20, 1912).

The Emergence of the Teen and Teen Market

Of particular relevance to this chapter's discussion of the activities of contemporary youth are a series of post–World War II developments that were associated with the emergence of a "teen" culture—a culture of youth intricately linked to consumer and popular culture. The most notable of these societal changes, according to Hall and Jefferson (1976), was the sharp increase in the birth rate from 1945 onwards (i.e., the "baby boom") that meant an increase in the proportion of young people in the population and a related rise in the number of youth enrolled in schools. Other relevant trends included the elimination of unskilled jobs in increasingly technologically sophisticated business environments, and the return of soldiers to positions previously held by youth. The net result of these changes was that teenagers were now spending more years in school and in isolation from the adult workforce. What this also meant was that an increasing number of young people spent an increasing proportion of their youth in age-specific peer groups. A key consequence of these developments was the increased opportunity for and impression of a distinct "youth-specific" culture. Elaborating on this point, Adams (1997) described how the psychologists, psychiatrists, physicians, sociologists, and journalists of the time further reinforced these perceived differences:

> Teenagers were new and interesting. Those who took an interest in them created special-ized niches for themselves in their various fields of study. So, for instance, psychiatrists and psychologists alike undertook studies to determine the boundaries of normal teenage development…Journalists and sociologists made mileage out of explaining teenagers to their elders, as did education film houses like the National Film Board…While adults were informed about a strange and baffling culture, teens were enlightened about appro-priate modes of behaving (p. 43).

Equally significant in this context was that the discretionary spending of youth during these years was on the rise, a development that did not go unno-ticed by businesses and advertisers. The result was the emergence of a "targetted" teen consumer (Hebdige, 1988). Rock and roll, teen magazines, records, clothing and other items were being marketed exclusively toward this younger demographic. At the same time that this new teen market was being exploited, the perceived gap between the parent/adult generation and the new youth cul-ture had become as wide as ever. As Hall and Jefferson (1976) put it, "the arrival of the whole range of distinctive styles in dress and rock-music cemented any doubts anyone may have had about a 'unique' younger generation" (p. 20).

This increasing cultural separation between adults and youth led to a new sense of trepidation about "out of control," hedonistic youth consumers who were embracing the pleasures associated with youth-oriented rock and roll music, dances, fast food, and "outrageous" clothing styles. When this new panic about teens "having too much fun" is considered in conjunction with existing concerns about youth delinquency (along with the perception of a "naturally" psychologically underdeveloped adolescent noted earlier), it becomes easy to see just how fluid, complex, and ambiguous the notion of youth had become.

Youth and Culture into the Twenty-First Century

From the 1950s to the present, these links between business, advertising, and teenage consumer culture solidified. This evolution is largely attributable to the increasing sophistication of the advertising industry. Evidence of this youth–advertiser connection is the development of the term "tweens" during the 1990s. Tweens, the 9 to14-year-old youth demographic, are now distinct from the 15- to 19-year-old "teens," a separation that is useful for advertisers attempting to more effectively target youth (Clark and Deziel, 1999). In general, millions of dollars have been spent to learn how to best connect with 9 to 19-year-olds, the fastest growing demographic in Canada and one that spent $13.5 billion in 1998 (Clark and Deziel, 1999).

This final point is important because it raises questions not only about the ways that contemporary youth are spending their time and about their relationships with consumer culture, but also about the nature of their ties with the "parent/adult generation" as we enter the twenty-first century. That is to say, it would seem that the adult world would be less relevant to the lives of teens who spend an increasing amount of time in youth-oriented educational settings, and who live in an increasingly consumption-driven and media-saturated world. Of course, to a certain extent this is only speculation. Until the actual meanings that young people give to their activities are considered (and potential for youth to be critical of and able to distance themselves from advertising images accounted for), we cannot speak decisively about Canadian youth and culture. For similar reasons, more information is needed about the variety of activities youth are involved in. In the following sections, we work through some of the existing research and theory on these topics with the goal of clarifying these issues.

WHAT ARE CANADIAN YOUTH DOING?: LEISURE PARTICIPATION PATTERNS IN AND OUTSIDE THE HOME

In this section we provide a broad overview of the most common leisure activities and consumption habits of Canadian youth, as reported by Canadian teenagers over the past several years. In doing this, we draw heavily on the work of Reginald Bibby (2001) and his book Canada's Teens: Today, Yesterday, and Tomorrow. Bibby's book includes an exemplary synopsis of the activities of Canadian teens, drawing on nine nationwide surveys of teens (aged 15–19) and adults spanning the years 1975 through 2000. In the process of doing this research, about 17 000 people were surveyed or interviewed. While we recognize that such an overview cannot possibly do justice to the diversity of young Canadians and their activities, this "big picture" does provide a platform from which to discuss the centrality of various popular culture-related activities in the lives of youth. In the same way, and while we recognize that identifying broad patterns of activity is quite different from explaining or interpreting these patterns of activity, our opinion is that these comprehensive statistics provide an excellent basis from which to consider how the activities of young people have been interpreted by social theorists who attempt to explain youth behaviour and culture.

Teen Trends and Cultural Activity: Bibby's Big Picture

According to the findings reported in Bibby's book, in 2000, the top three daily activities for Canadian teens, both male and female, were watching television (92 percent), listening to music (86 percent), and spending time with friends (60 percent). Number four on the list for females was doing home-work (54 percent), while for males it was using a computer (48 percent) (Bibby, 2001). On a daily to weekly basis, just over half (60 percent) of young people watch videos at home and about 70 percent of males play video/computer games. Four in ten females read books they want to read, as compared to three in ten males (Bibby, 2001). Attending a movie was the most popular activity on a monthly basis, with jamming or working on music receiving a similarly high rating (Bibby, 2001).

Music   Almost 90 percent of Canadian teenagers listen to music every day. The top three choices of music-genre for Canadian youth in 2000 were rap/hip-hop, alternative, and pop, while the three favourite performers were the Backstreet Boys, Blink 182, and DMX (Bibby, 2001). Bibby notes that a large number of contemporary Canadian youth view rock as a "retro style" when compared with the popular hip-hop, R&B, and pop and relates this to a fall in record sales of Canadian acts such as Amanda Marshall, Moist, and Our Lady Peace.

Canadian youth also enjoy music in different venues. For instance, about 20 percent of youth reported that they attend a music concert monthly or more often, and just over 20 percent of males and 15 percent of females attend a rave once a month or more (Bibby, 2001). Besides listening to music, today's teens also play and/or compose music. In fact, 42 percent of both females and males report that they jam or work on their own music monthly or more often (Bibby, 2001).

Television   Viewing television is reported as the top daily activity of teens. According to Bibby (2001), young people in Canada spend an average of 2.71 hours per day watching television, with little or no significant difference between males and females. Health Canada reports findings in a slightly different manner, noting that males between the ages of 12–19 watch nearly 10 hours of television per week, while females watch just over eight hours per week (Health Canada, 2000). It is also interesting to note that 32.4 percent of MuchMusic's viewers are between the ages of 12–17 (Health Canada, 2000), a finding that reinforces the above results as showing music to be extremely important to Canadian youth.

It is important to remember here that when youth spend time in front of the television set it also means that they are exposed not only to the programmes they are watching, but also to advertising and commercials. In fact, Canadian youth cite television as the key influence on their purchase decision, whether they buy the good themselves or ask their parents to buy it for them (Health Canada, 2000). In the same way, Canadian youth are exposed to an abundance of American-based programming and culture, with U.S.-based television being the primary source of television programming for Canadian teenagers (Health Canada, 2000).

Computer   The third most popular media-related daily activity (behind listening to music and viewing television) is computer use. Using the computer ranks as number five on the list of top daily activities, while using e-mail and accessing websites followed up at number six and seven, respectively. Time spent in front of the computer is reported to be 1.14 hours per day, with little gender differentiation. Findings about young people's "sources of enjoyment" showed using computers (47 percent) to outrank the Internet (42 percent), and e-mail (33 percent) (Bibby, 2001). It should be noted that males report higher levels of enjoyment from computers and the Internet than females, although more females receive greater enjoyment from using e-mail and socializing online (Bibby, 2001; Environics Research Group, 2001). It is speculated that a primary source of the increased level of enjoyment derived by males from computer use stems from the fact that they are much more apt to play computer games. Indeed, 69 percent of males reported playing video or computer games as a daily or weekly activity, as compared to 26 percent of females (Bibby, 2001).

Furthermore, about 80 percent of Canadian teenagers report that they have access to a computer at home (Bibby, 2001) and for all but 1 percent, this included Internet access (Environics Research Group, 2001). In addition, 99 percent of young people in Canada aged 9–17 report that they have used the Internet at some point (Environics Research Group, 2001). The three favourite websites of Canadian youth aged 13–17 were the e-mail websites hotmail.com and yahoo.com and the music-download website napster.com (Environics Research Group, 2001), while the top three online activities were playing and downloading music (57 percent), e-mail (56 percent), and surfing for fun (50 percent) (Environics Research Group, 2001). Finally, while only 38 percent of youth report that their parents know about the websites they visit, 71 percent of parents reported that they knew a great deal (http://www.media-awareness.ca).

Movies   Movies are another popular source of entertainment for teenagers. Bibby (2001) reports that 78 percent of 15 to19-year-olds attend a movie at least once a month, and in the U.S., teens aged 12–17 attend about 12 films per year, four times as many as adults (U.S. News and World Report, 1994). Part of the popularity of film amongst youth may stem from the fact that the North American movie industry aims many of its films at the teenage audience. Indeed, the movie industry takes in 40 percent of its revenue during the summer months when young people are out of school (Leonard, 2001) and "virtually every one of the top money-making movies of all time made most of its profits off teenagers" (Manning, 1995, p. 2).

Another likely lure of popular film is the youth-oriented venue in which they are increasingly being shown: the movie megaplex. In 1999, Famous Players, Canada's largest theatre chain, spent about $400 million to open 30 multi-screen complexes across the country. For instance, one popular design, the Colossus theatre, resembles a blinking UFO. It houses 18 floor-to-ceiling screens, as well as video arcades complete with virtual sports and car-racing games, various fast-food outlets, and TV screens playing music videos (Clark and Deziel, 1999). Although young people are under surveillance at these theatres (by staff and security), part of the lure of the megaplex may be that it is a youth-oriented, youth-friendly venue in a society in which public space is often synonymous with adult space (Skelton and Valentine, 1998).

Friends, Family, and Cultural Activity

While it is apparent that popular culture, especially mediated forms, plays a central role in the lives of Canadian teenagers, friends play a large part as well. When asked to rank important sources of enjoyment, the top answer for both males and females was friends (94 percent), and spending time with friends was the third most common daily activity of teens (as noted above). In addition, when given a list of characteristics and asked to indicate how personally important each one was, friendship and freedom tied for the top answer (85 percent) (Bibby, 2001). Furthermore, 78 percent of Canadian youth perceive friends of having "a great deal" of influence in their lives and finally, when faced with a serious problem, "friends" was the top choice (35 percent) for teens to turn to (Bibby, 2001). In fact, and importantly, Bibby concluded from his findings that although most teens value good relationships with their family, derive enjoyment from them, and "turn to them for support," they also indicated that they "feel distrust in dealing with adults in general," "feel they are not taken seriously and are unfairly stereotyped" (Bibby, 2001, pp. 76–77). Such observations are confirmed by research on mass media portrayals of youth by authors like Acland (1995).

EXPLAINING YOUTH CULTURAL ACTIVITY

It is clear from Bibby's research and the work of others that popular culture (e.g., popular media, music, games) plays a central role in the lives of Canadian youth. It would also be fair to suggest that while parents remain an important part of young people's lives, relationships with and approval from peers and friends are immensely important to youth. These trends and findings are the inspiration for many sociologists who attempt to understand how leisure and popular culture influence young people. In the following section we outline some of the key theoretical perspectives that speak to these trends and findings. As will become evident, these perspectives are somewhat diverse, with some scholars portraying youth as passive and impressionable consumers of various forms of popular culture, and others viewing youth as reactive and proactive agents who sometimes symbolically use cultural activities like listening to music and dancing, as well as stylistic expressions (e.g., embodied in hairstyles, clothing, and body alterations like piercing and tat-

BOX 3.1   SATELLITE CHILDREN: ETHNIC IDENTITY, FAMILY, AND LEISURE

According to Tsang et al. (2003), the term *satellite children* was first used in the late 1980s "to describe children whose parents are Chinese immigrants to North America [mainly from Hong Kong and Taiwan] and who have returned to their country of origin after immigration" (pp. 359–60). Typically, the father returns to the home country to ensure financial security for the family, while the mother and children remain in Canada. Because the family is separated by an "immense geographical distance" (p. 360), irregular visits occur and, as a result, the separated couples are commonly referred to as astronauts. Using a similar analogy, the children are referred to as *satellite children*.

A crucial point made by the researchers is that that ethnic identity is not something that people are born with. That is to say, it is something that is "socially constructed." For instance, some respondents reported that they are still Chinese even though they live in Canada, others classified themselves as Chinese-Canadians, and still others felt confused about the issue of ethnic identity. Furthermore, the acculturation process was found to be unique and differentiated for each respondent, although in most cases leisure activities and consumer items were crucial in the negotiation of ethnic identity. For instance, Chinese shopping malls, with karaoke bars, video rental shops, teahouses, and cinemas were credited with allowing satellite children to stay in touch with their culture of origin. Respondents in the study also reported that they are able to maintain a connection with their roots through local Chinese media structures, including Chinese TV and radio stations, newspapers, and magazines. Many respondents also felt that electronic communication technology such as the Internet, mobile phones, and e-mail "contributed to the ease of personal and cultural connections with the country of origin" (p. 373), especially with parents. Finally, it was noted that with the absence of parental guidance, peer influence became increasingly important in the development of ethnic identity among satellite children.

In short, the growth of Chinese communities and institutions in Canada, as well as the use of communication technology, enable satellite children to exist in a "hybrid cultural environment" (p. 377) that is a mixture of the host culture and the culture of origin. Furthermore, satellite children "are part of the growing ethnic population that created this new cultural milieu and contributed to its rapid development" (p. 377). Thus, instead of merely being conditioned and shaped by the existing Canadian culture, satellite children use leisure activities and consumption to actively create a new environment that eases their transition into Canada and helps them to cope with an altered family structure.

tooing) in order to: (a) resist "mainstream" influences and authority; (b) react to feelings of marginalization or disaffection; and/or (c) negotiate their ever-evolving identities.

Passive Youth and the Culture Industry

Implicit in many arguments that have been put forth about the negative impacts of, for example, video games and advertising on young people is the view that youth are "social dupes" who uncritically consume popular culture. This perspective of youth and consumers is not new. In fact, it is part of a long history of cultural criticism and writing that presumes that audiences (youth and others) have great difficulty resisting the evils of popular film and television. The most notorious proponents of this view were the social thinkers and theorists associated with the **Frankfurt School of Social Research**. The Frankfurt School, whose origins can be traced back to Germany in 1923, was best known for the critiques of modern capitalism put forth by the school's associates, especially Theodor Adorno, Max Horkheimer, and Herbert Marcuse. Members of the school fled to the United States (New York and California, in particular) in response to the rise of the Nazi party in Germany and the increasing intolerance to any ideas that were inconsistent with party ideology. What is especially interesting about this move is that the Frankfurt School's members, in escaping the Nazi ideologies of intolerance and control, found in America an extremely developed and sophisticated form of "control through culture" that formed the basis of subsequent work on the topic (Strinati, 1995).

This Frankfurt School's critique of the power of "mass culture" (e.g., mass mediated advertising, Hollywood film) emphasized the ways that commodity producers indirectly but forcefully manipulate consumer desires (Horkheimer and Adorno, 1972; Marcuse, 1964). Horkheimer and Adorno (1972), in their revered book *Dialectic of Enlightenment*, describe how pro-capitalist ideologies are supported through and within the "culture industry," the industry of technologies, commodities, and entertainments that impose wants and needs for material satisfaction on the "passive" consumer. According to the authors, within the culture industry, industrialized, mechanized, and standardized cultural products are given a seemingly individual character—a character that masks the reality of mass production, and, in turn, manipulates and subjugates the individual. For example, a television advertisement for a mass-produced product might be marketed in ways that lead consumers to think they will "stand out from the crowd" if they only purchase that item. Horkheimer and Adorno (1972) suggested, "in the culture industry the notion of genuine style is seen to be the aesthetic equivalent of domination" (pp. 129–30). In this way, the culture industry creates a homogenous culture of "social dupes," who, in being fascinated by and enamoured with elements of popular culture like Hollywood film and consumer items, have been lulled into an uncritical acceptance of present conditions (i.e., where identity is created and negotiated through consumption). Since the "concepts of order which it [the culture industry] hammers into people are always those of the status quo" (Adorno, 1991, p. 90), the masses—with youth being the most impressionable of the lot—are deceived into conformity and a loss of consciousness. That is to say, a life guided by and given meaning through the consumption of products and entertainment comes to be a taken-for-granted and unrivalled way of life.

Acknowledging that this portrayal of the Frankfurt School is necessarily brief and oversimplified, it is important to point out that there have been many critics of the school's view of the culture industry and the consumer over the years. Most pertinent to this chapter is the concern expressed by authors who feel that the Frankfurt School did not give sufficient credit to consumers—consumers who might well interpret popular culture-related messages and items in ways not intended by industry producers. As Douglas Kellner (1995) argued in his book *Media Culture*:

> The Frankfurt School position that all mass culture is ideological and debased, having the effects of duping a passive mass of consumers, is...objectionable...[One should] allow for the possibility that critical and subversive moments could be found in the artifacts of the culture industries...In addition, one should distinguish between the encoding and decoding of media artifacts, and recognize that an active audience often produces its own meanings and uses for products of the culture industries (pp. 29–30).

Many researchers have provided analyses of popular culture that responded to and contradicted those of the Frankfurt School. John Fiske (1989a, 1989b), in his books *Reading the Popular* and *Understanding Popular Culture*, celebrated the capacities of consumers who, for example, use shopping malls in empowering and resistive ways (e.g., by hanging out in the mall, but not shopping). Albert Cohen (1955), in his seminal research on youth and deviance, described how working-class youth who do not have the resources to measure up against "the middle-class measuring rod"—a status system essentially defined by academic and occupational achievement (and, by association, ownership of desirable consumer goods)—create their own "oppositional" value system (e.g., where disrespecting middle-class values come to be revered within the subcultural group).

Active Youth and Symbolic Resistance

It was at the **Centre for Contemporary Cultural Studies** (CCCS) at the University of Birmingham, England in the 1970s where a core of researchers and theorists developed a still-influential approach for understanding the ways that youth proactively respond to the power of mainstream culture and their related feelings of marginalization. Central to their analysis was the concept of **hegemony**, a term developed in the early twentieth century by Italian revolutionary Antonio Gramsci (1971). Hegemony, in simple terms, refers to the ways that groups in power (e.g., upper classes) are able to maintain their privileged position by developing strategies that ensure that marginal/oppressed groups consent to their power. By creating education systems that favour the status quo (e.g., that maintain standards oriented to the middle class), and by supporting the dissemination of media messages that both stigmatize groups that do not conform (e.g., youth) while maintaining a system of consumption that benefits only the most powerful, hegemony is maintained. As you might expect, for those who study hegemony and popular culture, research often focuses on how much input powerful groups have into the messages that are dispersed through mass media (e.g., by looking at relationships between media producers and big business).

At the same time that Gramsci described the power of dominant groups and classes, he more optimistically recognized the possibility for **counter-hegemony**, that is, the potential for marginal groups to fight back against the forces that oppress them. It was this potential for counter-hegemony that inspired the arguments made by those at the CCCS, who interpreted the spectacular and sometimes offensive styles and activities of youth subculture members to be proactive responses to these youths' marginalized positionings (i.e., positionings as both "youth" and "working class"). For example, Dick Hebdige (1979), in his classic book *Subculture: The Meaning of Style*, described how youth who were members of subcultures like the punk rockers and skinheads were expressing dissatisfaction with the status quo through style. That is to say, by dying their hair blue or purple, wearing intentionally torn clothes, adorning themselves with safety pins as nose-rings, and listening to music by bands like the Sex Pistols (a band whose lyrics challenged and mocked powerful institutions like the British monarchy), these youth were making purposeful attempts to challenge the sensibility of the establishment—or, as the title of another CCCS-based book relays, they were "resisting through rituals" (Hall and Jefferson, 1976).

It is important to acknowledge, however (as the CCCS members did), that these challenges were largely symbolic or "magical," and were not direct political challenges to authority. This concession could be interpreted in at least two ways. On one hand, it could mean that youth subcultures are not truly counter-hegemonic in the sense that their activities in no way alter the conditions that these young people are living with. In fact, it would seem that dominant groups would not be opposed to this kind of resistance because it would appear that young people "have a voice," when in reality existing social conditions that favour the privileged remain intact. On the other hand, to say that these activities do not "make a difference" is to be insensitive to the ways that young people are at least temporarily empowered by participation in alternative cultural activity. In the same way, it is important to consider that youth involvement in symbolically resistant subcultural activity is evidence that young people are active and critical recipients of cultural messages that circulate through, for example, mass media and educational settings. Paul Willis (1990) and Angela McRobbie (1994) are two authors who have specifically discussed how young people actively subvert aspects of consumer culture by, for example, taping music off the radio (or, more recently, downloading music off the Internet) or purchasing secondhand clothing.

Research and theory out of the CCCS has also been subject to a series of criticisms (c.f., Bennett and Harris, 2003). Most notably, CCCS-based theorists have been accused of "celebrating" the capacity of young people to resist mainstream cultural influences. That is to say, some critics argue that the youth depicted in some of the CCCS's work are given too much credit for their ability to think critically and respond proactively. Another issue identified by critics is that spectacular subcultures like punk rockers and skinheads are only a small sample of youth today, and that the everyday activities of young people might not be subversive in the ways described by some members of the CCCS (the work of Willis and McRobbie noted above notwithstanding). A related concern is that the research seemed to assume that all punks or skinheads interpreted their activities in the same way. As more recent (Canadian-based) research by sociologists like Young and Craig (1997) (who studied skinheads in Calgary) suggests, subculture members, while sharing broad philosophies, often participate in subcultures for quite different reasons and interpret their subcultural activities in distinct ways.

BOX 3.2   RACE, INTERPRETATION, ADVERTISING, AND YOUTH CULTURE

In the late 1980s and early 1990s, mass media reports about the "power of sneaker commercials" over youth began to surface. The impetus for these reports was a series of high-profile reports of violence over sneakers in the United States and Canada, including a well-documented case where one youth killed another for his Air Jordan Sneakers (c.f., Telander, 1990). A study by one of the authors of this chapter and his colleague considered the extent to which athletic apparel advertisements featuring celebrity icon athletes actually influenced young male basketball fans' perceptions of what is "cool" and the extent to which these youth felt they "needed" sneakers to "be cool" (Wilson and Sparks, 1996, 1999). An important addendum to this study was that the celebrity icon athletes (basketball players) in the commercials were in almost all cases African-American. For this reason, Wilson and Sparks focused on the ways that "black" youth in Toronto and "non-black" youth in Vancouver interpreted these commercials (using small focus group interviews in each city). What the researchers found was that the black youth were extremely enamoured with many of the sneaker commercials and the athletes featured in these commercials, and were clear about the importance of the name-brand (e.g., Nike) sneaker as a style-marker in their culture. It was also pertinent, though, that while appreciating the commercial and admitting to its influence, these same youth were also critical of the ways that blacks are portrayed in television, suggesting that there should be more "positive" non-athlete portrayals of blacks. Conversely, the non-black youth, who also enjoyed the commercials and admired the celebrity athletes, did not consider the sneakers to be as central to their cultural identities or as crucial in the construction of a "cool" persona among peers. As strikingly, these youth were largely uncritical of or ambivalent to the ways that blacks are portrayed in mass media. That is to say, unlike the black youth, for whom race-related issues (as they relate to African-American portrayals in particular) were a central part of their everyday lives, for the non-black youth, these concerns were not something they had thought much about—although the authors also found that some non-black youth appeared to learn about race from television. Conclusions offered by Wilson and Sparks (1996, 1999) in their two articles on the topic that are especially pertinent to this chapter are: 1) that young people are a complex group who interpret media in a variety of ways, depending on their cultural experiences and their social locations (i.e., their race and gender related identities; and their positioning as basketball fans living in different parts of Canada); and 2) that youth audiences are both critical (e.g., the black youth noticing the ways that African-Americans are portrayed in media) and impressionable (e.g., both youth groups enjoying the sneaker commercials, the non-black youth in some cases appearing to learn about race from television).

This understanding of youth subcultures as groups of young people who share many perspectives and cultural activities, but who also interpret cultural items (like clothing) and media messages in somewhat diverse ways is, in our view, a more balanced approach to explaining and describing relationships between youth and culture. In the next section, we explore this view of youth through a case study of the rave subculture in southern Ontario, referring to findings from research conducted by Wilson (1999, 2002a), one of the authors of this chapter. In this next section, Wilson also describes some of the findings from his research as a way of explaining some of the theories of youth cultural activity described here.

RAVE IN SOUTHERN ONTARIO: A CASE STUDY AND REFLECTIVE ACCOUNT

"Rave" is a culture of youth whose members are renowned for their interest in computer-generated "techno" music, use of amphetamine drugs, and attendance at all-night dance parties known as "raves." Over the course of my research on the southern Ontario rave scene from 1995 to 1999, I attended raves, interviewed ravers, rave-DJs, and rave party promoters, and read daily comments that appeared on rave-related newsgroups of which I was a member. In my Ph.D. dissertation (Wilson, 1999) and in a subsequent article (Wilson, 2002a), I reported findings from my research and, in conducting a sociological analysis of these findings, considered the extent to which raver-youth were either actively resisting aspects of mainstream culture (e.g., creating an alternative "neo-hippie" set of values in the rave) or passively participating in the scene (e.g., mindlessly escaping into the dance party and a drug-induced haze).

In essence, I found that although ravers shared a range of activities and perspectives, they also tended to participate in and interpret their experiences in diverse ways. At times this diversity manifested itself as differences between ravers, while other times it appeared that raver perspectives changed over time, as subculture members learned more about their scene. For example, many youth were aware of and generally supported the rave-related values articulated through the acronym **PLUR**, "Peace-Love-Unity-Respect." These values were operationalized in some of the following ways:

- *The "pick-up" culture that defines many dance clubs is less evident in rave, where ravers seldom "hit on" one another in the same way that people do at clubs, preferring to dance and listen to music.*

- *The macho norms of intimidation that are commonplace in many dance clubs are frowned upon in the rave. When strangers bump into one another on the dance floor, often an apology and friendly gesture or conversation will follow (instead of a scowl or physical confrontation).*

- *Uninhibited "communal" dancing to heavy and fast beated techno music was viewed as a way for ravers to "connect with one another" through ritual. When ravers are moving together to the music and, if they choose to do drugs, feeling the positive effects of the amphetamine drug Ecstasy (a drug that apparently allows people to lose inhibitions while giving them energy to dance), they are said to be "feeling the vibe." Many ravers claim that by feeling the vibe through this music and dance ritual, they are able to lose preconceptions about people—a state and perspective that at least partially explains why rave culture is also thought to be open to and accepting of all races and ethnicities, and to be especially empowering for women (c.f., McRobbie, 1993; Pini, 1997).*

For many of the youth I interviewed, rave culture was an alternative youth movement that was, for them, an escape from and a reaction against a mainstream culture where people are intolerant of one another and are poor communicators, and where day-to-day life is so intense that "letting go" is almost impossible.

Of course, not all ravers were this reflective about the meaning of their rave experiences, nor were they necessarily motivated by the "counter-cultural" possibilities of rave. Some of these youth viewed raves as places to go after the bars closed. At times these "drop-in" ravers were known to be either ignorant of or disrespectful of the informal norms of interaction in rave. Other youth viewed raves as little more than safe spaces to use drugs, a perspective frowned upon by "authentic" ravers who see drug use as only one component of an integrated ritual of dancing and music listening. Still others came to raves in hopes of "picking up" for a "one-night stand," a practice usually associated with more conventional nightclubs. One raver in the study labelled these disrespectful interlopers into the scene "toxic ravers," as a way of describing their effects on the culture and environment. The increased number of "outsiders" attending rave parties was a point of concern for many committed/"authentic" long-time ravers, who were upset about how, with the increased popularity of rave as a topic of discussion in mass media and a

BOX 3.3   RAVE AND TECHNOLOGY

The rave subculture is also a "pro-technology" subculture. Ravers advertise their parties over the Internet, often engage in chatroom discussions about upcoming and previous rave parties and about music, and enjoy and sometimes create music that is largely computer-generated. In some cases, virtual and real rave parties are held, where online ravers interact online with those at an actual party, with all participants listening to the same music and observing the same setting, albeit from different locations. In an article that I wrote recently with Michael Atkinson, we suggested that "online and offline" life for ravers had become increasingly blurred (Wilson and Atkinson, forthcoming). In fact, some DJs who play at rave parties will bring an entire "set of music" on their laptop computer, to be played for the raver-audience. Unlike many previous subcultures that were anti-technology, ravers celebrate technology (Kellner, 1995). In fact, ravers could be considered deviant and "subversive" because of their tendency to over-embrace technology (Wilson, 2002a).

"style" adopted by advertisers, people have begun to attend raves because it is the "cool" thing to do, not because of a desire to be part of a PLUR-inspired community (Wilson, 2002a).

In broad terms then, many youth attended raves for many different reasons. At the same time though, and as pertinently, many "committed" ravers described how their views on rave changed over their "careers" as a subculture member. For example, many interviewed members of the culture talked about how when they first entered the rave scene, they were enamoured with the music, drugs, and sense of community. As time went on though, some explained that they began to see that rave was actually more "political" than they thought, with rave promoters competing for raver-dollars and not always acting in the best interest of the community/participants (e.g., overcharging for bottled water, a necessary resource for those engaged in intense, all-night dancing). Others noticed some of their friends becoming too "into" the drug aspect of the scene and noticed how the "non-rave" lives of these peers were being negatively impacted. Others realized that the rave community was much more fragmented than they originally thought, with some ravers looking down on other ravers because of the specific type of techno music they listened to or the clothes they wore. The most common complaint was that rave was becoming too "commercialized," and that the alternative lifestyle they were seeking was not attainable in a rave scene that was now marketed in mainstream magazines and by money-hungry promoters. Certainly this latter view is a most cynical understanding of the scene, but it certainly represents the perspective of many ravers who became disillusioned over their subcultural careers (Wilson, 2002a).

Using Rave to Help Us Understand Youth Cultural Activity

It was clear from the research that rave was viewed and used in a variety of ways by the young people who participated in it. That is to say, rave represented, depending on to whom you talked and when you talked to them, anything from a weekend escape and "good party" to a proactive form of resistance and social movement. For example, some youth might attend raves because they saw a flashy "rave flyer" advertising what looked like a fun time, but did not view their participation as being a meaningful symbolic statement about or escape from an "overregulated and oppressive" mainstream culture. Conversely, there were many ravers who were dedicated to and supported the rave PLUR philosophy. These ravers often would not only attend raves, but also would also put up rave websites promoting PLUR-related views, and throw (sometimes non-profit) raves with titles like "Good Vibes" or "Unification of a Peaceful Nation." Many others, who were somewhere "in between" these extreme positionings, would express an awareness of rave values and would adhere to and enjoy the norms of interaction in raves, but only considered themselves to be weekend ravers who are not very committed to the subculture.

In other words, some youth were passive consumers of the rave party and music, akin to the consumers described by the Frankfurt School theorists (if we view more mainstream raves as leisure activities for mass consumption). On the other hand, some youth were proactive and committed participants in a culture that, for them, embodied counter-cultural values and symbolically challenged aspects of "the mainstream" that they find distasteful. Through the lens of CCCS theorists, these youth would be "resistant," using culture as a form of expression and potential disruption. Of course, there were also youth who inhabited a "middle ground," attending raves sometimes and adhering to rave norms when they do attend, but without a firm or long-term commitment to the scene or the counter-cultural ideology.

Although it is useful to outline these theoretical positionings, it is also important to point out that theorists committed to understanding the "hegemony" of the mainstream (e.g., the power of those who support the pro-commercialism values that ravers resist), would argue (cynically) that the symbolic resistance of ravers, even in its most proactive form, in no way alters the existing conditions of oppression or feelings of marginalization that some youth experience and resist. In other words, while some youth are empowered by their participation in rave, their "resistance," according to some theorists, is meaningless in the big picture (see Wilson, 2002a for a much more detailed discussion of these theoretical ideas).

CONCLUSION

In this chapter we described how youth have increasingly developed a cultural life separate from the "parent/adult generation," outlined a striking (albeit unsurprising) trend that mass media and popular culture have become an integral part of young people's lives, and discussed some ways that youth cultural activity has been explained. In working through these explanations, we referred to sociological theories developed by the Frankfurt School of Social Research and the Centre for Contemporary Cultural Studies in Birmingham, England, that theorized about young people's relationships with popular culture, peers, and the parent/adult generation. The rave subculture was used as a case study to interrogate some of these approaches and to ultimately argue that youth should be viewed as a diverse group who understand their social and cultural world in a range of ways, and that their perspectives change as they gain new experiences.

In reflecting on the developments, ideas, and assertions of this chapter on existing literature focused on "youth at the millennium," it seemed to us that much of what is written about young people's fascination with popular culture and the impacts of these fascinations on the family are quite negative. As noted earlier, authors like Furlong and Cartmel (1997) suggest that as youth become increasingly connected to the outside world through global media, they also come to be aware of social problems in ways that previous generations were not.

In the same way, these authors suggest that in spending time in the world of global media (and not within more conventional local peer and family-oriented groups), there is a weakened "sense of community" for young people, and, for this reason, youth feel more "on their own" than ever before.

While we agree that there is reason to be concerned, we also suggest that recent developments are not unconditionally negative. For example, the Internet has been described in some instances as a forum where young people, especially marginalized youth, can connect with one another, experience a sense of belonging that was missing in their "offline" lives, and express themselves in creative and productive ways (e.g., websites for bullied youth to attain information and get advice from peers about how to best deal with problems at school) (cf., Wilson, 2002b). In fact, the younger generation's literacy in computers and other media could be considered testament to their ability to adapt to new social and cultural circumstances in ways that many adults cannot or do not (Rushkoff, 1996). With these ideas in mind, Don Tapscott (1998), author of *Growing Up Digital: The Rise of the Net Generation*, offered a more optimistic approach to family relations in a society where young people's lives are intricately linked with media and technology. Tapscott argues that in order "to break down the walls between generations" there is a need to work toward more open and communicative families. Central to Tapscott's (1998) argument is that this openness is only possible if parents "understand the potential of new media" and, crucially, *accept* the part that it plays in youth culture (pp. 249–50). We would add to this that it is also important to recognize the diversity of ways young people interpret media and experience peer cultural relationships. In this way, parents and researchers can work toward a better understanding of youth and youth culture and, in turn, move away from a situation where young people are continually stigmatized and demonized.

Summary

- Youth are a complex and diverse group that negotiate, understand, and interpret the various cultural influences they encounter in different ways at different times.

- Conceptions of youth have changed through history; after World War II, a youth (teen) culture emerged linked to consumer and popular culture.

- In the twenty-first century, popular culture, which targets youth—music, television, computer activities, movies—and is enjoyed with friends, plays a central role in the lives of Canadian teenagers.

- There is a long history of analysts viewing youth as passive, uncritical consumers of popular culture; more recently theorists and researchers have articulated a perspective that suggests youth are active, critical recipients of cultural messages and may explicitly resist the dominant culture.

- Youth literacy with aspects of the new technology—the use of computers and other media—provides both for connection amongst youth and for the possibility of enhanced communication between generations if parents accept it as an integral part of youth culture.

- An examination of contemporary Canadian rave subculture suggests a diversity of youth groups—those who are simply passive consumers of the race party and music as well as those who are proactive and committed to a counter-cultural challenge to mainstream values.

Critical Thinking Questions

1. What does it means to say that the term "youth" is "socially constructed"?

2. Are youth more susceptible to the influences of popular culture than adults?

3. Why are youth often portrayed as either "troubled or troubling" in mass media reports?

Websites

Media Awareness Network
http://www.media-awareness.ca/english/index.cfm
    This site provides resources and support for those interested in media literacy programmes for youth. It includes links to several special initiative projects such as *Games for Kids* and *Young Canadians in a Wired World*.

Health Canada: Division of Childhood and Adolescence Webpage
http://www.hc-sc.gc.ca/dca-dea/7-18yrs-ans/index_e.html
    This webpage contains a range of information about issues to do with youth, children, identity, and health issues.

Suggested Reading

Mary Louise Adams. 1997. *The Trouble With Normal.* Toronto, ON: University of Toronto Press.
    Adams' book is one of the few recent Canadian books to consider youth culture with a specific focus on the historical construction of gender and heterosexuality in the lives of youth. Adams's book includes a useful discussion of the recent history of the social category "youth."

Tracey Skelton and Gill Valentine, eds. 1998. *Cool Places: Geographies of Youth Cultures.* London; New York: Routledge.

Skelton and Valentine's book is a collection of international studies of youth culture. The most notable contributions include: a geographical perspective on youth culture (i.e., focused on issues to do with youths' usages of social space), a specific inclusion of feminist perspectives on youth, and a discussion of globalization and youth.

Julian Tanner. 1996. *Teenage Troubles: Youth and Deviance in Canada*. Scarborough, ON: Nelson Canada.

This is a most comprehensive examination of deviance-related approaches to the study of youth in Canada.

References

Acland, C. 1995. *Youth, Murder, Spectacle: The Cultural Politics of 'Youth in Crisis.'* Boulder: Westview Press.

Adams, M. 1997. *The Trouble with Normal: Postwar Youth and the Making of Heterosexuality.* Toronto: University of Toronto Press.

Adorno, T. 1991. *The Culture Industry.* London: Routledge.

Bennett, A., and K. Harris, eds. 2003, forthcoming. *After Subculture: Critical Studies of Subcultural Theory.* New York: Palgrave.

Bibby, R. 2001. *Canada's Teens: Today, Yesterday, and Tomorrow.* Toronto: Stoddart.

Clark, A., and S. Deziel. (1999). "How teens got the power." *Maclean's* 112(12): 42–47.

Cohen, A. 1955. *Delinquent Boys.* Glencoe: The Free Press of Glencoe.

Coleman, J. 1992. "The Nature of Adolescence." In J. Coleman and C. Warren-Adamson, eds., *Youth Policy in the 1990s: The Way Forward* (pp. 8–27). New York: Routledge.

Environics Research Group. 2001. *Young Canadians in a Wired World: The Students' View.* Prepared for the Media Awareness Network and the Government of Canada.

Fiske, J. 1989a. *Reading the Popular.* Boston: Unwin Hyman.

————. 1989b. *Understanding Popular Culture.* Boston: Unwin Hyman.

Furlong, A., and F. Cartmel. 1997. *Young People and Social Change: Individualization and Risk in Late Modernity.* Buckingham, UK: Open University Press.

Gillis, J. 1974. *Youth and History.* New York: Academic Press.

Gramsci, A. 1971. *Selections from the Prison Notebooks.* New York: International Publishers.

Hall, S., and T. Jefferson. 1976. *Resistance through Rituals: Youth Subcultures in Post-War Britain.* London: Hutchinson.

Health Canada. 2000. Youth public opinion research study: Secondary analysis of current market research on youth ages 7–19. Retrieved from http://www.hc-sc. gc.ca/hppb/socialmarketing/2/youth/youth_e.pdf

Hebdige, D. 1979. *Subculture: The Meaning of Style*. London: Methuen.

———. 1988. *Hiding in the Light*. London: Routledge.

Horkheimer, M., and T. Adorno. 1972. *Dialectic of Enlightenment*. Trans. John Cummings. New York: Herder and Herder.

Kellner, D. 1995. *Media Culture: Cultural Studies, Identity and Politics between the Modern and the Postmodern*. New York: Routledge.

Kline, S. 1993. *Out of the Garden: Toys, TV, and Children's Culture in the Age of Marketing*. New York: Verso.

Leonard, D. 2001. "We Know What You're Doing Next Summer." *Fortune* 144(6): 117–19.

Manning, S. 1995. "The Power of Hollywood." *Scholastic Update* May 5, 2–3.

Marcuse, H. 1964. *One-Dimensional Man*. Boston: Beacon Press.

McRobbie, A. 1993. "Shut Up and Dance: Youth Culture and Changing Modes of Femininity." *Cultural Studies* 7(3): 406–26.

———. 1994. *Postmodernism and Popular Culture*. London: Routledge.

Pini, M. 1997. "Women and the Early British Rave Scene." In A. McRobbie, ed., *Back to Reality: Social Experience and Cultural Studies* (pp. 152–69). Manchester: Manchester University Press.

Rushkoff, D. 1996. *Playing the Future: How Kids' Culture Can Teach Us to Thrive in an Age of Chaos*. New York: HarperCollins

Skelton, T., and G. Valentine. 1998. *Cool Places: Geographies of Youth Cultures*. London; New York: Routledge.

Strinati, D. 1995. *An Introduction to Theories of Popular Culture*. London; New York: Routledge.

Tanner, J. 1996. *Teenage Troubles: Youth and Deviance in Canada*. Scarborough: Nelson Canada.

Tapscott, D. 1998. *Growing Up Digital: The Rise of the Net Generation*. Toronto: McGraw-Hill Ryerson.

Telander, R. "Senseless." *Sports Illustrated* May 14, 1990, pp. 36–38, 43–44, 46, 49.

Tsang, A., H. Irving, R. Alaggia, S. Chau, and M. Benjamin. 2003. "Negotiating Ethnic Identity in Canada: The Case of the 'Satellite children.'" *Youth and Society* 34(3): 359–83.

Tyyskä, V. 2001. *Long and Winding Road: Adolescents and Youth in Canada Today*. Toronto: Canadian Scholars' Press.

U.S. News & World Report. 1994. Database. *U.S. News & World Report* 116(23): 16.

Vancouver Sun. 1912. "May Ring Curfew for Children on Vancouver Streets at Night." *The Vancouver Sun*, 1(111), 1.

Willis, P. 1990. *Common Culture*. San Francisco: Westview.

Wilson, B. 1999. Empowering Communities or Delinquent Congregations?: A Study of Complexity and Contradiction in Canadian Youth Cultures and Leisure Spaces. Unpublished doctoral dissertation, McMaster University, Hamilton, Ontario, Canada.

———. 2002a. "The Canadian Rave Scene and Five Theses on Youth Resistance." *Canadian Journal of Sociology* 27(3): 373–412.

———. 2002b. "The 'Anti-Jock' Movement: Reconsidering Youth Resistance, Masculinity and Sport Culture in the Age of the Internet." *Sociology of Sport Journal* 19(2): 207–34.

Wilson, B. and M. Atkinson. forthcoming. "Rave Scenes and Straightedge Figurations: Exploring On-Line and Off-Line Experiences in Canadian Youth Subcultures." *Youth & Society.*

Wilson, B. and R. Sparks 1996. "'It's Gotta Be the Shoes': Youth, Race, and Sneaker Commercials." *Sociology of Sport Journal* 13(4): 398–427.

———. 1999. "Impacts of Black Athlete Media Portrayals on Canadian Youth." *Canadian Journal of Communication* 24(4): 589–627.

Young, K. and L. Craig 1997. "Beyond White Pride: Contradiction in the Canadian Skinhead Subculture." *Canadian Review of Sociology and Anthropology* 34(2): 175–206.

Chapter 4

Family Lives of Native Peoples, Immigrants, and Visible Minorities

Julianne Momirov and Kenise Murphy Kilbride

LEARNING OBJECTIVES

In this chapter, you will learn that:

1. families and their members face the impact of being racialized, ethnicized, and gendered;

2. immigrants, particularly women, face challenges in settling in Canada and trying to maintain their family lives;

3. immigration policy has affected and continues to affect family relations;

4. immigrant parents face challenges;

5. the children and youth in these families face particular challenges as they attempt to bridge two cultures.

INTRODUCTION

Many Canadians probably believe that having a family is a natural stage in the progression of human life. It is something that most, if not all, Canadians want in their lives at some point. We Canadians are socialized by numerous institutions to believe that having a family is our adult destiny, regardless of whatever else we might wish to do. Our culture reinforces this message in myriad ways. To have a family is "the right thing to do." A closer probe into this situation reveals, however, that the reality of having family rests on numerous factors besides intimate relationships and procreation, the most significant of these factors being economics and government policies that influence family life in various ways. For a significant number of Canadian citizens and those residing in Canada, family life is a difficult achievement. Frequently, having a family has out-and-out been denied these people in the past and, in less overt fashion, is still in some ways denied them today. Numerous other people who live in Canada find it extremely difficult to maintain a stable family life and provide their children with the resources that they will need in the future to be successful citizens.

To gain a true understanding of Canadian families, it is crucial to understand the role that immigration has played in Canadian life. As the Canadian Research Institute for the Advancement of Women (CRIAW) states in its fact sheet, "Only 4 percent of Canadians are not immigrants or descendants of immigrants. Only Aboriginal peoples are native to this land, and have lived and died here for 10 000 years" (No. 5-2003, 1). Although the figure of 10 000 years may be in dispute as being too recent, the sentiment is not disputed. For better or worse, immigrants are responsible for making this country into what it is today. Therefore, most Canadian families have been somehow shaped by immigration, past and present. Our migration experiences, no matter how distant in time, have helped to shape who and what our families are.

Canada is a pluralistic, or multicultural, nation. This condition is both reality and law. There is no reason to believe that at least the near future will change this reality since our birth rate, as noted in the 2001 Census, is low at an average of approximately 1.5 births per woman of childbearing age (The Daily, August 11, 2003), but our population must grow to sustain Canada's economic health and in order to support our social programmes. Canada counts on immigration for its current and continued well-being. For most of the past century, the foreign born have made up about 16 percent of the population. At present it is a little over 18.4 percent because of increased immigration in the 1990s. Indeed, that decade now stands as being historically the one of greatest immigrant arrival, with 2.2 million newcomers entering the country (Statistics Canada, 2003b, p. 5). Canada now ranks second only to Australia, which stands at 23 percent, in the proportion of foreign-born residents, and is far ahead of countries such as the United States (about 11 percent). Despite a figure that seems alarming to some native-born Canadians, the increase in immigration was by design and, in fact, Canada is not yet meeting its desired goal. Recent Ministers of Immigration have all mentioned plans to raise the annual immigration goal from 250 000 (including refugees) to 300 000. This figure will place the annual target at about 1 percent of the existing population.

With regard to refugees, contrary to popular opinion that sometimes portrays Canada as a country inundated by refugees and refugee claimants, this country does not accept a large number. In the spring of 2003, the Safe Third Country Agreement with the United States took effect. This agreement states that any refugee who enters Canada via what is considered a "safe third country," such as the United States, must be returned to that country to seek asylum there. Critics argue that this agreement will essentially keep refugee claimants out of Canada. The impact of this linkage will be assessed at the end of its first year in place, at which time we will see whether the differences in refugee policy between our two countries have had a negative impact on the treatment of refugees (CRIAW No. 5-2003, p. 4). Family life for refugees has often been destroyed by war or political persecution before they ever reach Canada. Re-establishing family life can be a particularly arduous process for these people.

Those Canadians who belong to what is known euphemistically as **visible minorities**, meaning those who state that they are not white and not Caucasian (but are not Aboriginal) in their descent, make up about 13.4 percent of the total population while, as noted above, about 4 percent have some Native, or Aboriginal, origins (Statistics Canada, 2003b and 2003f). Many visible minorities are immigrants and refugees.

In the past, the terms "race" and "ethnicity" have been used as if they were undisputed realities. It is no longer the case, however, among some sociologists who point out that "race" has no biological reality; therefore, its use in sociological literature helps to perpetuate a myth (Satzewich, 1998). More correctly, the term **"racialized"** should be used since it indicates the reality that some groups of people, due to their physical appearance and frequently because of the way they live, are categorized by a powerful or dominant group as being qualitatively different from it; so different, in fact, that they are held to belong to separate classes of beings (usually inferior), or "races." A similar process occurs when a group is designated as being "ethnic," although ethnicization involves the identification of cultural, not physical, characteristics. In both cases, the designations reveal power differentials between those who are labelled and those who have the power to label. Furthermore, gender and class complicate racialization and ethnicization, as feminists point out in their analyses.

THEORETICAL FRAMEWORK

The cornerstone of understanding the experiences and family lives of Natives, visible minorities, and immigrants/refugees is power relations and the resources that accrue to those with power. Because of their racialization and ethnicization, these people generally have less power than the dominant group that labels them in these ways. Their lack of power is manifested in lower socioeconomic status and prestige (or social honour), both of which frequently feed into one another, the result being multifaceted oppression. When gender oppression is added to this mix, it becomes obvious that racialized or ethnicized women who are immigrants or refugees, or Canadian women of colour or Aboriginal status, are among the most oppressed members of Canadian society. Their family lives are inevitably affected by their oppression. Since women bear most of the responsibility for family life through their reproductive labour, their multiple oppressions have a strong impact on the quality of life of the other members of their families. For this reason, it is vital that we employ a feminist perspective in the analysis of family lives of Natives, immigrants and refugees, and visible minorities.

To be a useful tool for analysis, a feminist perspective must holistically incorporate the multiplicity of oppressions that some women experience. This necessity leads us to antiracist feminism in its political economy form. The political economy approach examines how forms of oppression based in race, class, gender, and sexuality serve to situate groups of women in structured social relations. A form of oppression such as **racism** differs according to structural location. Oppressions have numerous meanings and manifestations. Antiracist feminism from a political economy perspective recognizes these diversities, their structural connections, and their implications regarding power relations and resources, and it attempts to address them in its analysis (Dua, 1999).

Miles et al. (2001; see also Mandell, 2001; and Dua, 1999) categorize antiracist feminism as a Third Wave feminism, meaning that it belongs to a contemporary generation of feminist theorizing that is characterized by the recognition of diversity among women and their experiences. Antiracist feminism promotes the notion that, in looking at gender relations, it is also imperative to examine how they intersect with racialized, ethnicized, and class relations. In other words, it acknowledges that where social boundaries exist and overlap in society, they must be accounted for and examined as a holistic entity, not in isolation from one another. There is no generic category of "woman" that is influenced solely by gender; women are also part of racialized groups, cultural groups, socioeconomic groups, religious groups, occupational groups, and so on. All of these factors, particularly when they are socially valued in different ways, have an impact on people's family lives. For instance, Cassidy et al. point out that, while women who belong to the dominant group in Canada have struggled for the right to have abortions, Native woman have struggled over the right to "give birth to and raise healthy children" (2001, p. 80). Furthermore, these authors note that, while the former group has fought to get out of the home and into the workforce, black women have long been forced to work outside their homes (often in the homes of the former group) and were not exclusively confined to the domestic sphere; their efforts have been focused on getting out of work ghettoes and obtaining better wages. Additionally, immigrant women have fought against restrictive immigration policies to enter Canada and reunite their families (Cassidy et al., 2001, pp. 86–87). When we take a Third Wave or antiracist feminist approach, we see that oppression is multifaceted and complex.

Furthermore, antiracist feminism focuses on family in a much more positive way than other, more mainstream feminisms have in the past. Rather than seeing family as first and foremost the site of women's oppression, antiracist feminists view the family as a more supportive and protective environment in which women are sheltered from the negative effects of racism. Antiracist feminists' concern is how the state acts in various ways to deny family life to some women of colour (cited in Mandell, 2001).

This chapter will attempt to address the following deceptively simple question: How has immigration to this land affected various peoples and their capacity to have a good quality of family life?

NATIVES

This section begins with a discussion of Native peoples. Some people like to call Native people immigrants, but for the purpose of this chapter, it will be considered that peoples who have inhabited a land for more than 10 000 years can claim to be indigenous. In order not to cloud the issue, the word "immigrant" will be used for those who came more recently, specifically in the last 500 years or so. Nevertheless, the immigration of Europeans and other peoples has affected Natives' lives on the whole and, in particular, their ability to maintain their own family forms, both historically and currently, as we shall see below.

Traditionally some nations preferred to live in extended families while others, such as the Mi'kmaq, were **patrilineal**, meaning that kinship is traced through the father's line. The *Haudenausaunee* (Iroquois) were all **matrilineal**, which means that they traced their kinship through the mother's line. The women of the Six Nations belonging to what is known as the Iroquois Confederacy were vested with a good deal of power, including the right to divest a chief of his authority. Among the longhouse people, women of the same family lived and worked together, with their husbands moving in with them (Steckley and Cummins, 2001). There was variety in the family forms adopted and practised by the various Native groups of North America. The variety of forms was changed when European missionaries and government administrators established themselves as the dominant group and imposed their own policies and laws upon Natives; Native families were forced to take on the patriarchal, nuclear form that was prevalent among their colonizers. That family form remains prevalent today, still reinforced by government policy and Canadian culture.

Sarah Carter (1996) writes of how Native women came to be relegated to the status of "squaw" when white settler women began to arrive in significant numbers in Western Canada after Confederation. Native women went from being sought-after "country" wives and mythical "Indian princesses" to being considered inferior in virtually every way to their white counterparts. Negative images were promulgated by government officials who openly stated that Native women were lazy and disliked cleaning their homes, preferring to live in tents rather than "proper" houses. They blamed Native mothers for the death of their babies and charged that they neglected their children, who grew up to be considered problems for Canadian society, rather than acknowledging that their own racist and sexist policies condemned these women and their children to living in squalor.

The Indian Act of 1876 has had the most powerful and lasting effect on the lives of Native peoples, demarcating the boundaries of their lives. Section 12(1)(b) stated that a woman married to anyone other than an Indian was not entitled to status as an Indian, nor were her children. If an Indian woman did marry an Indian man, she then became a member of his band and lost her position in her own band. Such a patriarchal law contravened the matrilineality of many Native peoples, disrupting family relations. Losing status for an

Indian woman meant that she and her children had no place on the reserve even if her marriage dissolved. She was, in effect, distanced from her community and family. She was now in a separate category from the rest of her family and friends—not an "Indian" any longer. Her children would have little knowledge or experience of the reserve community and its Native culture. Once severed from their community and family, Native women and their children could lose touch completely.

The reserve system was also established under the terms of the Indian Act of 1876. Those designated as being "Indians" as defined by the Act were relegated to the lands that had been set aside for them and, essentially, to the margins of Canadian society and its economy. It was considered by many that there was no place for these people in the contemporary society and economy. Much of the land on the reserves was inferior and farming barely yielded subsistence for many. In this way, the Canadian government effectively condemned Indians to occupy the lowest rungs of the economic ladder and, hence, the social ladder as well. Racist paternalism set the wheels of oppression into motion and racism continues to thwart many efforts by Natives to improve their social and economic conditions (Miller, 2000; Frideres, 1998).

Cognizant of the fact that life was changing around them and that there was nothing they could do to turn back the tide, the Natives requested that the government provide them with the skills and education they would need to survive under the new conditions. Officials quickly recognized that education was the simplest route to assimilation of the Natives so the form of education the government eventually established with the cooperation of several Christian denominations was the residential school. They removed children from their families and boarded them at these schools for most of the year, separating them from the "corrupting" influence of parents and community. Thus, the government and religious figures thought it better to separate Native families and break down family relations than to allow the children to continue to have a Native identity and practise Native culture. The quality of education was purposely reduced because leading Canadians feared that the Natives would be too well-educated and provide too much competition for jobs for the white population (Steckley and Cummins, 2001; Miller 2000). In this way, Natives were further marginalized economically, while being "educated."

Many of the Native children ultimately suffered physical, emotional, and sexual abuse in residential schools. Raised in institutions where authority and discipline were considered more important than nurturing and caring, having little contact with their families, including siblings in the same institution, and punished for speaking their languages or practising their cultural traditions, the majority of Natives grew up without any real notion of family life or parenting. Many of them went on to abuse or neglect their own children. The childrearing practices they had endured were in direct contrast to the generally non-interventionist and benign parenting style of many traditional Native cultures. In effect, the Canadian government had indicated that Native peoples did not have a natural right to family life, that assimilating Natives into Canadian society took precedence. The "dumbing down" of education in these schools had also ensured that Natives could not successfully compete for employment with white people.

A later attack on Native families occurred during what is known as the "Sixties (or sometimes the Seventies) Scoop." This occurred in the wake of a 1951 change to the Indian Act, which gave provincial governments responsibility for the welfare of Native children. In the 1960s this alteration began to manifest itself in more aggressive social welfare policies wherein Native children were taken from their families, communities, and cultures in alarming numbers. The statistics are shocking. In British Columbia 34.2 percent of the 1964 population of 4228 Native children were removed from their families while from 1971 to 1981 over 3400 Native children in Manitoba were taken not just from their families but also from the province itself (Steckley and Cummins, 2001, pp. 193–94). The children were often sent far away from their original locations and adopted out to non-Native families. A social worker's criteria for a good home would likely have been based on middle-class, Euro-Canadian standards, regardless of the reality that reserve Natives tend to be poor in comparison with non-Native Canadians (Steckley and Cummins, 2001). In essence, Natives were being punished for being poor and oppressed by having their families taken away from them, a situation not unknown to other impoverished people in Canada. However, racism is likely to have provided the incentive for social welfare authorities to go the extra step of ignoring cultural integrity and adopting out Native children to non-Native families, many in the United States. Furthermore, the essential "stealing" of Native children from their families by provincial authorities points to a complete lack of regard for the integrity of Native families, along with any parental or community rights to their children (see Fournier and Crey, 1997, for a full account of "the Scoop").

Overcrowded and inferior housing are two of the factors that contribute to poor health, particularly tuberculosis that is 43 times higher for Natives than for the general population. Ill health and death are more likely to disrupt Natives families than those of other residents of Canada. Poverty is another major contributor to illness and death. Natives earn considerably less income than do other Canadians: approximately $17 000 to a little over $24 000 respectively. Family incomes follow the same pattern. Over one-third of the income of on-reserve Natives comes from government transfers. The 1996 Census revealed that more than half of the Native population had incomes of less than $20 000 per annum and one-quarter of the Native population with income earned less than $5000. Unemployment is rampant on reserves and urban Natives do not fare much better in the labour market in cities and towns. Fifty-seven percent of on-reserve Natives are not in the labour force while 17 percent of off-reserve Natives were unemployed (Frideres, 1998).

BOX 4.1   A SOCIAL WORKER'S EXPERIENCE WITH NATIVE FAMILIES

CATHARINE CROW

REGISTERED SOCIAL WORKER, ALBERTA

Having worked in all of the Prairie Provinces at one time or another, I have seen considerable poverty, hardship, and desolation among Natives. As a social worker, [I find that] these are key factors in the needs of children. Although one cannot generalize about the social conditions, culture, political stability, and availability of resources on reserves, since each community is different and deals with its adversity in its own way, poverty is an indisputable fact on many reserves.

As a front line social worker in Alberta, I often faced situations in which Native parents could not provide "the necessities of life" to their children, particularly good nutrition. Generally there were options available, such as emergency funding for food and basic necessities or internal food banks, but the greatest problems arose in communities that did not have a social safety net for their people. In these cases, a social worker must be creative and seek out opportunities that would not normally be "acceptable."

It was not unusual to find a single mother, with perhaps four or five children, living on less than $1000 per month in a major city centre. In the cities, if a child attends school regularly without a lunch, it is virtually inevitable that somewhere down the line a social worker will be called. I remember one case in particular where a woman with four children was living in a major Alberta city and found herself in this situation. As an investigator, I was required to visit the woman at her home and inspect her cupboards. There was no food in the refrigerator, freezer, or cupboards. The woman had been at the food bank two weeks previously but in this city people were only eligible for food bank donations once per month. The woman also indicated that some family had come to visit for one of the children's birthdays so the food that she normally budgeted had been used. As a social worker, I had two options: break the rules and give the woman $20 so she could have food in her cupboards, or apprehend her children. There were no indications of abuse or maltreatment—only poverty. I gave the woman $20 of my own money and told her that I would return the next day. I also explained that, if she could not provide the children with "the necessities of life," I would have to take them until she could.

The next day I went to visit the woman and found that she had purchased a big bag of flour, a pound of lard, baking powder, a small bag of sugar, a big bag of rice, and a huge jar of peanut butter—all with the $20 that I had given her. The woman had already baked bannock and peanut butter cookies for her children. The children were no longer at risk and they remained at home. Shortly after this episode, the woman obtained a job at a local drycleaning business and no longer needed any child welfare involvement.

Another time the agency received a complaint that some homeless people were harassing an old lady and that the children had no place to live. Upon investigation, it was found that the old lady had offered the Native family her garage until they could find a more suitable place. The family had access to the woman's garden for fresh vegetables and they had a water barrel for washing clothing. They used the woman's hose outside for fresh drinking water and had the use of bathroom facilities in her unfinished basement. They had food, water, clean clothing, and shelter. There were no child protection concerns, despite the neighbour's objection to homeless people living in their neighbourhood.

Source: Catharine Crow, "A Social Worker's Experience with Native Families." Reprinted with permission.

Poverty also contributes to a lower marriage rate among Natives. Women are more likely to either marry in a traditional Native ceremony or to live common-law with a man than to go through formal, legal marriage (Frideres, 1998). Frideres (1998) also cites statistics that show Natives, as opposed to their non-Native counterparts, are less likely to live in husband-wife families, and more likely to live in female-headed single-parent families. Native families tend to be larger than non-Native families, principally among Inuit and on-reserve Indians. There are twice as many Native single-parent families than the Canadian average and Natives living off-reserve are more likely to live in such families. The data for 1986 reveal that Native single-parent families are most likely to be headed by females at a ratio of 5:1. The infant mortality for status Indians seems to be rising while it is dropping for other Canadians. For example, stillbirths and death during the first week of a baby's life are twice as high among Indian women as the rest of the population.

Native women in the labour force compared to non-Native women are distinguished by the fact that a large percentage, about one-fifth, are in service jobs compared to just above 10 percent of all Canadian women. Since most service jobs are notorious for being low-skilled, low-paying, dead-end jobs without benefits, and frequently seasonal in nature, it is apparent that twice as many Native women as non-Native women find themselves in this type of employment. The reason for this is likely to be found in the particular brand of discrimination that Native women face for being both Native and women. This fact also contributes to lower socioeconomic status among Native women (Frideres, 1998). Combined with the fact that Native women are more likely to be single mothers, low income and a lack of benefits make it difficult for these women to maintain their family lives.

In summary, Natives have been racialized as part of colonial oppression and have suffered a great deal of discrimination both historically and currently. Their disadvantaged position means that they have little or no capital of any type to pass on to their children, who will most likely replicate their parents' oppressed lives. Lacking capital and deprived in numerous ways, Natives endure poverty that negatively affects all other aspects of their lives, including housing, health, and marriage rates, as has been noted. Native women suffer even greater discrimination, due to gender inequity, racialization, and a piece of legislation that marginalizes them within their own communities, among their own people. Such abysmal conditions effectively deprive Natives of rewarding family lives.

IMMIGRATION POLICY, IMMIGRANTS, AND REFUGEES

Family life has always been a foundational element in the country that became Canada. Settlement of a territory is built on families because families tend to be more stable and less mobile than single persons. Families produce and reproduce, both much-needed activities for the ongoing viability of any settlement. Canadian families were begun by people who arrived as independent adventurers or as members of established families.

People came to this land for myriad reasons. They brought many class positions with them and established new ones in this country that affected their other experiences and those of their successors (Knowles, 1992). Men and women, even if they were from the same class backgrounds, were affected differently because of gender; women were commonly in worse economic situations than men because of their enforced dependency on men.

Isajiw (1999) states that, during the period of immigration from 1600 to the War of 1812, there were two main types of migrants, settlers and colonizers, and the task that concerned these migrants was establishing social structures. The first set of these two types of migrants was the French, who settled and colonized New France. The second set was the British, who superceded the French in New France and settled farther inland. The British were greatly concerned with attracting more settlers so that they could hang on to their new colony.

The influx of United Empire Loyalists who came to Canada because of the American Revolution was a boon to early immigration. These migrants, numbering about 40 000, settled in Nova Scotia and Quebec. Many of them were families who engaged in farming. Another group, enticed north by Lord Simcoe, who wanted to strengthen the British population, arrived around the turn of the nineteenth century, most settling around Lake Ontario to till the soil (Isajiw, 1999).

Although the first immigration acts of the nineteenth century were not explicitly restrictive of most groups, Canadian officials preferred to populate the country with British settlers for the most part and, to a lesser extent, with Northern Europeans. When circumstances called for it, they were willing to make allowances for other less "desired" groups, such as Eastern Europeans in the West. Yet, as more "undesirable" groups, such as blacks and Asians, entered the country, Canadian immigration acts became more and more exclusionary and special measures were enacted. Those policies that did not outright bar these groups from entry allowed only limited immigration, usually only males who were needed to work in particular industries. Without women, these groups could not form families and become part of the fledgling nation. The lasting effect of such policies on the excluded groups, according to Dua (1999), was that it disrupted their ability to participate in a family.

From the early years of the twentieth century, immigration acts contained clauses that specifically excluded from entry many different types of people and that allowed for the deportation of those already in Canada who were deemed "undesirable." The Immigration Act of 1910, for example, included Section 38, which specifically stated that the cabinet could forbid entry to immigrants belonging to any *race* that was considered to be unsuited to the climate or "requirements" of Canada. World Wars I and II and the Great

Depression contributed to the great limitations placed on immigration (Knowles, 1992; Isajiw, 1999).

World War II brought dramatic changes to the world. Empires were toppled, nationalism was discredited, and discrimination's horrors had been revealed. Gradually, as immigration acts were amended, the trend was to eliminate biases based on perceptions of "race" and "ethnicity" and to place more emphasis on economic criteria, such as education and occupational skills. Right after the close of the war, the main business occupying most countries was resettling refugees (Isajiw, 1999).

Refugees are people who have been judged by a refugee tribunal according to the United Nations Convention's definition of refugees: people with a well-grounded fear of persecution or danger on the specified grounds (ethnicity, race, religion, gender, and political affiliation are the most common). Since 1979, the approximately 20 000 people who enter Canada each year as refugees have been deemed by officials of the United Nations High Commission for Refugees (UNHCR) to be refugees; many, if not most, of them are in refugee camps operated by the UNHCR. Canadian officials visit the camps and interview those who apply for acceptance into Canada; those refugees whom they accept then enter Canada and become permanent residents, until they take out citizenship, as most of them do. Even in the refugee camps abroad, however, Canadian immigration officials attempt to make the same types of assessment of potential fit as they identify refugees whom the government will sponsor; well over 20 000 are admitted each year (Canadian Council for Refugees, n.d.).

Refugee claimants or asylum seekers are those people who have not yet been adjudged to be refugees, but who come to Canada and claim refugee status at our borders or within the country. Since Canada is a signatory to the Convention, we must give their claim a fair hearing. If the Canadian tribunal deems them to have met the criteria for refugee status, their claims are accepted. At that point, they become "protected persons." They must then apply for permanent residence, which could take six months and sometimes more. Students of family life, however, recognize that refugee claimant families awaiting the judgment of their claims are in particular difficulties, as they are not entitled to the settlement services provided for other immigrants, and they are far less employable than others, since they do not have a social insurance number. Their children, moreover, are sometimes denied entry into the local school system on the grounds that their parents are not yet here legally, but are in some kind of "legal limbo" (Canadian Council for Refugees, n.d.).

Since 1968 a merit points system has been in place with regard to application for immigration. Both independent and sponsored immigrants were to be assessed using the points system, although there would be differences between the two sets. Points were given for education, skills, occupational demand, knowledge of one of the official languages, and so forth, clearly demonstrating that immigration was important for meeting labour market needs (Isajiw, 1999). The result of the points system was that many more immigrants from Third World countries, who would come to be known as "visible minorities," were admitted to Canada, dramatically altering the face and faces of this country.

Under the Liberal governments, there has also been a move away from filling specific labour market niches with immigrants and their skills to admitting immigrants who have high levels of education and skills who will be able to adapt to the changing needs of the economy (Jakubowski, 1999). The Immigration and Refugee Protection Act of November 2001 has departed from the occupation-based model that has served Canada for most of the second half of the last century. Instead of a model that assigns points for language, skills, and the need for the job of the applicant, the new model looks to see if the education, training, and experience of the applicants have made them into the flexible, educated kind of people who can adjust well to a new setting. Economic immigrants have more and more been the preferred class of immigrants since about the mid-1990s, while family-class immigrants have been more peripheral (Li, 2003). Li (2003) asserts that family-class immigrants and refugees are considered not to have met the criteria relating to the labour market. There is an attitude in officialdom that these groups are not as valuable or desirable as economic-class immigrants.

To summarize, formal immigration policy has undergone a great deal of change. Overt discrimination against non-traditional, particularly non-white, source countries and groups of people has been eliminated. The emphasis has been on filling gaps in the economy. The result of these changes has been the enormous upsurge of immigration from Asian and Third World countries and the dramatic alteration of the composition of Canada's population.

A PROFILE OF TODAY'S IMMIGRANTS AND VISIBLE MINORITIES

In addition to the immigration of Europeans as outlined above, blacks, Asians, and people of colour from various countries have also immigrated to Canada since before Confederation. Their numbers were not as significant as they are today but they were substantial enough to cause distress among the white, European dominant class. Legislation was enacted from time to time to limit or out-and-out bar these groups from settling in Canada and forming families and communities. Discrimination against non-white, non-European

BOX 4.2   WOULD YOU QUALIFY AS AN IMMIGRANT TO CANADA?

Here's an exercise that might interest you. Go to the Citizenship and Immigration Canada website *http://www.cic.gc.ca/english/skilled/qual-1.html* and click on "Self-Assessment Tool." Take the test to see if you would qualify as a "skilled worker."

groups was the hallmark of immigration policy until the last half of the twentieth century. Canada's immigration policies denied family lives to these people. Nevertheless, the presence of the earlier immigrants and the introduction of the merit points system have meant that Canada is now home to large numbers of visible minorities.

Between 1956 and 1976, 63.6 percent of immigrants had come from Britain and Europe and only 11.9 percent from Asia. In the next quarter century this ratio was reversed, as only 18.9 percent of immigrants came from Britain and Europe while 53 percent came from Asia, 18 percent from Africa and the Middle East, 7.5 percent from South and Central America and the Caribbean, and 2.6 percent from the United States.

The 2001 Census data show us that our immigration policies are even more important than ever before. First, in the previous five years, the rate of population increase by birth was lower by about a third from what the last census had revealed. Second, our growth rate over that period, a little over 4 percent, was also smaller. Immigration, therefore, the major source of that small growth, is clearly the most important source of Canada's economic well-being. Our last census showed that about 60 percent of immigrants were **economic immigrants** applying based on their qualifications.[1] Another 25 percent to 30 percent were **family reunification** immigrants, entering as relatives sponsored by others. Approximately 10 percent entered as refugees.

Today's immigrants, no matter where they come from, are bound for Canada's metropolises, for the most part, making metropolitan areas very cosmopolitan indeed. For instance, the Toronto urban area now has the highest concentration of immigrants of any metropolitan centre in North America. In 2001, immigrants comprised 43.7 percent of the Toronto Census Metropolitan Area (CMA) population, and 43 percent of all newcomers to Canada during the 1990s settled there. Similarly, 35 percent of Vancouver's population and 18 percent of Montreal's were born outside of Canada, but in Quebec we see the greatest concentration of an immigrant population, since almost 90 percent of all immigrants there live in metropolitan Montreal. Toronto attracted nearly three times more new immigrants than its share of the Canadian population (Statistics Canada, 2003b, p. 7). Refer to Figure 4.1.

It should be noted, however, that it is true for all Canadians, immigrants and native-born alike, that we are increasingly an urban population. Canada is one of the most urban nations on the face of the earth, with four out of five Canadians living in a large city.

The most recent census shows that 18.4 percent of the total population of Canada, or 5.4 million people, was born outside Canada, the highest proportion since 1931. In 2001, approximately 1.8 million people, or 6.2 percent of the population, who were living in Canada as immigrants had arrived since 1991. Fifty-eight percent of these recent arrivals were from Asia, including the Middle East. Another 11 percent were from the Caribbean,

Figure 4.1 **FOREIGN BORN AS A PERCENT OF TOTAL POPULATION: TORONTO, VANCOUVER, MONTREAL**

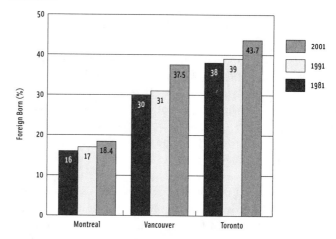

In 2001, 94 percent of immigrants who arrived during the 1990s were living in cities, three-quarters of whom lived in Toronto, Vancouver, and Montreal. Toronto received the largest share of newcomers, 43 percent (Statistis Canada, 2003c, p. 8).

Source: Based on data from Statistics Canada.

Central and South America, 8 percent were from Africa, while the remainder hailed from Europe and the United States (Statistics Canada, 2003b).

"The visible minority population is growing much faster than the total population" (Statistics Canada, 2003b, p. 10). As has already been noted above, the changes to immigration policy have been largely responsible for this striking growth. According to the 2001 Census, 73 percent of the immigrants who came to Canada in the 1990s were members of visible minorities. Only three out of ten visible minority group members are born in Canada. Blacks and Japanese are more likely to have been born in Canada rather than to be immigrants. If the rate of growth in the visible minority population remains steady, projections indicate that by 2016 one-fifth of Canada's population will consist of visible minorities. The Chinese are the largest visible minority group, surpassing the one million mark, comprising 3.5 percent of the total population, and 26 percent of the visible minority population (Statistics Canada, 2003b, pp. 10–11).

Statistics Canada's Ethnic Diversity Survey (2003e, p. 16) notes that about three times more visible minorities than those who are not visible minorities report that they feel uncomfortable in Canada at least sometimes because of "their ethnicity, culture, race, skin colour, language, accent or religion" (24 percent as opposed to 8 percent non-visible minorities). Eighty-four percent of visible minorities are first generation, meaning that they had immigrated to Canada. About 7 percent of visible minorities felt that they had sometimes or often experienced discrimination or unfair treatment in the past five years. Blacks were more likely to report such feelings, followed by South Asians and

Chinese people (Statistics Canada, 2003e, p. 18). About 71 percent of those who stated that they had sometimes or often experienced discrimination gave race or skin colour as the reason, either singly or in combination with other reasons. The most commonly stated situation in which discrimination was perceived was in the workplace or when applying for a job or a promotion (Statistics Canada, 2003e, p. 21). Elabor-Idemudia (1999) documents the ghettoization of, and discrimination against, African black women in the labour market where they get no recognition of their educational credentials, cannot get into educational institutions to upgrade their credentials, must shoulder the burden of a double day, and frequently experience abuse within their family setting. For these women, who are accustomed to working outside the home and being self-reliant, being forced to be dependent on their husbands was a tremendous drain.

It is worth noting that the Longitudinal Survey of Immigrants to Canada (LSIC) (Statistics Canada, 2003a) includes 67 percent of economic-class immigrants comprised of 56 percent principal applicants (those who qualify under the points system) and 44 percent spouses and dependants. Seventy-seven percent of the principal applicants were men while those admitted as a spouse or a dependant were more likely to be women. "Women made up 75 percent of the 47 900 individuals in the category of economic-class spouse or dependant" (Statistics Canada, 2003a, p. 6). Six out of ten family-class immigrants were women. Principal applicants in the economic class had the highest employment rate among the LSIC participants, while spouses and dependants

BOX 4.3   "THE OLD RUN-AROUND"

An African woman who was a veterinarian in her country described her experience in Canada since her arrival five years previously as the "run-around."

Before she had immigrated, she had had three years of work experience in her field. She attempted to upgrade her skills in order to write a qualifying exam. She was interviewed by an Ontario university but was not admitted. She was advised that she should take some correspondence courses in order to be better qualified for admission the following year. She followed this advice but still was not admitted the following year. She did not even get an interview the second time. When she inquired about this, she was told that she had not actually needed the correspondence courses for admission.

"They only served as a way of assessing your capacity to function at a certain educational level," she was told.

She is still trying to get accepted into a university to upgrade her veterinary skills but is working at an Ontario Humane Society as a secretary in order to be in the environment that she loves.

Source: Adapted from Patience Elabor-Idemudia. 1999. "The Racialization of Gender in the Social Construction of Immigrant Women in Canada: A Case Study of African Women in a Prairie Province." *Canadian Woman Studies*, Volume 19, Number 3, 38–44.

of the economic-class immigrants and family-class immigrants, primarily women, had significantly lower rates of employment. They were also much more likely to work part-time as opposed to full-time (Statistics Canada, 2003a, pp. 27–28). Thus, according to this survey, it is apparent that women immigrants are more likely than men to be dependants, placing them at a disadvantage in terms of the way that immigration policy treats them. Being dependent on their husbands can put immigrant women into particularly vulnerable positions.

Diversity, then, is a metropolitan characteristic rather than a pan-Canadian characteristic. Most medium-sized and small towns remain wholly populated by Canadians who are not members of visible minorities—or not members of the current groups of visible minorities.

Incomes of immigrants who came to Canada in the 1990s suffered a downturn due to economic conditions. One of every two recent immigrants earned less than $20 000 in 1995. Improvement was recorded in 2000 with only four of every ten earning below this figure. "The average earnings in 2000 of male immigrants aged 25 to 54 who arrived in Canada between 1990 and 1999 was $33 900, almost 25 percent lower than that of the Canadian-born. This level was well below the average of $40 100 among male recent immigrants who arrived in Canada two decades earlier" (Statistics Canada, 2003c, p. 12). Female immigrants of the same age fare worse than their male counterparts, suggesting that sexism and possibly racism are at play in this situation. At an average of $21 959, their income is almost 25 percent lower than that of the native born. It represented a slightly higher amount than recent female immigrants earned in the 1970s, probably reflecting high levels of education. As noted by Statistics Canada (2003c), the earnings of recent immigrants have suffered a drastic decline. "In 2000, male immigrants who had been in the country one full year made 63 cents for every dollar made by those born in Canada. Immigrants who had been in the country 10 years made 80 cents for each dollar earned by Canadian born workers" (Statistics Canada, 2003c, p. 12; see also Reitz, 1998, 2001; Kazemipur and Halli, 2000). Considering that under the points system immigrants are chosen for their educational credentials and skills, such declines in income for recent immigrants and difficulties in achieving parity with Canadian-born counterparts even after 10 years suggests that something is decidedly amiss. Again, it should be noted that immigrant women, despite their high levels of education, are not reaping the rewards of their educational status.

A disturbing aspect of the recent decline in earnings of immigrants lies in the fact that during the 1990s, 40 percent of immigrants from the ages of 25 to 54 held university degrees compared to only 23 percent of the Canadian-born population between the same ages. Knowledge of an official language meant that recent immigrants earned more but, again, not as much as they had in earlier decades. Eighty-two percent of the new immigrants included in the LSIC

(Statistics Canada, 2003a) stated that they were able to converse in at least one of Canada's official languages. However, of the 18 percent that could not speak English or French, women were more likely than men to have little or no knowledge of an official language. With the decline in income-earning power, immigrant women who do not speak one of the official languages may not have the luxury of spending time in language classes, if such are available, to upgrade their language skills. They may have no choice but to work at any job they can find in order to supplement the family income so that the family can afford adequate housing and other necessities, and allow the children to concentrate on their schoolwork instead of on part-time work.

Isajiw (1999) states that immigrants with higher education have the problem of their credentials not being accepted as being the equivalent of Canadian credentials. Here the issue of racialization also plays a part, as access to well-paying jobs and promotions comes more slowly for visible minorities (Hou and Balakrishnan, 1996; Pendakur and Pendakur, 1998; Persad at al., 2002). According to LSIC (Statistics Canada, 2003a), many immigrants were not employed in the same occupational field as before they came to Canada. Sixty percent of both male and female immigrants were working in a different occupational group after they immigrated. Country of origin and official language skills played a role in whether immigrants could find jobs in their previous occupational fields. For instance, about 63 percent of immigrants born in the United States and 68 percent of those born in Australia, New Zealand, and other parts of Oceania were employed in the same occupational groups, while only 33 percent of immigrants born in Asia and the Middle East, and 36 percent of immigrants from Central and South America were. About 40 percent of those who could speak one of the official languages were likely to work in the same employment field as they had worked in prior to coming to Canada. Educational level did not seem to have an impact.

Another disquieting aspect of the decline of recent immigrants' incomes is how it affects children. In 2000, 33 percent of children with at least one parent who had immigrated in the past 10 years were living at a low rate of income. In 1990 the figure had been 27 percent and in 1980 it had been 20 percent. The low-income rate was higher when both parents were recent immigrants: 39 percent in 2000 as opposed to 33 percent in 1990 and 22 percent in 1980. Low-income rates for children with Canadian-born parents were 16 percent in 2000, 17 percent in 1990, and 19 percent in 1980 (Statistics Canada, 2003d, p. 11).

LSIC (Statistics Canada, 2003a) offers valuable insights into occupational distribution among immigrants. The largest concentration of jobs was in the sales and service area. One-quarter of the immigrant men who had found jobs six months after coming to Canada worked in this area. Twenty-two percent of immigrant men were employed in processing/manufacturing jobs in Canada while only 4 percent of them had worked in such jobs before immigration. The pattern was similar for female immigrants. The percentage of immigrant women working in management positions dropped from 8 percent prior to their arrival to 3 percent after their arrival. The largest concentration of immigrant women was found in sales and service occupations. "The 37 percent of employed women in this occupational group represented three times the proportion employed in this field prior to immigration" (Statistics Canada, 2003a, p. 31). LSIC (2003) goes on to report that both men and women (although more of the former than the latter) were looking for alternative employment, especially those who were working in occupations different from those they had held before immigration. The most commonly-cited problem impeding their efforts at finding better employment was the lack of job experience in Canada. Twenty-six percent of the immigrants reported this barrier, while 24 percent cited transferability of foreign qualifications or experience (Statistics Canada, 2003a, p. 34). Only 34 percent of immigrants from the United States and Oceania countries reported these difficulties related to employment. Therefore, it is apparent from the survey that recent immigrants face discrimination in employment relating to their credentials and experience when they are not from Anglo-origin countries. Immigrant women suffer additional discrimination, since gender plays a role in all women's employment experiences, placing them at a further disadvantage in comparison to men.

FAMILY DYNAMICS, YOUTH, AND CHILDREN

As antiracist feminists point out, mainstream feminists have argued that the nuclear family is responsible for the oppression of women. Antiracist feminists, conversely, contend that family is experienced differently based on class, racialization/ethnicization, and sexual orientation. In a racist society, family is frequently a bulwark for minority women, a refuge from the oppressions they must endure in the public realm. Many minority women do not seek to escape the nuclear family, but to exercise their right to have one (Dua, 1999). Immigrants frequently struggle to maintain their family life in the face of numerous challenges and pressures, changes, conflicts, and losses. Studies have shown that a positive family experience can be highly beneficial during the integration process, particularly in the case of children and youth.

Family life undergoes changes when immigrants come to Canada. As has been noted above, today's immigrants go to large metropolitan centres to live; if they work, they tend to work in occupations that are of lower status and lower pay than those they had in their home country, despite their high levels of education. A significant number of women do not speak one of the official languages, adding to their difficulty in obtaining better employment. Women tend to be sponsored family members rather than principal applicants in the immigration process, causing them to be dependent on husbands and their sponsorship. **Culture shock,** a sense of bewilderment with a new way of life and that one is a "foreigner," is a serious matter that many immigrants encounter, but women, some of whom may have been more sheltered in their home countries, may have a more trying time adjusting to Canadian society and culture because of their double day. Culture shock also occurs within families, as parents realize that their children no longer support or share their values and norms. Culture shock can lead to self-doubt, disorientation, and alienation from loved ones (Isajiw, 1999, p. 101).

Since children enter the school system and are generally exposed to Canadian culture and language, they tend to overtake their parents in their knowledge of these matters. As such, parents must rely on their children to act as their interpreters. This can be distressing for both generations as parents fear their authority being undermined and children experience embarrassment over their parents' lack of knowledge. Immigrant mothers are sometimes overprotective of their children while the children seek more independence to emulate their Canadian peers (Isajiw, 1999; see Anisef and Kilbride, 2003b; Janzen and Ochocka, 2003; and Tyyskä, 2001). Gaps develop between parents and children sometimes because the school may not give value to immigrants' language or culture, giving children the impression that these things are inferior to those of Canadians. Parents can feel insulted or denigrated by this attitude. Conflicts may also develop between parents and youth over Canadian dating patterns that emphasize individuals going out together rather than groups of adolescents, a pattern often encouraged in other countries (Isajiw, 1999, p. 103; Anisef and Kilbride, 2003b). Tyyskä (2001, pp. 103–05) cites studies indicating that both gender and ethnocultural background affect the amount of conflict between parents and youth. That is, among some groups, girls have much less freedom than do boys. Even within immigrant groups there are differences as to how conservative parents, and how rebellious youth, are. One study on youths' impact on parents revealed that children of parents from the Caribbean, the British Isles, or Israel did not think any impact they had was linked to parents' immigrant status whereas others, particularly females, thought they had had great impact on Italian, Greek, and Portuguese immigrant parents. Tyyskä also argues that parental reliance on interpretive skills of children may bring the two generations closer.

Dynamics change between husbands and wives as well. Often wives who did not work in the home country must work in Canada to supplement the family income or as sole breadwinners. It is not uncommon for these women to feel empowered and to want to participate in decision-making, as well as to insist that their husbands help out in the home. Husbands may regard their gender role as being threatened, which can lower their self-esteem. Conflict and violence against women can ensue, causing estrangement between parents or the breakdown of the family. Fear of deportation and various other barriers, plus distrust of the Canadian system, keep many abused immigrant women from seeking help (Isajiw, 1999; McDonald, 1999; Kamateros, 1998).

BOX 4.4   IMMIGRANT VOICES: THE STRUGGLES OF FAMILIES

"We have lost our status socially and economically after coming to Canada. We were brought here as professional immigrants but after coming here, our education was de-recognized and we were forced to do unrelated [to professional training and experience] jobs. Even our wives were forced to do jobs they never did at home. Our children observe us doing this labour and developed hatred for the system. This may affect their personality..."

"Securing [even a] bare existence, in my opinion, is the hardest thing parents face upon arrival to Canada. Finding themselves and making a living takes all of their time. In all that, how much time they can find for their children?"

"I think it is very important for her to value where she is coming from, to value her culture, her roots, and the Spanish language. My daughter has to value her cultural heritage, because this will give her an identity as a person and it will give her a sense of belonging to a community."

"I have brought them to Canada at a tender age. Their most formative years will be in this country. My main fear is ...during their learning process, whether they will understand where we have come from and that there are different sets of religious and cultural instructions in our ethos. My fear is how much of our culture would they keep with themselves once they have grown up."

Source: Voices of immigrant parents contributing to various research projects conducted by K.M. Kilbride and others in the late 1990s.

Immigrant women may also be reluctant to reinforce negative stereotypes about their communities. Furthermore, shelters have not been culturally specific, and services in general do not address the whole issue of immigration and its relationship to abuse (McDonald, 1999). Mohamed (1999) argues in her study of Somali refugee women that the situation of settlement in Canada is worse for refugees because of all the trauma they have already suffered and shifting gender roles between couples can bring on conflict. Elabor-Idemudia (1999) believes there is hope for racialized women to solve their problems, including labour market troubles, because more services are becoming sensitive to the needs of racialized communities.

Immigrant children and youth themselves face many issues; most children and youth share some while others are specific to being immigrants. For instance, Canadian youth generally experience the pressure to do well in school and the stress of facing a high unemployment rate. They are making a major transition in their lives to adulthood. Immigrant youth face all these pressures and stresses and, in addition, the added demands of settlement and integration into a new society, which increase the strain. It has been found that youth well-being rests chiefly on being part of a "strong and loving family." Studies have also shown that a stable income improves the family's likelihood of living in a safe neighbourhood with good schools for youth to attend. The fact that for many immigrant families attaining a stable and adequate income has become arduous means that immigrant youth are likely to be at greater risk for suffering stress. High levels of stress can lead to depression and other negative behaviours, such as dropping out of school (Anisef and Kilbride, 2003a).

Some of the specific challenges that immigrant youth must deal with are: (1) visible minority youth feel that teachers discriminate against them and do not encourage them to succeed; (2) seeing their parents' negative employment experiences may make youth feel like they should drop out of school and find work in order to contribute to the family income; (3) youth experience high unemployment due to such factors as a lack of Canadian work experience, deficient language skills, and the lack of a social network to help them find work (Kunz, 2003); (4) for refugee youth, coping with emotional trauma and loss of family members, in addition to the many things immigrant youth must deal with, adds to their strain; (5) being from a low socioeconomic background increased the discrimination youth had to cope with, along with subjecting them to public housing and bad neighbourhoods, both contributing to low self-esteem (Anisef and Kilbride, 2003a; Anisef and Kilbride, 2003b; Janzen and Ochocka, 2003; Peera, 2003; Tyyskä, 2001).

Youth in several studies identified English as a Second Language (ESL) classes as being very helpful not only because they learned the language but also because they could be with other immigrants to share experiences and exchange information about the way the Canadian school system worked. Some also wanted help in losing accents, while Caribbean youth, who considered themselves native English speakers, found it demeaning to be placed in such classes (Anisef and Kilbride, 2003b). Flexible schools that were willing to adapt to the needs of immigrant youth were beneficial in integrating them, as was parental support and having friends to help them learn about the Canadian system. Since immigrants are twice as likely to live in multigenerational families, and grandparents can provide stability and another close and loving relationship for children and youth, it is likely a benefit to them to have these additional family members around (Milan and Hamm, 2003). Studies also revealed that a positive sense of their ethnocultural background and involvement in their community helped youth overcome their problems with school and achieve success (cited in Anisef and Kilbride, 2003a). Research also indicated that academic progress was part of positive integration (Anisef and Kilbride, 2003a). Clearly, it would seem that support from family, friends, community, and social institutions are very important in the integration process for immigrant youth, for whom the transition to adulthood is especially onerous compared to their Canadian counterparts.

CONCLUSION

After briefly examining the conditions facing Natives, immigrants, and visible minorities in this country, it becomes apparent that family life is a struggle for many people. In the face of racialization and ethnicization and all that goes with being labelled in these ways—along with sexism and classism, which feed into the former and magnify the intensity of the prejudice and discrimination—we can see that residence in Canada can be harrowing for some. The impact on family life is to weaken its material underpinnings. Though family relations might be strong and positive in the light of such diversity, the ability to maintain a stable family life, which rests on economic stability, affordable housing, a sense of belonging, and so on, erodes when these are not in place or are being undermined. Native families have been overtly broken by policies of various levels of government. Visible minorities and immigrants have to face tremendous barriers that make it difficult to obtain a secure home life, including discrimination in various guises, their struggles to integrate into Canadian society, the lack of support for some, such as women and youth, and numerous others that have been noted above.

As we have seen, women in all these categories suffer the most because of the multiplicity of oppressions they are forced to endure. Since women are still entrusted with the majority of family responsibilities, their families experience the backlash from these oppressions. What happens to women happens to the men, children, and other women who are related to them. When those women are forced to work in low-paying, no-benefit, dead-end jobs without hope of promotion, or they have to live in inadequate or overcrowded housing in dangerous neighbourhoods, or they are humiliated because of their culture or physical characteristics, or any one of the other numerous incidents of discrimination, they are not the only ones who bear the negative consequences; their families also bear those negative consequences. Family relations are frequently a source of strength and self-esteem for these women, but sometimes they can be strained and full of conflict for some, adding to the oppression that these women already endure. Social and community resources need to be in place to give extra support for such women.

Immigrant, refugee, and visible minority youth face the same problems that their native-born Canadian counterparts face but with the added dimension of trying to integrate successfully into Canadian society and culture. High unemployment is a serious problem for all youth but immigrant, refugee, and visible minority youth are confronted with greater challenges in finding employment, such as discrimination, lack of Canadian work experience, a deficient social network, problems with language proficiency, and so on. Their task is to overcome these hurdles, maintain a sense of self-esteem, and attempt to attain educational credentials and compete with native-born youth—a tall order, indeed. Youth themselves have identified some of the external supports they need to accomplish these goals. Internally, one of their greatest sources of strength, self-esteem, and support is their family. Hence, immigrant families must be sustained and successfully integrated into Canadian society if this country is to be productive and prosperous. The well-being of all Canadians will ultimately be enhanced if we can ensure the well-being of immigrants and their families.

Summary

- For native peoples, immigrants, and visible minorities in Canada, achieving a family has been and often continues to be a difficult proposition as a result of racialization, ethnicization, sexism, and classism.

- The experiences of Natives, visible minorities, and immigrants/refugees are best understood in terms of their power relationship vis-à-vis the dominant groups.

- Native and immigrant families, especially women and children in these families, are often beset by poverty and related problems of poor health and inadequate housing, as well as marginal employment.

- Historically, immigration policy has restricted which "types of people" would be admitted to Canada.

- In recent years, the point system along with the occupation-based model in immigration policy has meant that many more Third World immigrants have been admitted to Canada.

- As a result of immigration, many urban areas in Canada have high concentrations of immigrants and visible minorities.

- Research suggests that recent immigrants, especially immigrant women, face employment discrimination.

- Exposure to Canadian culture and language may lead to conflict between the immigrants and their more Canadianized children as well as between spouses.

- Immigrant, native, refugee, and visible minority youth often experience difficulty integrating into Canadian society, as reflected in patterns of unemployment.

- Families are often important sources of support and strength for immigrant, native, refugee, and visible minority individuals and should be supported through policy initiatives.

Note

1. Economic immigrants include skilled workers, immigrants nominated by specific provinces as needed, self-employed persons, entrepreneurs, and investors.

Critical Thinking Questions

1. How has the immigration of Europeans influenced the family lives of Native peoples?

2. How has immigration policy changed and what impact has it had on Canada's families?

3. Explain how and why women are among the most oppressed in Canadian society.

4. Discuss the challenges that immigrant families, particularly their younger members, have to face.

5. How have racialization, ethnicization, sexism, and classism worked together to make family life drastically different for some Canadians?

Websites

National Longitudinal Study of Children and Youth

http://www.hrdc-drhc.gc.ca/sp-ps/arb-dgra/publications/nlscy/v4n1.pdf
National Longitudinal Study of Children and Youth. Vol. 4 (1)

Metropolis Project

http://www.metropolis.net
The Metropolis Project of the federal government has created four national centres of excellence for research on immigration, settlement, and integration into the metropolis. They are located in Montreal, Toronto, Edmonton, and Vancouver, and their extensive research on immigrant families may be reached through this central website or through its links to the centres' sites.

Settlement Directorate

http://www.settlement.org
This site is created by the Settlement Directorate in Ontario and run by the (non-governmental) Ontario Council of Agencies Serving Immigrants.

Human Resources Development Canada

http://www.hrdc-drhc.gc.ca/sp-ps/arb-dgra/metropolis/lit.shtml
Additional research may be accessed through the portal of Human Resources Development Canada, which presents its own funded research in the area of immigrant children and youth.

Suggested Reading

P. Anisef and K. M. Kilbride. 2003. *Managing Two Worlds: The Experiences & Concerns of Immigrant Youth in Ontario.* Toronto: Canadian Scholars' Press.

Examines the experiences of immigrant youth aged 16 to 24 and their families in Ontario.

P. S. Li. 2003. *Destination Canada: Immigration Debates and Issues.* Don Mills: Oxford University Press.
Gives an excellent overview of the major issues confronting immigrant families today.

Statistics Canada. 2003. *Longitudinal Survey of Immigrants to Canada: Process, Progress and Prospects.* Ottawa: Minister of Industry.
Excellent statistical portrait of immigrants in Canada.

References

Anisef, P., and K. M. Kilbride. 2003a. "Introduction." In *Managing Two Worlds: Immigrant Youth in Ontario.* P. Anisef and K.M. Kilbride, eds. Toronto: Canadian Scholar's Press. Pp. 1–36.

————. 2003b. "Overview and Implications of the Research." In *Managing Two Worlds: Immigrant Youth in Ontario.* P. Anisef and K.M. Kilbride, eds. Toronto: Canadian Scholar's Press. Pp. 235–72.

Canadian Council for Refugees. n.d. "State of Refugees in Canada." *http://www.web.net/ ~ccr/state.html.*

Canadian Research Institute for the Advancement of Women. *Immigrant and Refugee Women.* No. 5-2003.

Carter, Sarah. 1996. "Categories and Terrains of Exclusion: Constructing the 'Indian Woman' in the Early Settlement Era in Western Canada." In *Gender and History in Canada.* Joy Parr and Mark Rosenfeld, eds. Toronto: Copp Clark Ltd. Pp. 30–49.

Cassidy, Barbara, Robina Lord, and Nancy Mandell. 2001. "Silenced and Forgotten Women: Race, Poverty, and Disability." In *Feminist Issues: Race, Class, and Sexuality.* Nancy Mandell, ed. 3rd ed. Toronto: Pearson Education Canada Inc. Pp. 75–107.

Dua, Enakshi. 1999. "Beyond Diversity: Exploring the Ways in Which the Discourse of Race Has Shaped the Institution of the Nuclear Family." In *Scatching the Surface: Canadian Anti-Racist Feminist Thought.* Enakshi Dua and Angela Robertson, eds. Toronto: Women's Press. Pp. 237–59.

Elabor-Idemudia, Patience. 1999. "The Racialization of Gender in the Social Construction of Immigrant Women in Canada: A Case Study of African Women in a Prairie Province." *Canadian Woman Studies,* Volume 19, Number 3, 38–44.

Fournier, Suzanne, and Ernie Crey. 1997. *Stolen From Our Embrace: The Abduction of First Nations Children and the Restoration of Aboriginal Communities.* Vancouver/Toronto: Douglas & McIntyre.

Frideres, James S. 1998. *Aboriginal Peoples in Canada: Contemporary Conflicts.* 5th ed. Scarborough: Prentice Hall Allyn and Bacon Canada.

Hou, F., and T.R. Balakrishnan. 1996. "The Integration of Visible Minorities in Contemporary Canadian Society." *Canadian Journal of Sociology*, 21(3), 307–26.

Isajiw, Wsevolod W. 1999. *Understanding Diversity: Ethnicity and Race in the Canadian Context.* Toronto: Thompson Educational Publishing, Inc.

Jakubowski, Lisa Marie. 1999. "'Managing' Canadian Immigration: Racism, Ethnic Selectivity, and the Law." In *Locating Law: Race/Class/Gender Connections*. Elizabeth Comack, ed. Halifax: Fernwood Publishing. Pp. 98–124.

Janzen, Rick, and Joanna Ochocka. 2003. "Immigrant Youth in Waterloo Region." In *Managing Two Worlds: Immigrant Youth in Ontario*. P. Anisef and K.M. Kilbride, eds. Toronto: Canadian Scholar's Press. Pp. 37–68.

Kamateros, Melpa. 1998. "The Isolated Immigrant Family." *Transition*, Volume 28, Number 3, 13–14.

Kazemipur, A., and S. S. Halli. 2000. *The New Poverty in Canada: Ethnic Groups and Ghetto Neighbourhoods*. Toronto: Thompson Educational Publishing.

Knowles, Valerie. 1992. *Strangers at Our Gates: Canadian Immigration and Immigration Policy, 1540–1990*. Toronto and Oxford: Dundurn Press.

Kunz, Jean Lock. 2003. "Being Young and Visible: Labour Market Access Among Immigrant and Visible Minority Youth." Ottawa: Human Resources Development Canada.

Li, P. S. 2003. *Destination Canada: Immigration Debates and Issues*. Don Mills: Oxford University Press.

Mandell, Nancy. 2001. "Women, Families, and Intimate Relations." In *Feminist Issues: Race, Class, and Sexuality*. Nancy Mandell, ed. 3rd ed. Toronto: Pearson Education Canada Inc. Pp. 193–218.

McDonald, Susan. 1999. "Not in the Numbers: Domestic Violence and Immigrant Women." *Canadian Woman Studies*, Volume 19, Number 3, 163–67.

Milan, Anne, and Brian Hamm. 2003. "Across the Generations: Grandparents and Grandchildren." *Canadian Social Trends*, Winter, No. 71, 2–7.

Miles, Angela, Goli Rezai-Rashti, and Lisa Bryn Rundle. 2001. "Third Wave Feminism: Transnationalists, and Young Feminists Speak Out." In *Feminist Issues: Race, Class, and Sexuality*. Nancy Mandell, ed. 3rd ed. Toronto: Pearson Education Canada Inc. Pp. 1–22.

Miller, J.R. 2000. *Skyscrapers Hide the Heavens: A History of Indian-White Relations in Canada*. 3rd ed. Toronto: University of Toronto Press.

Mohamed, Hamdi S. 1999. "Resistance Strategies: Somali Women's Struggles to Reconstruct Their Lives in Canada." *Canadian Woman Studies*, Volume 19, Number 3, 52–57.

Peera, Rishma. 2003. "Employment Needs of Newcomer Youth in West End Ottawa." In *Managing Two Worlds: Immigrant Youth in Ontario.* P. Anisef and K.M. Kilbride, eds. Toronto: Canadian Scholar's Press. Pp. 69–95.

Pendakur, K., and R. Pendakur. 1998. "The Colour of Money: Earnings Differentials Among Ethnic Groups in Canada." *Canadian Journal of Economics* 31 (3): 519–48.

Persad, J. et al. 2002. *"No Hijab is Permitted Here"—A Study on the Experiences of Muslim Women Wearing Hijab Applying for Work in the Manufacturing, Sales and Service Sectors.* Toronto: Women Working with Immigrant Women.

Reitz, J. G. 1998. *Warmth of the Welcome: The Social Causes of Economic Success for Immigrants in Different Nations and Cities.* Boulder: Westview Press, 1998.

————. 2001. "Immigrant Skill Utilization in the Canadian Labour Market: Implications of Human Capital Research." *Journal of International Migration and Integration,* 2(3): 347–78.

Satzewich, Vic. 1998. "Race, Racism and Racialization: Contested Concepts." In *Racism & Social Inequality in Canada.* Vic Satzewich, ed. Toronto: Thompson Educational Publishing, Inc. Pp. 25–45.

Statistics Canada. 2001. The Daily. "Births, 2001." Monday, August 11, 2003. http://www.statcan.ca/Daily

————. 2003a. *Longitudinal Survey of Immigrants to Canada: Process, Progress and Prospects.* Ottawa: Minister of Industry.

————. 2003b. *Canada's Ethnocultural Portrait: The Changing Mosaic.* Ottawa: Minister of Industry.

————. 2003c. *Earnings of Canadians: Making A Living in the New Economy.* Ottawa: Minister of Industry.

————. 2003d. *Income of Canadian Families.* Ottawa: Minister of Industry.

————. 2003e. *Ethnic Diversity Survey: Portrait of a Multicultural Society.* Ottawa: Minister of Industry.

————. 2003f. "2001 Census Analysis Series: Aboriginal Peoples of Canada: A Demographic Profile," Minister of Industry, 2003. Catalogue no. 96F0030XIE2001007.

Steckley, John L., and Bryan D. Cummins. 2001. *Full Circle: Canada's First Nations.* Toronto: Pearson Education Canada Inc.

Tyyskä, Vappu. 2001. *Long and Winding Road: Adolescents and Youth in Canada Today.* Toronto: Canadian Scholars' Press.

Part 2

Living Inside Families

Chapter 5

Rethinking Intimate Questions: Intimacy as Discourse

Debra Langan and Deborah Davidson

LEARNING OBJECTIVES

In this chapter, you will learn that:

1. taken-for-granted, ideological assumptions are embedded in popular notions of "intimacy" in Western society;

2. much of the literature on intimacy has involved descriptions of gender differences and therapeutic approaches to dealing with these differences;

3. understanding intimacy as discourse offers alternative ways to approach questions around intimacy;

4. Intimacy Discourse has implications for men and women's lived experiences.

INTRODUCTION

In Western society, we think of love as a driving force for romantic relationships. Literature treats **romantic love** as something we find difficult to define. Even though we may not agree on a definition of "love," most of us can cite examples of relationships in which we were romantically "in love." Romantic love justifies marriage and partnerships and incites legal contracts. Romantic love validates sexual activity within or outside of marriage. We are socially conditioned to think of love as liberating and as the answer to dissatisfaction with being single (Langford, 1999). We value "the couple" as the most basic intimate relationship and valorize "romantic love" as "a means of salvation" (Langford, 1999, pp. xi, 153).

While love is conceptualized as a driving force in creating and maintaining romantic relationships, **intimacy** is widely understood as a desirable goal for romantic relationships. Yet intimacy seems difficult to achieve, as the extensive self-help literature reveals. Sociological literature on families and partnerships largely fails to include a consideration of intimacy. In this chapter, we challenge the taken-for-granted, **ideological assumptions** that characterize the most widely held beliefs on intimacy. We argue for a broader understanding of "intimacy" that incorporates and critiques dominant intimacy discourse that is popular in contemporary Western society. Dominant discourse emphasizes the importance of developing intimacy in romantic relationships. It neither questions intimacy as a desirable goal nor considers alternative ways in which intimacy might be experienced. Our critique is important because **Intimacy Discourse** has different but equally profound implications for the expectations and lived experiences of men and women. Women take up most of the **intimacy work** in relationships, while men are criticized for their lack of attention to intimacy.

IDEOLOGICAL ASSUMPTIONS ABOUT INTIMACY

"Intimacy" is rarely defined or problematized.[1] However, the "taken-for-granted" assumptions about "intimacy" that appear in popular culture and that are enshrined in ideologies contain the following themes:[2]

- Intimacy is a desirable, subjective experience.
- Intimacy is achieved in romantic relationships.
- Romantic relationships are also sexual relationships.
- Sexual relating is restricted to one monogamous couple relationship.
- Intimacy is linked to **heteronormativity** (i.e., heterosexual relationships are the "natural" home for intimacy).
- Intimacy naturally develops in the evolution of a healthy relationship.
- Intimacy develops over time.
- Intimacy requires "mutual self disclosure and an appreciation of others' unique qualities" (Jamieson, 1999, p. 477).
- In order for intimacy to be achieved, propinquity (i.e., being physically close) is necessary.[3]

These assumptions ignore the *contextual features* of interactions or relationships, such as current practices, historical locations, or the pressures of day-to-day life in contemporary society. Rather than uncritically accepting these prescriptions, we present an intimacy critique that is similar to that of Adrienne Rich (1980) in her critique of "compulsory heterosexuality." Rich suggests that our ideas about intimacy are conflated with heterosexual romance, and this dramatically restricts the ways in which we think about, and engage in, relationships with others. Following Rich, we argue that heterosexuality continues to be framed as a "natural" sexual orientation, which limits our field of possible partners and presents heterosexual romance as our greatest "adventure, duty and fulfillment" (Rich 1980, p. 654).

GENDER DIFFERENCES IN THE QUEST FOR INTIMACY

"He was a boi. She was a girl. Can I make it any more obvious?" Avril Lavigne, 2002, from her song, "Sk8ter Boi" on her CD, Let Go.

Gender shapes private, love relationships. The desire for intimacy is not equally shared, and the contouring of intimate relations varies for men and women. Not only do the above lyrics by 2003 Juno award winner Avril Lavigne highlight this notion of boys and girls as "obviously" different, but the song implies that, because of their sex difference, boys and girls will "obviously" be romantically, and/or sexually, attracted to one another. So, how do men and women differ? Adie Nelson and Barrie W. Robinson's review of the literature reveals "males tend to be more idealistic about love than are females...[who]...are more realistic, pragmatic, and practical about the nature and power of love" (2002, p. 279). But it seems that the "tables turn" once women have "acknowledged being in love, [for then] women tend to experience the emotions of their relationship more intensely than do men" (Dion and Dion, 1973; Kanin et al., 1970 in Nelson and Robinson, 2002, p. 279). Once they are involved in romantic relationships, women want intimacy and understanding through the self-disclosure of feelings. In contrast, men want independence, sex, and non-disclosure of "feelings" (Cancian, 1987; Duncombe and Marsden, 1993; Hare-Mustin, 1991; Hite, 1987; Mansfield and Collard, 1988; Tannen, 1997; Tavris, 1992; Wood, 1997). Women prefer to be more "connected," while men prefer to be more autonomous and withdrawn.

Some contemporary researchers challenge these findings, suggesting they reinforce and replicate traditional gender norms. Reis, Senchak, and Solomon (1985) found the desire for intimacy is situationally bound. They compared male and female evaluations of the criteria that constitute intimate interactions; their labelling of interactions; whom they select for intimate interactions; and their preference for intimate interactions. They concluded, "males are capable of interacting as intimately as females when the situation makes it desirable to do so...[however] males are relatively more likely to choose not to interact intimately...despite an equivalent capacity for intimacy" (1985, pp. 1215–216).

Anthony Giddens (1992) agrees that men have the capacity for interacting intimately. He argues that couples are experiencing what he labels "a transformation of intimacy" that is fostering more equality both in personal relationships and at the structural level. Our increasing preoccupation with bodies and sexuality accounts for this transformation of intimacy, and signals a move toward what he calls "the pure relationship." According to Giddens, women are the driving force behind these changes.

While these findings are appealing, other critics wonder if heterosexual relationships have equalized to the extent that Giddens suggests (Jamieson, 1999). Undoubtedly, the widely shared cultural belief is that both men and women want equality and intimacy. For example, consider the success of reality romance television shows that showcase women picking their favourite men (e.g., *The Bachelorette*) and men picking their favourite women (e.g., *Joe Millionaire*). As illustrated in the excerpt taken from *The Bachelorette*: Episode Guide (Box 5.1), Charlie, who has "a career in finance," is described as having a vulnerable side ("He thinks he's at a crossroads in his life") and as striving for equality in his relationships with women (He "is comfortable if his wife made more money than him, and has no issue staying at home to be a Mr. Mom"). Shows like this provide details of couples' interactions that would typically only be known by those who were involved in intimate relationships. They allow us to engage as voyeurs of couples' intimacy and thus gain information, often titillating, that we otherwise would not possess. In the excerpt (Box 5.1), the sense is that Trista and Charlie are becoming intimate by talking with one another, exchanging personal information (Trista also clarifies how she feels about Charlie and another suitor, Ryan), and ultimately retiring to Trista's room "for some much needed privacy." The account suggests that their interaction was romantic, openly communicative, and perhaps sexual in nature, some of the assumptions that accompany the popular notion of what it means to achieve intimacy.

THERAPEUTIC ANALYSES OF INTIMACY

Therapeutic analyses of intimacy elaborate how gender differences manifest in interaction. These analyses take up the project of offering solutions to address the behavioural outcomes of gender differences. Like the gender difference analyses, most of this therapeutic literature focuses on interactions within heterosexual couple relationships. The most popular theme is that men and women fail to have intimacy because they are unable to communicate effectively and satisfactorily. Failure to communicate causes conflict, unhappiness, and sometimes dissolution (Tannen, 1997). Even when men and women try to reinforce intimacy, their efforts often result in a **failure of intimacy**. According to Tannen, "Trying to trigger a symmetrical communication, they end up in an asymmetrical one" (1997, p. 190).

Because of this asymmetry, women feel that men lack "emotional participation" in the relationship. Women are irritated when men intellectualize, but do not appear to experience, emotion. This commonly reported "problem" conveys a particular idea of what qualifies as legitimate "emotional" involvement and signals a set of assumptions condoned by the therapeutic community. This analysis is gendered in that men's "emotional needs" (perhaps, for example, the emotional need to intellectualize) are discounted while women's emotional needs are prioritized. Moreover, women's needs are privileged over those of men. That is, there is a privileging of a specific way of relating, one "way" (the woman's way) that is condoned as better than another "way" (the man's way).

BOX 5.1 *THE BACHELORETTE:* EPISODE GUIDE

02/19/03 –

St. Louis with Charlie

Charlie arrives in St. Louis, and is greeted by Trista. They go for a date in the park, and reconnect. Trista confesses it feels great with Charlie no matter what they do, and Charlie asks her if he's her boyfriend. They then go to meet Trista's family...

They head into the living room and get to know Charlie a little better, talking about Charlie's career in finance; Charlie explains he thinks he's at a crossroads in his life. They go off to dinner with a bowl filled with questions that Trista's mom has written, with the idea of randomly picking questions out of the bowl.

Charlie takes their questions in stride, and reveals that he's a morning person, is comfortable if his wife made more money than him, and has no issue staying at home to be a Mr. Mom. Charlie is then given the opportunity to ask Trista's family a question; he opts to ask them to reveal something about Trista that she wouldn't reveal on her own. Her stepmother reveals a picture of Trista as a young lady, complete with braces. As the questions resume, Charlie proves he doesn't get embarrassed by answering a question about what non-facial parts of his body he shaves.

Trista's father can clearly see that they are a couple, and at ease with each other, and Trista's stepmother thinks he would be truly devoted to Trista. Charlie feels he's done well with her parents, and feels good about his chances; Trista thinks her family really liked Charlie.

In the limo back to Trista's, she tells Charlie that she needs the freedom to be intimate with Ryan, so she can learn who's best for her; she tells Charlie she's totally with him, but she also has feelings for Ryan. Charlie understands what she is saying, and is OK with it. They then enter her room for some much needed privacy.

Next...

[St. Louis with Ryan is next, and we are left to imagine what happened in Trista's room!]

Source: *The Bachelorette:* Episode Guide, February 2003, ABC, October 4, 2003, *http://abc.go.com/primetime/bachelorette*

Doherty (1991) labelled this analysis "deficit model of manhood." It has important implications for therapeutic interventions because it signals how "problems" are socially constructed and addressed.

Women who experience a lack of intimacy typically become turned off by sex (Duncombe and Marsden, 1993). Since the men's desires for sex are no longer being met, the conflict in couple situations intensifies. The therapeutic responses from counsellors, typically psychologists and social workers, help couples in therapy resolve their difficulties and learn new ways of working toward intimacy. Case Study 5.1: "Cheryl and Rob" typifies the therapeutic approach by addressing barriers to mutual self-disclosure and issues of sexuality. In this case study, a counsellor works with a couple, and encourages the man to emotionally participate more (i.e., become more intimate) in the relationship. The result is an enhancement of the woman's desire for and participation

CASE STUDY 5.1   CHERYL AND ROB

It was February 14, and Cheryl was very excited. She and Rob had been dating for almost a year now, and they were about to celebrate their first Valentine's Day together. They had talked about getting married someday, maybe when they both finished university. Cheryl met Rob at the door, and told him that she had a surprise for him. "Come into the kitchen!" she coaxed. "Sure" he replied, glancing nervously at his watch. "What's going on?" he asked. Cheryl pointed to the table, set for two with flowers and lit candles in the centre. "I thought we could have a romantic dinner together, just the two of us. I've been cooking all day! You sit down, and I'll open the wine" she said. "But I thought we were going to the bar" said Rob. "I told the guys that we'd meet them there at six. We can grab something to eat when we get there."

Cheryl went to the table, pulled out a chair, and sat down. She suddenly felt sick to her stomach. "When we talked about what we were going to do on Valentine's Day," she said, "I thought we agreed that we were going to spend some time together, alone. Now you are telling me that you've made plans to go to the bar, with the guys! Some Valentine's Day this is going to be!" she retorted, as tears filled her eyes. "You haven't even given me a card!" she cried. Rob seemed surprised. "When we talked about what we were doing tonight, we said that *we* were going to have dinner together, so when the guys called, I said that *we* would join them, so it's not like I'm going out without you! Come on, Cheryl, let's go and have a good time. Don't ruin it by making me feel guilty!" By now, Cheryl was really crying. Rob hated it when she cried, and he reconsidered his position. Maybe he was being insensitive. There were many times during the past year when they had had similar arguments, and it was always such a drag.

Rob looked at his watch again. There was still time to solve this. It was only 5:30. At this point, Cheryl got up from the table to go to the stove. A pot had boiled dry, and an unpleasant burnt smell filled the room. Dinner needed her attention or it would all be ruined. As she walked across the room, Rob reached out to Cheryl and put his arms around her. His embrace made her feel hopeful and she stopped crying. Maybe this wouldn't be such a bad Valentine's Day after all. Maybe her plan for dinner and a romantic evening would go ahead. Then Rob began to unbutton Cheryl's blouse, moving his hands across her breasts. Disbelieving, she pulled back. He then put one hand between her legs. Cheryl began to cry uncontrollably and sat down again on the chair. "I don't get it," was all that Rob could say.

Over the next few weeks, things got worse between Cheryl and Rob. It seemed like they couldn't talk anymore, even when Rob tried to pay more attention to Cheryl. Their relationship seemed doomed to fail. When Cheryl suggested that they see a counsellor at the University Centre, Rob reluctantly agreed. The counsellor told them that they had been doing a "dance" that had to stop. Cheryl, he said, had been what therapists called a "pursuer" who was trying to establish intimacy and Rob had been a "distancer" trying to avoid intimacy. The therapist explained that they would need to change the way in which they related to one another in order to achieve intimacy in their relationship. In the days that followed, they tried to take the counsellor's advice. Cheryl stopped trying to create romantic situations, and focused more on her schoolwork, and her female friendships. Rob stopped initiating sex, and instead tried to be more emotionally sensitive toward Cheryl. Rob really missed the sex, but as things started to get better between them, Cheryl began to feel better about their relationship and began to initiate sex.

in sex. (The Critical Thinking Questions at the end of this chapter will help you to analyze the case study using the theories on intimacy.)

DISCOURSE ANALYSIS

Some theorists, therapists, sociologists, and postmodernists question traditional conceptions of intimacy by suggesting a theoretical framework within which they can be critiqued. Discourse analysis, a type of social constructionism that has emerged within postmodernism, provides a useful way to analyze intimacy. According to Weingarten (1991, p. 288), discourse:

1. consists of ideas and practices that share common values.

2. reflects a specific world view.

3. constrains what we can feel, think, and do.

4. shapes our experience

5. evolves through collective conversations people have about their lives.
    Barbara Hudson also emphasizes the complexity of discourse:

> [D]iscourse is] not just a unity of themes, or a grouping of knowledge, a professional terminology or a set of concepts, but an interrelationship of themes, statements, forms of knowledge, and... positions held by individuals in relation to these (1984, p. 33).

DISCOURSE ANALYSIS APPLIED TO INTIMACY

There are two main discourses on the subject of intimacy (Weingarten, 1991). The first discourse is called the "Individual Capacity Discourse," and involves the idea that achieving intimacy depends upon an individual's ability to talk about his or her private thoughts and feelings of intimacy. The second discourse, called the "Quality of Relatedness Discourse," involves the idea that intimacy grows out of long-term, committed relationships, it does not depend on the characteristics of the individual (Weingarten 1991, p. 292). Weingarten maintains that both of these discourses work against people's ability to engage in intimate interactions for the following reasons: The "Individual Capacity Discourse" suggests that the self is a coherent entity, and Weingarten argues that the self is socially constructed through narratives, and this means that individuals sometimes may have the capacity to be intimate, and sometimes may not (Weingarten, 1991, p. 289). The "Quality of Relatedness Discourse" suggests that a "relationship" is a static entity, rather than a series of evolving interactions, giving the impression that your relationship either is or is not intimate. Weingarten posits that an understanding of self and relationships as more fluid phenomena would better reflect people's fluctuating potentials for, and experiences of, intimacy.

Weingarten's conceptualization of intimacy challenges the aforementioned heterosexist, couple-oriented assumptions. She advocates thinking of intimacy as taking place at the level of interactions, so that the potential for intimate (as opposed to "non-intimate") relating, increases. By locating intimacy firmly within the context of interaction, Weingarten moves beyond essentialist depictions of what is and isn't intimate, and who is and isn't intimate. Her approach allows for a range of interactions to count as intimate, and broadens the possibilities with respect to how intimacy can be achieved. She argues, "Intimate interaction occurs when people *share meaning* or *co-create meaning* and are able to coordinate their actions to reflect their mutual meaning-making" (1991, p. 287). In addition to co-creating meaning, Weingarten notes the importance of *coordinating action*. For example, "[p]eople select a range of activities as ones in which it is likely that intimate interaction will occur between themselves and the people who participate with them" (1991, p. 292). Viewed in this way, any activity can be intimate if those involved in the activity are both co-creating meaning and coordinating action. To illustrate, Weingarten offers the following experiences (see Box 5.2).

Conceptualizations that challenge taken-for-granted assumptions about intimacy move away from heterosexist understandings to include lesbian, gay, transgender, and transsexual relating. The experience of marginalization for gays impedes their desire to achieve intimacy (Meneses, 2000), particularly in cultures that hold static definitions of gender identity (i.e., you are *either* male or female). When same-sex couples are compared to heterosexual couples, emotional intimacy is more salient for women than it is for men, regardless of sexual orientation. Schreurs and Buunk (1996) argue that lesbian relationships are characterized by greater emotional intimacy than are heterosexual relationships. In the latter, women compromise their desire for intimacy. Mackey et al. (2000) reported a similar finding in their study of whites, blacks, and Mexican-Americans, with Catholic, Jewish, and Protestant religious backgrounds. They found that, regardless of racial or religious identity, women in lesbian relationships, compared to their heterosexual and gay counterparts, are more likely to report that psychologically intimate communication characterized their relationships. Carroll et al. (1999) reached a different conclusion in their argument that there are no differences in intimacy (which they refer to as "relational connectedness") when heterosexual, gay, and lesbian couples' perceptions are compared.

The links between intimacy and sexuality are explored in literature researching gay and lesbian relationships. This line of inquiry challenges the assumption that sexual activity is a prerequisite for the achievement of intimacy. Similar to heterosexual relationships, same-sex relationships can be sexual, but lack intimacy. For example, a collection of essays on the masculine gay subculture in Greenwich Village (New York City) during the late 1970s suggests that, like heterosexual men, gays during this period lacked the

BOX 5.2   WEINGARTEN'S EXPERIENCES OF INTIMACY

"Experience 1: My second child had serious health problems at birth and we didn't know if she was going to live or die. I was also very sick after the birth, and asked my father, who lives in a distant city, to wait to visit until I felt better. Waiting was stressful and difficult for him. After three days, I felt well enough to have him come to see us, and he did. He looked at me, looked at the baby, sat in a chair, and promptly fell asleep.

Experience 2: Several years ago, my husband and I had a particularly wonderful vacation. Each in excellent health, we hiked and read and kept a running conversation. We were each talking about topics that were of great intellectual, political, and emotional interest to us. One day, late in the afternoon, I began talking with him about thoughts that I had about my own funeral. With as much laughter as tears, we planned my funeral.

Experience 3: Recently, my 11-year-old daughter had minor surgery that necessitated general anesthesia. In the aftermath, she had a lot of discomfort, and over the course of the several hours I was with her, my attention faltered and I felt impatient and bored. Her surgeon had insisted that she and I could go to a play that evening, and because she was eager to do so, we went. During intermission, out on the lawn on this lovely summer's evening, she began vomiting, and she vomited more than I have ever seen in my whole life. Both of us got covered with her vomit. Just as she started to feel better, but before either of us was clean, and on the periphery of a group of what I can only imagine must have been horrified spectators, we began to laugh, and then roar until we had trouble standing up."

Source: Excerpted from Kathy Weingarten. 1991. "The Discourses of Intimacy: Adding a Social Constructionist and Feminist View," *Family Process*, 30(3): 295–96.

required emotional skills to maintain long-term, emotionally intimate relationships (Bhugra, 1997). Most of the studies that report on intimacy within gay subculture have focused on the relationship between AIDS (either having AIDS, or the threat of AIDS), sexual activities, and gays' desire for intimacy. A common finding is that unsafe sex practices (e.g., not using a condom) symbolize love and trust within a relationship, and are inspired by the desire for intimacy by gay partners (Sandstrom 1996; Flowers et al., 1997; Diaz and Ayala, 1999; Cannold et al., 1995; Martin and Knox, 1995; Fontaine, 1995; Powell-Cope, 1995; Robinson, 1994; Paradis, 1991).

Other analyses point to the ways in which lesbians often enjoy intimacy in their friendships with and/or without being sexual (e.g., Weinstock and Rothblum, 1996; Diamond, 2000). For example, in Case Study 5.2: "Marcia and Martha," we read of two lesbians who enjoy intimacy in their relationship together and who are sometimes sexual and at other times not sexual with one another. In addition, they are also non-monogamous, and not always living in close physical proximity, thus challenging two other assumptions about the prerequisites for intimacy. Gabb points to the ways in which those who identify as lesbian engage in relationships that challenge the normalcy of (hetero)sexuality: "Lesbian sexual narratives, because they do not operate

---

CASE STUDY 5.2 MARCIA AND MARTHA

"Martha McPheeters and Marcia Munson request the pleasure of your company at their 21st Anniversary Party.... We are celebrating 21 years of open love, uncommitted sex, firm friendship, and wild adventures."

As we read over the invitation, we knew that our friends would focus on the phrase "uncommitted sex." Because we have both been in open relationships, various lesbian communities have seen us as "loose women" over the years. But sex, though fun, has never been central to our relationship. First of all, we have been friends. The words that inspired us most were "wild adventures." Both of us have done plenty of wilderness travel over the last two decades, but very little of it has been together. As we embarked on the adventure of planning our anniversary party two months away, we dreamed of seeing more wild landscapes together in the future.

...From the start we knew we wanted to each wear evening gowns for part of the night and tuxedos for the rest of the party. Political discussions of butch/femme, butch/butch, femme power, and gender-bender got pushed aside once we realized comfort was the real issue. Marcia would start out in a tux, Martha in a dress. To get everyone's attention we would switch, right before our non-commitment ceremony.

To help us celebrate open love, we each planned to bring a date to our anniversary party. We wanted to emphasize the point that we were not, nor had we ever been, a couple...

Source: Marcia Munson. 1996. "Celebrating Wild Erotic Friendship: Marcia and Martha," pp. 124–32 in Jacqueline S. Weinstock and Esther D. Rothblum, eds., *Lesbian Friendships for Ourselves and Each Other*. New York: New York University Press.

---

with what is seen to be 'natural,' displace the sexual as the determining factor of love, and support the postmodern academic analyses that posit friendship as the primary source of emotional support" (2001, p. 318). Furthermore, Gabb argues that lesbians are far more likely than heterosexuals to retain relationships with past sexual partners.

Adrienne Rich deconstructs the heterosexual/lesbian distinction, and highlights the importance of intimacy among women generally. She speaks of the "lesbian continuum," referring to a range of women who identified "many forms of a primary intensity between and among women, including the sharing of a rich inner life…" (1980, p. 649). Her vision of a lesbian continuum is much more inclusive than the phrase might suggest: "[W]omen exist on a lesbian continuum, we can see ourselves moving in and out of this continuum, whether we identify ourselves as lesbian or not" (1980, p. 651). Similarly, Esther Rothblum (1999) argues that a shift in emphasis from lovers to friends more accurately reflects the realities of lasting commitment within most adult lives, regardless of sexual orientation (in Gabb, 2001, 318). Jessie Bernard (1985) has also noted the importance of both male and female same-sex relating, which she argues "is more **homophilic** (i.e., based on friendship) than homosexual." "Such woman-to-woman and man-to-man related-ness grows through communicational sharing as well as through joint problem solving" (Wynne and Wynne, 1986, p. 390).

Research on lesbian families supports the argument that love is not biolog-ically determined, and that its "natural" home is not exclusively in heterosexual, nuclear families. Love is seen as an *elective* property. Romantic love between adults is not afforded a privileged position to mother–child(ren) love or to love and intimacy that is developed in friendships. Rather, mother–child(ren) relation-ships and/or friendships gain legitimacy as possibly the only, and/or the most important, love relationship(s) in a woman's life.

In her analysis of lesbian families, Gabb focuses on intimacy in the les-bian's relationships with their children. She highlights the mother–child(ren) relationship as "a positive and active response to the inherent failings of het-erosexual love" (Langford, 1999 in Gabb 2001, p. 315). Gabb argues that tra-ditional discourses of love stratify our emotions and intimate relations into socially prescribed categories, wherein "mature love" (read adult love) is con-flated with sex and desire (2001, p. 313). This "stratification of intimacy" means that adult "love" experiences have become privileged over mother–child(ren) love experiences. Focusing on mother–child(ren) relation-ships "challenges the binary logic that underpins heterosexual society and makes evident the artificiality of competing hierarchies of love" (2001, p. 314). Lesbian families with children provide an opportunity to witness the disruption of this "stratification of love." Gabb argues that mother–child(ren) relationships are important sites for intimacy irrespective of sexual orientation. An appreciation of love within all mother–child(ren) units suggest that women have an innate need for intimacy, and that these needs can be fulfilled through their relationships with their children (2001, p. 316). Of course, the "rules of engagement" differ (i.e., rules demand that mothers do not have sexual rela-tionships with their children) (Gabb, 2001, p. 317), but Gabb's research shows that sex is not necessary for the achievement of love and intimacy.

These kinds of critical analyses make room for innovative conceptualizations of who can be involved in creating intimacy. They challenge the ideological parameters of who can constitute "family" (Gabb, 2001, pp. 324–25). Legislative changes in Canada also pose profound challenges to traditional ideas about who "legitimately" constitutes a family. In June 2003, the Ontario appeals court ruled as unconstitutional Canada's heterosexual-only definition of marriage, thereby legalizing gay marriages. This court decision marks significant social change that will undoubtedly enhance possibilities for elective relationships.

In addition to contesting heterosexist assumptions, Weingarten's approach, because it casts intimacy as contingent on the sharing of meaning-making, allows for more than two people to be involved in the creation of an intimate interaction (Weingarten 1991, p. 295). This approach challenges the idea that intimacy is achievable only in monogamous, couple relationships.

Information on support groups (e.g., Alcoholics Anonymous, bereavement groups, etc.) supports the idea that more than two individuals can come together and create intimate interactions. Case Study 5:2: "Marcia and Martha" is an example of how individuals can (un)structure their relationship(s) in ways that defy societal norms, yet still produce intimacy.

QUESTIONING THE DOMINANT DISCOURSE ON INTIMACY

Both the therapeutic and descriptive analyses of "intimacy" presented thus far are premised on the assumption that intimacy is an innate, desirable goal for romantic relationships. This point is difficult for us to imagine otherwise, or for many of us to appreciate, for we have been socialized to accept, without question, the value of intimacy.[4] By understanding how families, sex, and intimacy have changed over time, we can appreciate the way in which "intimacy" as a historical, social construction has come to be valued in contemporary society. In what follows, we begin to question the importance placed on intimacy in Western culture by arguing that intimacy is discourse.

Although some of the aforementioned analyses (e.g., Weingarten, 1991; Jamieson, 1999; Gabb, 2001) profess to offer a discursive analysis of intimacy, what they really offer are different ways to describe intimacy: they do not question the dominant discourse on intimacy per se. A critical analysis focuses on the way in which language contributes to the cultural construction of intimacy, and questions how "intimacy" as a type of discourse (hereafter we offer as "Intimacy Discourse")[5] has shaped both our ideas about what is important in romantic relations, and our behaviour in romantic relations.

What we offer as dominant "Intimacy Discourse" involves the ideological assumptions that were outlined at the beginning of this chapter. In brief, intimacy is an innate human need that can be achieved through mutual self-disclosure and the appreciation of the other's unique qualities in romantic, sexual, couple relationships characterized by propinquity. When understood as a discourse, "intimacy" is no longer viewed, in an essentialist way, as any of these things. Intimacy is no longer a need or a state of being. Rather, as discourse, intimacy is framed as a cultural and historical construction that is "mediated by social processes...[and]... inextricably linked to the other discourses— discourses of gender, power, domination, and sexuality" (Weingarten 1991, p. 287). Intimacy Discourse conveys particular ideologies that are connected to power and that are embedded in language (Fairclough, 1989, p. 2).

Weingarten observes that whether or not an interaction gets defined as intimate depends upon the availability of discourses of intimacy. She notes that people are able to invest in discourses, if they have been exposed to them. Our access to discourses depends, in great part, on the discourses that are popular at any given point in history. Once we have access to a discourse, we can invest in it to varying degrees. The dominant Intimacy Discourse, as we have presented it, is the one that most people have access to most of the time.

When framed as discourse, then, intimacy is understood as a social, cultural, political, and historical construction. Intimacy Discourse, we believe, demands thoughtful interrogation because of the implications that it has for men and women.

HISTORICAL EVOLUTIONS OF FAMILIES, SEXUALITY, AND INTIMACY

Understanding the historical development of ideas provides insight into how Intimacy Discourse has come to be culturally valued. Charles Lindholm describes how expectations and beliefs about romantic love develop out of specific cultural backgrounds and historical trajectory (1998). Drawing on cross-cultural analyses, Lindholm demonstrates that "the beloved is very rarely the person one marries, and reproduction and romantic attraction usually do not coincide" (1998, p. 246). For example, in Victorian times, sexual desire was not fulfilled in middle class marriage; rather, married women were expected to remain virginally pure, and married men were expected to satisfy their sexual passions with prostitutes. Sexual contact between husband and wife was seen as "an unfortunate necessity of marriage" (1998, p. 247).

Prior to the Industrial Revolution, family members lived and worked together; "intimacy," as it is commonly understood, characterized all aspects of their daily relations. Wynne and Wynne draw on the historical analysis of Gadlin (1977) and note that in earlier times, "...people's lives were completely intertwined in close physical proximity...persons were intertwined in every waking and sleeping moment....Under such circumstances, self-disclosure did not take place in isolated rare moments, but as a part of the continuous stream of life experiences" (Wynne and Wynne, 1986, pp. 388–89). Family relations were based on work and economics, such that each family member had a specific task and contribution, their activities were closely coordinated, and one member was subordinated to another (Beck-Gernsheim, 1999). As a result, family members were exposed to similar experiences, pressures, and common efforts, resulting in what Elizabeth Beck-Gernsheim calls "an obligation of solidarity" (1999, p. 58).

The Industrial Revolution

In the nineteenth century, the Industrial Revolution transformed family relationships from "obligations of solidarity" (Beck-Gernsheim, 1999, p. 58) to "obligations of individualism." Rapid urbanization and industrial development severed the world of work from the world of home (Beck-Gernsheim, 1999, pp. 56–58). The family no longer functioned mainly as an economic unit, for men became chiefly employed outside the home, in the public realm. Women, on the other hand, were relegated to home and children, in the private sphere, and women became dependent on men's earnings. Thus the family's relationship to work and economics changed because individuals within families assumed their own relationships with the labour market—

men were paid for their work; women were not. Another historical development that contributed to individualism toward the end of the nineteenth century involved the rise of the welfare state. Social control mechanisms like pension and welfare gave some protection and material assistance to those in need, and meant that individuals did not have to rely as much on their families as they had historically (Beck-Gernsheim, 1999, p. 58).

Wynne and Wynne's evaluation of this historical transformation showed "[c]hanges in social structure brought disconnectedness between both persons and the parts of an individual's life. One result...was the painful loss of what had previously often been onerous: As a result of the changes, intimacy became recognized as a 'need' when it became more difficult to achieve" (Wynne and Wynne, 1986, p. 389). It is interesting to note Wynne and Wynne's argument that the origin of intimacy as a need resulted from the loss of too much intimacy ("the painful loss of what had previously often been onerous," italics ours). If, in pre-industrial times, the intimacy (although not a linguistic concept at that time) was often onerous, one might expect that when familial relations individualized and became less intense (i.e., less onerous), people would have become relieved of, rather than in need of, intimacy. This kind of hearkening back to "the good old days" is a phenomenon noted by Stephanie Coontz in her book, The Way We Never Were (1992). She notes the tendency for people to romanticize past familial relations, even when there is abundant evidence to the contrary.

A discourse analysis of the rise of the need for intimacy asks the following questions: To what extent does this historical portrayal reflect people's interpretations of what has been called "an obligation of solidarity?" To what extent are these meanings imposed through an author's social construction of what occurred historically? An analysis of intimacy as discourse renders irrelevant the question of the extent to which people have "needed" or "experienced" intimacy, and focuses instead on how, as economic conditions changed and familial relations individualized, the notion of "intimacy" was "born." As noted previously, discourses evolve relative to changing social conditions and the collective conversations people have about their lives.

The Sexual Revolution

A historical analysis of developments in love and sex since the 1960s (Wouters, 1998), serves to further contextualize our notions about intimacy in contemporary society. From the 1920s onward the desexualization and desensualization of love began a reversal to asexualization of love and an eroticization of sex. Until the mid century, gender differences in how love was interpreted were apparent in what Cas Wouters calls the "lust balance"—a social code that represented a lust-dominated sexuality for men and a romantic love or relationship-dominated sexuality for women.[6] In the 1950s, the notion of female sexual pleasure and gratification gained attention, followed by a diminution in fear of sexuality in the 1960s. Wouters uses the concept of "lust balance" to "focus on the relationship between sex and love…the attempt to find a satisfying balance between the longing for sex and the longing for love" (1998, p. 189). Wouters's analysis demonstrates the growing empowerment of women during the last 50 years, and the growing trend for women to exercise more agency in making individualistic choices with respect to their sexuality. Still, these changes have not meant that the "lust balance" has completely equalized. Traditional romantic ideologies, as evidenced in Intimacy Discourse, have continued to perpetuate gendered ideologies and practices that reinforce inequality in the sexual arena, even as women's sexuality has become more liberated. As will become apparent later in this section, these changes in sexuality are in keeping with the ways in which family relations have become increasingly individualistic.

Contemporary Society

According to Lindholm, in our contemporary society, romantic love occupies an ambiguous place in our thoughts (1998). While love is not necessarily sexual, it often assumes a sexual nature, or is thought to lead to sexual involvement. "Love is akin to a religious experience—a vision of the beloved other as a unique, transcendent and transformative being who can 'complete' one's own life…the fountainhead of all that is beautiful, good, and desirable" (1998, pp. 247–48).

Lindholm sees parallels between our current Western society and those of primitive societies with respect to the ways in which individuals are self-reliant and isolated (1998, p. 255).

Other historical analyses of the family support the argument that the rise of individualism has had a major impact on the relations among members of the same family. Beck-Gernsheim argues that the family is acquiring a new historical form, less obliged to external, imposed rules, and more elective in nature. Similarly, Gabb argues that familial relations have increasingly become relationships of choice. Jamieson notes, "[I]ndividuals are in fact restructuring friendships into 'voluntaristic and altruistic bonds of disclosing intimacy': developing networks that support or even usurp the former emotional privilege afforded to 'the family'" (in Gabb, 2001, p. 319). The rise in divorce and remarriage rates signals that love and family relations have become more elective in nature, and the promise to love another "until death do you part" becomes suspect. Similarly, the proliferation of other-than heterosexual families illustrates the trend toward choice in the construction of family relationships. For example, Gabb points to the ways in which lesbian mothers and their children exercise agency in the development of strategies for dealing with situations, for unlike heterosexual families, they have no social "blue print" in place. "Living outside the social scripts of traditional family life, they are given no choice but to construct a series of identity kits for immediate assembly and equally instant dismantling" (Gabb, 2001, p. 323). Beck-Gernsheim sums it up well: "Paradoxically, we could say that the contours of a '**post-familial family**' are taking shape" (1999, p. 54).

So, how do changing family relations impact the quest for intimacy? As noted previously in our discussion of the impact of the Industrial Revolution, the usual response in the literature to this question is that without the traditional structures of imposed family relations in place, individuals "may find meaning and emotional warmth in the mutuality of romantic relationships" (Lindholm, 1998, pp. 255–56). "The couple is idealized as the ultimate refuge against the hostile world, and functions as the necessary nucleus of the atomized social organization" (Lindholm, 1998, pp. 255–56). Beck-Gernsheim makes a similar argument: "[I] ndividualization and choice in family relations 'fosters a longing for the opposite world of intimacy, security and closeness'" (Beck-Gernsheim, 1999, p. 67).

It is important to note the ways in which this historical portrayal is discursively constructed. We are presented here with the case that, because of increasing individualization, the family has become "a haven in a heartless world" (Lasch, 1977). The idea that people would long for the "opposite world of intimacy" is grounded in structural functional theorizing. This approach is premised on the idea that society has particular needs, and societal phenomena can be explained by understanding the nature of social organization. The historical portrayals suggest that the onset of the need for intimacy resulted from the rise of individualism and the resulting weakened social ties among family members. This explanation is reminiscent of Durkheim's analysis of "anomie."[7] Berger and Kellner (1964) have offered a similar analysis of intimate relations in their description of marriage as protection against anomie. The research on gender difference can be used to further elaborate this argument by highlighting the fact that it is women, not men, who appear to have this inherent need. Social structural changes and one's location within the social structure are used to explain why there is a need for intimacy, and who within the society manifests this need. The reasoning is tautological—society evolves to meet needs, and these changes create new needs that lead to societal evolutions, which lead to new needs, etc. The question that emerges from all of this is: do we accept the idea that society has "needs?"

The "need" theory is dispelled when we move to an analysis of how Intimacy Discourse serves to perpetuate patriarchal relations. The historical record suggests that "intimacy" was an unspoken state of affairs in familial relations prior to the Industrial Revolution. With the Industrial Revolution and the increasing autonomy of family members, people longed for "the good ol' days" (Coontz, 1992), and discursively constructed depictions of past familial relations as harmonious, and present familial relations as lacking. Intimacy, even though reportedly it had been onerous, became a valued cultural construction, and the notion of a need for intimacy, with all of the ideological assumptions previously detailed in this chapter, developed. Individualism and intimacy are conceptualized here as binary opposites (as noted above, in the words of Beck-Gernsheim (1999), "a longing for the *opposite* world of intimacy," italics ours) both in the historical portrayals, and we would argue, in everyday discursive constructions. We can begin to see the lack of fit between discourses of individualism and intimacy within contemporary society. These are competing discourses: Individualism Discourse demands *independence*, while Intimacy Discourse demands *interdependence*.

While Intimacy Discourse perpetuates idealized notions of the family, and romantic couple relationships more generally, as locations for us to seek refuge, it fails to acknowledge the broader societal contexts in which these exist. Although a complete elaboration of the societal contexts is not possible here,[8] the changing nature of employment provides one example of the demands that characterize our day-to-day living. Dual-career marriages are now the norm rather than the exception (Wynne and Wynne, 1986, p. 341). This puts added pressures on family members to manage a myriad of domestic affairs that traditionally were the exclusive domain of the women (primarily the mothers) in the family. Such demands on individuals make the achievement of intimacy difficult. "With the recent rapid increase in the numbers of women working outside the home, the allocation of tasks and roles within the household has generated a need for a sophisticated, creative and uncharted approach to problem-solving by both partners" (Wynne and Wynne, 1986, p. 386). Thus, for families to be successful interpersonally, they must create ways in which to negotiate and plan together, and this requires their ingenuity and cooperation, for there is no "road map" on how this is to be done. As Wynne and Wynne note, major societal changes require joint problem solving by husbands and wives, "but [men and women] have no models from the immediately preceding generation for resolving the division of tasks and authority...." (1986, p. 392). The "uncharted territories" of family matters strain family relations because individuals have not learned ways of successfully dealing with these situations.

INTIMACY WORK FOR WOMEN

Feminist critiques have asserted that romantic love "traps women in false expectations and psychologically crippling demands" (Evans 1998, p. 265) such that in heterosexual relationships, "love" as an ideology is one of the primary means through which women are subordinated to men (e.g., Gabb, 2001; Jackson, 1993; Rich, 1980). Critics argue that women invest more in love and give more affection than they receive (de Beauvoir, 1972; Firestone, 1972), and that they are overburdened with domestic responsibilities. Women become "everybody's Mummy" (Langford, 1999, p. 88). As noted by Langford, in love relationships, women end up submitting, men end up withdrawing: "Although initially love seemed like a shared project, eventually the heroine finds herself deciding what the hero should have in his sandwiches while he shows more interest in his computer" (Langford, 1999, p. 87). Love is linked to women's search for identity and value in a society in which they are marginalized. The literature on gender differences supports the idea that men and women cannot meet one another's needs, and that it is women who become the victims of love (Gabb, 2001, p. 316).

Intimacy Discourse promotes particular expectations as to how primary relationships should be realized and reinforces patriarchal relations. As noted by Duncombe and Marsden (1993), gender differences in emotion behaviour result in differences in "emotion work," (or as we have named it more specifically here, "intimacy work"). "In heterosexual couple relationships, women express men's unwillingness to do emotion work necessary to maintain the relationship, and they point to the unspoken assumption that women will take on this work" (Duncombe and Marsden, 1993, p. 222). As we have argued, women hold expectations about intimacy, and engage in intimacy work not because their experiences are profoundly shaped by Intimacy Discourse. By investing in or "buying into" Intimacy Discourse, women engage in an inordinate amount of "intimacy work," expending considerable time and energy pursuing the ideological, and frequently unrealizable, dream of intimacy.

Rich argues that "[t]he ideology of heterosexual romance…[is] beamed at [girls] from childhood out of fairy tales, television, films, advertising, popular songs, [and] wedding pageantry" (Rich, 1980, p. 645). Throughout maturation, girls are bombarded with messages that perpetuate heterosexuality and they become inundated with the notion of intimacy as a goal in romantic relationships. Ads abound for "intimate apparel" as the key to securing a (male) partner. Advice columns in magazines reinforce the idea that it is up to the woman to create situations in romantic relationships that will entice, and then retain, a man. Valentine's Day, roses, and candlelit dinners (Jackson, 1993, p. 207), wine, sexy lingerie, and readiness for sexual intimacy are just some of the "tickets" to successful intimacy, and therefore, a successful relationship. As discussed previously, reality-based television programmes provide supposedly "close up and personal" insights into what individuals will do together, even in "intimate moments," in any number of situations. The television series The Bachelor, The Bachelorette, and Survivor are good examples of how media aims to create the illusion of intimacy, allowing us to watch male and female hopefuls talk, walk, kiss, etc. their way through romantic encounters. This illusion arguably has become as alluring as the intimacy that is sought through in-person interactions (see Wilson, 1999 on a "celebration of fakery"). This is not to say that we do not challenge televisions portrayals of intimacy. Most of us argue that we "know" reality-based TV is not really "real." Still we are influenced by the allure of intimacy that is suggested. Furthermore, the construction of intimacy in popular culture, with some exceptions, encourages women to manufacture situations that will inspire intimacy. The relationship between ideologies (that are communicated through popular culture) and subjectivities is complex. Intimacy Discourse, and our experiences of it, is not unitary, but wrought with contradictions.

EXPERIENCING CONTRADICTORY INVESTMENTS

Dominant discourses on love and intimacy impact women at the level of experience in complex and contradictory ways. For many, the idea of Intimacy Discourse, while it makes sense intellectually, is counter-intuitive to their own experiences of, or aspirations for, intimacy in a relationship. Similarly, many resist theories that point to inequalities as impediments to intimacy, because to acknowledge this is to surrender a valued belief in our culture that we are "all equal." For example, we find that women frequently admit to their desire for, and their efforts toward, the attainment of intimacy in their own relationships with males.[9] They also allude to the "fact" that they have been less than successful in this regard. When we have suggested that gender "inequalities" impede the development of intimacy, the overwhelming response from these same women is the rejection of inequality as the culprit. Contradictions, then, can be seen within people's discursive productions (i.e., gender differences both *are*, and *are not*, impediments).

Contradictions are also evident in people's investments in discourse and the material circumstances of their relationships. Many couples attest to intimacy in their relationships; however, these claims may not fit in large part with their lived experiences together as a couple. According to Jamieson, therapeutic understandings, or discourses on the achievability of intimacy, are reflected in everyday "talk," even though these "truths" about intimacy do not coincide with people's everyday experiences. Couples often overlook their inequalities and define their relationships as intimate even though they are contributing differentially to the maintenance of their relationships (Jamieson, 1999, p. 484).

Frigga Haug et al. also point to contradictions when they describe how women take pleasure in simultaneously submitting to and resisting their subjection and oppression: "they saw themselves taking pleasure in the very process of being trained into particular dominant structures rather than feeling tyrannized by them" (1987, p. 81) Haug et al. did not arrive at this analysis of contradictions easily, and point to [their] "own [initial] incapacity to see two sides at once; for us, women were either victims, or active agents who could never be seen as subordinate" (1987, p. 145). Haug et al.'s reflections on their analytic process highlight the ways in which we tend to look for consistency in others' subject positions.

The tendency for people to hold contradictory or competing discursive positions simultaneously on topics other than intimacy is exemplified by Margaret Wetherell et al.'s study of university students' aspirations with respect to future careers and family (1987). They found that it was typical for a student to simultaneously, and unproblematically, present contradictory discourses. While a student would advocate "equal opportunities" for women and men in terms of workplace, careers, and children (e.g., men and women should have equal pay, should share the childcare equally), at the same time the student pointed to "practical considerations" (e.g., women are naturally more suited to stay home with the kids, so should give up their careers) that made such opportunities unachievable. Wetherell et al. concluded that these competing discourses serve to "naturalize and justify inequality" while at the same time achieving for the participants "a positive self-presentation in terms of moral principles" (1987, p. 69).

CONCLUSION

As mentioned at the outset, we are arguing for a conceptualization of intimacy as discourse, similar to the way in which Adrienne Rich argued for a conceptualization of "heterosexuality" as an institution. Rich outlined her reason for doing so: "To take the step of questioning heterosexuality as a 'preference' or 'choice' for women—and to do the intellectual and emotional work that follows—will call for a special kind of courage in heterosexually identified feminists, but...the rewards will be great: a freeing-up of thinking, the exploring of new paths, the shattering of another great silence, new clarity in personal relationships" (1980, p. 649). We hope that our critique of Intimacy Discourse will achieve similar ends.

While we are not suggesting that you abandon the quest for intimacy in your lives, we *are* arguing that it is prudent to reflect on ways to understand intimacy; the contradictory and fluctuating nature of investments in discourses on intimacy and the social importance that is placed on achieving intimacy in romantic relationships. Perhaps it is useful to distinguish between the *experience* of intimacy and the *quest* for that experience. The "quest for intimacy" can mean, particularly for women, an inordinate amount of work that is possibly aimed at a subject who is not similarly oriented toward the same goal. While intimacy, however you define it, may constitute an enjoyable emotional experience, working hard on getting it can be a misspent use of time and energy, especially in relationships that are characterized by inequality. As Bittman and Lovejoy (1993) argue, a lot of creative energy is used to disguise inequality rather than to undermine it (in Jamieson, 1999, p. 485).

The harder one strives to create intimacy, the more elusive it is. Lyman Wynne makes this point: "....[P]reoccupation with intimacy as a goal, as with simultaneous orgasm, interferes with its attainment and also distracts, at the very least, from attention to other forms of relatedness" (Wynne, 1985, p. 311 in Wynne and Wynne, 1986, p. 385). Therefore, to make the achievement of

BOX 5.3   APPLYING CRITICAL ANALYSES

We suggest the following:

1. Work individually and collectively toward social change that would rectify social inequalities (since equality seems to be a key feature for achieving intimacy in relationships). Wynne and Wynne argue that experiences of intimacy are associated with deepened mutuality in families that work collaboratively on home and work issues (1986, pp. 386–87).

2. Seek intimacy in places other than romantic, heterosexual relations, since men tend to be uninterested in achieving intimacy, and other relationships can offer intimacy.

3. Seek intimacy through other than in-person interaction (through online communities; through memories; through pets).

4. Re-conceptualize intimacy as achievable through other than mutual, interpersonal, self-disclosure (e.g., through activity-based interactions).

5. Lessen the cultural importance placed on intimacy and make something other than the achievement of intimacy a primary goal. Wynne and Wynne (1986) make the following point in this regard: "[P]rofessionals in the marital and family field should take the leadership in challenging the enshrinement of 'intimacy' as the primary goal" (p. 392 in Weingarten, 1991, p. 302).

intimacy a primary goal may be to automatically undermine its possibility. In Box 5.3, we make a number of suggestions that we hope will help you think critically about your own and others' social experiences.

Summary

- Intimacy is a desirable goal in romantic relationships that is based on a number of ideological assumptions.

- Most of the literature on intimacy reflects these assumptions, and focuses on gender differences in the desire for intimacy and therapeutic approaches to the conflicts caused by these differences.

- Critical analyses broaden our notions of how, where, or with whom intimacy can be realized, and consider how intimacy is experienced in non-romantic interactions; gay and lesbian relationships; friendships; adult–child relationships; non-monogamous relationships; non-coupled relationships; and long-distance relationships.

- Intimacy Discourse came into being following the Industrial Revolution, as family relations became individualized and elective.

- Intimacy Discourse perpetuates patriarchal relations—women invest time and energy in "intimacy work" in relationships, men are faulted for not contributing to "intimacy work."

- Intimacy Discourse is an idealized way of relating that is difficult to achieve because of competing demands that characterize life in contemporary society.

- Our investments in Intimacy Discourse are complex and contradictory.

- Think critically about ways to understand intimacy and to question the social importance that is placed on achieving intimacy in romantic relationships

Notes

1. Wynne and Wynne (1986, p. 384) are one exception. In their article: "The Quest for Intimacy," they define intimacy as "a subjective relational experience in which the core components are trusting self-disclosure to which the response is communicated empathy" (italics in the original). Later in that article, they note, "intimacy is not so much a process as it is the subjective corollary of any of the more basic relational processes" (1986, p. 386).

2. Fairclough defines ideologies as "common sense assumptions which are implicit in the conventions according to which people interact linguistically, and of which people are generally not aware..." (1989, p. 2).

3. Research on Internet relationships is challenging the notion of propinquity as necessary for the development of intimacy; still it is a common assumption within the literature, and in the society more generally.

4. In fact, it was not until we were well advanced in our research for this chapter that we came to question the taken-for-granted assumption that the quest for intimacy was a "good thing."

5. The phrase, "Intimacy Discourse" has been purposefully capitalized to emphasize the idea that "Intimacy Discourse" (as opposed to "intimacy") has an empirical reality, and to convey the sense of importance that this discourse has on subjectivity.

6. Wouters took the term from Norbert Elias who used it in a wider sense, i.e., the whole lust economy (Wouters, 1998).

7. Durkheim studied suicide rates among various groups and concluded that the more socially integrated groups had lower rates of suicide. Groups that were not as socially integrated experienced what he called "anomie" and this was a factor in their higher suicide rates.

8. See Rubin, 1983 and Gergen, 1991 (noted in the References at the end of this chapter) for an analysis of the hectic, complex nature of contemporary society and the implications for social relationships.

9. While working on this chapter, when asked by other women about the topic of the chapter, we would say, "It's about love and intimacy." Typically, they reacted by saying things like, "Oh! I sure could stand to

read that when you're done!" or, "I could really use that!" followed by typically some joking that suggested, in our opinion, that women felt as if they had "failed" to achieve an ideal level of intimacy in their heterosexual relations with their partners.

Critical Thinking Questions

In Case Study 5.1: "Cheryl and Rob," a couple encounters problems in their marital relationship.

1. In terms of "gender difference" theorizing, what is the source of Cheryl and Rob's problems?

2. From a therapeutic perspective, how can their problems be solved?

3. How might critical analyses of intimacy as discourse explain Cheryl and Rob's problems?

4. To what extent is the social context of Cheryl and Rob's relationship considered in this case study (i.e., what factors might improve or interfere with their efforts to achieve intimacy, and are these addressed)?

5. Considering this case study as a text, what ideological assumptions about intimacy are perpetuated? What ideological assumptions are challenged?

Websites

Dr. Phil on Intimacy
http://www.drphil.com/advice/advice_landing.jhtml?section=Relationships/Sex
Dr. Phil's advice on relationships is a good example of how dominant ideological assumptions about intimacy are reinforced in popular culture.

Achieving Intimacy in Life: Learning to Develop Lasting Relationships
http://www.mtnviewhospital.com/Health%20Information%20Library/PFF%20Achieving%20Intimacy%20in%20Life.htm
This website adopts a therapeutic approach to achieving intimacy that ignores the social contexts of relationships.

Long Distance Relationships (LDRs) websites
http://directory.google.com/Top/Society/Relationships/Long_Distance/?tc=1
These websites cover a range of issues and strategies for couples that are trying to achieve and/or sustain intimacy in long-distance relationships.

Suggested Reading

Kenneth Gergen. 1991. *The Saturated Self: Dilemmas of Identity in Contemporary Life.* New York: Basic Books.

Gergen provides an analysis of contemporary Western society that high-lights the way in which technology has increased the complexity of everyday experience.

Adrienne Rich. 1980. "Compulsory Heterosexuality and Lesbian Existence." *Signs* 5(4): 631–60.

In this groundbreaking article, Rich interrogates heterosexuality as a political institution based in patriarchy, and argues that while hetero-sexual coupling and marriage are presumed to be the "sexual preference" of "most women," this choice is bound by sex roles and social prescrip-tions for women that are born out of economic necessity.

Lillian B. Rubin. 1983. *Intimate Strangers: Men and Women Together.* New York: Harper and Row.

Rubin notes the ways in which the social institutions have changed the social roles and responsibilities of men and women, and how this has resulted in a contradiction: a lack of fit between the old dreams and the new realities of romantic relationships.

References

Beck-Gernsheim, Elizabeth. 1999. "On the Way to the Post-Familial Family: From a Community of Need to Elective Affinities," pp. 53-79. In Mike Featherstone, ed., *Love and Eroticism.* London: Sage.

Berger, P.L., and H. Kellner. 1964. "Marriage and the Construction of Reality." *Diogenes,* 1–23.

Bernard, Jessie. 1985. "The Marital Bond vis-à-vis The Male Bond and The Female Bond." *Newsletter of the American Family Therapy Association* 19: 15–22.

Bhugra, Dinesh. 1997. "Coming Out by South Asian Gay Men in the United Kingdom." *Archives-of-Sexual-Behavior* 26: 547–57.

Cancian, F.M. 1987. *Love in America: Gender and Self Development.* New York: Cambridge University Press.

Cannold, Leslie, Bill O'Loughlin, Geoff Woolcock, and Brian Hickman. 1995. "HIV as a Catalyst for Positive Gay Men's Desire for Clarification, Enhancement and Promotion of Intimacy in Significant Relationships." *Journal of Psychology and Human Sexuality* 7: 161–79.

Carroll, Lynne, Natalia Hoenigmann-Stovall, Joseph A. Turner, and Paula Gilroy. 1999. "A Comparative Study of Relational Interconnectedness, Merger, and Ego Development in Lesbian, Gay Male, and Heterosexual Couples." *Journal of Gay and Lesbian Social Services* 9: 51–67.

Coontz, Stephanie. 1992. *The Way We Never Were: American Families and the Nostalgia Trap.* New York: Basic Books.

De Beauvoir, S. 1972. *The Second Sex*. Harmondsworth: Penguin.

Diamond, Lisa M. 2000. "Passionate Friendships among Adolescent Sexual-Minority Women." *Journal of Research on Adolescence* 10: 191–209.

Diaz, Rafael M., and George Ayala. 1999. "Love, Passion and Rebellion: Ideologies of HIV Risk among Latino Gay Men in the USA." *Culture, Health and Sexuality* 1: 277–93.

Dion, K.L, and K.K. Dion. 1973. "Correlates of Romantic Love." *Journal of Consulting and Clinical Psychology* 41: 51–56.

Doherty, William J. 1991. "Beyond Reactivity and the Deficit Model of Manhood." *Journal of Marital and Family Therapy* 17: 29–32.

Duncombe, Jean, and Dennis Marsden. 1993. "Love and Intimacy: The Gender Division of Emotion and 'Emotion Work:' A Neglected Aspect of Sociological Discussion of Heterosexual Relationships." *Sociology* 27(2): 221–41.

Evans, Mary. 1998. "'Falling in Love with Love is Falling for Make Believe': Ideologies of Romance in Post-Enlightenment Culture." *Theory, Culture & Society* 15(3-4): 265–75.

Fairclough, Norman. 1989. *Discourse Analysis*. Cambridge: Polity Press.

Firestone, S. 1972. *The Dialectic of Sex*. London: Paladin.

Flowers, Paul, Jonathan A. Smith, Paschal Sheeran, and Nigel Beail. 1997. "Health and Romance: Understanding Unprotected Sex in Relationships between Gay Men." *British Journal of Health Psychology* 2: 73–86.

Fontaine, Michele M. 1995. "Issues of Isolation and Intimacy for the HIV Infected, Sexually Addicted Gay Male in Group Psychotherapy." *Journal of Psychology and Human Sexuality* 7: 181–90.

Gabb, Jacqui. 2001. "Querying the Discourses of Love: An Analysis of Contemporary Patterns of Love and the Stratification of Intimacy within Lesbian Families." *European Journal of Women's Studies* 8(3): 313–28.

Gadlin, H. 1977. "Private Lives and Public Order: A Critical View of the History of Intimate Relationships in the United States." In G. Levinger & H.L. Raush, eds., *Close Relationships: Perspectives on the Meaning of Intimacy*. Amherst: University of Massachusetts Press.

Gergen, Kenneth. 1991. *The Saturated Self: Dilemmas of Identity in Contemporary Life*. New York: Basic Books.

Giddens, Anthony. 1992. *The Transformation of Intimacy: Sexuality, Love and Eroticism in Modern Societies*. Cambridge: Polity Press.

Hare-Mustin, R.T. 1991. "Sex, Lies, and Headaches: The Problem is Power." In T.J. Goodridge, ed., *Women and Power: Perspectives for Therapy*. New York: W.W. Norton.

Haug, Frigga et al. 1987. *Female Sexualization: A Collective Work of Memory*. London: Verso.

Hite, S. 1987. *Women in Love: A Cultural Revolution in Progress*. New York: Alfred A. Knopf.

Hudson, Barbara. 1984. "Femininity and Adolescence." In A. McRobbie and M. Nava, eds., *Gender and Generation*. London: Macmillan.

Jackson, S. 1993. "Even Sociologists Fall in Love: An Exploration in the Sociology of Emotions." *Sociology* 27: 201–20.

Jamieson, Lynn. 1999. "Intimacy Transformed? A Critical Look at the 'Pure Relationship.'" *Sociology* 33(3): 477–94.

Kanin, E. J., K.R. Davidson, and S.R. Scheck. 1970. "A Research Note on Male–Female Differentials in the Experience of Heterosexual Love." *The Journal of Sex Research* 6: 64–72.

Langford, Wendy. 1999. *Revolutions of the Heart: Gender, Power and the Delusions of Love*. London: Routledge.

Lasch, C. 1977. *Haven in a Heartless World. The Family Besieged*. New York: Basic Books.

Lindholm, C. 1998. "Love and Structure." *Theory, Culture & Society* 15: 243–63.

Mackey, Richard A., Matthew A. Diemer, Bernard A. O'Brien. 2000. "Psychological Intimacy in the Lasting Relationships of Heterosexual and Same Gender Couples." *Sex Roles* 43: 201–27.

Mansfield, Penny, and Jean Collard. 1988. *The Beginning of the Rest of Your Life?* London: Macmillan.

Martin, James I., and Jo Knox. 1995. "HIV Risk Behavior in Gay Men with Unstable Self-Esteem." *Journal of Gay and Lesbian Social Services* 2: 21–41.

Meneses, Ines. 2000. "Intimacy, Norm and Difference: Gay Modernity in Lisbon; Intimidade, norma e diferenca: a modernidade gay em Lisboa. *Analise Social* 34: 933–55.

Munson, Marcia. 1996. "Celebrating Wild Erotic Friendship: Marcia and Martha," pp. 124–32. In Jacqueline S. Weinstock and Esther D. Rothblum, eds., *Lesbian Friendships for Ourselves and Each Other*. New York: New York University Press.

Nelson, Adie, and B.W. Robinson. 1995. "The Quest for Intimacy," pp. 231–48. In Adie Nelson and B.W. Robinson, eds., *Gender in the 1990s: Images, Realities, and Issues*. Scarborough: Nelson Canada.

———. 2002. *Gender in Canada*. Toronto: Pearson Education Canada.

Paradis, Bruce A. 1991. "Seeking Intimacy and Integration: Gay Men in the Era of AIDS." *Smith College Studies in Social Work* 61: 260–74.

Powell-Cope, Gail M. 1995. "The Experiences of Gay Couples Affected by HIV Infection." *Qualitative Health Research* 5: 36–62.

Reis, Harry T., Marilyn Senchak, and Beth Solomon. 1985. "Sex Differences in the Intimacy of Social Interaction: Further Examination of Potential Explanations." *Journal of Personality and Social Psychology* 48: 1204–217.

Rich, Adrienne. 1980. "Compulsory Heterosexuality and Lesbian Existence." *Signs* 5 (4): 631–60.

Robinson, C. Sean. 1994. "Counseling Gay Males with AIDS: Psychosocial Perspectives." *Journal of Gay and Lesbian Social Services* 1: 15–32.

Rothblum, Esther. 1999. "Poly-Friendships," pp. 71–83. In Marcia Munson and Judith P. Stelboum, eds., *The Lesbian Polyamory Reader: Open Relationships, Non-Monogamy, and Casual Sex*. New York: Harrington Park Press.

Rubin, Lillian B. 1983. *Intimate Strangers: Men and Women Together*. New York: Harper and Row.

Sandstrom, Kent L. 1996. "Relationships of Gay Men Living with HIV/AIDS." *Symbolic Interaction* 19: 241–62.

Schreurs, Karlein M.G., and Bram P. Buunk. 1996. "Closeness, Autonomy, Equity, and Relationship Satisfaction in Lesbian Couples." *Psychology of Women Quarterly* 20: 577–92.

Tannen, Deborah. 1997. "You Just Don't Understand," pp. 186–91. In Estelle Disch, ed., *Reconstructing Gender: A Multicultural Anthology*. Toronto: Mayfield Publishing Company.

Tavris, C. 1992. *The Mismeasure of Women*. New York: Simon and Schuster.

The Bachelorette: Episode Guide. February 2003. ABC. October 4, 2003. http://abc.go.com/primetime/bachelorette

Weingarten, Kathy. 1991. "The Discourses of Intimacy: Adding a Social Constructionist and Feminist View." *Family Process* 30: 285–305.

Weinstock, Jacqueline S., and Esther D. Rothblum. 1996. *Lesbian Friendships for Ourselves and Each Other*. New York: New York University Press.

Wetherell, Margaret, Hilda Stiven, and Jonathan Potter. 1987. "Unequal Egalitarianism: a Preliminary Study of Discourses Concerning Gender and Employment Opportunities." *British Journal of Social Psychology* 26: 59–71.

Wilson, Robert. 1999. "Playing and Being Played: Experiencing West Edmonton Mall," pp. 82–90. In Lynne Van Luven and Priscilla L. Walton, eds., *Pop Can: Popular Culture in Canada*. Scarborough: Prentice Hall Allyn and Bacon Canada.

Wood, J. 1997. *Gendered Lives: Communication, Gender, and Culture*, 2d. Belmont: Wadsworth.

Wouters, Cas. 1998. "Balancing Sex and Love since the 1960s Sexual Revolution." *Theory, Culture, and Society* 15: 187–214.

Wynne, L.C. 1985. "Mutuality and Pseudomutuality Reconsidered: Implications for Therapy and a Theory of Development of Relational Systems." In D. Schwartz, J. Stacksteder, and Y. Akabane, eds., *Attachment and the Therapeutic Process*. New York: International Universities Press.

Wynne, Lyman C., and Adele R. Wynne. 1986. "The Quest for Intimacy." *Journal of Marital and Family Therapy* 12(4): 383–94.

Chapter 6

Family Violence: A Twenty-First Century Issue

Ann Duffy and Julianne Momirov

LEARNING OBJECTIVES

In this chapter, you will learn that:

1. in the last several decades, family violence has emerged as a central theme in the sociology of the Canadian family;

2. recent research advances have provided an increasingly accurate and disturbing portrait of the frequency and dimensions of family violence in Canada;

3. our societal responsiveness to family violence has been undermined, in part, by the long historical acceptance of family violence as normative;

4. family violence is increasingly understood as a global phenomenon in which the weakest members of the family—children, women, elderly, disabled—are the principal victims;

5. sociological and feminist analyses—especially those that examine the global dimensions and diversities of family violence—are generating an increasingly sophisticated theoretical understanding of family violence and its societal roots;

6. societal-level theorizing suggests that we examine the fundamental structures of the society and global interrelations—the economic order, patterns of social inequality, and so on—to understand the aetiology of family violence.

INTRODUCTION

Family violence is commonly understood as the hurt or suffering (physical, emotional/psychological, economic, sexual) inflicted by family members on other family members. In this sense, it has become part of the popular lexicon. Canadians would be hard-pressed to find a daily newspaper that does not contain some coverage of wife abuse, child abuse, elder abuse, or any of the other manifestations of conflict in intimate relations. TV movies and talk shows have broached every aspect of family violence, from incest and femicide, to sibling violence and child murder. Academic research has grown exponentially in this area, and numerous publications are now entirely devoted to specific topics such as child abuse. Numerous policy initiatives have been launched, often at great public expense, both to explore the dimensions of family violence and to hew out some solutions to the violence. Only the most isolated members of our society have been untouched by the deluge of information on what was once an invisible issue.

Here, we set forth a general outline of the current state of knowledge on several dimensions of family violence. Tremendous work has been accomplished in naming and defining the nature of family violence. Where once a man beating his wife or parents smacking their child was a normative part of patriarchal social existence, these actions are now much more likely to be identified as unacceptable and abusive. Further, the parameters for understanding abuse have been extended well beyond simple physical violence to include emotional, psychological, and other forms of abuse. As the conceptualization of family violence and its constituent parts have been clarified, examinations of the dimensions of violence, including frequency and patterns, have dramatically improved. Today, we have a much greater appreciation of how routine and widespread violence among family members is and how much it is a global phenomenon. Not surprisingly, the improved conceptualization of family violence has been accompanied by increasingly complex and sophisticated theoretical explanations of the causes, consequences, and patterns of abuse. As we explore these formulations it becomes clear that the roots of family violence may not ultimately rest in the hands or hearts of individual abusers but rather in the societal arrangements—notably, systemic patterns of societal and global inequality—that create the arena for the family violence drama.

A PROFILE OF FAMILY VIOLENCE IN CANADA

Not surprisingly, it is enormously difficult to accurately capture the rates and patterns of domestic violence. On an individual level, victims frequently are embarrassed by their victimization, and intimidated by their victimizers, while perpetrators fear prosecution. On an institutional level, these problems are further compounded by the lack of agreement on basic definitions of key concepts such as "abuse" and "violence." As a result, traditional techniques of social research, such as questionnaires and personal interviews, have met with uneven success. It was only in the 1990s that significant strides were made in creating reliable databases that detail some of the rates and patterns of family violence (Statistics Canada, 1998).

Of particular importance was the 1993 Canadian Violence Against Women Survey (CVAWS). This internationally acclaimed study employed in-depth interviews to survey a nationally representative sample of Canadian women about their experiences with violence, especially violence at the hands of intimates. Anonymity was assured by computer-generated telephone sampling, and interviewers were provided with specialized training to elicit sensitive information. The result is a landmark research document that reveals a disturbing picture of pervasive and persistent violence against women.

According to the CVAWS almost one in three women experienced violence from an intimate partner. It also found that 29 percent of women who had ever married or lived in a common-law relationship revealed at least one episode of violence by a husband or live-in partner (Johnson, 1996, p.136). CVAWS data also indicated that assaults on wives occur with alarming frequency. Two-thirds (63 percent) of women reporting violence stated that it had occurred more than once, and one-third (32 percent) revealed more than 10 episodes (Johnson, 1996, p. 138). This research also underscored the seriousness of the violence involved. In almost half (44 percent) of all violent relationships, a weapon was used at some point. Not surprisingly, in one-third (34 percent) of these cases, the women stated that they feared their lives were in danger (Johnson, 1996, p. 140).

The CVAWS study has not been replicated but the 1999 General Social Survey (GSS) asked the same or similar questions. However, unlike its predecessor, the GSS interviewed both women and men and like many similar surveys it excluded a variety of potential respondents, including anyone who did not speak either English or French, anyone who did not have access to a telephone (the homeless, women in transition, many disabled and Aboriginal women living on remote reserves) (Jiwani, 2000). Keeping these limitations in mind, the 1999 GSS suggests that some rates of violence have declined. It reported that 8 percent of female and 7 percent of male respondents indicated they had been the victims of one or more spousal assaults in the preceding five years (compared to 12 percent in the CVAWS). When extrapolated to the larger population, this means that hundreds of thousands of women and men have been physically or sexually assaulted by their spousal partner. Not surprisingly, troubled Aboriginal communities report even higher rates of violence with 25 percent of Aboriginal women (and 13 percent of men) indicating they were victims of spousal assaults in the past five years. In short, the research, like its predecessor) convincingly documents that intimate male/female relationships remain rife with conflict and violence.

It is important to point out that the results, contrary to some media coverage, do not suggest that domestic violence claims equal numbers of male and female victims. Indeed, the GSS indicates that twice as many women as men reported being beaten, five times as many women as men reported being choked, almost twice as many women as men reported having a weapon used against them, and six times as many women as men reported sexual assault (Jiwani, 2000). Similarly, police-reported data overwhelmingly indicate that violence significant enough to warrant police intervention routinely involves female victims and male perpetrators (Federal/Provincial/Territorial Ministers Responsible for the Status of Women, 2002). A variety of extensively documented research consistently finds the violence women are subject to in their families is more extreme, dangerous, and frequent than any such violence against men. (See Table 6.1.)

Progress has also been made in exposing the dimensions of child abuse in Canada. Indeed, initially, Canadian research was at the international forefront of investigations into sexual violence against children (Badgley, 1984), but this early initiative has lead to primarily regional and provincial studies. It was only in 2001 that the first national study of the incidence of child abuse and neglect reported to and investigated by child welfare services was presented in *The Canadian Incidence Study of Reported Child Abuse and Neglect* (CIS) (Trocme and Wolfe, 2001). Prior to this material, analysts relied on police reports of violence against children and youth that, understandably, tend to dramatically underrepresent the actual incidents of child abuse. Despite the fact that provincial legislation seeks to ensure that all professionals (and, in some locales, all citizens) are legally required to report any suspected instances of child abuse, national data on all reported cases of child abuse are not available. This is largely the result of both the private nature of the offence, the position of children in Canadian society, and the lack of consensus on operational definitions of child abuse. As a result our understanding of the national dimensions and patterns of abuse are in some respects still in their infancy.

The CIS does provide an invaluable statistical summary of instances of child abuse and neglect that involve child welfare services in Canada. Twenty-two forms of maltreatment categorized under the four classifications of physical abuse, sexual abuse, neglect, and emotional maltreatment are included in the report. Important to note is the fact that the study focused on the number

Table 6.1   TYPES OF SPOUSAL VIOLENCE EXPERIENCED BY WOMEN AND MEN, 1999

	Women	Men
Sexually assaulted	20%	3%
Attacked with a gun or knife	13%	7%
Choked	20%	4%
Beaten	25%	10%
Hit with something	23%	26%
Kicked, bit, hit	33%	51%
Slapped	40%	57%
Pushed, grabbed, shoved	81%	43%
Something thrown	44%	56%
Threatened to be hit	65%	61%

Source: Derived from Federal/Provincial/Territorial Ministers Responsible for the Status of Women, *Assessing Violence Against Women: A Statistical Profile.* Ottawa: Status of Women Canada, 2002.

of investigations of child maltreatment, not the number of children themselves; there may be children included who have been investigated a number of times. Another caveat is that each case does not represent a family being investigated, but a child within a family. If more than one child in the same family was involved in an incident, each child would constitute a separate investigation.

For every 1000 children in Canada, there were 22 investigations of child abuse and almost half (45 percent) of these investigations were substantiated by the child welfare agent. Child neglect—the failure to provide adequate supervision, food, shelter, and clothing—was the most common reason for investigation, representing 40 percent of all investigations. Physical abuse followed at 31 percent, then emotional maltreatment at 19 percent, with sexual abuse comprising 10 percent of the investigations. The highest substantiation rate (over 50 percent) was for emotional maltreatment—acts such verbal threats and put-downs, intimidation, isolation, and terror. The majority of substantiated physical abuse entailed inappropriate punishment while fondling of the genitals was the most common type of sexual abuse. The form of neglect most commonly substantiated by investigation was failure to supervise the children properly leading to physical harm. Interestingly, the exposure of children to family violence—exposing children to violent spousal conflict—was cited in the CIS as the most common example of emotional maltreatment, at over one-half of substantiated cases. Biological parents were most likely to be the perpetrators in the various types of child maltreatment, with the exception of sexual abuse. In the case of this particular type of maltreatment, other relatives and non-related persons were far more likely to be sexual abusers of children, although they gained access to these children through their connections to the family.

The CIS, along with data from police reports, suggests that boys and girls are almost equally likely to be victimized. However, boys are much more likely to be the victims of physical abuse, constituting 60 percent, while in the case of sexual abuse, 69 percent of the victims are girls. Sexual abuse appears to target boys when they are younger and girls as they mature. Young boys (from 4 to 7 years old) are three times more likely to be victims of sexual abuse than other age groups of boys (Trocme and Wolfe, 2001; Locke, 2002).

Not surprisingly the families in which these children lived were often beset by a variety of problems. Single parents were more likely to be the head of the families in which child maltreatment was substantiated. One-third of the families were dependent on social assistance for their income. About 20 percent of the children in the cases of maltreatment were living in unsafe housing. The caregivers of maltreated children were likely to have problems such as alcohol and/or drug abuse, mental health issues, a history of childhood abuse, and spousal violence. It appears that substantiated cases of child maltreatment often involve children from some of Canada's most vulnerable and struggling families. Given that poor families are more likely to be scrutinized by social welfare authorities and to be defined as a highly problematized part of society, it is not surprising that child abuse is more likely to be identified in these families while remaining less visible in many others (Knowles, 1996).

The research record on elder abuse, sibling abuse, and teen abuse—the least well known and most recently identified manifestations of family violence—is less well developed. Among these, elder abuse has captured the greatest attention and is furthest along the road to social recognition and policy responses. Currently, research estimates depend upon victimization surveys based upon self-reported accounts of violence and police statistics. Both approaches are quite limited since they leave out many of the more subtle manifestations of elder abuse noted in Box 6.1, however, they have revealed some suggestive information. According to the General Social Survey (GSS) on victimization in 1999, 7 percent of seniors surveyed indicated they had been the victims of some form of emotional or financial abuse by an adult child, caregiver, or spouse in the preceding five-year period and only 1 percent indicated they had been the victims of physical or sexual abuse. The abuse cut across all obvious lines of difference: men and women, wealthy and poor, well or poorly educated were all vulnerable to victimization (Dauvergne, 2002).

Statistics based on police reports suggest somewhat different patterns. Overall, seniors (65 and older) are at the lowest risk of any age group of being a victim of violent crime. Amongst seniors who were victimized, women accounted for the clear majority of older victims of family violence. Common assault was the most common criminal offence perpetrated on seniors by family members. Males comprised the clear majority (82 percent) of those accused of violently victimizing an older family member. This finding is consistent with the view that in many instances, elder abuse is "wife abuse grown old," that is, when aging husbands continue to abuse their elderly wives, the violence is re-categorized as elder abuse. Among cases of family violence, senior males were more likely to be victimized by their adult children and senior females were as likely to be victimized by their spouse as their adult children (Au Coin, 2003).

Other manifestations of family violence—notably, teen abuse and sibling violence—have received much less research attention. However, this appears to be changing and the dynamics of these forms of family violence are being clarified. A 1996 exploratory study of parents abused by their teenaged children defines parent abuse as "any act of a child which is intended to cause physical, psychological or financial damage to gain power and control over a parent" (Health Canada, 1996). According to this research parent abuse is not "normal" teenage behaviour and it often begins as verbal abuse but usually progresses to other forms, particularly if the teenager is using drugs or alcohol. Some parents note that their teenagers express remorse and self-hatred but the majority reports that the teenagers are completely remorseless.

BOX 6.1 CATEGORIES OF ELDER ABUSE

Physical abuse—use of physical force resulting in pain, discomfort, or injury, e.g., slapping, tying up the individual.

Psychological or emotional abuse—actions that diminish the identity, dignity, and self-worth of the older individual, e.g., attacking self-esteem, intentional frightening.

Financial abuse or exploitation—frauds, scams, and misuse of money or property, e.g., misusing credit cards, forging signature on cheques.

Sexual abuse—unwanted sexual activity, e.g., not respecting personal privacy, fondling.

Medication abuse—the misuse of an older person's medications and prescriptions, e.g., withholding medication, over-medication.

Neglect—the failure or refusal to meet the needs of an older adult, e.g., denial of food, water, clothing, medical treatment.

Other categories—restricting freedoms and civil rights; asserting adult/male privilege ("I" know best); spiritual abuse.

Source: Dianne Kinnon. 2001. "Community Awareness and Response: Abuse and Neglect of Older Adults." *National Clearinghouse on Family Violence Publication.* Ottawa: Health Canada.

The study indicates that both boys and girls are equally likely to engage in parent abuse and frequently start to abuse at about age 12. The teenagers are involved in other deviant activities as well, including shoplifting, violent crime, and prostitution.

All kinds of families experience parent abuse but mothers and stepmothers are the most frequent victims in all of the families, regardless of their structure. In addition, parents with disabilities, including fathers, are frequent victims, as well as other vulnerable members of the family and pets. Not surprisingly, abused parents experience many conflicting emotions. They fear their teenaged children but, at the same time, many fear for their children as well. They may feel guilty if police have to be called. They feel depressed, anxious, and ashamed that they have not been better parents or because they are unable to control the family situation. Parents' personal and work relationships often suffer from the strain of the abuse and how to handle it. Abused parents must also worry about the effect of their child's violence on other children in the family. Once again, researchers draw attention to a complex interplay of personal and societal factors as possible explanations for teen abuse of parents: an underlying medical condition, such as ADHD; poor parenting practices and/or unhealthy family structures in which parents fail to take charge or to pay enough attention to their children; emotionally or physically absent or abusive fathers; lack of support for parents from the justice system; a dangerous school environment that promotes a culture of violence; and the use of drugs and alcohol (Health Canada, 1996).

In sum, a substantive body of literature on family violence in Canada is being constructed. There is not, however, unanimity concerning the value of that literature. Certainly, there appear to be often clear limitations in research sampling, conceptualizations of key terms, and quality of results (Jiwani, 2000). In particular, the relative recency of research efforts means that we have very little sense of trends over time and, as a result, little understanding of whether current social policies are making important inroads into family violence. For example, from 1975 to 2000 the spousal homicide rate decreased from 16.5 to 8.3 women per million couples and by more than half for men from 5.9 to 2.1 men per million couples (Patterson, 2003, p. 7). However, in 2001 for the first time in six years the spousal homicide rate increased. There were 86 such homicides, with 69 men, 16 women and one same-sex partner accused of killing their spouse. This indicates a 33 percent increase over one year in the number of men accused of killing their wife or ex-wife ("Homicides," 2002). Other evidence suggests that the more extreme manifestations of family violence are in decline. Although 31 children and youth were killed by family members in 2000, this was the lowest number (and rate) in 27 years. Homicides of seniors committed by family members also display a steady downward trend between 1974 and 2000. (Dauvergne, 2002). However, these are the more extreme manifestations of family violence.

Trends in more routine expressions are much less promising. In 1993, Bill C-126 created criminal harassment as a criminal offence. Although not gender specific, this law was intended, in part, to protect women who are victims of domestic violence from being stalked, intimidated, and threatened. Charges of criminal harassment by intimate partners increased overall from 1995 to 2001 by 53 percent and the overwhelming majority of these victims of criminal harassment continue to be female (Beattie, 2003, p. 11). Similarly, the number of spousal violence incidents reported to the police tended to increase from 1995 to 2001 (Patterson, 2003, p. 5). Research in specific locales also suggests continued problems. Ontario reported that substantiated child maltreatment cases doubled between 1993 and 1998, that child abuse cases leading to criminal charges increased from 2100 in 1993 to 4000 in 1998 and the number of children in the custody of children's aid societies increased from 10 000 in 1996 to 17 000 in 2002 (Orwen, 2002).

To recap, while family violence is out of the closet and Canadians know a great deal more than they did only two decades ago, the most solid conclusions that can currently be drawn is that family violence is a pervasive and serious issue in numerous Canadian families and that the weakest members of the family are most vulnerable to victimization.

HISTORICAL ROOTS OF FAMILY VIOLENCE

The institutional structures and beliefs and values that sustain family violence have a long history. For centuries, those who were physically, economically, and socially most vulnerable in the family have been subject to violence and mistreatment and have been kept in their place by both violence and the threat of violence. In 2500 B.C., a man could engrave his wife's name on a brick and use it to beat her for the heinous crime of talking back to him (DeKeseredy and MacLeod, 1997, pp. 7–9). Scolding, nagging, or talking back were grounds for being burnt at the stake in the Middle Ages, along with adultery. Pregnant women did not escape such a fate. In her work on the history of women in Western Europe from 1500 to 1800, Olwen Hufton (1995, pp. 266–91) recounts stories of women taking abusive husbands to court but effectively being on trial themselves. Although husbands were not free to treat their wives as abusively as they pleased without risking court action, they were considered to be legally superior to their wives. Neighbours approved of a husband's violence against his wife if she violated her gender role. Indeed, complainant wives risked chastisement by the court if they were judged to have overstepped the strict confines of their gender role. In fact, a woman had to be flawless to have any plausibility as a complainant in court against her abusive husband. Of course, this degree of perfection was rarely attainable, particularly since their flaws were largely due to the abuse they had suffered. In other words, if they had been raped, beaten, abused, or impregnated, they were deemed to be defective, a judgment that negatively influenced their credibility, despite the fact that they were in court seeking redress from the man who had rendered them so.

The abuse of children has similarly gone on for centuries under the guise of "parental discipline." Many of us are familiar with the admonition that sparing the rod will "spoil the child" (Greven, 1990). Such treatment of children is likely the result of the historical notion that children, like women, were the property of men. Being the head of the household and family, the man was expected to be in control of those over whom he ruled. As a result, he had every right to use any amount of force he deemed necessary to ensure obedience. Furthermore, as the undisputed authority over the family, the patriarch was expected to do what was, in his opinion, best for its well-being. That well-being, at times, may have had to be achieved at the expense of particular members, such as its youngest ones. For example, infants may have been killed or allowed to die if there were already too many mouths to feed or if the babies themselves had some sort of defect. Alternatively, children may have been sold if the family were in dire need. From about the eighteenth century onward, Western religious beliefs have frequently admonished parents to break the will of children to attain complete obedience and control over them (Duffy and Momirov, 1997, p. 55). It is only since the mid-twentieth century that child abuse has been "discovered" and socially constructed as a serious social problem warranting medical, legal and social action (Kramar, 2003) (see Box 6.2, "Reconstructing 'Spanking': Contemporary Social History").

Other expressions of family violence, such as elder abuse and sibling abuse, were similarly embedded in the historical traditions of Canadian society. Sibling abuse, for example, was dismissed as "sibling rivalry" until quite recently, considered to be normal behaviour among brothers and sisters unless it went to extremes. Violent and abusive behaviour of many different sorts between siblings is well known in Western society. Judaeo-Christian literature recounts stories about one brother killing the other, another brother tricking his brother out of an inheritance, and several brothers selling their father's favourite son (and their brother) into slavery, meanwhile advising their father that his favourite had been killed. The history of royal houses in Western Europe is riven with the same types of stories of thoroughly nasty behaviour. The sheer length of time and breadth of geographical space in which such abusive behaviour among family members has occurred has probably contributed to its tacit acceptance by so many. History and geographical prevalence have helped to normalize family violence to such a degree that ironically it has become virtually unnoticeable.

Given these deep historical roots, it is not surprising to find ample evidence of the "normalization" of violence and abuse in the history of Canadian families. In the 1800s, in Canada, a woman seeking divorce after repeated beatings by her husband was often chastised for not having left after the first beating; yet women who did leave their marriages after only a couple of beatings were chastised for not being patient enough with their husbands. Judgments frequently implied that the women themselves were at fault when they appeared in court as complainants against their abusive husbands. Because women were supposed to conform to their husbands' standards, if a husband were violent, it was considered to be a wife's responsibility to change him. Courts in Canada were even less sympathetic to the plight of women who suffered male violence in common-law relations, usually due to the fact that these women were deviating from domestic ideals (Prentice et al., 1988, p.148).

English common law and its principle of "marital unity" were at the heart of such inhumane treatment by the judicial system. Marriage by law made husband and wife one person—that was, of course, the husband. Rooted in the longstanding concept of coverture, through marriage the woman became feme covert, meaning that she was figuratively "veiled," protected by her husband but also obscured by his legal identity (Dolan, 2003). A woman, as a result, could not sue her husband, regardless of what he did to her, for it would be tantamount to suing herself. Or, more to the point, it would be as if he were suing himself. It must have seemed a ridiculous notion to nineteenth-century Canadians that a man could be so harsh to "himself" as to warrant being sued in court. Furthermore, wives could not be sexually assaulted within marriage because it was believed that, having married, they have given irrevocable consent to sexual intercourse at all times for the rest of their married lives. Any potential objections to such a legal position were silenced after the Canadian Parliament hurriedly passed legislation stating that a Canadian man could not be convicted of raping his wife (Backhouse, 1991, pp.177–78).

Nineteenth-century women and men did not meekly accept this systemic sexism; numerous personal and public efforts were made to demand more egalitarian marriage relations. While the suffrage movement focused primarily on women's right to vote, its supporters were aware that increased legal equality was the key to challenging the abuse of women in the home. Similarly, the Woman's Christian Temperance Union, which called for the abolition of alcohol, based their campaign on the belief that the abuse of alcohol consumption by men leads to physical violence against women and children in the home. Their efforts and those of other early social reformers who sought to protect the welfare of children remind us that while the history of family violence is long and dreary, it is also highlighted by persistent individual and social acts of conscience and courage.

BOX 6.2   RECONSTRUCTING "SPANKING": CONTEMPORARY SOCIAL HISTORY

The public debate over spanking provides an interesting glimpse into the current evolution of public thinking about family violence. Well into the twentieth century, spanking a child was seen by many Canadians as not only a parental prerogative but also a parental responsibility. Parents who did not physically punish their children were at risk of being seen as overly-indulgent and, potentially, negligent. In the course of the twentieth century these ideas have been roundly challenged. Numerous family violence experts have stepped forward to admonish parents not to use violence. Research, they say, clearly indicates that physical punishment does not work as well as alternative measures (such as time-outs, communication) and tends to encourage the child to use violence in their own interpersonal relations (Straus, 2000). Indeed, some analysts argue that the main lesson learned from spanking is to distrust someone larger and stronger.

Internationally, the anti-spanking arguments have been considered persuasive and a growing number of nations—Sweden (1979), Norway (1987), Iceland (2003), Finland (1984), Denmark (1997), Austria (1989), Germany (2000), Scotland (2001), Italy (1995)—have banned spanking (UNICEF, 2003). In these countries, the emphasis is not so much on punishing parents who spank but educating them about the potential harm to their children and the alternatives available to them. In Sweden, for example, a 16-page educational pamphlet was sent to all parents with young children and "responsible parenthood" lessons became part of Swedish education at all levels. A recent evaluation of the Swedish experience indicates that the numbers of children reporting they had been hit in the last year had dropped from over 50 percent in 1980 to under 10 percent in 2000 and public support for spanking has declined from 55 percent of the population to just over 10 percent. Needless to say, whether these are actual changes that are the result of the 1979 law is hotly debated. Bullying, for example, does not appear to have

(continued)

(*continued*)

decreased and it is not clear if youth violence has changed since there have been changes in prosecuting and recording systems. What is clear is that Swedish society has not fallen into disarray and the clear majority of Swedes continue to support the ban (UNICEF, 2003).

The Canadian spanking dispute gained momentum through the late 1990s. A very active lobby sought to have Section 43 of the Criminal Code (which allows parents to physically discipline their children) rescinded. Health Canada weighed in with an educational pamphlet which stated "it is never okay to spank your child." In 1995, a United Nations monitoring committee on the Convention of the Rights of the Child recommended that Canada review its Code so that physical punishment of children in families was prohibited. However, many Canadians remained unconvinced. In 2002, 70 percent of Canadians polled indicated they opposed any law that would prohibit parents from spanking their children and 47 percent of parents indicated they condone spanking as a regular form of punishment for young children.

Spanking became a front-page item in January 2004 when the Canadian Supreme Court ruled in response to a Charter challenge to Section 43 that parents, their stand-in caregivers and teachers may use "reasonable force" if it is for educational or corrective purposes. The court also issued guidelines at the same time indicating that spanking teenagers and children under age two, hitting a child on the head, or using objects like belts or rulers were unacceptable and that teachers should only use physical force to remove a disruptive child from a classroom or to get children to comply with instructions. Not surprisingly, this did not signal the end of the spanking dispute. The Supreme Court decision was split 6–3 and the three dissenting Supreme Court justices' opinions lent support to the view that spanking infringes on the equality rights of children to equal protection under the law. As well, child advocacy groups continued to point to social science evidence that parental violence against children under the guise of discipline is ineffective and damaging and that it puts children at risk for abuse. In response to the ruling, opponents of the physical punishment of children vowed to take their struggle to the Prime Minister and Parliament and demand a full review.

Sources: Goddard, 2003 and 2004; McKenzie, 2002; "U.S. parents," 2000; Semanak, 2000; MacCharles, 2004a and 2004b.

FAMILY VIOLENCE IN A GLOBAL CONTEXT

Not only does family violence have a solid historical foundation, it pervades almost every country and culture. Even the most cursory review of global events quickly reveals sobering testimony to its presence. Children and young women are sold into the global sex industry by their impoverished parents in Thailand, Indonesia, the Philippines, eastern Europe, and the former Soviet bloc; wives are the victims of disfiguring acid attacks by their disgruntled husbands in Pakistan and India; young women in India are set afire by in-laws dissatisfied with the dowry payments; women (and, as a result, their children) are infected with HIV by sexually abusive husbands in Uganda; newborn girls are the victims of infanticide in India and China; young girls in Kenya, Egypt, Somalia, and elsewhere are subject to genital mutilation by their parents or other family members (Miles, 2003; Poulin, 2003; Rudd, 2001; Pande, 2002;

Karanja, 2003; Munala, 2003; Sharma, 2003; Neft and Levine, 1997). Further, in many fiercely patriarchal countries, women, as wives and daughters, are subject to harsh physical punishment, even death, if they are seen by family members to be dishonouring the family by rejecting an arranged marriage, leaving an abusive husband, or engaging in sexual relations outside marriage (Akpinar, 2003). Of course, typical North American patterns of family violence—wife beating, child neglect, and elder abuse—are also found around the globe (Castro et al., [Mexico] 2003). (See Table 6.2.)

Global research also suggests that family violence may be increasing. The World Health Organization (WHO) reports that in every country (where reliable statistics have been collected) between 10 and 50 percent of women indicate they have been physically abused by an intimate partner at some time in their life. Research also indicates that between 12 and 25 percent of women have experienced attempted or completed forced sex by an intimate partner or ex-partner in their lifetime. Further, statistical sources suggest that trafficking of women and children for sex and sex tourism has grown dramatically in recent years (WHO, 2000).

Further, the globalization of the economy, advances in information technology, and global migration mean that family violence flows effortlessly across borders. North American sex-tourists make use of children farmed out for prostitution by their families and Canadians create and exchange child pornography with citizens around the globe. Forms of familial abuse have even been imported. In a number of instances in Europe and North America,

Table 6.2 PATTERNS OF DOMESTIC VIOLENCE ACROSS THE GLOBE

Country	Percentage of Women Who Say They Have Experienced Physical Abuse by a Male Intimate
Canada	29
United States	25–31
Mexico	17–40
Nicaragua	28–69
Egypt	34
India	26–40
Australia	23–38
South Africa	13–29
Portugal	53
Japan	59
South Korea	38

Note: The author points out we have only sketchy data on domestic violence globally. Evidence does indicate, however, that domestic violence is "the most ubiquitous constant in women's lives around the world" (Seager, 2003, p. 26).

Source: Seager, 2003, pp. 26–27.

the daughters of immigrant families have been the victims of **honour killings** when they were perceived to be dishonouring their family (by challenging their husbands' or fathers' authority) (Akpinar, 2003). Recently, parents in St. Catharines, Ontario were charged after they allegedly arranged to have genital mutilation performed on their 11-year-old daughter at the family's home ("Parents charged," 2002).

Of course, there have also been efforts to resist the globalized nature of family violence. In St. Catharines, the local Somali community responded to the above incident by organizing an educational forum to discuss and oppose genital mutilation. On a national scale, Canada was the first (1993) country (followed by the United States and Australia) to accept female asylum-seekers on the grounds of gender persecution. Women who have been sold into marriage by their families, subjected to female genital mutilation, or been the victims of long-term spousal abuse have been accepted into Canada as refugees from gender violence (Knight, 2003, p. A23).

By viewing family violence from a global perspective, it becomes easier to see the ways in which violence and abuse are embedded in social arrangements rather than individual pathology. Global comparisons reveal the ways in which certain social arrangements lend themselves to increased violence in the family while other societies are able to effectively reduce rates of abuse and violence. Not surprisingly, nations, as well as communities, struggling with widespread poverty, extreme patterns of social inequality, unemployment, racism, colonialism, and military upheaval are likely to report high rates of social disorder, including intimate violence. If these societies embrace strong **patriarchal** traditions—traditions that hold men's rights as pre-eminent—it is likely that violence against women and girls in the family is common. For example, the customary use of female genital mutilation to control a girl's sexuality so that she can be married and serve as a suitable wife to her future husband reveals an important intersection between family violence practices and generalized social beliefs. The girl who is not circumcised is not suitable for marriage; if unmarried, she threatens to become a burden on her family's meagre resources or an economic outcast since there are few economic options for single women.

Within this patriarchal-economic structure, it is understandable that women and men actively participate in the practice of female genital mutilation on girls; just as, in Pakistan, mothers-in-law as much as husbands and fathers-in-law defend their family's economic interests by abusing new brides whose dowry is deemed insufficient (Seager, 2003). Women's role in the abuse speaks to the importance of understanding the structural realities of patriarchal societies. As Candib (1999) explains, women may find themselves caught "within the webs of culture and patriarchal control" and required to choose either to harm their daughters for what they see as "their own good" or to save themselves at the risk of harming their daughters—those are the only socially constructed choices. A global and societal perspective allows us to vividly see this connection between personal lives and suffering of individual family members and the larger societal and international realities.

A macro-level orientation not only reveals the larger social forces at work, it suggests the possibility of challenging those forces. In a recent report, UNICEF examined the patterns of child maltreatment deaths in rich nations. Each year about 3500 children under age 15 die as a result of physical abuse or neglect in the industrialized world. Although this death rate appears to be in decline in most industrialized countries, it is still the case that children, especially very young children are at risk. What is interesting is that the risk varies from one nation to another. A small group of countries—Spain, Greece, Italy, Ireland, and Norway—have exceptionally low rates of child maltreatment deaths. Similarly, a small group of countries—the United States, Mexico, and Portugal—have rates between 10 and 15 times higher than the average for the leading countries. Evidence suggests that countries with lower rates of child maltreatment deaths have lower rates of generalized violence (as reflected in exceptionally low adult death rates) and vice versa. Further, child abuse rates appear to be interconnected with poverty, stress, and alcohol and drug abuse (UNICEF, 2003). Countries that provide a stronger safety net for their citizens (and thereby reducing poverty and related stresses) have lower rates of child abuse deaths. Two recent U.S. studies, for example, found that an increase from 10 percent to 15 percent in the proportion of children living in extreme poverty was associated with a 22 percent increase in child abuse. These researchers also found that reductions in welfare benefits are correlated with increased numbers of children in foster care and more children substantiated as victims of neglect (Paxson and Waldfogel, 2002, 2003). To the degree that a society or a global community does not address issues of poverty and social inequality, it invites family violence to flourish.

Theorizing Family Violence

As apparent from the above discussion, documenting the extent of family violence is intimately connected with efforts to both understand the roots of the family and reduce the victimization. While it is not possible to do justice here to the complex array of theoretical explanations emerging in the academic literature, several major themes will be identified.

Understandably, individual-level explanations (and solutions) have been extremely popular. Considerable attention has focused on individual victims and perpetrators and explanations have often been couched in psychiatric or psychological terms. Men who batter women, for example, have been described as suffering from poor impulse control, addiction, depression, and low self-esteem. These personal pathologies are then often traced back to the abuser's family of origin, with its "angry and ambivalent mother" and "shaming and rejecting father" (Dutton, 1995). Appropriately, this theoretical approach seeks to develop psychological scales for identifying potential individual abusers (Dutton et al., 2001). Similarly, the behaviour of child abusers has been explained in terms of various psychological aspects such as self-centredness or simply as an expression of mental illness (Tower, 1999). In many instances, this theoretical perspective offers a satisfying explanation of unimaginable acts—why would any man kill his wife and children and then commit suicide; why would a mother drown her five children? Individual pathology—depression, psychosis—along with the clearly implied solutions—counselling, medication, and psychotherapy—does not challenge our "**familialism**." We can continue to believe in the family as a warm, loving, and stable relationship, where abuse and violence are pathological and rare.

These individualistic explanations, of course, imply a person-by-person solution. For example, the abuser is subject to psychological counselling, anger management, and/or criminal charges; the victim is provided with shelter (foster homes for abused children, shelters for abused women), counselling, and support during any criminal proceedings. However, just as much as food banks help individual poor people to survive, they do not address systemic patterns of social inequality; individual solutions to family violence are typically flawed and inadequate, particularly when even these scant measures are not adequately resourced by the state.

Individual-level approaches may have a place, particularly in addressing the most extreme instances of intra-family violence. They cannot, however, account for the sheer volume of abuse that has already been identified. Hundreds of thousands of families in Canada and millions globally experience some form of violence and abuse and the victimization often follows, as noted above, easily identifiable patterns, such as women are more likely the victims of serious spousal violence, boys are subject to sexual abuse at a younger age than girls, poor and marginalized communities experience higher rates of family violence, and so on. To approach these concerns, analysts have necessarily moved towards more institutional and societal frameworks.

From the **social interaction vantage point**—midway between individual and societal levels of explanation—abuse is located not simply within the abuser and his or her personal characteristics, but in the idiosyncratic nature of the relationship between the abuser and the abused. Concretely, this perspective calls attention to specific aspects of the abusive relationship. For example, in explaining the aetiology of child abuse, analysts focus on relationship elements such as unwanted and unhealthy pregnancy, difficult labour, physical illness or disability in the child or parent (Tower, 1999). From this situational perspective, abuse may be triggered by specific aspects of the relationship and its relationship to institutional structures—medical or social welfare supports. In the absence of specific triggers, the same individual may not display abusive behaviour. The net result of this interactive approach is a line of analysis that is more broadly framed and flexible than purely psycho-dynamic approaches.

BOX 6.3   THE LIMITATIONS OF INDIVIDUALISTIC AND UNDERFUNDED RESPONSES TO FAMILY VIOLENCE

A) FROM ANGER MANAGEMENT TO CRIMINALIZATION

The case of Loletta Bressette Landry (London, Ontario) exemplifies the interwoven problems. In 1999 Loletta went to live with her uncle and his family. In his custody, unknown to any child protection agency, she was slapped, thrown, hit with a belt, and burnt with cigarettes. One evening, according to her uncle's testimony, he pulled her out of bed to make sure she had on her pajamas. He shook her and threw her on the bed. Her head hit the floor and she suffered catastrophic brain injuries. Now in the care of her grandparents, she is severely physically and mentally disabled and has numerous daily seizures; she receives 24-hour-care, is unable to walk, talk, or go to the bathroom herself. She is fed through a tube. Her uncle was convicted of attacking Loletta and, in contrast to Loletta's life sentence, was sentenced to six and a half years in jail. In the course of his trial, information came out that in 1991 the uncle's 2-month-old daughter, Jasmine, had been taken to hospital with injuries consistent with shaken-baby syndrome. The child was taken into the custody of the children's aid society and the uncle received a two-year supervision order that required him to take an anger management course and counselling. He was not criminally charged. When he offered to assume custody of Loletta in 1999 he did not inform the authorities of his past, nor was his past record investigated ("Man jailed," 2000). This and many other instances are testimony to an inadequate societal response—lack of investigation, lack of protection, lack of punishment—and behind these inadequacies—lack of funding, lack of staff, and lack of political will.

B) NO ROOM AT THE SHELTER

Underfunded and inadequate services for victims of family violence are frequently in the news. Recent reports in Ontario indicate that women and children who are fleeing domestic abuse may find that their local shelter has no place for them. The Ontario Provincial Auditor reported that staff at one of the Ontario shelters indicated that in 2000 over 1000 women and children had been turned away. In addition, eight of nine Ministry of Community and Social Services regional offices indicated that women and their children had been turned away from abuse shelters and sent to shelters for the homeless. Even if they gain admission to a shelter, services such as crisis intervention, emergency transportation, and counselling may not be available. According to the Auditor's report, waiting times for counselling services frequently range from three to six months. As a result, abused women and their children may have little choice but to continue to live in their violent homes (Boyle, 2002, p. A18; Miller and Du Mont, 2000).

Socialization literature is a particularly prominent ingredient in this mid-level theorizing. It has been helpful, for example, in explaining the "**intergenerational transmission**" of violence. Viewed from this "**social learning** perspective," growing up in an abusive family socializes children to become victimizers or victims (Tower, 1999). Violence is normalized and rationalized in the family of origin and, as a result, violent patterns of interaction are more likely to be played out in the family of procreation. Socialization is the underlying theoretical perspective in the growing literature on "male support theories." Put simply, this perspective examines the ways in which social ties (friendships) with abusive peers may be associated with higher rates of woman abuse. When a man's friends encourage him to use physical force to dominate his wife or girlfriend, he is more likely to engage in this behaviour and vice versa. Needless to say, many other factors may enter into this equation. Membership in all-male organizations such as fraternities and the use of alcohol may, for example, intensify the relationship between male support for abuse and actual violent behaviour. Currently theories are being developed and tested to reflect this complexity (DeKeseredy and MacLeod, 1997).

Another mid-level theoretical perspective—**symbolic interactionism**—has also provided some valuable insights into the ways in which violence is conceptualized, "framed," and justified by abusers. For example, abusers may call upon a socially acceptable vocabulary of motives to rationalize their behaviour. Researchers interviewed 122 Scottish men who had been convicted of at least one incident of violence against their partner using Goffman's concept of "remedial work" (Cavanaugh et al., 2001). Remedial work in this sense can be equated to "damage control" used by the participants to save their sense of self and to attempt to maintain control over the way their female partners interpreted and understood their experiences with the abuse. The researchers found that the men denied being violent, some by stating that what they had done should not be considered violent because they only acted that way with their female partners. They frequently blamed the women for their violence, although some of them blamed alcohol and the culture of violence in their community. Many of them minimized their violence because they did not consider it to be severe, or they refused to recognize the effects of their violence, blaming injuries on their partners' vulnerability. The majority of participants also used apologies and splitting the responsibility for the violence with their female partners to mitigate the damage their behaviour had inflicted on the relationship. Requesting in advance of using violence ("do you want me to hit you?!") to make it seem as if the woman were somehow in control of the choice to use violence was another example of remedial work. Cavanaugh et al. (2001) point out that the "requests" are really men's demands premised on the threat of violence; if women fail to comply with these "requests," they are held by their violent male partners to have taken the responsibility for instigating the abuse, thus absolving the men of such responsibility.

A similar study was done by Eisikovits et al. (1999) with 20 married couples (aged 23–51 years) from Northern Israel. They found that "accounts" were used by the couples to allow them to continue their relationship. The couples constructed a symbolic meaning to the violence that minimized any threat to the marital relationship. The couples tended to present themselves as normal, despite the presence of violence in their relationships. They presented their narrative accounts of the violence as being infrequent (thus marginal-izing it), short in duration (thus just a slip), low in intensity (thus not dam-aging), and with minimal consequences (thus not very violent). Why the violence occurred was accounted for as a loss of control, therefore having a short temper, a stressful life, anger, "nerves," and situational factors. Accounting for violence on the part of the husband as due to a loss of control means that the violence can be effectively separated from him as a person/husband and from the "normal" marital relationship. Regulating con-trol between the partners was another accounting device used by the couples to normalize the husband's use of violence against his wife. For example, the women were expected to comply with the husbands' expectations; when they did not, violence could be justified as a way to bring them back into line. By exploring the actual accounts used by couples to conceptualize the violence, the symbolic interaction approach draws our attention to the ways in which "interpersonal violence" is socially constructed using socially acceptable beliefs and values.

Sociologists have also sought to develop mid-level theories that seek to incorporate the role of major institutions into their analysis of family vio-lence. **Exchange/social control theory** works from the premise that individ-uals seek rewards and avoid punishment or costs. From this perspective, family members engage in violence "because they can." In other words, vio-lence is used in the family when its rewards outweigh its costs. However, this cost/reward calculation does not simply depend on personal factors such as who is bigger and stronger. Clearly, this perspective allows for inclusion of other variables, such as who is employed and, therefore, has greater financial assets; who receives more education; and who is likely to be supported by agencies of social control (police, social welfare officers). If the use of vio-lence is likely to be punished by the police and/or stigmatized by the com-munity; if the victim is in a position to inflict financial, social, or religious penalties on the abuser; and if there are other effective means of action at the disposal of the abuser, violence is less likely to be employed. Conversely, if the violence is likely to be kept secret, if the punishment is non-existent or light, or if there are rewards for being violent, then the likelihood of a violent out-come is increased (Gelles and Cornell, 1990).

Family stress theory and **resource theory** also seek to navigate between family violence and its relationship to institutional structures. In the former, domestic violence might be seen as the result of a pileup of stressors—unwanted pregnancy, loss of employment, and so on. These stressors are clearly related to the institutional context—the availability of childcare, employment opportunities, and so on. From the resource perspective, conflict over the lack of resources in the family—poor housing, inadequate employ-ment, insufficient income—may lead to family violence. Once again, institu-tional structures—the role of the state in the provision of low-cost housing, social welfare assistance, and so on may be seen as crucial to setting the stage for violence. Research from these two perspectives has been helpful in explaining the connections between poverty, unemployment, economic marginalization, and increased rates of family violence (Fox et al., 2002).

These, and other efforts at sociological theorizing, suggest that sociologists continue to seek an increasingly sophisticated and complex analysis of family violence. However, theorizing that occupies a mid-point between individual and society-level analyses can still be critiqued as unresponsive to the larger societal ingredients, which may be crucial in setting the stage for abusive, dysfunctional families or, conversely, for supportive, non-violent families. Violent family scripts are not randomly distributed through the general population or around the globe. Rather, they are complexly influenced by patterns of social inequality—social class, ethnicity (race), age, disability, and, in particular, gender; by hegemonic ideologies—racism, sexism, ablism, ageism and, fundamentally, by the material conditions of people's lives—the ways in which societies produce and reproduce the means of their own survival.

It is precisely these macro-level issues that have stimulated an outpouring of sociological and feminist theorizing on family violence and have generated some of the most innovative and challenging perceptions.

Feminist Initiatives

Sociological efforts to develop an understanding of family violence have received a tremendous impetus from the evolution of feminist theorizing. Feminists of the second wave, coming of intellectual age in the late 1960s and early 1970s in both the United States and Canada, began to problematize gender and power relations between men and women. They promoted public recognition that women were second-class citizens and they questioned the underlying assumptions of social and cultural structures. By meeting together and sharing their personal experiences, these women realized that male violence and child abuse was quite common—not the rare pathology traditional belief had promoted (Thorne-Finch, 1992; Firestone, 1970). They protested this violence against women (and their children), taking the blame from the shoulders of the victims and firmly placing it upon the male and adult perpetrators. In practical terms, by the 1970s they had laid the foundation for the shelter movement, and by the 1980s had established wife abuse, and to a lesser degree, child abuse, in Canadian public consciousness. Most important, feminists demonstrated that, in contrast to popular notions about the rarity of family violence and its relation to "sick" individuals, violence within families was common in its various forms.

While modern feminists were pivotally important in "naming and problematizing" woman abuse, feminist analysis has had a dramatic, if uneven, impact on theorizing family-violence issues. In particular, feminists have underlined the role of patriarchal culture in legitimating and perpetuating male violence against both women and children. Understanding intimate violence as either pathology or innate human trait was explicitly rejected and, instead, the violence was conceptualized as a manifestation of particular social arrangements and specific patterns of gender socialization. In particular, considerable attention focused on the ways in which violence—physical, economic, sexual, and so on—were deployed to maintain men's power and control in the family. More recently, this perception has generated an enormous outpouring of research and analyses on "masculinities" (Messerschmidt, 1993; Miedzian, 1991).

An interesting Canadian example of this research is Totten's (2000) study of male youth who abuse their girlfriends. The research explores why these young men, ranging from 14 to 17 years of age and "economically and socially marginal" (p. 65), engage in violent actions towards girlfriends and the social nature of these actions. Totten's ultimate sample consisted of in-depth interviews with 30 youth. He found that the majority of respondents were raised in families with rigid, patriarchal gender roles, held homophobic and sexually-objectifying heterosexual attitudes, believed that an ideal man without a job could still save his manhood through "fucking and fighting," and had been physically and emotionally abused as children, and witnessed their mothers being similarly abused. When asked about their future economic prospects, half of the young men cried openly, indicating their despair. They had little or no hope of getting good jobs and having an adequate quality of life in adulthood, yet they balked at the thought of women taking over the traditional economic role of men. It appeared to threaten their masculinity that, in turn, brought out their abusiveness towards females. Abuse, it seems, was one of the few resources at their disposal to save their masculine identity. Totten's (2000) study adds to our understanding of how masculinities are socially constructed, how patterns of employment, education, and personal shame intersect and how these patterns may connect to the male's use of violence against women with whom they are intimately involved.

This emphasis on masculinity and gender is an explicit rejection of trends in some mainstream sociological analysis to minimize any gendered dimension to family violence. As sociologists focused on developing research instruments to count the numbers and types of violent episodes in families (most notably, the Conflict Tactics Scale; see, for example, Table 6.1), they increasingly were seen to be arguing that family violence was gender-neutral (Tutty, 1999). Research that tallied up the numbers of slaps, the number of shouts, and so on frequently concluded that both men and women engaged in interpersonal violence in the family. Explicitly rejecting a feminist analysis, some sociologists began to discuss spouse/partner abuse and marital violence rather than woman or wife abuse. Similarly, research into child abuse (often neglect) frequently reported that it was mothers, the principal parents, who were identified as the responsible adults. Again, these findings appeared to challenge any feminist position on understanding family violence.

In response, feminist analysts have developed a more nuanced and complex theoretical position. In part, as noted above, this has involved dissecting patterns of abuse and pointing to evidence that the most serious expressions of violence—acts that resulted in injury and, in some instances, death—were typically perpetrated by men. Further, men's use of violence was presented as not simply an expression of physical power but also the political, economic, religious, and social power men as a group enjoyed in most societies. In addition, men's complex relationship to power and violence was deconstructed in a new literature that examined "masculinities." Given that men are not "naturally" violent, the complex historical traditions—in particular, men's role in paid employment, men's traditional responsibilities in the military—were teased apart and the argument was advanced that hegemonic masculinities have tended to embrace the use of violence and the need for power and control. It is through this deconstructing of masculinity, for example, that analysts seek to understand what motivates men to take advantage of the opportunity provided by patriarchy to abuse women (Seymour, 1998; Silberschmidt, 2001; Connell, 2000).

DIVERSITIES AND STRUCTURAL ANALYSIS

Recent feminist analyses that have targeted the diversities of family violence—lesbian battering, family violence in Aboriginal, immigrant, and minority communities, abuse of immigrant and minority women, abuse of the disabled—have also served to challenge narrowly framed theoretical positions and to emphasize the importance of macro-level, structural analysis.

There is now, for example, extensive evidence that woman-on-woman abuse does occur in lesbian relationships (Ristock, 2002). While it was important for lesbians to be simply heard on the issue of intimate violence, ending the silence had a momentous impact on feminist analysis. On the one hand, it pushed feminists to focus on the power and control perspective rather than the interplay of genders. Any essentialist analysis of men or women as perpetrators or victims had to be abandoned; clearly, intimate violence was socially constructed by a myriad of factors that included but were not restricted to gender roles. Other elements in the larger social context had to be scrutinized.

In particular, the experience of lesbian battering must be located in a multi-faceted, homophobic social context, where police, social-service agencies, and even friends, may be not only unsympathetic, but also openly antagonistic to hearing charges of lesbian violence. Victims may be loath to act not only because they fear the victimizer or mistrust the social-support system, but also because they fear stigmatization as a lesbian, because they don't want to contribute to homophobia, and because they expect their accounts to be trivialized and minimized. Lesbian women who come out about abuse may be seen as "'airing dirty laundry' outside the lesbian community" (Faulkner,

1998, p. 53) and as contributing to the pathologizing of lesbians and their relationships. Lesbian battering also gives anti-feminists, male and female, a golden opportunity to showcase that "women are just as bad as men" when it comes to violence against intimate partners (Ristock, 2002). Understanding lesbian violence necessitates exploring these complex and, sometimes, contradictory realities.

A useful parallel might be drawn to the structural context in which intimate violence in visible minority communities occurs. Black-on-black violence in U.S. neighbourhoods cannot be understood simply in violence and gender terms. For example, a whole array of myths and stereotypes are immediately mobilized when police respond to domestic violence in a black neighbourhood. Research suggests that police often believe arresting abusive black men is a "waste of time" since violence is a way of life for black women. If black women resist the violence they are more likely to be seen as responsible for their victimization and less likely to be considered truthful (Harrison and Esqueda, 1999). Further, black men and women living in America are much more likely to confront a myriad of social factors related to higher rates of domestic violence. They are more likely to live in disadvantaged neighbourhoods, which in turn have implications for quality and opportunity for education, criminal victimization, and availability of employment in desirable jobs. In short, the complex, interconnected structure of a racist society sets many black men and women up for increased risk of intimate violence, violence that then is most likely to be inflicted on women. The experience of family violence is conditioned not simply by gender or by poverty but by "the persistent, structural racism that is deeply institutionalized in this culture" (Fox et al., 2002, p. 806).

Precisely the same conclusion is suggested by recent feminist research on immigrant women's feelings about police intervention (known as the "policing solution") in cases of abuse. Using data from focus groups held in New Brunswick in 1997, researchers found that, of the approximately one-third that had suffered abuse from their intimate male partners, a number of the women stated that calling the police could mean isolation from their friends and community, make them feel as if they had lost control over the situation (since, when they arrived on the scene, the police took over and decided how to deal with the abusive partners according to their procedures and guidelines), and put them into a subordinate position with individuals in whom they had no trust (Wacholz and Miedema, 2000). In other words, the policing solution was not a solution at all, and could increase their problems with abuse. Calling the police could bring shame upon the family and the ethnic community, damaging or destroying important relationships. Past experiences in their countries of origin may have taught them that police were not to be trusted and could harm them; thus, having to rely on them for assistance in Canada during episodes of violence places them in an even more stressful and frightening position. The immigrant women in the study also expressed their fears about what calling the police could ultimately mean for their own and their families' status as immigrants in Canada. In short, their experience of family violence and their perception of solutions could only be understood when framed in terms of the complex relationships of race and social class embedded in contemporary Canadian society.

A similar line of analysis has been developed by analysts, often feminist researchers, who have explored Aboriginal women's experiences of abuse—both as children and as adults. Much of this research also works from a macro theoretical perspective. Violence against Aboriginal women and family violence in Aboriginal communities is not simply an expression of general patterns of violence in Canada. It is violence framed by centuries of oppression and conditioned by ongoing racial antagonisms. Concretely, this means the violence may be rooted in disadvantaged communities besieged by unemployment, poverty, and addiction; it may be conditioned by a history of abusive schools and unsympathetic social services, by the routine derogation of Native culture and traditions, and by Native exclusion from mainstream realities. As McGillivray and Comaskey remind us, "The contest [between group and individual rights] is fought out in the larger political areas of race, feminism, self-determination, and rights, but the ground of the battle is the bodies of children and women"(1999, p. 147). While patriarchy may be the critical ingredient, it is filtered through the important prisms of racism, colonialism, and classism that are, in turn, lived out in the personal lives of women, men, and children and rooted in the realities of contemporary capitalist economies. This perspective is echoed by indigenous people around the globe—Maoris in New Zealand, Australian Aborigines, and so on—it is clear that family violence, while it strikes at the centre of personal life, cannot be fully understood outside of its historical, economic, and cultural context (Blagg, 2000; Smallwood, 1996; Cutts, 1996).

CONCLUSION

Today, much more is known about family violence in Canada than a generation ago. The problem has been named, numbers are being collected, and action is being taken. Important advances in our understanding of family violence have also been achieved. However, in so many regards—from our basic grasp of the dimensions of the problem to our theoretical analysis—much remains to be done. In particular, societal efforts to address family violence issues continue to rely on individualistic, after-the-fact responses and even these efforts are often underfunded and understaffed. A broader analytical framework that is based in the social-economic foundation to family life and intimate relations, and that works from the premise of supporting "good" families and positive relationships rather than eradicating violent family members, has yet to be articulated. Such an analysis of family would make connections to the structural conditions—such as patterns of growing social inequality in Canada and globally; the state's corporatist rather than human agenda; the perpetuation of systemic patriarchy, racism, classism, agism and so on in Canada and globally—all of which provide such a rich environment for intimate violence.

Summary

- Since the late 1960s, family violence has emerged as a central issue in the sociology of the Canadian family.

- As a result of this recognition, an increasingly accurate statistical database on forms of family violence is emerging.

- Confronting family violence entails coming to terms with our collective history, in which many expressions of violence were considered socially acceptable, even desirable.

- Family violence is linked to traditional family practices around the globe; globalization has merely intensified the victimization.

- While mainstream sociology has contributed to our understanding of family violence, social-structural analyses, such as feminist analyses of diversities, provide a stronger theoretical analysis.

- Success in articulating solutions (policies) for family violence has been difficult to achieve and underscores the need for a more broadly framed theoretical perspective.

Critical Thinking Questions

1. Consider in what ways the status of women in society—economic, political, religious, educational, social—has an impact on women's experience of family violence and renders it significantly different from men's. Are there important parallels to the relationships between children and adults?

2. How well do you think the Conflict Tactics Scale (see Table 6.1) captures the realities of family violence situations? How would you suggest a researcher develop a more sensitive and thorough instrument for "getting at" family violence? In your discussion consider the categories of elder abuse in Box 6.1.

3. Analysts have become increasingly aware of the "diversities" in experiences of family violence. Consider the ways in which social class, sexual

orientation, and race affect women and children's experiences of abuse. Outline specific ways in which social policy might respond to these differences in experience.

4. If you were asked to design a community project around the issue of family violence, what one direct or indirect issue (teen abuse, poverty, and so on) would you target, and why?

5. With the increasing proportion of elderly, and especially older elderly in the population, abuse of the elderly is likely to become increasingly prominent as a family-violence issue. Identify some concrete steps that might be taken at both the societal and the community level to help reduce the abuse of our seniors.

6. Discuss the ways that men justify victimizing their female partners. In your opinion, are their justifications associated with the findings of Leslie Tutty in her study of husband abuse? Explain.

7. How does the deteriorating economic situation influence the way that young men perceive their masculine identity? What are the implications of their perceptions for the future in terms of family violence?

Websites

National Clearinghouse on Family Violence
http://www.hc-sc.gc.ca/hppb/familyviolence/
>   The National Clearinghouse on Family Violence is a national resource centre for all Canadians seeking information about violence within families and looking for new resources—including publications, video collection, and links.

BC Institute Against Family Violence
http://www.bcifv.org/
>   The focus is not just on family violence in the province of British Columbia but on the larger social problem as well. Again, lots of information and publications.

Canadian Research Institute for the Advancement of Women (CRIAW)
http://www.criaw-icref.ca/indexFrame-e.htm
>   Broadly based, informative, feminist site with a fact sheet on family violence with the basics and articles dealing with more sophisticated issues as well. Also, articles on poverty, racism, and other matters that are associated with family violence.

Suggested Reading

Elly Danica. 1988. *Don't: A Woman's Word*. Toronto: McClelland & Stewart.
A riveting and disturbing first-hand account of one woman's experience with childhood abuse.

Walter DeKeseredy and Linda MacLeod. 1997. *Woman Abuse: A Sociological Story*. Toronto: Harcourt Brace & Company.
An invaluable combination of sociological theory, current research, and personal experiences relating to women's experience of violence.

Ann Duffy and Julianne Momirov. 1997. *Family Violence: A Canadian Introduction*. Toronto: James Lorimer.
The first Canadian text to provide an overview of Canadians' experience with and understanding of woman, child, elder, and other family abuse.

Holly Johnson. 1996. *Dangerous Domains: Violence Against Women in Canada*. Toronto: Nelson Canada.
A detailed analysis of woman abuse, drawing in particular on the data generated by Statistics Canada's *Canadian Violence Against Women Survey*.

Anne McGillivray and Brenda Comaskey. 1999. *Black Eyes All of the Time: Intimate Violence, Aboriginal Women, and the Justice System*. Toronto: University of Toronto Press.
Just as the title states, a study of Aboriginal women, intimate violence, and the justice system.

Janice L. Ristock. 2002. *No More Secrets: Violence in Lesbian Relationships*. New York: Routledge.
Excellent Canadian study and in-depth discussion of lesbian abuse showcasing their first-hand accounts.

Leslie Timmins, ed. 1995. *Listening to the Thunder: Advocates Talk about the Battered Women's Movement*. Vancouver: Women's Research Centre.
The voices of 22 grass-roots activists discussing their experiences and strategies.

References

Akpinar, Aylin. 2003. "The Honour/Shame Complex Revisited: Violence Against Women in the Migration Context." *Women's Studies International Forum* 26 (5) (September-October): 425–442.

Au Coin, Kathy. 2003. "Family Violence Against Older Adults". Pp. 21–32 in H. Johnson and K. Au Coin, eds. *Family Violence in Canada: A Statistical Profile 2003*. Ottawa: Statistics Canada.

Backhouse, Constance. 1991. *Petticoats and Prejudice: Women and Law in Nineteenth-Century Canada.* Toronto: Women's Press (for The Osgoode Society).

Badgley, Robin F. 1984. *Sexual Offences Against Children in Canada*, vols. 1, 2, and *Summary.* Ottawa: Minister of Supply and Services.

Beattie, Sara. 2003. "Criminal Harassment." Pp. 8-13 in H. Johnson and K. Au Coin, eds. *Family Violence in Canada: A Statistical Profile* 2003. Ottawa: Statistics Canada.

Blagg, Harry. 2000. *Crisis Intervention in Aboriginal Family Violence: Strategies and Models for Western Australia.* University of Western Australia: Crime Research Centre.

Boyle, Theresa. 2002. "Too Many Turned Away from Shelters, MPP Says." *Toronto Star.* March 1, p. A18.

Candib, Lucy M. 1999. "Incest and Other Harms to Daughters Across Cultures: Maternal Complicity and Patriarchal Power." *Women's Studies International Forum* 22(2): 185–201.

Castro, Roberto, C. Peek-Asa, and A. Ruiz. 2003. "Violence Against Women in Mexico: A Study of Abuse Before and During Pregnancy." *American Journal of Public Health* 93 (7)(July): 1110–117.

Cavanaugh, Kate, R. Emerson Dobash, Russell P. Dobash, and Ruth Lewis. 2001. "'Remedial Work': Men's Strategic Responses to Their Violence Against Intimate Female Partners." *Sociology* August, Vol. 35, Issue 3: 695 (first page).

Connell, R.W. 2000. *The Men and the Boys.* Berkley: University of California Press.

Cutts, Christine. 1996. "A Torres Strait Islander Perspective on Family Violence." In R. Thorpe and J. Irwin, eds. *Women and Violence: Working for Change.* Sydney: Hale & Iremonger.

Dauvergne, Mia. 2002. "Family Violence Against Older Adults." Pp. 26–33 in Canadian Centre for Justice Statistics, *Family Violence in Canada: A Statistical Profile* 2002. Ottawa: Statistics Canada.

DeKeseredy, Walter S., and Linda MacLeod. 1997. *Woman Abuse: A Sociological Story.* Toronto: Harcourt Brace & Company.

Dolan, Frances E. 2003. "Battered Women, Petty Traitors, and the Legacy of Coverture." *Feminist Studies* 29 (2) (Summer): 249–78.

Duffy, Ann, and Julianne Momirov. 1997. *Family Violence: A Canadian Introduction.* Toronto: James Lorimer.

Dutton, Donald G. 1995. *The Batterer: A Psychological Profile.* New York: Basic Books.

Dutton, Donald G., Monica A. Landolt, Andrew Starzomski, and Mark Bodnarchuk. 2001. "Validation of the Propensity for Abusiveness Scale in Diverse Male Populations." *Journal of Family Violence* 16 (1) (March): 59–73.

Eisikovits, Zvi, Hadass Goldblatt, and Zeev Winstok. 1999. "Partner Accounts of Intimate Violence: Towards a Theoretical Model." *Families in Society: The Journal of Contemporary Human Services* November, Vol. 80, Issue 16: 606 (first page).

Faulkner, Ellen. 1998. "Woman-to-Woman Abuse: Analyzing Extant Accounts of Lesbian Battering." Pp. 52-62 in K. Bonnycastle and G. Rigakos, eds. *Unsettling Truths: Battered Women, Policy, Politics and Contemporary Research in Canada.* Vancouver: Collective Press.

Federal/Provincial/Territorial Ministers Responsible for the Status of Women. 2002. *Assessing Violence Against Women: A Statistical Profile.* Ottawa: Status of Women Canada.

Firestone, Shulamith. 1970. *The Dialectic of Sex.* New York: William Morrow and Company.

Fox, G.L., M.L. Benson, A.A. DeMaris, and J. Van Wyk. 2002. "Economic Distress and Intimate Violence: Testing Family Stress and Resources Theories." *Journal of Marriage and the Family* 64 (August): 793–807.

Gelles, Richard J., and Claire Pedrick Cornell. 1990. *Intimate Violence in Families,* 2nd ed. Newbury Park, CA: Sage.

Goddard, John. 2003. "Spanking Case Opens in Supreme Court." *Toronto Star,* June 6, p. A23.

———. 2004. "Spanking decision may hit home." *Toronto Star,* January 24, p. A23.

Greven, Philip. 1990. *Spare the Child: The Religious Roots of Punishment and the Psychological Impact of Physical Abuse.* New York: Alfred A. Knopf.

Harrison, Lisa A., and Cynthia Willis Esqueda. 1999. "Myths and Stereotypes of Actors Involved in Domestic Violence: Implications for Domestic Violence Culpability Attributions." *Aggression and Violent Behavior* 4(2): 129–38.

Health Canada. 1996. *Parent Abuse: The Abuse of Parents by Their Teenage Children.* Ottawa: Family Violence Prevention Division.

Homicides by spouses on the rise. (2002, September 26). *Toronto Star,* p. A27.

Hufton, Olwen. 1995. *The Prospect Before Her: A History of Women in Western Europe, 1500–1800.* New York: Alfred A. Knopf.

Jiwani, Yasmin. 2000. "The 1999 Gender Social Survey on Spousal Violence: An Analysis." *Canadian Woman Studies* 20(3) (Fall): 34–40.

Johnson, Holly. 1996. *Dangerous Domains: Violence Against Women.* Toronto: Nelson Canada.

Karanja, Lisa W. 2003. "Domestic Violence and HIV Infection In Uganada." *Human Rights Dialogue* 2 (10) (Fall): 10–11.

Kinnon, Dianne. 2001. "Community Awareness and Response: Abuse and Neglect of Older Adults." *National Clearinghouse on Family Violence Publication.* Ottawa: Health Canada.

Knight, Stephen. (2003, March 7). A Safe Haven for Women. *Toronto Star,* p. A23.

Knowles, Caroline. 1996. *Family Boundaries: the Invention of Normality and Dangerousness.* Peterborough: Broadview.

Kramar, K.J. 2003. "Vengeance for the Innocents: The New Medico-Legal Designation of 'Infanticide' as 'Child Abuse Homicide'." Pp. 182–208 in D. Brock, ed. *Making Normal: Social Regulation in Canada.* Toronto: Thomson Nelson.

Locke, Daisy. 2002. "Violence Against Children and Youth." Pp. 34–43 in Canadian Centre for Justice Statistics, *Family Violence in Canada: A Statistical Profile 2002.* Ottawa: Statistics Canada.

MacCharles, Tonda. 2004a. "Ruling Allows Parents to Spank." *Toronto Star.* January 31, pp. A1, A23.

———. 2004b. "Judges Say Law Vague and Charter Violation." *Toronto Star.* January 31, pp. A22.

Man jailed 6 1/2 years for attacking niece. (2000, November 13). *Toronto Star,* p. A4.

McGillivray, Anne, and Brenda Comaskey. 1999. *Black Eyes All of the Time: Intimate Violence, Aboriginal Women, and the Justice System.* Toronto: University of Toronto Press.

McKenzie, Donald. 2002. "Right to Spank Backed in Poll." *Toronto Star,* February 11, p. A6.

Messerschmidt, James W. 1993. *Masculinities and Crime: Critique and Reconceptualization of Theory.* Lanham: Rowman & Littlefield.

Miedzian, Myriam. 1991. *Boys Will Be Boys: Breaking the Link between Masculinity and Violence.* New York: Doubleday.

Miles, Angela. 2003 "Prostitution, Trafficking and the Global Sex Industry: A Conversation with Janice Raymond." *Canadian Woman Studies* 22 (3,4) (Spring/Summer): 26–37.

Miller, Karen-Lee, and Janice Du Mont. 2000. "Countless Abused Women: Homeless and Inadequately Housed." *Canadian Woman Studies* 20(3) (Fall): 115–22.

Munala, June. 2003. "Combating FGM in Kenya's Refugee Camps." *Human Rights Dialogue* 2 (10) (Fall): 17–18.

Neft, Naomi, and Ann D. Levine. 1997. *Where Women Stand: An International Report on the Status of Women in 140 Countries, 1997–1998.* New York: Random House.

Orwen, Patricia. 2002. "Child Abuse Caseload 24,000 and Growing." *Toronto Star,* May 8, p. A2.

Pande, Rekha. 2002. "The Public Face of a Private Domestic Violence." *International Feminist Journal of Politics* 4 (3) (December): 342–67.

Parents charged. (2000, February 15). *Toronto Star,* p. A6.

Patterson, Julienne. 2003. "Spousal Violence." Pp. 3-8 in H. Johnson and K. Au Coin, eds. *Family Violence in Canada: A Statistical Profile 2003.* Ottawa: Statistics Canada.

Paxson, C., and J. Waldfogel. 2002. "Work, Welfare and Child Maltreatment." *Journal of Labor Economics* 20 (3): 435–74.

———. 2003. "Welfare Reforms, Family Resources and Child Maltreatment." *Journal of Policy Analysis and Management* 22 (1): 85–113.

Poulin, Richard. 2003. "Globalization and the Sex Trade: Trafficking and the Commodifiction of Women and Children." *Canadian Woman Studies* 22 (3,4) (Spring/Summer): 38–47.

Prentice, Alison, Paula Bourne, Gail Cuthbert Brandt, Beth Light, Wendy Mitchinson, and Naomi Black. 1988. *Canadian Women: A History.* Toronto: Harcourt Brace Jovanovich.

Ristock, Janice L. 2002. *No More Secrets:Violence in Lesbian Relationships.* New York: Routledge.

Rudd, Jane. 2001. "Dowry-Murder: An Example of Violence Against Women." *Women's Studies International Forum* 24 (5): 513–22.

Seager, Joni. 2003. *The Penguin Atlas of Women in the World.* Toronto: Penguin Books.

Semanak, Susan. 2000. "The Case Against Spanking." *Toronto Star,* May 20, p. F5.

Seymour, Anne. 1998. "Aetiology of the Sexual Abuse of Children: An Extended Feminist Perspective." *Women's Studies International Forum* 21 (4): 415–27.

Sharma, Dinesh C. 2003. "Widespread Concern over India's Missing Girls." *Lancet* 362 (9395): 1553.

Silberschmidt, Margrethe. 2001. "Disempowerment of Men in Rural and Urban East Africa: Implications for Male Identity and Sexual Behaviour." *World Development* 29 (4): 657–71.

Smallwood, Margaret. 1996. "This Violence Is Not Our Way: An Aboriginal Perspective on Domestic Violence." In R. Thorpe and J. Irwin, eds. *Women and Violence:Working for Change.* Sydney: Hale & Iremonger.

Statistics Canada. 1998. *Family Violence in Canada: A Statistical Profile, 1998.* Ottawa: Minister of Industry. Catalogue no. 85-224-XPE.

Straus, Murray A. 2000. "Corporal Punishment and Primary Prevention of Physical Abuse." *Child Abuse and Neglect.* 24 (9): 1109–114.

Thorne-Finch, Ron. 1992. *Ending the Silence: The Origins and Treatment of Male Violence against Women.* Toronto: University of Toronto Press.

Totten, Mark D. 2000. *Guys, Gangs, & Girlfriend Abuse.* Peterborough: Broadview.

Tower, Cynthia Crosson. 1999. *Understanding Child Abuse and Neglect,* 4th ed. Boston: Allyn and Bacon.

Trocme, N., and D. Wolfe. 2001. *Child Maltreatment in Canada: Selected Results from the Canadian Incidence Study of Reported Child Abuse and Neglect.* Ottawa: Minister of Public Works and Government Services.

Tutty, Leslie. 1999. *Husband Abuse: An Overview of Research and Perspectives.* Ottawa: Family Violence Prevention Unit, Health Canada.

UNICEF. 2003. "A League Table of Child Maltreatment Deaths in Rich Nations." *Innocenti Report Card* No. 5, September. Florence: UNICEF Innocenti Research Centre.

U.S. parents condone spanking, survey finds. (2000, October 6). *Toronto Star*, p. D4.

Wachholz, Sandra, and Baukje Miedema. 2000. "Risk, Fear, Harm: Immigrant Women's Perceptions of the 'Policing Solution' to Woman Abuse." *Crime, Law & Social Change* 34: 301–17.

World Health Organization (WHO). 2000. "Violence Against Women." Fact Sheet No. 239. June 2000.

Chapter 7

Lesbian and Gay Parents

Katherine Arnup

LEARNING OBJECTIVES

In this chapter, you will learn that:

1. attitudes toward sexuality in and out of marriage, especially gay and lesbian sexuality, have changed dramatically over the past 40 years;

2. the recent legalization of same-sex marriage marks a significant shift in the legal recognition of gay and lesbian relationships;

3. legal and social practices regarding children in gay and lesbian families have been dramatically reformed;

4. while in the past, gaining custody of children from prior heterosexual unions was the principal avenue by which gay men and lesbians became parents, today donor insemination, adoption, and surrogacy offer new options;

5. although the presence of children in gay and lesbian families remains a hotly contested social issue, research suggests that gay and lesbian parents are as capable as heterosexual parents of providing for the healthy psychological, social, and sexual development of children.

INTRODUCTION

For people born in the past two or three decades, the pace of cultural and social change may not seem particularly fast. Coming of age when the public debate was whether or not to legally recognize gay marriages and when annual Lesbian and Gay Pride Parades were established traditions across Canada, many young people take lesbian and gay relationships for granted. We've seen pictures on the front page of our newspaper depicting gay men and lesbians celebrating their wedding ceremonies, gay men taking charge of heterosexual men's wardrobes on *Queer Eye for the Straight Guy*, and Melissa Etheridge and her partner on the cover of *Newsweek* proclaiming, "We're having a baby!" (November 4, 1996). Today, for many, the presence of lesbian and gay

176

parents is a non-issue—they merely represent one more variation in the ever-changing Canadian family.

For others, however, both the rate and scope of change in sexual mores is nothing short of staggering. It is important to remember that, until 1968, abortion in Canada was illegal, and the dissemination of birth control information and devices was punishable under the Criminal Code. Although some provinces had provisions for the legal separation of married couples, there was no federal Divorce Act. Couples living together without benefit of marriage were said to be "shacking up," or, worse still, "living in sin," their unions earning condemnation and social and legal sanctions. Their children were born "out of wedlock," "illegitimate" in the eyes of the law, and "bastards" in the eyes of their neighbours and classmates—subject to both social stigma and financial and personal privation. Non-heterosexual sexual acts were more harshly treated. Private sexual acts between consenting adults of the same sex were subject to prosecution under the Criminal Code. Gays and lesbians were fags, homos, deviants, objects of ridicule and personal attacks. Should their sexual orientation become known, they risked losing their jobs, their housing, their families and friends, and even their children.

Starting in 1968, many of the basic assumptions and beliefs surrounding families and sexuality have been challenged. Justice Minister Pierre Trudeau's Omnibus Bill (1968) legalized both birth control and abortion, and decriminalized private sexual acts between consenting adults. In an oft-cited remark, Trudeau argued, "the state has no place in the bedrooms of the nation." The 1982 passage of the Charter of Rights and Freedoms reinforced these changes since now unmarried opposite-sex couples, gay men and lesbians, and a host of other groups were able to challenge discriminatory laws that excluded them from full participation in society and denied them full legal protections. Today, for example, lesbians and gay men can, in most provinces, foster and adopt children. In 2003, the Ontario Court of Appeal, along with the British Columbia courts, ruled that lesbian and gay couples have access to full marriage rights. Dozens of couples from across Canada, the United States, and even parts of Europe have flocked to Ontario to "tie the knot."

Many Canadians likely take this avalanche of change more or less for granted (see Box 7.1). But for some, these changes feel very threatening, raising the spectre of the decline of civilization, the demise of marriage and the family,

BOX 7.1   POLLS SUPPORT SAME-SEX MARRIAGE

A Canadian Press/Leger Marketing survey reported that in 2001 65.4 percent of Canadians supported same-sex marriage. Not surprisingly, younger people were strongly in favour with 80.5 percent of those aged 18 to 34 supporting the recognition of same-sex marriage.

Source: Mawhinney, J. (2002, September 28). Gay Unions Garner Public Support. *Toronto Star*, p. K4.

and a rejection of the teachings of the Bible and the church. The legalization of gay and lesbian marriages, for example, prompted a storm of protest on talk radio and in letters to the editor. It was clear that, for some Canadians, marriage was strictly reserved for heterosexuals and the inclusion of gays and lesbians was seen as both unacceptable and unnatural. The loud and often intemperate debate over whether or not gay and lesbian marriages are "real" marriages clearly reveals that the family itself remains "contested terrain."

In this chapter I look at the issues that surround lesbian and gay families. Lesbians and gay men enter into relationships and become parents in what is often a hostile social climate and, at best, an unclear legal context. With this in mind, I first address lesbian and gay family experiences in terms of the relevant legal, social, and demographic changes that have occurred over the past 20 years. Most significant have been the shifts in laws and policies governing child custody and adoption as they pertain to gay and lesbian couples. As the research record has made increasingly clear, earlier fears about negative outcomes for children raised in gay and lesbian families have been refuted. However, despite these important advances, gays and lesbians and their children still must confront public and private **homophobia**.

LESBIAN AND GAY FAMILIES

Prior to the 1970s, few people outside of the homosexual community even knew of the existence of lesbian and gay parents. If they thought about homosexuality at all, most people falsely assumed that homosexuals led lonely, empty lives, devoid of long-term attachments of any kind. In just over three decades, both the perception and the reality of lesbian and gay lives have changed dramatically. Widely cited figures suggest that approximately 10 percent of women are lesbians and that between 20 and 30 percent of lesbians are mothers. In addition, untold numbers of gay men have become parents— in heterosexual relationships prior to "coming out," in co-parenting arrangements with female friends, and through adoption, fostering, and surrogacy arrangements. In the 2001 Census, information was collected for the first time on the numbers of same-sex couples across Canada. The results, which likely grossly underestimate the number of gays and lesbians in the Canadian population, indicate that 34 200 couples self-identified as "same sex." Of these couples, almost half (45 percent) were female and one in seven of these lesbian couples indicated they have children. Only 3 percent of the male same-sex couples indicated that they have children (*Globe and Mail*, October 23, 2002, p. A7). While the 1990 and 2000 U.S. census results unearthed an equivalently small number of lesbian and gay couples, estimates suggest that there are between "three and eight million gay and lesbian parents, raising between six and 14 million children" (Martin, 1993).

Today, lesbian and gay parents are highly visible at child-care centres, school concerts, soccer fields, and shopping centres across the country. They

BOX 7.2 MARRIAGE

While marriage does not of necessity involve children, in both law and the public mind the two institutions are deeply intertwined. Proponents of marriage rights for lesbian and gay couples frequently seek marriage rights in order to secure their relationships with their children or in anticipation of forming a family. Opponents of gay marriage argue vehemently that marriage rights are but an aspect of the slippery slope of homosexual recruitment and proselytizing.

In Western society, marriage stands as the recognized marker of stability, commitment, and social acceptance. Marriage provides a measure of community support for a relationship, an opportunity for the public welcoming of a couple into their families. In addition, it is seen as an effective means of providing for the security and stability necessary for the raising of children, through the host of legal protections and rights, benefits and responsibilities that accompany marriage.

Since the first Canadian case, *North v. Matheson* (1974), governments in Canada have repeatedly rebuffed efforts by lesbians and gays to codify their relationships through marriage. In each case, officials have cited the opposite-sex requirement of marriage in the federal legislation. Three recent cases in Ontario, Quebec, and British Columbia reversed that trend. In all three cases, appeal courts have ruled that the opposite-sex requirement of marriage is unconstitutional. In June 2002, Quebec enacted Bill 84, which created a new status of **civil union partners** (open to both unmarried opposite-sex and same-sex conjugal partners). The status accords almost all the same benefits and obligations as married couples. Nonetheless, civil unions are not marriages and the law makes it clear that some provisions related to marriage (including the division of property upon separation) do not apply to civil unions. As a result, even in those jurisdictions, activists have continued to pursue full marriage rights.

In June 2003, the Ontario Court of Appeal set aside the heterosexual definition of marriage with immediate effect and ordered the Toronto city clerk to issue marriage licences to several gay couples who had applied for them. The decision was one of three in 2003 by appeal courts in provinces across the country. A decision in May 2003 by the British Columbia Court of Appeal had given the federal government until July 2004 to change the law to include homosexual marriages. (A similar decision was reached in a Quebec case.) In the Ontario case, the court ruled that to provide a waiting period would have the effect of further denying the couples their constitutional rights. The court redefined the common-law definition of marriage as "the voluntary union for life of two persons to the exclusion of all others," substituting "two persons" for "one man and one woman." The three-person court ruled that the law limiting marriage to heterosexuals violated the Charter of Rights and Freedoms. The court ruled, "The common law definition of marriage is inconsistent with the Charter to the extent that it excludes same-sex couples."

In response, the federal government stated that it would not appeal the decision of the Ontario Court of Appeal and that it would act quickly to legalize same-sex marriage. The Justice Department delivered draft legislation and three constitutional questions to the Supreme Court of Canada. The government has asked the Court to give a non-binding legal opinion on whether the proposed legislation complies with the Charter of Rights. A recent challenge to these rulings was unsuccessful. As of this writing, it appears that marriage rights for gays and lesbians will be encoded in Canada.

are forming families and raising their children, facing many of the same challenges that confront any parent in the twenty-first century. At the same time, however, these parents continue to be profoundly affected by the political and legal climate within which they live and raise their children. Although in Canada same-sex sexual activities conducted in private between consenting adults were decriminalized 35 years ago, the larger social reality continues to be openly hostile. For example, in many jurisdictions in the United States and throughout the world, homosexuality remains a "crime against nature" and criminal charges and imprisonment are still employed (Bowers v. Hardwick, 1986). The recent Vatican pronouncement condemning homosexuality and same-sex marriage and expressing concern about the impact of gay and lesbian parents on their children speaks to the continuing negative atmosphere in which Canadian gay and lesbian families must function. Further, "not being illegal" in Canada did not result in a clear set of legal rights and obligations. Until very recently, lesbians' and gay men's relationships with each other and with their children remained largely outside of the law. Lesbian and gay couples were effectively legal strangers to one another, unable to claim health or workplace benefits, and even prohibited from visiting a dying partner in hospital. This marginalization had profound implications for lesbians and gay men and their children. Co-parents enjoyed few if any legal rights in relation to the children they were parenting and lesbian and gay parents were often denied the social and financial support any adult relationship might need.

Custody and Access Issues

Although it is likely that there have always been lesbian and gay parents, prior to the 1970s, few contested custody in court. For the most part, these were women who had conceived children within heterosexual marriages, prior to either acknowledging or "discovering" their sexual orientation. For many men and women, heterosexual marriage seemed to be the only route to family life. As a result, even when they experienced homosexual desire, many women and men suppressed these feelings in hopes of leading a "normal" life. The end of a heterosexual marriage, falling in love with someone of their own sex, or meeting a lesbian or gay man, could lead men and women to embrace (albeit often in secret) a lesbian or gay life. If there were children of the marriage, however, the discovery of one's sexual orientation presented a major challenge. Fearing public exposure and recognizing that they were almost assured of defeat at the hands of a decidedly homophobic legal system, many relinquished custody in exchange for "liberal" access to their children. On occasion, lesbian mothers were able to make private arrangements with former husbands, often concealing their sexual orientation in order to retain custody of the children. Such arrangements are still common today, although the numbers are impossible to determine, given the necessarily private nature of the agreements.

During the 70s and 80s, with the support of the gay and lesbian movements and of feminist lawyers and friends, lesbians began to contest and, in a limited number of cases, win the custody of their children conceived within heterosexual marriages. In addition, increasing numbers of gay men attempted to secure reasonable access to and, in some instances, custody of their children. Gay fathers' groups began to form in the late 1970s to support these men in their efforts to retain parental ties with their children. In their deliberations in these cases, judges adopted a range of approaches. As author Robert Beargie notes, "at one end of the scale is the *per se* category in which a parent's homosexuality creates an unrebuttable presumption that the parent is unfit" (Beargie, 1988). Such an approach means that homosexuality in and of itself renders a parent unfit, regardless of any evidence to the contrary.

Although (as seen in Box 7.3) in a limited number of American jurisdictions homosexuality per se remains a bar to custody and access, judges in Canada and in many American states have adopted what is known as the **nexus approach**: here, the court seeks to determine what effect, if any, the parent's sexual orientation will have on the well-being of the child (Gross, 1986; Arnup, 1989). In a key 1980 decision in the Ontario Court of Appeal, Mr. Justice Arnup explained:

> In my view homosexuality, either as a tendency, a proclivity, or a practiced way of life is not in itself alone a ground for refusing custody to the parent with respect to whom such evidence is given. The question is and must always be what effect upon the welfare of the children that aspect of the parent's makeup and lifestyle has (Bezaire v. Bezaire, 1980).

In the nexus approach, then, each case is judged on the basis of its evidence. In order to deny custody or access to a homosexual parent, it must be demonstrated that the parent's sexual orientation will have a negative effect upon the child.

How can we resolve the apparent contradiction between the fact that, in most jurisdictions, homosexuality per se is no longer a barrier to custody and access, and the fact that, until very recently, many lesbian and gay parents continued to face discrimination in the courts? The answer lies in large measure in the enormous amount of judicial discretion that is afforded to judges in family court matters. Under current family law provisions in Canada and the United States, the paramount standard applied in custody and access disputes is "the **best interests of the child**."[1] To date, no precise rule or formula exists, however, for determining which household or family arrangement operates in the child's best interests. Until the 1980s in Canada, and still in many jurisdictions in the United States and elsewhere, parental fitness represented a key element of the "best interests" criteria. Judges relied on a variety of factors for determining the "fitness" of each parent, including past and present sexual conduct, the grounds for the termination of the marriage, the guilt or innocence of each party, and the "quality" of the home to assist them in determining the best custody arrangements for the children. These tests were routinely used to brand virtually every lesbian and gay man who attempted to gain custody as an "unfit" parent.

With the passage of family law reform legislation in the 1980s, criteria for determining custody were amended and, as a result, parental behaviour in *and of itself* could no longer be considered a bar to custody. In Ontario, for example, the Children's Law Reform Act specifies that the "best interests of the child" shall be the determining factor. The legislation directs the judge to consider "all the needs and circumstances of the child," including the relationship between the child and those persons claiming custody, the preferences of the child, the current living situation of the child, the plans put forward for the child, the "permanence and stability of the family unit with which it is proposed that the child will live," and the blood or adoptive links between the child and the applicant. The section explicitly states that "the past conduct of a person is not relevant to a determination of an application...unless the conduct is relevant to the ability of the person to act as a parent of a child" (Children's Law Reform Act, 1980, Sec 24).

While the family law reforms might appear to improve a lesbian or gay parent's chances for success, these provisions may be used to rule against their application for custody. First, a judge may refuse to recognize a "homosexual" family as a permanent and stable family unit. Until the June 2003 Ontario

BOX 7.3   UNITED STATES: *LAWRENCE v. TEXAS*

The year 2003 was a year of tumultuous change for lesbians and gay men throughout the western world. Much of this change has been effected at the level of the judiciary, rather than through legislative change. On June 26, 2003, the United States Supreme Court found that the constitutional rights of John Lawrence had been violated when the police entered his apartment, found him engaged in a consensual sexual act with another man, and charged him with a violation of the state sodomy act. The charge was based on outmoded sodomy statutes the legality of which had been confirmed by the infamous 1986 Supreme Court decision in *Bowers v. Hardwick* in which the court determined that sodomy statutes did not violate the privacy provisions of the constitution. Although many of the remaining sodomy statutes do not explicitly target gays, in fact it is only gay men who have been charged under these statutes. On this basis, in a groundbreaking 6–3 decision, the Supreme Court found that the statutes violated Lawrence's right to due process and equal protection under the Constitution.

Sodomy statutes have implications far beyond the regulation of private sexual acts. Such statutes have been used to justify the denial of custody to lesbian mothers and gay fathers, to support bans on gay adoption and foster parenting, to refuse medical and other health care benefits, and to exclude lesbians and gay men from marriage. As Mr. Justice Kennedy wrote in the majority decision, "The stigma this criminal statute imposes is not trivial." Erasing **sodomy laws** may help to undermine discriminatory adoption, custody, and employment decisions and laws—perhaps even including the ban on lesbians and gay men serving openly in the military.

Court of Appeal decision, and in most jurisdictions still, gays and lesbians are not permitted to marry and therefore can not meet this standard heterosexual measure of "stability." The "closeted" nature of many gay and lesbian relationships and the absence until 2001 of a census category to "capture" same-sex partnerships also render it virtually impossible to offer statistical evidence of the longevity of same-sex relationships. Given these obstacles, a lesbian or gay parent may well be unable to demonstrate the "permanence and stability" of his or her "family unit."

Political involvement in the lesbian and gay movements has also been used to find that a lesbian or gay parent is unable to provide a "suitable" home. Coupled with a lack of "discretion" on the part of a lesbian or gay parent, political activity often spells the death of the custody application of a lesbian or gay parent. *Case v. Case*, the first reported Canadian case to deal specifically with the issue of lesbian custody, exemplifies this result. In July 1974, Mr. Justice MacPherson of the Saskatchewan Queen's Bench granted custody of the two children to their father. In considering the significance of the mother's lesbianism, the judge rejected the *per se* approach, noting that "it seems to me that homosexuality on the part of a parent is a factor to be considered along with all the other evidence in the case. It should not be considered a bar in itself to a parent's right to custody." That statement is contradicted by the judge's discussion of the mother's "lifestyle." Describing the father as a "stable and secure and responsible person," the judge added, "I hesitate to put adjectives on the personality of the mother but the evidence shows, I think, that her way of life is irregular." In considering her role as vice president of the local gay club, he added, "I greatly fear that if these children are raised by the mother they will be too much in contact with people of abnormal tastes and proclivities." Thus, while Mrs. Case's lesbianism was not in itself a bar to custody, her lesbian "lifestyle" was. In similar cases, judges have deemed activities like attending rallies and dances, exposing children to other lesbians and gay men, and discussing political issues openly in the home to be negative factors in considering the application of lesbian mothers for custody of their children (*Case v. Case*, 1974).[2]

In marked contrast to the politically active lesbian or gay parent stands the "good" homosexual parent, a person who is "discreet," and appears to the outside world to be a single (read: heterosexual) parent. Discretion on the part of a homosexual parent has repeatedly been cited as the rationale for awarding custody to a lesbian or gay parent. In *K. v. K.*, a 1975 Alberta custody dispute, the judge drew a comparison between Mrs. K. and Mrs. Case (the mother in the preceding case):

> The situation before this court is, in my view, different. Mrs. K. is not a missionary about to convert heterosexuals to her present way of life. She does not regard herself as gay in the sense that heterosexuals are "morose"... Mrs. K. is a good mother and a warm, loving, concerned parent (K. v. K., 1975, p. 64).

Having had the opportunity to examine both Mrs. K. and her partner, the judge concluded, "their relationship will be discreet and will not be flaunted to the children or to the community at large." On that basis, Mrs. K. was awarded custody of her child.

Discretion played an important role in a 1991 Saskatchewan case in which custody of two children was awarded to their aunt, a woman who had

BOX 7.4 RECENT COURT VICTORIES IN THE LEGAL RECOGNITION OF GAY AND LESBIAN RELATIONSHIPS

Jim Egan and Jack Nesbit lived together in a committed relationship from 1948 until their deaths a few months apart in 2000. They shared their financial resources, owned property together, and were devoted to and took care of one another. When Jim reached the age of 65 in 1987, he applied for the spousal allowance for his partner under the Old Age Security Act. His request was turned down on the grounds that Jim and Jack's relationship did not qualify under the definition of spouse given in the Act. The couple challenged the decision on the basis of the Charter of Rights and Freedoms, taking the case to the Supreme Court of Canada. In a landmark ruling, the Court declared that sexual orientation, although not one of the enumerated grounds for protection, was nonetheless an analogous ground for protection against discrimination under the Charter. The Court was deeply divided on the issue, and ultimately decided that, although the Act did discriminate against lesbians and gay men, that discrimination was justified under Section 1 of the Charter. The 1995 decision remains a pivotal one in the struggle for relationship recognition in Canada, as it recognized that discrimination on the basis of sexual orientation was prohibited under the Charter of Rights and Freedoms.

Thus, although Egan and Nesbit were ultimately unsuccessful in their benefits claim, their challenge laid the groundwork for the key legal victories that followed. In determining that sexual orientation was an analogous ground under the Charter or Rights and Freedoms, the Supreme Court of Canada declared that sexual orientation in and of itself was no longer a justification for discrimination.

In a case that built on the decision in *Egan*, *M. v. H.* concerned the rights of lesbian and gay ex-partners to receive spousal support (formerly termed alimony) in the event of the termination of a relationship. The case involved a lesbian couple that had separated following the dissolution of a decade-long relationship. *M.* sought relief and support on the basis of the spousal provisions of Ontario's Family Law Act. Her initial application was turned down because of the opposite-sex definition of spouse contained in the Act. On May 20, 1999, the Supreme Court of Canada declared that the opposite-sex definition of spouse in Ontario's Family Law Act was unconstitutional. In its decision, the Court gave the Ontario Government six months to amend the offending law. The case was a landmark because for the first time the Supreme Court ruled that a law was unconstitutional on the grounds that it failed to treat same-sex couples equally. In response to the decision, the Ontario government passed "An Act to Amend Certain Statutes to Ensure their Constitutionality Because of the Supreme Court Decision in *M. v. H*." The Ontario Conservative government was reluctant to pass the legislation, noting that they were only introducing the legislation to comply with the Supreme Court decision. Provinces across the country amended their legislation with varying degrees of reluctance.

been involved in a lesbian relationship for 12 years. In discussing the relationship between the two women, the judge noted:

> I found these two women to be rather straightforward. Their relationship does not meet with the approval of all members of society in general. They were neither apologetic nor aggressive about their relationship. They are very discreet. They make no effort to recruit others to their way of living. They make no special effort to associate with others who pursue that lifestyle. In short, D. and H. mind their own business and go their own way in a discreet and dignified way (D.M. v. M.D., 1991, p. 672).

Although these observations may seem antiquated, the attitudes they reflect have by no means disappeared from the Canadian landscape. Comments like "I'm not homophobic; but why do they have to flaunt their sexuality?" can still be heard in corridors, lunchrooms, and courtrooms across the country. It should be noted that commonplace behaviour like holding hands in public, embracing upon first seeing a loved one, or talking openly about one's life partner have all been considered "flaunting" when placed in the context of a lesbian or gay relationship.

On occasion, where concern has arisen that homosexuality may negatively affect the children, a judge has attempted to minimize its effects by preventing the lesbian or gay parent from engaging in an open, same-sex relationship. In a classic 1980 Ontario case, the trial judge ordered a lesbian mother to live alone. "I am attempting to improve the situation," he explained, "and this includes negativing any open, declared, and avowed lesbian, or homosexual relationship" (MacMahon, 1980). When Mrs. B. failed to meet this condition, the original order granting her custody of her two children was quickly reversed.

Imposing such conditions has been a common practice in cases involving a lesbian or gay parent, although a far less frequent occurrence since the success of lesbian and gay Charter claims in the 1990s. The practice is based on the assumption that a parent's homosexuality may negatively affect the child, but that those effects can be overcome if the parent meets certain conditions, such as not co-habiting or sharing a bedroom with a lover, and not showing affection of any kind in front of the child. On occasion, judges have ordered that visitation take place only in the absence of the same-sex partner. Such practices are more in evidence in cases involving gay men than lesbian mothers, perhaps because of the incorrect associations of gay men with pedophilia and child abuse. Author Paula Brantner (1991) explains the unfairness of these conditions, "Heterosexual parents are not routinely asked to forgo sexual relationships with other adults to obtain custody of their children—lesbian and gay parents are" (p.105). The impact of these conditions on the lives of lesbian and gay parents is severe. Brantner (1991) notes, "...gay parents are forced to make impossible and intolerable decisions. Parents who fail to comply with the court's restrictions may lose their children. If they do comply, they may lose their partners or the ability to be openly gay and to maintain contact with other gay persons, which takes its own psychological toll" (p. 107).

The judicial effort to limit or terminate a lesbian or gay relationship is particularly disturbing in light of the research suggesting that lesbian mothers' psychological health and well-being is associated with their ability to be open about their sexual orientation "with their employer, ex-husband, children, and friends, and with their degree of feminist activism" (Patterson, 1996, p. 281). As well, living with a partner was, not surprisingly, correlated with both parental happiness and financial stability, factors that, presumably, would also contribute to the well-being of the children.

The contradiction between the rejection of the *per se* approach and the setting of punitive conditions is evident in dozens of cases involving lesbian and gay parents. A 1989 British Columbia decision provides particularly dramatic evidence of the persistence of these practices. Ian Jeffrey Saunders enjoyed regular access with his child for four years following the dissolution of his marriage until his ex-wife discovered that, in the words of Judge Wetmore, "the father had entered into a complete homosexual relationship with one E.L." Following this discovery, the mother refused to allow any overnight access. In the initial hearing on the case, the judge decided against the father, largely based on the fact that the men were living in a single-room apartment. Shortly thereafter, the men's relationship ended and access resumed informally. Eventually, the two men re-established their relationship, and moved into a two-bedroom apartment. On the basis of the improved accommodation, the father applied once again for overnight and holiday access. His claim was rejected by Provincial Court Judge B.K. Davis, who chose to ignore the social worker's conclusion that "the two [men] would be as discreet as heterosexual couples when children are in the home." Saunders' appeal of that judgment was dismissed.

In his judgment dismissing the appeal, Judge Wetmore noted, "Saunders and Leblanc are unwilling to hide their relationship from the child, by LeBlanc being absent during overnight visits." "Surely it cannot be argued that the exposure of a child to unnatural relationships is in the best interests of that child of tender years," the appellate judge opined. Noting that he was charged with the responsibility of assessing "community standards as reflected by the thinking members of society," he concluded:

> I am not convinced, and neither was the Provincial Court Judge, that the exposure of a child of tender years to an unnatural relationship of a parent to any degree, is in the best interests of the development and natural attainment of maturity of that child. That is the issue, not the rights of homosexuals (Saunders v. Saunders, 1989, sec. 368).

As these cases suggest, regardless of how "good" a parent a lesbian or gay man may be, they may find it difficult to be a "good enough" parent unless they are willing to abandon or, at the very least, hide their same-sex relationship. As *Saunders v. Saunders* reveals, lesbian and gay parents must be willing to forgo the possibility of a committed sexual relationship, at least while the children are present. Their children must be their first, and indeed their only priority, even if it means the demise of their committed homosexual relationships. As Judge MacKinnon noted in denying custody to a lesbian mother in a 1987 British Columbia case, in resuming cohabitation with her partner "without leave of the court," "she left no doubt as to the priority of her relationship with her companion. It was the paramount consideration. She wanted custody. It was, however, not at the sacrifice of the homosexual relationship" (Elliott v. Elliott, 1987).

These judicial approaches present lesbian and gay parents seeking court-ordered custody with a number of difficult choices. If, for example, a woman presents herself in court as an "avowed lesbian," if she admits to coming out at work or at her children's school, she stands less chance of winning custody of her children, especially if she meets a determined challenge from her ex-husband. Within this legal context, most lesbians "choose" to act as "straight" as possible to win custody of their children. Such strategies tell us a great deal about the attitudes and prejudices of the courts.

Within the last two decades, the legal status of lesbian and gay parents has improved considerably, notably with the advent of the Charter of Rights and Freedoms and moves toward equality for lesbians and gay men. On this measure, Canada is far ahead of most jurisdictions in the United States (e.g., the U.S. has no federal protection against discrimination for lesbians and gay men, even in areas of employment and services). Nonetheless, we must bear in mind that attitudes, practices, and policies are apt to be more liberal in urban areas with significant gay and lesbian populations. Lesbian mothers in small or remote regions of Canada continue to report experiencing discrimination at the hands of judges, neighbours, and ex-husbands, treatment reminiscent of the experiences from the 1970s and 1980s.

Gay Fathers

Although both lesbians and gay men are affected by homophobic laws and policies, gender remains an important factor in determining the impact of family law on our lives. As feminist legal scholar Susan Boyd and I have argued elsewhere, "[i]n the realm of reproduction, women and men, regardless of their sexual orientation, are undeniably constituted differently. Indeed, for lesbians and gay men, these differences may be even more significant than for heterosexual men and women" (Arnup and Boyd, 1995). Lesbians can choose to conceive and give birth to children. In contrast, gay men cannot father a child without the intimate cooperation of a woman, in either a co-parenting or a surrogacy relationship. These fundamental biological differences mean that issues such as access to **donor insemination** and other reproductive technologies may be of primary concern to lesbians, while **surrogacy**, foster parenting, and adoption may be priorities for gay men seeking to become parents. Furthermore, because women tend to be the primary caregivers within heterosexual marriages,[3] custody has been the paramount legal issue for lesbian mothers upon divorce, while access and visitation have been the main areas of contention for gay fathers.

It has been argued that gay men face much more judicial resistance to their parental relationships than lesbian mothers. Darryl Wishard claims, "more courts have granted lesbian mothers the right to custody of their children than have granted custody to homosexual fathers" (Wishard, 1989). Perhaps the reason for this discrepancy lies in the fact that many gay men choose not to seek custody, either because they are afraid that they will be unsuccessful, or because they, like their heterosexual counterparts, do not wish to have primary care and custody of their children.[4]

It is clear that in the past 20 years the spectre of HIV and AIDS has been a deterrent to gay men's efforts to forge relationships with their children following separation and divorce.[5] This would appear to be the case even when a father is not HIV positive, presumably because of the strong ideological connection between gay men and AIDS and the resulting presumption that gay fathers will inevitably expose their children to the virus. In judicial decisions, particularly in the United States, HIV-positive fathers have been ordered to refrain from kissing their children and to visit with their children only under supervision. A California court ordered a gay man to be tested for HIV before visitation was determined.[6] While in this respect, at least, gay fathers face an almost insurmountable burden of proof, I would argue that, despite the vast discrepancy in the rate of HIV infection between lesbians and gay men, the custodial claims of both gay men and lesbians are hampered by the "automatic" connection in the public (and judicial) mind between homosexuality and AIDS, as well as by the alleged (and false) connections between homosexuality and **pedophilia**.[7]

The Lesbian Baby Boom

While in the past most lesbian mothers who came to public attention were women who had conceived and given birth to children within heterosexual partnerships or marriages, in the past 20 years, increasing numbers of lesbians have chosen to conceive and bear children, either on their own or within a lesbian relationship.

Lesbians who wish to conceive through alternative insemination can apply for services through a fertility clinic, using an anonymous or known donor, or they can undertake a home insemination. Since the late 1970s, an undetermined number of lesbians have requested artificial insemination services at infertility clinics and sperm banks across North America. Many of these requests were denied once the applicant's sexual orientation was revealed. In some instances women were informed that the clinic had decided not to inseminate *any* single woman, claiming that they feared single mothers would launch child support suits against the medical facility should the insemination be successful or that they would become embroiled in a legal contest should the lesbian couple's relationship subsequently dissolve (Arnup, 1994).

To date, no court decisions have been issued with respect to infertility clinics that discriminate against single women or lesbians. In Canada, the British Columbia Council of Human Rights upheld a complaint in August 1995. The complaint, alleging discrimination on the basis of sexual orientation and family status, was filed by Sandra Benson and Tracy Potter against Dr. Gerald Korn for his refusal to provide artificial insemination services to them solely on the grounds that they are lesbians ("Lesbian Couple," 1993). The B.C. Council of Human Rights awarded Benson and Potter $2500 as compensation for emotional injury and $896.44 for expenses.[8] The B.C. Supreme Court found that there were no grounds to review the decision and dismissed the physician's application for judicial review (*Korn v. Potter*, 1996). Although applicable only in British Columbia, the decision represents an important precedent in the struggle for the provision of donor insemination services for lesbians.

Attaining access to donor insemination is only the first step in the struggle for lesbian parents. When donor insemination is carried out through a clinic, the identity of the donor remains unknown. As a result, in registering the birth of the resulting offspring, a parent faces a blank space where the identity of "father" is requested. In the heterosexual context, a woman merely inserts her husband's name and the form is processed without question. For lesbians, the matter is not quite so simple. For some time, untold numbers of lesbian couples have attempted to write the name of the lesbian co-parent in the spot designated "father." Repeatedly those forms have been rejected as invalid. In the late 1990s, two B.C. couples challenged this practice. Both Verna Ann Gill and her partner Margaret Maher, and Bren Murray and her partner Karen Popoff completed their child's birth registration forms by filling in the name of the non-biological co-parent in place of the name of the biological father. The Vital Statistics Branch rejected both submissions. The women challenged the policy, lodging complaints with the B.C. Human Rights Tribunal. The Tribunal ruled in their favour in August 2001, determining that they had the right to register both of their names on the birth certificates of their children, thereby eliminating the need for a second parent adoption. This decision, which is not binding on other jurisdictions, would enable lesbian parents to avoid lengthy and costly legal proceedings in an effort to protect their families.

Donor Insemination and the Rights of Sperm Donors Since many hospital clinics have not been welcoming, it is not surprising that lesbians have often chosen to make private insemination arrangements. In addition to technical difficulties and potential health and safety concerns, one of the many issues faced by lesbian parents using private arrangements is the legal status of the sperm donor. In the context of heterosexual marriage, the courts recognize the child as the legitimate offspring of the recipient's husband, provided he has consented to the insemination procedure. The husband is thereby accorded all the rights and obligations of a legal parent. Most legislation now specifies that the paternal rights of the husband replace the parental rights and obligations of the donor.

The issues are considerably more complex in the case of a lesbian or unmarried heterosexual woman and a known donor. In such instances, women who arrange a private insemination—most of whom are lesbians— face the risk of paternity claims by the man who donated sperm. A number of American cases involving lesbian mothers and sperm donors have been reported during the past two decades. In the vast majority of these cases, sperm donors seeking paternity rights have had at least some of their claims upheld by the courts. The decisions have ranged from placing the sperm donor's name on the child's birth certificate to granting access rights ("Sperm Donor," 1991; see also Arnup, 1994; Arnup and Boyd, 1995). Such decisions have been made *even* in cases where the insemination was performed by a licenced practitioner, thereby ignoring relevant legislation that extinguished the rights and obligations of donors.

While all of the cases to date have involved only the issues of access and a declaration of paternity, the implications extend far beyond those claims. A declaration of paternity can accord any or all of the following: sole or joint physical or legal custody, visitation, decision-making in such areas as education, religion, and health care, custody in the event of the mother's death, denial of permission to change residence or to adopt, obligation to provide child support, and inclusion of the donor's name as father on the child's birth certificate (National Center for Lesbian Rights, 1993). As the National Center for Lesbian Rights has noted, "in our system of law there are only two options. Either the donor is merely a donor, with no parental rights or relationship with the child whatsoever, or he is a father, with all of his parental rights intact. There are no gray areas in the law here, and, when in doubt, the courts tend to grant donors full parental rights in cases involving single mothers" (National Center for Lesbian Rights, 1993, p. 543). That fact was made abundantly clear in a recent London, Ontario case, in which a lesbian couple with a known donor sought an order recognizing the parental roles of all three parents. Since the donor had already been recognized as a legal parent on the child's birth certificate (along with the biological mother) and the statute contemplates that a child can have, at most, two parents, the court refused to extend parental rights to the lesbian co-mother (see *A.A. v. B.B.*, 2003).

The issues involved here are clearly complex ones that involve important issues of public policy. Can a child have more than two parents? Can a person be a parent without having full parental rights? Does every child have the right to a father? As increasing numbers of lesbians and gay men seek to become parents, through a variety of means, these issues will continue to appear before the courts.

Lesbian Co-Parents In marked contrast to sperm donors, the legal status of **non-biological lesbian mothers** has historically been denied by the courts in both Canada and the United States (Polikoff, 1990–91). Disregarding non-biological mothers' often substantial contributions to childcare and financial support, courts repeatedly refused to grant their claims for visitation rights upon dissolution of the lesbian relationship or custody rights upon the death of the biological mother.

In an early Canadian case (*Anderson v. Luoma*) dealing with this issue, the judge rejected a lesbian mother's application for support for herself and her children born during a relationship with her former lesbian partner. The court sided with the ex-partner on the grounds that she had no legal obligation to support the mother or the children. Indeed, the judge appeared taken aback by the ex-partner's stance, noting that she downplayed her involvement with the children "almost to the point of being a disinterested bystander." Echoing sentiments heard in heterosexual divorces, the ex-partner suggested that the mother had been on a "frolic of her own when she had the children." Despite the court's conclusion that the lesbian couple and their children had "worked and played as a 'family like' unit," the judge did not impose a financial obligation for support on the ex-partner. As a result, as Karen Andrews has pointed out, "*Anderson v. Luoma* stands for the unhappy proposition that a lesbian can behave as despicably as a man who evades her parenting and child support obligations and because she is outside the statutes she can get away with it" (Andrews, 1995, p. 367).

The second Canadian case reverses this direction. In 1997, Margaret Buist, a well-known London, Ontario, lawyer and feminist, sought sole or joint custody of the child she and her partner had been raising since his birth, as well as an order that he not be removed from the province (Ontario) where he and his mother resided. Her former partner counterclaimed for child support, as well as for sole custody. The judge awarded the biological mother sole custody of the child and permission to relocate to British Columbia to pursue a job opportunity. Buist was ordered to pay child support in the amount of $450 per month, and was granted generous access to the child. The case was the first in which a lesbian co-parent had been ordered to pay child support (Schmitz, 1997).

As more and more lesbian couples become parents, courts have increasingly been faced with the issue of the rights and responsibilities of non-biological lesbian mothers. Many areas of both children's and parents' lives are affected, including medical authorization, visitation, support, custody upon dissolution of the parental relationship, and guardianship in the event of the death of the biological mother. In the absence of access to marriage rights, and in an effort to secure legal rights for the non-biological parent, lesbian parents have sought a variety of legal mechanisms including guardianship, joint custody, and **second parent adoption**.

Second Parent Adoption

Second parent adoption allows a "new" parent to assume rights and responsibilities without requiring the original parent of that sex to forfeit his or her parenting status. Lesbian and gay parents have increasingly used such an option. In May 1995, lesbian parents in Ontario won an important legal victory when Judge Nevins granted second parent adoptions to four lesbian couples (Re. K., 1995). In a far-reaching decision, Judge Nevins rejected all of the standard arguments used to deny parental rights to homosexuals, concluding:

> When one reflects on the seemingly limitless parade of neglected, abandoned and abused children who appear before our courts in protection cases daily, all of whom have been in the care of heterosexual parents in a "traditional" family structure, the suggestion that it might not ever be in the best interests of these children to be raised by loving, caring and committed parents, who might happen to be lesbian or gay, is nothing short of ludicrous (Re. K., 1995, p. 708).

Ontario thus joined the growing list of jurisdictions in which second parent adoptions can be granted to lesbian and gay couples. Although that case has now been superseded by legislation in the area, it remains an important statement about the merits of lesbian and gay families, particularly in the midst of renewed opposition.

Adoption and Foster Parenting

In addition to giving birth to children, for untold years, lesbians and gay men have become parents through adoption and foster parenting. Unfortunately, legal measures designed to limit homosexuals' access to children because of fear and prejudice have forced prospective adoptive or foster parents to present themselves to social service agencies as single individuals, regardless of their actual relationship status. The question of adoption reveals in a dramatic fashion that many segments of society still harbour irrational and unfounded fears and prejudices about the dangers posed by relationships between lesbians or gay men and children. Those fears persist despite the almost complete lack of evidence of child abuse perpetrated by lesbians or gay men. Indeed, side by side with marriage, adoption, especially "stranger" or third-party adoption, is the most contentious issue in the struggle for lesbian and gay rights.

During the 1990s, with the emergence of anti-discrimination policies and legislation, lesbians and gay men began to successfully adopt children, both privately and through state agencies, both from within Canada and internationally. In 1996, a new adoption act was proclaimed in B.C. that allowed all adults over the age of 19 to apply to adopt a child and permitted a child to be placed for adoption with one adult or two adults jointly, thus removing the barriers that discriminated against common-law and same-sex couples. In all cases, the "best interests of the child" are deemed to be the sole determinant of an adoption order. Similar initiatives have taken place in Ontario, Quebec, Manitoba, Alberta (only second parent adoption), Nova Scotia (court-imposed), Saskatchewan, and the Yukon, both through legislation and court decisions. In the Yukon, only spouses can adopt (although the law is silent on the meaning of spouses). At the time of this writing, lesbians and gay men in New Brunswick, Prince Edward Island, and Nunavut are prohibited from adoption. In 1999, Newfoundland passed a law allowing adoption to same-sex partners but it never received royal assent.

Because of the shortage of newborn babies available for adoption within Canada, increasing numbers of lesbians and gay men are turning to international adoption—a costly and time-consuming option. In China and many Latin American countries, lesbians and gay men encounter profound homophobia, and are forced to present themselves as single (heterosexual) parents in order to secure an adoption.

Foster Parenting[9]   The first openly acknowledged placements of children in gay or lesbian foster homes were of teenagers who had been evicted from their families because they were lesbian or gay. As well, "hard-to-place" or special needs children were sometimes placed with a single lesbian or gay man or same-sex couple. In contrast to adoption, however, where there is generally a surplus of applicants for most children, in fostering, there are fewer and fewer applicants wishing to foster children. Thus, agencies across North America are often more "flexible" in their views of appropriate foster parents, particularly for so-called hard-to-place children, such as children who were born HIV-positive.

As with adoption, the number of lesbian and gay men who have fostered children is impossible to determine. There is no law in any province or territory in Canada that prohibits lesbians or gay men from fostering children. However, officials (case workers and so on) with local agencies operate with enormous discretion in this area. In recent decades, the shortage of appropriate foster parents (largely the result of women's increased labour force participation and the decline in the number of stay-at-home mothers) has led agencies to approve foster parent arrangements for single parents. In some areas, however, if a foster parent is discovered to be gay or lesbian, that arrangement is terminated. In 1997, for example, Alberta's Social Services Department announced that it would no longer place foster children with Mrs. T., who had been a foster parent for 17 years, because they discovered she was a lesbian ("Gay Kept," 1997). Mrs. T. launched an appeal of the decision. In 1999, Alberta Social Services Minister Lyle Oberg announced that the government would allow children to be placed in same-sex homes, provided that the placement officer could demonstrate that the placement was

BOX 7.5 HOMOPHOBIA AND THE U.S. COURTS: IMPLICATIONS FOR CANADIAN GAY AND LESBIAN FAMILIES?

During the past 10 years, a number of cases have highlighted the differences between the Canadian and the American judicial approaches to lesbian and gay families. In September 1993, Richmond, Virginia, Judge Buford M. Parsons Jr. awarded custody of Tyler Doustou to his maternal grandmother, removing the 2-year-old child from the care of his biological mother and her lesbian partner. His ruling was based solely on the fact that the child's biological mother is a lesbian. In his judgment, Parsons relied on a 1985 Virginia Supreme Court case that found homosexual parents to be unfit parents with no custodial rights to their children (*Roe v. Roe*, 1985).[10] In that case, the court had found that living with a lesbian or gay parent placed "an intolerable burden" on a child. The court also took notice of the fact that same-sex sexual activities were illegal in Virginia (under the existing sodomy statute), thus rendering every lesbian and gay parent a potential lawbreaker. While Bottoms was successful in her initial appeal of the decision (see Wartik, 1993),[11] that ruling was overturned by the Virginia Supreme Court, which determined that the appeals court had not given enough attention to the facts of the case (*Bottoms v. Bottoms*, 1995).[12] A bid to appeal that ruling was unsuccessful and Tyler remains in the custody of his grandmother. Sharon Bottoms's efforts to expand visitation with Tyler have been thwarted, as Judge Parsons instead tightened visitation, changing weekly visits to every other weekend, and forbidding Bottoms's partner to have any contact with the child (GLPCI Network, 1996).

An equally dramatic decision was reached in a Pensacola, Florida, contest between a lesbian mother and her former husband, a convicted murderer. In August 1995, Judge Joseph Tarbuck granted custody of an 11-year-old girl to her father, John Ward, a man who murdered his first wife, apparently in the midst of a bitter custody dispute. In removing the girl from her mother's home, where she had been living since her parents' separation in 1987, Judge Tarbuck declared that it was important to give the girl a chance to live in "a non-lesbian world" ("Judge Gives," 1996). Apparently, in the eyes of the court, a murderer was preferable to a "sex deviant." The decision was upheld on appeal.

In 2002, the Alabama Supreme Court unanimously agreed to grant custody of the children of a lesbian mother to their father, whose disciplinary practices had been deemed equivalent to violence. The Chief Justice described homosexual behaviour as "a crime in Alabama, a crime against nature, an inherent evil and an act so heinous that it defies one's ability to describe it" (*D.H. v. H.H.*, 2002).

in the child's best interests. Social workers who place children in lesbian and gay foster homes, however, are required to provide a written rationale for their decision within two working days of the placement (Jeffs, 1999).[13]

For gay men, for whom fewer avenues to parenting are available, these barriers may be especially punishing. But the ban has important implications for the children involved as well. It is not uncommon for foster parents to decide to adopt a child in their care. If their foster parents are unable to adopt them, then children fostered by gay parents risk "bouncing" around the child welfare system for their entire childhoods, unable to secure a permanent home. It is difficult to see the logic behind a decision that determines that gay men and women are eligible to foster children and not to adopt them.

Surrogacy

In recent years, an increasing number of individuals and couples have turned to surrogacy in order to bring a child into their lives. While it raises a number of complex ethical and legal issues, surrogacy offers the opportunity for at least one of the parents to have a biological connection to the child. There are two types of surrogacy: traditional surrogacy, in which a surrogate mother is artificially inseminated, either with sperm from the intended father or from an anonymous donor, and carries the baby to term; and gestational surrogacy, during which an egg is removed from the mother and fertilized with the sperm of the intended father or anonymous donor. The fertilized egg is then implanted in the womb of the surrogate mother who carries the baby to term. This method offers the potential for both members of a lesbian couple to have a genetic connection to a child, as it enables one member of the couple to donate her egg and the other to carry the baby to term. The couple could then apply for a joint adoption to secure their legal relationships to the child.

Surrogacy is a particularly attractive option for gay men who cannot otherwise have a genetic connection to a child. Since 1996, the website *growinggenerations.com* has been facilitating surrogacy arrangements within the gay community, assisting hundreds of lesbians and gay men to have children. Surrogacy arrangements are costly, however, ranging from $50 000 (US) for traditional surrogacy, to $70 000 (US) for gestational surrogacy. Once again, legislation (Bill C-13) governing the sale of reproductive matter may limit the use of this practice in Canada, as surrogacy is among the practices that will be banned.

CHILDREN IN GAY AND LESBIAN FAMILIES: WHAT THE RESEARCH REVEALS

New means by which gays and lesbians may choose to become parents, ever more powerful gay and lesbian rights movements, and an increasing presence of gay and lesbian themes and celebrities in the media have all contributed to growing public awareness of gays and lesbians. Newspapers, television shows, and movies almost routinely acknowledge gay and lesbian perspectives. Ellen DeGeneres not only "comes out" in her television series but also includes lesbian romance as a theme. Talk show host Rosie O'Donnell comes out as both a lesbian and a devoted lesbian mother. *Queer as Folks, Will and Grace*, and other gay-themed television series suggest that gay and lesbian reality has been accepted as part of the mainstream. However, controversy continues to swirl, particularly about the presence of children in the lives of gays and lesbians. When the public debate centres on custody rights, fostering, and adoption, homophobes are heard making dire pronouncements about the fate of the children. Whatever the root causes of this fear—the unfounded association of gays with pedophilia, an extension of the stigmatization associated with AIDS, or a longing for the "simple" old days of patriarchal heterosexuality—the research conducted over the past 30 years strongly demonstrates that children are not imperilled by living in a gay or lesbian family.

Despite the "lesbian baby boom" and the increasing visibility of lesbian and gay parents, the research on gay parenting remains limited. Virtually all of the existing research is American or British. The only Canadian research on lesbian and gay families consists of case law analysis of custody cases involving lesbian and gay parents (Arnup, 1989; Gross, 1986) and a number of small, qualitative studies involving in-depth interviews with lesbian parents (Epstein, 1993; Kirby, 2000; Nelson, 1996). Thus, I will rely primarily on the American psychological literature that has emerged in the past two decades.

When researchers compare the parenting skills and values of homosexual parents to heterosexual parents, they found them to be essentially the same. In a comprehensive article that reviewed the existing studies of gay and lesbian parenting skills, psychologists Green and Bozett concluded that the homes of lesbians and gays were as healthy—morally, physically, and psychologically—as those of non-gays. Social science research conducted during the 1990s has supported this finding.

Numerous studies have demonstrated that, on a range of measures, lesbian mothers appear to be as psychologically healthy as their heterosexual counterparts (Lewin, 1993). Furthermore, studies have confirmed that lesbian mothers are as capable of effective parenting as heterosexual mothers. In a 1995 study, psychologist David Flaks and his colleagues compared 15 lesbian-mother-led families and 15 heterosexual-parent families. All of the lesbian families were "planned lesbian families;" that is, families comprised of a lesbian couple who made the decision to have children as a couple—after coming out. On a Parent Awareness Skills Survey (PASS), the lesbian mothers were found to have "more parenting awareness skills than [the] heterosexual parents" in the study (Flaks, Ficher, Masterpasqua, and Joseph, 1995). No other significant differences were found between the lesbian mothers and heterosexual parents or their children.

While relatively little scholarly attention has been given to gay fathers, the studies that do exist indicate that gay fathers, like lesbian mothers, are caring, loving, capable, and committed parents. In a 1999 article, Jerry J. Bigner, a prominent researcher and author in the field, concludes, "It has been clearly established by a number of investigations using a variety of measurement methods that sexual orientation of an adult is an invalid variable in determining the ability to parent children and provide for their care effectively" (Bigner, 1999, p. 64). Reviewing the studies conducted in the past two decades, Bigner (1999) reports that the parenting styles and behaviours of gay fathers have been "consistently found to be similar to heterosexual fathers in many respects" (p. 64). "When differences are noted, the distinguishing factors tend to depict gay fathers in a positive manner in comparison with heterosexual fathers." Gay fathers, for example, were found to be "more astute to children's needs, more nurturant in providing caregiving, and less traditional than heterosexual fathers." "Gay fathers are repeatedly described in studies as having warm and positive relationships with their children." Their home lives were described "as stable and highly structured," and their parenting style strict but not authoritarian (Bigner, 1999, p. 64). Other researchers have reported similar findings in the area (Bozett, 1989).

Such results should not be surprising given the fact that, for lesbians and gay couples, the decision to become parents is one that requires considerable planning and consideration. As author Cheri Pies (1990) notes, for gay men and lesbians, "[d]eciding to become a parent is a conscious choice; it rarely happens by accident. It is often a carefully orchestrated undertaking, with focused attention to the personal, social, psychological, ethical and practical considerations" (p. 139). Pies also notes that all of the methods used by lesbian and gay parents are ones that require "a considerable amount of planning and co-ordination."

Given the similarities between the parenting abilities of heterosexuals and gay men and lesbians, it is not surprising that research has demonstrated that children of lesbian and gay parents are not significantly different from other children. As psychologist Charlotte Patterson (1993) notes, "There is no evidence to suggest that psychosocial development among children of gay men or lesbians is compromised in any respect relative to that among offspring of heterosexual parents" (p. 1036). Many other authors have echoed these findings.

In short, not one study has found children of gay or lesbian parents to be disadvantaged in any significant respect relative to children of heterosexual parents. Although small sample sizes and the difficulty of obtaining random samples limit the impact of particular studies, the collective weight of the research unquestionably supports the conclusion that children of gay or lesbian parents are as happy, healthy, and well-adjusted as their counterparts raised by heterosexual parents.

Study upon study has confirmed that children's psychological development is not negatively affected by growing up in a lesbian or gay household. In a 1998 study, Chan et al. examined the relationship between family structure (number of parents in the household; sexual orientation of the parents etc.) and family process (parental depression, stress, quality of the parental relationship) and the psychological development of children in 80 families who used donor insemination. The study's results indicated, "children's outcomes were unrelated to parental sexual orientation." Indeed, "[o]n the basis of assessments of children's social competence and behavior problems...it was impossible to distinguish children born to and brought up by lesbian versus heterosexual parents." "In short," the authors concluded, "our results are consistent with the view that qualities of relationships within families are far more important than parental sexual orientation as a predictor of children's adjustment" (Chan, Raboy, and Patterson, 1998, p. 454).[14]

European researchers came to a similar conclusion in a 1997 study. Comparing 30 families headed by two lesbian parents with a child aged 4 to 8 years of old and conceived through donor insemination (DI) to matched groups of 38 heterosexual-parent families with children of the same age conceived through DI, and 30 heterosexual-parent families with children who were not conceived through DI, researchers found no differences in the behavioural adjustment of the children in the three groups. "The most important conclusion emerging from all these findings with regard to family functioning is that children in lesbian mother families have been growing up for the first years of their lives in a warm and secure family environment, just like the children in the heterosexual control groups" (Brewaeys, Ponjaert, Van Hall, and Golombok, 1997, p. 1356).

In a number of articles resulting from the Bay Area Families Study, Charlotte Patterson (1998) reported similar findings. The study involved 37 participating families, with a total of 66 lesbian mothers. Using a variety of standard measures, Patterson found that the children scored within the normal range for all measures (Patterson, 1998). The only area in which the children of lesbian mothers differed (while still remaining within the normal range) was in self-concept. Children of lesbian mothers "reported more reactions to stress (e.g., feeling angry, scared, or upset), but also a greater sense of well-being (e.g., feeling joyful, content, and comfortable with themselves) than did same-aged children of heterosexual mothers." Patterson suggested that this measure may reflect the fact, "children of lesbian mothers were better able to acknowledge both positive and negative aspects of their emotional experience" (Patterson, 1998, p. 159).

Researchers Fiona Tasker and Susan Golombok conducted one of the most comprehensive studies, the British Longitudinal Study of Lesbian Mother Families. In their initial 1976–77 study, Golombok and Tasker compared a group of 27 lesbian mothers and their 39 children with a single-parent group of equal size. They found no significant differences between the children of lesbian mothers and those of heterosexual single mothers with respect to emotional difficulties, conduct difficulties, unsociability, or hyperactivity (Golombok, Spencer, and Rutter, 1983). A follow-up study conducted in 1990–92 with the children raised by lesbian mothers found no differences between the children (now young adults) raised by lesbian mothers and those from heterosexual family backgrounds on the measures of anxiety, depression, or stress. Furthermore, "young adults from lesbian families were no more likely than those from heterosexual single-parent backgrounds to have sought professional help for mental health problems" (Tasker and Golombok, 1996, p. 212).

Like psychological development, social development and peer relations do not appear to be negatively affected by growing up in a gay or lesbian family. While most observers have assumed that the children of lesbian and gay parents will experience harassment and peer pressure because of their parents' sexual orientation, the social science research on this issue does not in fact bear out this supposition.

In the first phase of the British Longitudinal Study of the children of lesbian parents referred to above, "[n]o differences in quality of friendships were identified between children raised in lesbian mother families and those raised in heterosexual mother families" (Tasker and Golombok, 1996, p. 86). In their follow-up study with the young adults raised by lesbian mothers, they found, "[y]oung adults from lesbian mother families were no more likely to remember peer group hostility than were those from heterosexual single-parent homes. Furthermore, for those who reported peer group hostility, there was no group difference in the recollected seriousness of the episode" (Tasker and Golombok, 1996, p. 87). Numerous studies have reported similar results (Huggins, 1989; Hotved and Mandel, 1982).

Anecdotal evidence and in-depth interviews with small samples of children of lesbian mothers have found reports of teasing and the fear of peer harassment (Arnup, 1998). A Nova Scotia study of lesbian families included the following statement by a child of lesbian mothers:

> Having gay parents isn't always easy for me. I often hide the fact that I have two mothers instead of a "normal" mother and father or even a single parent. Kids at school or camp, even fairly close friends, say things like, "Oh gross, she's a lesbian," or "He's gay," and the people around them laugh. I feel really awkward at times like this because if I laugh, it's like I'm laughing at my parents for being who they are, and if I don't laugh, the kids will make fun of me (Nova Scotia Advisory Council on the Status of Women, 1996, p. 26).

This child added, "On the other hand, having two mothers is wonderful. I'm very close to both my biological mother and my non-biological mother. I wouldn't give either of them up for anything" (Nova Scotia Advisory Council on the Status of Women, 1996, p. 26).

In her 1993 article, Ann O'Connell reported that, among the teenagers she interviewed, fears of losing friends or being judged were common. Many of the teens resorted to "secret-keeping and guardedness, in order to maintain friendships." As one girl reported, "In high school, constantly as soon as the subject changed to moms, you were on your toes about everything... Sometimes I would try to change the subject" (O'Connell, 1993, p. 290).

How can we explain the apparent discrepancy between the results of the research studies and anecdotal evidence? First, the reports of teasing (or, more accurately, fears of teasing) are often made by children who have recently changed schools or neighbourhoods and/or by children whose mother has recently "come out" as a lesbian. These children are attempting to integrate the reality of their family into a new and unknown environment. Children who were born into "planned lesbian families" may experience fewer fears in this area, as the nature of their family is more widely known and accepted.

British researchers Tasker and Golombok remind us, "being bullied by peers is not an uncommon experience for schoolchildren" (Tasker and Golombok, 1997, pp. 87–88). A parent's appearance, race, accent, style of dress, even age, can be perceived as a potential source of embarrassment by a child, and can, in fact, become a source of ridicule. We ought not to overestimate the uniqueness of such teasing among the children of lesbian and gay parents. Furthermore, we must bear in mind that all of the existing studies found no significant differences in self-esteem or the quality of peer relationships between the children of lesbian and gay parents and the children raised by heterosexual parents.

Not only does the research suggest that psychological and social development is not impeded, it also raises the possibility of positive outcomes. The experience of being "different" may, in fact, have beneficial effects upon the children of lesbian and gay parents. Some studies have suggested that these children grow up to be more tolerant of others and show a greater sensitivity to issues of difference and diversity. The report on lesbian families from Nova Scotia makes the following observation: "Because of their own experiences of growing up in a homophobic culture, the children of lesbians can be more sensitive to discrimination against others, and more open-minded about people who are different from them." As one child noted, "I think I understand more about how it feels to be different from most people. I've made a lot of friends from different cultures" (Nova Scotia Advisory Council on the Status of Women, 1996, p. 27).

A study of Manitoba lesbians published in 2000 offered similar findings. The authors noted, "In all cases, lesbian mothers see themselves as a positive influence on their children, and in two cases, even suggest that the marginality of Moms, by virtue of their sexual orientation, produces children who are more accepting, more open and stronger individuals" (Kirby, Streu, Riley, and Simpson, 2000, p. 41).

The concern most often cited about children growing up in gay or lesbian families is that they too will grow up to be gay or lesbian. On the one hand, this is an odd position since the overwhelming majority of gays, lesbians, bisexuals, transsexuals, and transgendered individuals grew up in heterosexual homes. On the other hand, it is, of course, an implicit condemnation of gays and lesbians since the implication is that growing up to be gay or lesbian is somehow a dire fate.

Social science research has not uncovered any differences between the children of lesbian and gay parents and the children of heterosexual parents in terms of gender identity and sexual orientation. In 1996, Charlotte Patterson and her colleague reviewed four studies on the gender identity, eight studies on the gender-role behaviour, and thirteen studies on the sexual ori-

BOX 7.6   SURREY BOARD OF EDUCATION

In 1996, James Chamberlain, a kindergarten teacher with the Surrey Board of Education, sought approval for the use of three books depicting same-sex families in his classroom. The books in question were *Asha's Mums*, *Belinda's Bouquet*, and *One Dad, Two Dads, Brown Dads, Blue Dads*. On April 10, 1997, the Board of Trustees of School District #36 (Surrey) denied the request and used the opportunity to pass a resolution requiring that school administrators, teachers, and counsellors be informed of any lesbian and gay materials to be used in the Surrey School District. The Board refused to allow the books to be used anywhere in the district, stating there were parents who had complained that their religious beliefs would be offended by acknowledging in the classroom that there are children who have same-gender parents. With the support of GALE (Gay and Lesbian Educators), parents, and colleagues, Chamberlain launched a petition to the British Columbia Supreme Court to have the resolution rescinded. The petition garnered the support of noted authors Robert Munsch and Dennis Lee, and the B.C. Civil Liberties Association; in all, more than 60 groups and individuals submitted affidavits in support of Chamberlain. Seventeen of the 20 families in Chamberlain's class signed a petition in support of the use of the materials. Chamberlain et al. were successful at the B.C. Supreme Court; the judge ruled that the Board had breached the School Act in failing to act in a secular manner. The Board chose to appeal that decision, and they were successful at the B.C. Court of Appeal (1999). The case was finally heard at the Supreme Court of Canada in June 2002, and a decision upholding the use of books discussing same-sex families in the classroom was released on December 20, 2002. "Tolerance is always age appropriate," Chief Justice Beverley McLachlin noted in the 7–2 majority decision. "Children cannot learn [tolerance] unless they are exposed to views that differ from those they are taught at home," she concluded.

On June 12, 2003, the Surrey School Board announced that it had decided that none of the three books in question was acceptable for classroom use because of the inconsistent grammar and spelling and potentially confusing messages allegedly contained in the books. Mary Polak, Chair of the Board of Trustees, indicated that the Board would be looking for alternative materials during the summer break. On June 26, 2003, the District Standing Advisory Committee for Learning Resources approved two other books, *Who's in a Family* by Robert Skutch and *A Family Alphabet* by Bobbie Coombs as learning resources. Two other books were referred for further research. Following the June 26 announcement, Trustee Heather Stilwell indicated that she had been inundated by complaints from parents about the decision.

entation of the children of gay or lesbian parents. They concluded that these studies of over 300 children of gay or lesbian parents revealed, "no evidence has been found for disturbances in the development of sexual identity among these individuals" (Patterson and Redding, 1996, p. 41). Extensive research suggests that sexual orientation is determined by a complex array of factors and not by the sexual identity of your parents.

This is not a surprising result, in light of the anecdotal evidence from lesbian mothers. In the Manitoba study referred to above, "[w]hen asked about the sexual orientation of their children, the lesbian mothers uniformly responded that sexual orientation was their children's choice." Leona, one of the women interviewed in the study, told researchers, "I don't care whether my daughter loves a man or a woman as long as she is happy" (Kirby et al., 2000, p. 51).

This is not, of course, to suggest that if parental sexual orientation *did* affect children's sex role development or sexual orientation, parenting by lesbian or gay parents would be problematic. While psychological difficulties or peer harassment may present public policy issues, same-sex sexual orientation or "atypical" sex role behaviour does not, as long as the children are otherwise healthy and well-adjusted.

In short, the wealth of scientific research that has been devoted to examining children in gay or lesbian families has failed to disclose much in the way of differences from heterosexual couples. Gays, lesbians, and heterosexuals appear to be equally capable of providing a sound basis for the psychological, social, and sexual development of a child.

CONCLUSION

While the struggle betweens lesbians and gays and their opponents continues in the legislatures, courtrooms, and every other public and private space in our society, it is important to remember that we are not discussing whether there should be lesbian and gay families. The fact is that these families exist and the children growing up in them are entitled to the support and protection the law provides for every child in this country.

Despite many gains, in some jurisdictions, lesbian and gay parents still risk losing their children and many of their children face daily harassment. Recognition in the courts continues to be an important key in securing the equality rights of these families.

Summary

*   Although gays and lesbians have formed families for generations, there has been a significant shift in social and legal recognition of gay and lesbian families in recent decades.

*   The recent legalization of same-sex marriage has both enshrined new legal rights and prompted an outpouring of homophobia.

*   While children have long had gay and lesbian parents, until recently they were usually the result of heterosexual unions.

*   Custody, adoption, and fostering procedures tended to disadvantage gays and lesbians seeking to parent children.

*   Donor insemination and surrogacy offer gay men and lesbians new alternatives for family; however, both are expensive and subject to future legislation.

- However gays and lesbians become parents, the research suggests that they are as capable as their heterosexual counterparts in providing for the psychological, social, and sexual development of their children.

Notes

1. This test replaced the "tender years" doctrine, which dictated that maternal custody was always in the best interests of the child, particularly in the case of young children.

2. Although this case was decided prior to the family law reforms referred to above, the judicial reasoning applied by Mr. Justice MacPherson would still be allowed under current family law.

3. These gender differences in caregiving are, of course, largely the result of socialization rather than biology. As well, the lower earning capacity of women frequently means that the mother becomes the stay-at-home parent during the first few years of her children's lives.

4. For a discussion of the differential impact of family law on lesbians and gay men, see Jenni Millbank, "Lesbian Mothers, Gay Fathers: Sameness and Difference," *Australian Gay and Lesbian Law Journal* 2 (Spring 1992), 21–40.

5. See, however, *Droit de la famille* 63 (1989), Quebec Superior Court, Melancon J at 27–28, in which the judge found that the HIV-positive status of the father was not a deterrent to access.

6. See Michael T. Isbell, *HIV and Family Law: A Survey* (Lambda Legal Defense and Education Fund ed., 1992) for a discussion of these issues in Bernstein, "Two mothers...and a donor with visitation," 11.

7. For a discussion of the impact of AIDS on lesbian and gay parenting, see Kath Weston, "Parenting in the Age of AIDS," in *Families We Choose: Lesbians, Gays, Kinship* (New York: Columbia University Press, 1991).

8. In the Matter of the *Human Rights Act* S.B.C. 1984, c.22 (as amended) and In the Matter of a complaint before the British Columbia Council of Human Rights between Tracy Potter and Sandra Benson AND Gerald W. Korn and/or Korn Management Ltd. I am grateful to Susan Boyd for supplying me with this reference.

9. On foster parenting, see Bryn Sheridan and Katherine Stuart, "A 'Blended Family'," in *Lesbian Parenting: Living with Pride and Prejudice*, ed. Katherine Arnup (Charlottetown: Gynergy Books, 1995), 134–47, which describes the experiences of a B.C. couple who have fostered and adopted a number of children. See, also, Wendell Ricketts and Roberta Achtenberg, "Adoption

and Foster Parenting for Lesbians and Gay Men: Creating New Traditions in Family," *Marriage and Family Review* (1990), 105. For a discussion of the Florida case, see *www.lethimstay.com*

10. The Virginia Supreme Court found that living conditions would "impose an intolerable burden upon her [the child] by reason of the social condemnation attached to them." The court noted as well, "the father's unfitness is manifested by his willingness to impose this burden upon (his daughter) in exchange for his own gratification." 694.

11. For an initial report on the case, see Nancy Wartik, "Virginia Is No Place For Lesbian Mothers," *Ms.* (November/December 1993), 89. The appeals court decision overturning Judge Parsons's original order was unanimous. Judge Sam W. Coleman III wrote, "a child's natural and legal right to the care and support of a parent and the parent's right to the custody and companionship of the child should only be disrupted if there are compelling reasons to do so." (*AP wire service*, June 21, 1994). Nonetheless, the Virginia Supreme Court overturned that ruling, reinstating Judge Parsons's original order.

12. The Supreme Court judges noted, "We have held ... that a lesbian mother is not per se an unfit parent." Nonetheless, "conduct inherent in lesbianism is punishable as a Class 6 felony in the Commonwealth [of Virginia]...; thus, that conduct is another important consideration in determining custody."

13. Jeffs indicates that the rationale must be provided within five working days. A memorandum from the Alberta Family and Social Services Department indicates that the rationale must be provided within two working days. (Memorandum CWH-06-02-02, dated 15/08/99.)

14. Fifty-five of the families were lesbian-headed; twenty-five were headed by heterosexual parents. Fifty of the families were headed by couples; thirty by single parents. Because all of the children had been conceived through donor insemination, all of them were biologically related to the mother and not to the other parent.

Critical Thinking Questions

1. How has the social and legal context in which lesbian families live changed since 1968?

2. Why have some areas of the United States, in contrast to Canada, retained such restrictive and outdated approaches to lesbian and gay parents?

3. Has the presence of lesbian and gay celebrities helped or hindered the struggle by gay and lesbian parents for equal parental rights?

4. What role have legal decisions played in the evolution of lesbian and gay families?

5. What elements in society are likely to affect the future of lesbian and gay families?

Websites

Family Pride Canada
http://familypride.uwo.ca
National online resource centre for LGBT parents and their children.

Lesbian Mothers Association of Quebec
http://www.aml-lma.org/an_home.html
A bilingual group of lesbian mothers and mothers-to-be, formed in 1998.

COLAGE—Children of Lesbians and Gays Everywhere
http://www.colage.org
The only international organization in the world specifically supporting young people with gay, lesbian, bisexual, and transgendered parents.

Family Pride Coalition
http://www.familypride.org
American-based organization with international links, supporting and protecting the families of gay, lesbian, bisexual, and transgendered parents.

Lesbian Mothers Support Society
http://www.lesbian.org/lesbian-moms/text.html
A non-profit group that provides peer support for lesbian parents and their children as well as for lesbians wanting to become parents. Based in Calgary, Alberta, the site provides excellent information and links to other groups and sites.

Suggested Reading

Katherine Arnup, ed. 1995 and 1997. *Lesbian Parenting: Living with Pride and Prejudice.* Charlottetown: Gynergy Books.
A collection of essays both personal and scholarly about the experiences of lesbian parents in Canada.

Mary Bernstein and Renate Reimann, eds. 2001. *Queer Families, Queer Politics: Challenging Culture and the State.* New York: Columbia University Press.
A collection of 24 articles on issues ranging from activism to transgendered parenting.

Suzanne M. Johnson and Elizabeth O'Connor. 2002. *The Gay Baby Boom: The Psychology of Gay Parenthood.* New York: New York University Press.

A review of the major psychological literature on lesbian and gay parenting and a presentation of the findings of the Gay and Lesbian Family Study, the largest American assessment of gay and lesbian headed families.

April Martin. 1993. *The Lesbian and Gay Parenting Handbook.* New York: Harper.
The classic book on lesbian and gay parenting. A virtual "Dr. Spock" for lesbian and gay parents.

Fiona Nelson. 1996. *Lesbian Motherhood: An Exploration of Canadian Lesbian Families.* Toronto: University of Toronto Press.
Based on interviews with 30 lesbian mothers in Alberta.

Richard Sullivan, ed. 1999. *Queer Families, Common Agendas: Gay People, Lesbians, and Family Values.* New York: Harrington Park Press.
A collection of essays, including two Canadian contributions, on a range of issues including adoption, custody, lesbian parenting, and gay fatherhood.

References

A.A. v. B.B., Ontario Superior Court of Justice, Family Court, April 11, 2003.

Allyson, J. 1999, March 24. "Best Interests of Child Onus on Gay Homes." *Edmonton Journal.*

Andrews, Karen. 1995. "Ancient Affections: Gays, Lesbians, and Family Status." In K. Arnup, ed. *Lesbian Parenting: Living with Pride and Prejudice.* Charlottetown: Gynergy Books.

Arnup, K. 1989. "'Mothers Just Like Others': Lesbians, Divorce, and Child Custody in Canada," *Canadian Journal of Women and the Law* 3, 18–32.

———. 1994. "Finding Fathers: Artificial Insemination, Lesbians, and the Law." *Canadian Journal of Women and the Law* 7, 1, 97–115.

———. 1998. "'Does the Word LESBIAN Mean Anything to You?' Lesbians Raising Daughters." In S. Abbey and A. O'Reilly, eds., *Redefining Motherhood: Changing Identities and Patterns.* Toronto: Second Story Press, 58–68.

Arnup, K., and Boyd, S. 1995. "Familial Disputes? Sperm Donors, Lesbian Mothers, and Legal Parenthood." In D. Herman and C. Stychin, eds., *Legal Inversions: Lesbians, Gay Men, and the Politics of Law.* Philadelphia: Temple University Press.

Beargie, R. 1988. "Custody Determinations Involving the Homosexual Parent." *Family Law Quarterly* 22, 1 (Spring), 71–86.

Bezaire v. Bezaire (1980), 20 R.F.L. (2d) 365 (Ont. C.A.).

Bigner, J. 1999. "Raising Our Sons: Gay Men as Fathers." In T. Richard Sullivan, ed., *Queer Families: Common Agendas: Gay People, Lesbians, and Family Values.* New York: Harrington Park Press.

Bottoms v. Bottoms, 457 S.E. 2d 102 (Va 1995).

Bowers v. Hardwick, 106 S.Ct. 2841 (1986).

Bozett, F. 1989. "Gay Fathers: A Review of the Literature." *Journal of Homosexuality* 18, 1/2, 153–54.

Brantner, P. 1991. "When Mommy or Daddy is Gay: Developing Constitutional Standards for Custody Decisions." *Hastings Women's Law Journal* 3, 1 (Winter), 105.

Brewaeys, A., I. Ponjaert, E. Van Hall, and S. Golombok. 1997. "Donor Insemination: Child Development and Family Functioning in Lesbian Mother Families." 12 *Human Reproduction*, 1356.

Case v. Case (1974), 18 R.F.L. 138 (Sask. Queen's Bench).

Chan, R., B. Raboy, and C. Patterson. 1998. "Psychosocial Adjustment among Children Conceived via Donor Insemination by Lesbian and Heterosexual Mothers." *Child Development* 69, 2 (April), 454.

Children's Law Reform Act, R.S.O. 1980, c. 68, section 24.

D.H. v. H.H., Alabama Supreme Court, 2002.

D.M. v. M.D., 94 Sask. R. 315; [1991] S.J. No. 672.

Droit de la famille 63 (1989), Quebec Superior Court, Melancon J. at 27–28.

Elliott v. Elliott, [1987] B.C.J. No. 43 (B.C.S.C.), 22.

Epstein, R. 1993. "Breaking with Tradition," *Healthsharing* (Summer/Fall), 18–22.

Flaks, D., I. Ficher, F. Masterpasqua, and G. Joseph. 1995. "Lesbians Choosing Motherhood: A Comparative Study of Lesbian and Heterosexual Parents and Their Children." *Developmental Psychology* 31, 1, 111.

"Gay Kept from Foster Role." 1997, July 15. *Globe and Mail*, A4.

Globe and Mail, October 23, 2002, p. A7.

GLPCI Network, Fall 1996 Issue, p. 3.

Golombok, S., A. Spencer, and M. Rutter. 1983. "Children in Lesbian and Single-parent Households: Psychosexual and Psychiatric Appraisal." *Journal of Child Psychology and Psychiatry* 24, 551–72.

Gross, W. 1986. "Judging the Best Interests of the Child: Child Custody and the Homosexual Parent." *Canadian Journal of Women and the Law* 1, 505–31.

Hotved M., and Mandel, J. 1982. "Children of Lesbian Mothers." In W. Paul, J. Weinfrich, J. Gonsiorek, and M. Hotved, eds., *Homosexuality—Social, Psychological and Biological Issues*. Beverly Hills: Sage Publications, 275–86.

Huggins, S. 1989. "A Comparative Study of Self-Esteem of Adolescent Children of Divorced Lesbian Mothers and Divorced Heterosexual Mothers." *Journal of Homosexuality* 17, 123.

Isbell, M. 1992. *HIV and Family Law: A Survey*. Lambda Legal Defense and Education Fund, ed.

"Judge Gives Killer Custody Because Wife Is A Lesbian." 1996, February 3. *Ottawa Citizen*.

K. v. K. (1975), 23 R.F.L. 63 (Alta. Prov. Ct.), 64.

Kirby, S., H. Streu, S. Riley, and J. Simpson. 2000. *Manitoba Struggle for Rights: Lesbians and Their Families*. Ottawa: CRIAW.

Korn v. Potter (1996), 134 D.L.R. (4th) 437 (B.C.S.C.).

"Lesbian Couple Charge Doctor and College with Discrimination." 1993. *Gazebo Connection* 14, 8 (September), 2.

Lewin, E. 1993. *Lesbian Mothers: Accounts of Gender in American Culture*. Ithaca: Cornell University Press.

MacMahon, Judge, cited in *Bezaire v. Bezaire* (1980), 20 R.F.L. (2d) 365 (Ont. C.A.).

Martin, A. 1993. *The Lesbian and Gay Parenting Handbook*. New York: Harper.

Mawhinney, J. 2002, September 28. "Gay Unions Garner Public Support." *Toronto Star*,

Millbank, J. "Lesbian Mothers, Gay Fathers: Sameness and Difference." *Australian Gay and Lesbian Law Journal* 2 (Spring 1992), 21–40.

Memorandum CWH-06-02-02, dated 15/08/99.

National Center for Lesbian Rights. 1993. "Lesbians Choosing Motherhood: Legal Implications of Donor Insemination and Co-Parenting." Reprinted in William B. Rubenstein, ed., *Lesbians, Gay Men, and the Law*. New York: New Press, 543.

Nelson, F. 1996. *Lesbian Motherhood: An Exploration of Canadian Lesbian Families*. Toronto: University of Toronto Press.

North v. Matheson, 20 R.F.L. 112, 53 D.L.R .(3d) 280 (Man. Co. Ct.) (denial of capacity to marry did not violate Manitoba Human Rights Act).

Nova Scotia Advisory Council on the Status of Women. 1996. *Letting in a Little Light: Lesbians and Their Families in Nova Scotia*. Halifax: Nova Scotia Department of Supply and Services, 26.

O'Connell, A. 1993. "Voices from the Heart: The Developmental Impact of a Mother's Lesbianism on her Adolescent Children." *Smith College Studies in Social Work* 63, 3, 290.

Patterson, C. 1993. "Children of Lesbian and Gay Parents." *Child Development* 63, 1036.

———. 1996. "Lesbian and Gay Parents and Their Children." In R. Savin-Williams and K. Cohen, ed., *The Lives of Lesbians, Gays, and Bisexuals: Adults to Children*. Orlando: Harcourt Brace.

———. 1998. "The Family Lives of Children Born to Lesbian Mothers." In C. Patterson and A. D'Augelli, eds., *Lesbian, Gay, and Bisexual Identities in Families: Psychological Perspectives*. New York: Oxford.

Patterson, C., and R. Redding. 1996. "Lesbian and Gay Families with Children: Implications of Social Science Research for Policy." *Journal of Social Issues* 52, 3.

Pies, C. 1990. "Lesbians and the Choice to Parent." *Marriage and Family Review* 14, 139.

Polikoff, N. 1990–91. "This Child Does Have Two Mothers: Redefining Parenthood to Meet the Needs of Children in Lesbian-Mother and Other Nontraditional Families." *Georgetown Law Journal* 78, 459–575.

Re. K. (1995), 23 O.R. (3d) 679 (Ont. Ct. Prov. Div.).

Ricketts, W., and R. Achtenberg. 1990. "Adoption and Foster Parenting for Lesbians and Gay Men: Creating New Traditions in Family." *Marriage and Family Review*, 105. For a discussion of the Florida case, see www.lethimstay.com

Roe v. Roe, 228 Va. 722, 324 S.E. (2d) 691 (1985).

Saunders v. Saunders (1989), 20 R.F.L. (3d) 368 (B.C. Co. Ct.).

Schmitz, C. 1997, 18 July. "Lesbian Co-Parent Must Pay Biological Mother Child Support." *Lawyer's Weekly*, 21.

Sheridan, B., and K. Stuart. 1995. "A 'Blended Family'." In *Lesbian Parenting: Living with Pride and Prejudice*, ed. Katherine Arnup. Charlottetown: Gynergy Books, 134–47.

"Sperm Donor Wins Fight with Lesbians." 1991, July 26. *The Toronto Star*, p. F1.

Tasker, F., and S. Golombok. 1996. "Adults Raised as Children in Lesbian Families." *American Journal of Orthopsychiatry* 65, 2 (April), 212.

———. 1997. *Growing up in a Lesbian Family*. New York: Guilford Press.

Wartik, N. 1993. "Virginia Is No Place For Lesbian Mothers." *Ms.* (November/December), 89.

"We're Having a Baby." 1996, November 4. *Newsweek*, cover.

Weston, K. "Parenting in the Age of AIDS." 1991. In *Families We Choose: Lesbians, Gays, Kinship*. New York: Columbia University Press.

Wishard, D. 1989. "Out of the Closets and into the Courts: Homosexual Fathers and Child Custody." *Dickinson Law Review* 93, 420.

Chapter 8

Divorce: Options Available, Constraints Forced, Pathways Taken

Carolyne A. Gorlick

LEARNING OBJECTIVES

In this chapter, you will learn that:

1. divorce is increasing and is associated with marriage duration;

2. (mis)perceptions are apparent in divorce discussions;

3. controversy exists as to the long-term impacts of divorce on children;

4. changes are proposed to the Divorce Act emphasizing the best interests of the child and parental responsibility;

5. frequently missing from the divorce literature are the voices of divorced women and children in defining, framing, and guiding their experiences.

INTRODUCTION

Divorce is likely to be viewed as an ending rather than a beginning. Clearly it is an end to some relationships; it weakens some and strengthens others. Divorce may also initiate an interactive process of individual and social realignments, strains, hopes, and expectations combined with perceptions of available options, institutional and individual constraints, and paths chosen. Divorce is also a process in which gender inequities persist and are sustained. In this context, it is useful to recognize everyday interactions and their effects on the lives of family members, relatives, and friends. In that light, the life experiences of divorced women guide the discussion in this chapter.

The first section of the chapter addresses conclusions drawn from the divorce literature and their influence on policy assumptions and reform activities. The second section offers an illustration of the options perceived, the constraints forced, and some of the pathways taken by a particular group of low-income female single parents who found themselves characterized as "welfare moms."

Canada has one of the highest divorce rates along with Sweden, Denmark, and the United Kingdom. Although the numbers of divorces fluctuated in the 1990s, at the turn of the century more Canadian families experienced divorce. In 2000, there were 71 144 divorced couples, an increase of 3 percent from 1998. Four out of ten Canadian marriages end with divorce and seven out of ten divorced Canadians are likely to remarry. Divorce relates to marriage duration with the lowest risk after the first wedding anniversary (5.1 percent) increasing to 17 percent after the second, 23.6 percent after the third, and a peak of 25.5 percent after the fourth anniversary. In 1999 and 2000, 60 percent of divorced couples were married less than 15 years (Statistics Canada, 2003a).

Discussions of divorce rate trends also include the impact of legal divorce reforms such as family-law changes, expanded judicial services, and shortened waiting periods. Other explanations focus on women's financial independence, through increased participation in the labour force, as a factor in women's decision to divorce. Yet other explanations emphasize supportive societal attitudes regarding divorce. Still others view the increase in divorce as a disruption of traditional family values and as comparable to an epidemic or disease.

Whether one is offering explanations for divorce rate trends or attitudes, it is also useful to address conclusions drawn from the divorce literature and their influence on policy assumptions and reform activities.

(MIS)PERCEPTIONS OF DIVORCE

Perceptions of divorce have been framed and challenged by individual, familial, and societal experiences and reinforced through the media and professional and research information. Divorce has been categorized and described in numerous academic/professional writings (several journals focus specifically on divorce) and self-help/how-to-survive-divorce books, which have proliferated as the number of individuals experiencing divorce has increased. Much of the social-psychological information may be grouped under two general approaches: divorce viewed as initiating negative and pathological responses, and divorce as a positive self-realization experience (Arendell, 1986).

Is Divorce a Pathological Response or a Positive Self-Realization Experience?

How people adjust to divorce has received significant theoretical and speculative attention. Some theories promote a **deviance model of divorce** characterized by stages of denial, mourning, anger, and readjustment; by a significant, continuous loss of self-esteem for women (Weiss, 1975); and as creating long-term negative consequences for children and a period of "diminished parenting" (Wallerstein and Kelly, 1980). This traditional monolithic model pathologizes divorce by describing the divorcing family as deviant and emphasizing the problems emerging from this deviance (Eichler, 1993). Elements of this approach have been found in professional responses (some therapeutic and casework activities) that emphasize divorce as a crisis as opposed to a lengthy, continuous process of adjustment (Strauss, 1988).

The reverse of the deviancy model is the view of marital separation as an opportunity for personal growth. Divorce is seen as challenging individuals to increase or reinforce their adaptive abilities by interacting with and responding to the challenges and crises that are integral to divorce (Weitzman, 1985; Strauss, 1988). Several possibilities exist, such as enlarging, not decreasing, supportive family ties with remarriage: children may have more than two parents and a greater number of relatives. An expansion of friendship ties and opportunities is also viewed as a possibility. Divorce may also be understood as a mass resistance of women against oppressive familial and social structures. It may certainly have a liberating outcome for women, men, and children leaving a hostile family environment.

In any case, it is misleading to emphasize either greater personal-growth opportunities or negative and pathologizing divorce outcomes, for each places the onus for adaptability or change on the individual. For the individual responding to changes in the aftermath of divorce, however, it is less a question of ability than one of opportunity, with women frequently having fewer economic, legal, and labour market opportunities than men (Eichler, 1993, 1997). Furthermore, to picture divorce as primarily either positive or negative is to overlook the complexity of the process itself and the differing concerns and capacities of individual family members. For example, when women leave a physically and/or emotionally abusive relationship, the initial relief at separation and the degree of predictability in the aftermath of departure have the possibility of translating into enhanced self-worth. This possibility exists along with the personal stress, fear, and worry about money, housing, and legal outcomes that accompany the departure.

Missing from both of these assumptions is the significance of race and ethnicity for divorcing families. It is undoubtedly more difficult for recent female immigrants to initiate and obtain a divorce. Why is this, and what solutions should be forthcoming? Are some racial or ethnic groups more supportive of divorce than others? If so, what forms of support exist? And what are the policy and advocacy implications of these differences? Also, how might a woman who is disabled define and respond to the divorce process? The questions are numerous; the answers in the research literature are few.

In spite of the contradictions and omissions in these two general assumptions, they underlie much of the divorce literature. The following discussion of some myths and realities surrounding divorce emphasizes the pervasiveness of these assumptions.

Is Divorce a Commonality of Negative Experiences?

Divorce in this "commonality of experiences" context is a life-cycle transition experienced negatively by all involved individuals (former spouses, children, grandparents, friends, and other family members) (Ahrons and Rogers, 1987). The social and psychological impact is difficult for everyone, with no individual or group suffering more or adapting better than another. Timing of individual and familial adaptation is also significant. Two to three years is frequently perceived as the crucial period of "adaptability" for most members of divorced families.

Recognizing the diversity of individual experiences and understandings, hopes and expectations, and strains and stresses throws into question arguments for commonality in adaptation and timing. Furthermore, to view divorce as another life transition masks the different short- and long-term outcomes experienced by gender (husband versus wife, son versus daughter). For example, missing from the commonality of experiences discussion is the economic vulnerability of women (and their children) and its direct link with their post-divorce experiences. In sum, overemphasizing the commonality of experiences ignores the differing divorce realities and the diversity of experiences of family members. Stating that the experiences of divorcing family members are entirely negative offers a picture of the family as coming to an end, with few constructive or positive initiatives forthcoming.

Are Post-Divorce Problems Transitional Because the Parent is Likely to Remarry?

As noted, the deviancy model of divorce presents this family type as short-term, aberrant, and "no longer intact." Frequent comparisons are drawn between "intact" families—the preferred, normative, and "necessary family structure"—and "not intact" families. The divorced family presumably becomes "intact" again if divorced spouses remarry and form another nuclear family, sometimes referred to as blended, step-, reconstituted, or bi-nuclear. The **blended family** contains spouses who may have been divorced, widowed, or never married, and with or without children. Within this family unit are various configurations of stepparents and stepadopted siblings, as well as stepgrandparents and an array of stepaunts, uncles, and cousins.

Most children living in stepfamilies are in a blended form of the couples' biological children and the wife's child(ren) from a previous marriage. Nine percent of children under 12 years of age are members of a stepfamily, with approximately 50 percent being stepchildren and 50 percent born or adopted into the stepfamily (Statistics Canada, 1997a). By 2001, there were 503 100 stepfamilies representing 12 percent of all Canadian couples with children, up from 10 percent in 1995 (Statistics Canada, 2003a).

The most frequent steprelationship was that of stepfather–stepdaughter, with stepfathers outnumbering stepmothers five to one. In spite of the fact that stepmother–stepdaughter was the least frequent relationship, the "wicked stepmother" myth, emerging from folk tales and children's stories such as "Cinderella" and "Snow White," persists. Cheal (1996) discovered that National Longitudinal Survey of Children and Youth (NLSCY) data did not support the traditional stepmother myth (Cheal, 1996). Stepmothers were not harsher or more inconsistent in their interactions with their stepchildren than were biological/adopted mothers with their biological/adopted children. It appears that the majority of children in stepfamilies have moderate to good relationships with their parents, which is remarkable given the various permutations of interactions and complexities that might emerge as family members negotiate their roles and positions. Ferri and Smith (1998), in acknowledging the stresses and strains experienced by stepfamilies, argue for greater support of these families, such as recognition of particular circumstances, the myriad and complex relationship structures and processes, and the formidable time and financial-resource challenges. Ferri and Smith (1998) maintain that the challenge facing those in stepfamilies is particularly great, not only because of the complex new relationships involved, but also because, for biological parents at least, and for many stepparents too, the failure of earlier relationships may have left a vulnerable legacy in terms of material hardship and emotional insecurity.

The literature on stepfamilies, although growing, tends to use a comparative (that is, blended versus nuclear family) approach, or contains descriptions of emerging personality and familial traits, or presents hurdles overcome in spousal or parental relationships. In short, the measuring stick remains the nuclear family and the degree to which the blended family is able to approximate it.

The possibility increasingly exists for a child or an adult to move in and out of a variety of family structures over time. Remarriage is increasing. When compared to first-time brides and grooms from 1979 to 1999, the proportion of brides and grooms previously divorced had increased from 14 percent to 21.6 percent for females and from 15.6 percent to 22.1 percent for males (Statistics Canada, 2003a). More than a quarter of individuals in common-law relationships are divorced. From the 1990s, common-law families increased the fastest of any other family structure. Compared to all families, common-law couples with children (under the age of 25) at home increased from 2.1 percent in 1981 to 7.4 percent in 2001. In contrast, married couples with children decreased from 60 percent of all couples in 1981 to 44 percent in 2001 (Statistics Canada, 2003a).

In response to the perception that single-parenting is transitional, there are two final considerations. First, the labour force participation of females (and, for some, greater financial independence) may lead to a postponement of remarriage or influence a decision not to remarry. Second, it is not entirely clear that remarriage will resolve any or most post-divorce problems. Indeed, remarriage may lead to another divorce.

Does Divorce have a Long-Term Negative Impact on Children?

The assumption here is that, although divorcing spouses ultimately tend to adapt to marital separation, children are more likely to experience emotional and physical trauma for a long time. The "missing" father and the "emotionally overwrought" mother are to blame, and there are long-term negative consequences of divorce and growing up in an "aberrant" single-parent family. The hypothesis that the absence of the non-resident parent is harmful to children of divorce has been challenged by research evidence indicating no clear association between paternal visitation frequency and child well-being (Bernardini and Jenkins, 2002). However, these authors note

> ...other dimensions of father involvement, such as payment of child support, authoritative parenting and feelings of closeness, can and do have positive effects on children's adjustment following divorce. Therefore what a father does with his children when he is with them is much more important than the amount of time he spends with them.

Other factors, such as the age of the child, have been discussed as indicators of long-term negative impacts on children. A 1998 Statistics Canada study of 23 000 children under the age of 11 noted that 20 percent of children ages 10–11 saw their parents separate before they were five years old. This was an increase from 12 percent of a similar group in 1973, and 6.5 percent in 1962. Subsequently the number of young children witnessing divorce had tripled during this period. Is the child's age at divorce a risk or protector or not significant?

Another risk factor is parental conflict. A study that tracked 2000 families over 20 years discovered that children of high-conflict divorces fared better than children of apparent low-conflict divorces where marital hostility was not overt (Amato and Booth, 1997). Divorce in the latter family situation was more of a surprise and jarring for children who experienced a diminished sense of trust leading to psychological distress in later years. Others argue that child-adjustment factors relate to income, level of couple animosity, and custodial parents' childrearing skills (Ambert, 1989). Still others contend that children of divorce are sick more than children in two-parent families. Statistics Canada (1992a) found that 56 percent of children of single-parent families have at least one health problem, compared with 49 percent of children from two-parent families.[1] The implication is that children in two-parent families have safe and comfortable environments, and those in single-parent families do not. Another study concluded that the majority of children in single-mother families did not have more emotional and behavioural problems and academic and social difficulties than children from two-parent families, although it did argue that risk factors and rates were greater for children of single-parent families (Lipman, Offord, and Dooley, 1996).

What is much less clear is whether these health or behavioural conditions are a direct result of divorce or a drop in the standard of living, or some combination that might ensue from divorce. Also, what is defined as long-term versus short-term negative effects and how might these be delineated or measured over time? Studies also reveal that comparable negative impacts are observed in both discordant two-parent families and high-conflict divorces.

Certainly, there are several intervening and controlling factors beyond the implied assumption that, by divorcing, parents will make their children sick. Nevertheless, those kinds of links are made and compounded. For example, it is sometimes said that, if a parent works, she is likely to cause harm to her children. An employed mother seeking custody may frequently discover that working fathers are lauded as dedicated, responsible parents for providing child support, while working mothers are not necessarily viewed in a favourable manner.

Controversy over whether divorce has long-term negative impacts on children seems to have altered public opinion. More specifically, there appears to be an attitude shift regarding divorce and its effect on children among certain age groups. Statistics Canada (1997b) noted that 44.5 percent of 15- to 29-year-olds said they would remain in a bad marriage for their children, compared with 39.5 percent of 30- to 49-year-olds. Of those over the age of 50, 52 percent consistently reported they would remain in bad marriages for the children's sake. Overall, 40 percent of adult Canadians would stay in an unhappy relationship for their children, with 60 percent of males choosing to remain, compared with 33 percent of females. It is difficult to predict the extent to which these changing attitudes will have an impact on marital separation in the future. Those most willing to stay in a relationship for the children's sake, such as the 15- to 29-year-old group compared with the 30- to 49-year-old group, may not have married and are predicting their possible behaviour.

What interventions are currently in place to assist children undergoing divorce? Legal representation consists of three models: the advocate, the litigation guardian, and the amicus curiae (Bessner, 2002). The amicus curiae is a lawyer whose allegiance is primarily to the court and subsequently perceived as silencing the child's voice rather than enhancing. Critics have tended to view the amicus curiae as not suitable for custody and access decisions. The litigation guardian offers information on the best interests of the child from his/her perspective and not necessarily the child's preferences. It is the child advocate whose role is to give the child a direct voice in the divorce proceedings.

Recently proposed changes to the Divorce Act (Bill C-22) and shifts in custody arrangements are likely to impact on children experiencing divorce. Guiding the Divorce Act's "best interests of the child" criteria has been a fundamental assumption defined as "the court shall take into consideration only the best interests of the child of the marriage as determined by reference to the condition, mean, needs and other circumstances of the child" (Divorce Act, section 16.8). With this lack of clarity, several interpretations emerged, including perceived fathers' rights to access the child in situations of violence by non-resident fathers (Greaves et al., 2002). Bill C-22 includes proposed amendments to the best interests criteria with guidelines to be weighed by the court and dependent on the specific case. Refer to Box 8.1.

BOX 8.1   THE CHILD-CENTRED FAMILY JUSTICE STRATEGY

The Child-Centred Family Justice Strategy or Bill C-22 articulates a number of proposed Divorce Act changes. These changes are based on the recommendations of the Special Joint Committee on Child Custody and Access to avoid presumptions regarding which parental arrangement was in the best interests of the child. These include:

PARENTING RESPONSIBILITIES

The terms "custody" and "access" will be replaced by "parental responsibility" and "parental order." The former includes decisions regarding child's education, health, religious affiliation, and parenting time. The latter occurs during court proceedings and decision-making.

BEST INTERESTS CRITERIA

While the fundamental principle of the best interests of the child in custody decision-making will be maintained, this offers further guidelines for the courts to base their decisions. The best interests criteria proposed include the child's preferences and perceptions to the "extent they can be reasonably ascertained," greater emphasis on the child's well-being and safety in family violence, and emphasis on the spouse's "willingness to support the development and mainte-nance of the child's relationship with the other spouse" as well as the child's need for emotional and physical stability.

CONTACT ORDERS

The bill includes the provision of contact between the child and others, including grandparents and older siblings. These orders would also be based on the best interest of the child criteria.

LAWYERS

The bill offers emphasis on and expansion of the lawyer's role through non-adversarial dispute resolution interventions and including information dissemination regarding mediation services and family justice services such as parent education courses.

INTERPROVINCIAL VARIATION OF SUPPORT ORDERS

The bill attempts to address parents living in different provinces or territories via the option of a written application to replace two court hearings in the applicant's and respondent's jurisdiction.

To implement these proposals, the federal government will offer $16.1 million for 62 new judges and expand the Unified Family Courts to promote "a holistic approach to each family's situation."

Source: *Family Justice Newsletter*, vol 1 Spring 2003, Department of Justice Canada, p. 1–4,
http://canada.justice.gc.ca/en/ps/pad/news/052003.html

Trends in the custody of children have also shifted. In two out of three divorces, couples either decided on custody arrangements outside of divorce proceedings or did not have children. Of those children (N = 37,000) in 2000 whose custody was determined through divorce proceedings, 53.5 percent were awarded to the mother—a decline from 75.8 percent in 1988. Also in 2000, custody of 9.1 percent of dependants was awarded to the father, down from 15 percent in 1986. One explanation for these trends might be found in the rise of joint custody arrangements in divorce proceedings. For 37.2 percent of children, joint custody arrangements were identified in divorce proceedings. Although this trend has been increasing over the last 14 years, it does not signify that children are spending equal amounts of time with each parent (Statistics Canada, 2003b). Also unclear is the impact of joint custody arrangements on, for example, finances, housing, childcare, family relationships (parent–child, sibling, grandparents, other family, and friends), and parental work patterns. More recently, "parallel parenting" has emerged in custody and support discussions and legal interventions. Refer to the accompanying Case Study 8.1: "Parallel Parenting."

Do legal interventions and participation in divorce proceedings precipitate harm to children? If there are risks, how might they be addressed? In addition to greater accommodation in legal proceedings, including definitions of competency, child-friendly courtrooms, and preparing the child for courtroom appearances, there are attempts at identifying and implementing a dispute resolution continuum. Necessary is a multidisciplinary effort (lawyers, psychologists, and social workers) focusing on the best interests of the child and the family's needs and responses at each stage of separation and

CASE STUDY 8.1　PARALLEL PARENTING

The Ontario Court of Appeal has ruled in the case of *Lefebvre v. Lefebvre* using a new option called "parallel parenting," in which parents are given equal status after divorce, but exercise rights and responsibilities independently. For instance, in the *Lefebvre* case, Ontario Superior Court Justice Heidi Levenson Polowin ordered parallel parenting of the 3-year-old child, giving the mother final say on medical and dental decisions but the father responsibilities in other areas.

Some see the concept of parallel parenting as anticipating the upcoming changes to the Divorce Act (Bill C-22, 2003), under which the terms "custody" and "access" will be replaced. Family law expert Julia Cornish has said parallel parenting provides equal involvement of mother and father even if the parents are hostile to each other. Under the concept, one parent may handle education and religious decisions while the other handles decisions over recreation and health care. Other lawyers have said that the concept goes against the legal premise that warring parents should not be awarded joint custody.

Source: Beverley Smith, 2003. *http://canadiansocialresearch.net/caregiving.htm*

divorce. Although elements of the dispute resolution continuum have been introduced, most interventions occur after with less continuous emphasis before, after, and following family crisis (Birnbaum, in press).

What are the long-term implications for children of parents staying together, or remarrying, compared with divorcing? Perhaps what makes this a difficult period for some children and not others is not the act of marital separation but myriad influences. Some of these influences include family relationships, income decline, separation/divorce proceedings, and residential changes combined with the child's age and gender. In addition to the number and type of influences, it is also their interactive and cumulative effects over time that may be significant. Perhaps analysis in the divorce literature should stress "mother presence" rather than "father absence" to draw a clearer picture of the ambiguities surrounding these questions. Perhaps a greater emphasis on context and interaction of factors should be pursued. Perhaps also worth revisiting is whether only cross-sectional data provide sufficient answers to time-based questions. And perhaps a greater effort in listening to divorce experiences interpreted by children is a direction worthy of pursuit.

Do Divorced Fathers Offer Sufficient and Consistent Alimony and Child Support?

The argument here is that divorced, non-custodial fathers have been sufficient and consistent in their alimony and child-support payments. In fact, downward financial and social mobility has been the experience of most women and children after divorce, and this decline is directly linked to inadequate, erratic, and missing financial support. Public recognition of the numbers of female single-parent families relying on social assistance has led to accusations against a group referred to as **"dead-beat dads."** Some, however, believe that dead-beat dads are a myth. The co-chairperson of the Special Joint Committee on Child Custody and Access contends: "the idea of deadbeat dads, I find objectionable…that is a myth created by the feminist agenda. There are just as many deadbeat mothers as there are deadbeat fathers" ("Deadbeat Dad," 1998). This is an interesting observation, given the significantly higher numbers of custodial mothers compared with custodial fathers.

Provinces and territories have implemented a variety of punitive measures responding to support orders in default. Before the implementation of the Family Support Plan in Ontario, 85 percent of family-support orders were in default. With the introduction of the mandatory deduction order under the Family Support Plan, the number of defaults began to decline. Several measures have been put in place to collect owing child support. Ontario has increased efforts by suspending driver's licences, and in some cases jail sentences have been imposed. Other possible methods of solving the arrears problem include seizing lottery winnings over $1000 (although one wonders how many child-support orders this would affect), withdrawing half the money held by delinquent parents in joint bank accounts, and allowing courts to collect money from a third party found hiding defaulting parents' assets. With significant fines to both the non-custodial parent and his or her employer, a clear responsibility is placed on the parent who has been issued an alimony/child-support order and the employer to ensure that the order agreement is fulfilled. In 1993, the Ontario government extended the garnishee of wages from one year to five years to minimize the need for yearly renewals. As well, up to half of Employment Insurance benefits may be garnisheed for support payments.

Nevertheless, in spite of court orders and other measures, Ontario has a total of $1.3 billion in support arrears (Ontario Ombudsman Report, 2002–2003). The details of why this trend is occurring are not clear. There is some speculation that at least one segment of those parents in arrears over child support are members of the working poor whose incomes may be based on seasonal or part-time employment. The Family Responsibility Office (FRO), established to correct the problem of child-support arrears, has come under criticism from custodial parents, women's support groups, opposition MPPs, and the province's ombudsman. Much of this criticism rests with the "inequitable and inadequate" delivery system that leaves some families without income support that has been garnisheed from the non-custodial parent's wages. Although the Family Responsibility Office has privatized some of its services, the current $1.3 billion in support arrears is an increase from $1.2 billion in support arrears in the latter part of the 1990s.

Another possible consideration for non-custodial parents and their child-support decisions is the financial incentive to obtain 40 percent of child custody. As Greaves et al., 2002 maintain,

> In practice, obtaining at least 40 percent custody on paper (this is not necessarily reflective of where the child actually lives and is cared for) means at least a reduction in child support payments, if not absolution of the requirement to pay, depending on the income of each party.

Legal reforms such as "no-fault" divorce have failed to ameliorate the financial crisis experienced by custodial parents and their children. In fact, the post-separation income discrepancy between former spouses has continued. There are many conceptual and methodological difficulties in measuring the economic impact of divorce. Some of the studies are based on differing research designs (cross-sectional or longitudinal) and varying income measures (drop in income, drop in expected income, negative-income events, or additional "need" measures). Also the politics of poverty-line definition influence discussions of depth of poverty for female single-parent families. Questions worth pursuing include: Do younger divorced women experience a greater drop in standard of living than older divorced women? Do upper-income divorced women experience the same relative decline as lower-income divorced women? And what influence do socioeconomic status and age have on men's economic experiences after divorce? Do race, ethnicity, or disability influence a woman's income drop? Or are predetermined factors before divorce at work?

Regardless of the omissions and inconsistencies in the literature on economic decline in the aftermath of divorce, the family wage becomes the husband's wage as the measuring stick in alimony/child-support decisions. Even before divorce, however, the family wage does not always reflect an equitable sharing of household resources.

In sum, although there is no clear consensus on the extent of economic decline (or how to measure it), a drop in standard of living does occur for the custodial mother. This drop depends on the non-custodial father's pattern of financial support, and legal processes that enhance or detract from that support. Furthermore, it has been concluded that there is a clear association between the father's payment of child support and positive child outcomes (Amato and Gilbreth, 1999).

Do Custodial Mothers Choose to Work or Parent Full-Time?

A prevailing policy assumption is that there is an element of choice for female single parents between paid employment and full-time parenting. For those families receiving minimal alimony and unpredictable child support payments, full-time parenting for the custodial parent was never an option. Recognition of traditional unpaid women's labour such as childrearing seems light years away. Only 15.8 percent of all Canadian families have used the federal Child Care Expense income tax deduction as many are dependent on relatives for caregiving or are working from home (Smith, 2003). Female lone-parent families are particularly vulnerable to income and employment pressures. In 2000, more two-parent families with children fell into poverty and needed an additional $10 032 to reach the poverty line. In the same year, although female lone-parent families saw some income increases, they would still need an additional $8500 to reach the poverty line (Canadian Council on Social Development, 2002). Both types of families in need of social assistance find themselves in an alternate policy world of defining and redefining the caregiving role.

The replacement of social assistance programmes with provincial/territorial welfare to work activities has led to the targeting of female single parents receiving social assistance (Gorlick and Brethour, 1998). Within this context, employability is redefining parenting. The definition of caregiving is up for grabs as parenting is defined by programme convenience. The age of a child or children as the key to lone-parent employability varies between jurisdictions. In the past, the age markers for employability had been in some provinces 18 to 19 years while current age markers have shifted downward to preschool or school age (Gorlick, 2002). Thus, a female single parent's entitlements are predicated upon her role as an employee as opposed to parent. It is also expected that full-time employment be obtained.

Federal employment-related policies often do not support part-time and low-income workers. A recent legal challenge to the restrictive eligibility of the 1996 Employment Insurance (EI) Act was denied by the Supreme Court overturning the EI "Umpire" decision, which found that the regulations violated the equality guarantee of section 15 of the Charter of Rights and Freedoms (Chic, 2003). Kelly Lesiuk maintained that the tightening of EI rules discriminated against women and parents. The number of unemployed individuals receiving EI benefits declined from 74 percent in 1989 to 37 percent in 1999, largely as a result of eligibility restrictions. In addition to losing her case, Lesiuk was ordered by the Supreme Court to pay the costs associated with her appeal (Chic, 2003).

In sum, a custodial mother is frequently placed in a no-win position in which she attempts to balance parental and work responsibilities with economic pressures. There may appear to be a choice between parenting and employment; the reality is there is no such choice.

Are Mothers Who Do Not Seek or Are Not Granted Custody Immoral and Unfit Parents?

The mother is most often the custodial parent. However, countervailing trends are emerging. An increasing number of fathers are requesting custody of their children and joint custody arrangements. There is also a greater awareness of mothers who are not seeking or who are not granted custody.

Predominantly ignored in the divorce literature are the experiences of non-custodial mothers. Edwards's (1989) study is an exception; it identifies the variety of choices made by, and the perceptions of, non-custodial mothers, including the following: "I still feel most people do not understand children not living with their mothers. There is an automatic stigma. What must be wrong with her? She must not be a very loving or dedicated person or mother. She must be a drunk or prostitute or something evil" (Edwards, 1989, p. 30).

Some of the non-custodial mothers in the Edwards study lost custody battles, some chose to be the non-custodial parent, some regained custody, some developed positive relationships with their children, others did not. Many are living in new family configurations; some are living alone. Their accounts show a diversity of reasons and myriad responses. Clearly, though, blaming the mother prevails when women are non-custodial, while the single custodial father is portrayed in the media as long-suffering, thoughtful, and responsive to his children's needs. It must be remembered that, in spite of the array of television shows featuring single custodial fathers, this group is a statistical minority, as are non-custodial mothers.

A recent study focused on mothering under duress, particularly those mothers dealing with family violence, substance abuse, and mental heath concerns (Greaves et al., 2003). The authors concluded that legal, policy, and media sectors have placed the mother's rights below the child's, relied on evidence that draws from expert and professional knowledge rather than from women themselves, and viewed children as independent of their relationships with others. Frequently women in these situations of duress find themselves isolated, scorned, and victimized by court custody decisions against them. Necessary is a mothering framework ensuring the recognition, respect, and restoration of the mother–child unit in divorce policy debates (Greaves et al., 2003). Have new divorce reform proposals moved in this direction?

Are Reformed Divorce Laws Removing the Gender Biases in Divorce?

Until 1968, divorces in Canada were granted if one of the spouses had committed adultery, if desertion or imprisonment had taken place, or if spouses had lived apart for three years. A relative liberalization of divorce laws after 1968 led to increased divorce rates. In 1985, the **"no-fault" divorce law** was passed, and in the 10 weeks immediately after its passage the number of divorce cases in Canada tripled, to 49 000. The new law reduced the waiting period to apply for a divorce to one year, and granted an uncontested divorce after a three-year separation.

One of the outcomes of the legal reforms has been a **"get self-sufficient quick"** orientation primarily directed to those women who have interrupted their employment for marriage and/or childcare. This approach assumes that in most current marriages both spouses have careers, and that wives generally have kept working full-time or intermittently throughout the marriage. This orientation, reinforced by judicial indifference to gender wage inequities, influences decisions regarding retraining periods for the dependent spouse. Frequently, the time frames for education or retraining are unrealistic, given the duration of academic or professional training, demands of single parenting, and lack of opportunity to engage full-time in these educational and retraining programmes.

A 1992 Supreme Court decision influenced the "get self-sufficient quick" approach in divorce settlements. In delivering the decision on the *Moge* case, in which the husband argued that his wife had time to become self-sufficient, Justice Claire L'Heureux-Dubé found that the financial consequences of the end of a marriage extend beyond the simple loss of future earning power or losses directly related to the care of children. They will often encompass loss of seniority, missed promotions, and lack of access to fringe benefits such as pension plans and insurance. This decision was based on the assumption that support payments should function as a vehicle for an equal sharing of the economic consequences of marriage and divorce. In some instances, support payments may continue for an indefinite period. Frequently, however, there is not sufficient income for long-term substantial support. In the *Moge* case, for example, the former wife's monthly support is $150. Thus, the extent to which this initial and other similar decisions will balance the financial inequalities that emerge in most families is questionable.

In a legal context, it is not useful to examine women's approach to economic support after divorce primarily in terms of whether or not they seek employment. As MacLean (1991) suggests,

> we have to stop thinking of the woman's role as head of household after divorce as not financially dependent or independent, working or not working, and begin to perceive it as negotiating an income package from a variety of sources, public and private, collective and individual. The divorced woman then would have to contend with only the cost of being a woman, rather than the cost of divorce as well.

As of May 1997, changes to the federal Divorce Act led to child support being calculated using the income of the non-custodial parent based on average awards in each province. Also, federal Income Tax Act changes meant that child support will not be tax deductible for non-custodial parents, and custodial parents will not have to pay income tax on the money they receive. Critics of these changes contend that they take away the discretionary powers of the courts regarding child support and provide for an annual review of the orders that may be very stressful for some women, particularly those who have been abused. Furthermore, these changes may increase the possibility of litigation; may lead to more parents lobbying for joint or sole custody rather than paying child-support costs; and may result in a significant federal tax grab, given that non-custodial parents usually have a higher income than custodial parents.

Divorce mediation, intended to minimize the hurdles of the process, has not been entirely successful. Mediation assumes an equal bargaining power, and has led some women to forgo the legal protection of the adversarial system. And, whether voluntary or ordered by the court, mediation may reinforce psychological and economic inequalities between spouses (Strauss, 1988).

Similarly, joint custody was intended to equitably divide the financial and emotional burdens of child custody. Consistent and sufficient support payments, it was thought, would accompany this arrangement as a result of the father's greater involvement in his children's lives, in turn reducing conflicts over money and parenting responsibilities. The expectation of a friendly and co-operative relationship either at the time of divorce or soon thereafter is not a reality for many divorcing spouses. Subsequently, joint custody is infrequently an option in hostile divorces. Furthermore, family violence appears to escalate at the time of marital separation, with abused women often at risk of being seriously hurt or killed and children at risk for abduction by abusers. Bill C-22 has proposed that in "the best interest of the child" any family violence should be taken under consideration, including:

- The safety of the child and other family members.
- The child's general well-being.
- The ability of the person who engaged in family violence to care for and meet the needs of the child.

- The appropriateness of making an order that would require the spouses to co-operate on issues affecting the child (*Family Justice Newsletter*, vol 1, 2003, p. 2).

Will these new child custody and access proposals ease or promote gender inequities in the divorce process and outcome? Have past divorce reforms eased gender inequities? Twenty-five years after Canada's Divorce Act was introduced, 86 percent of children from separated/divorced families lived with their mothers, and 7 percent lived with their fathers. Seven percent lived in joint custody or with other relatives, or were cared for by social agencies. A startling 42 percent of children rarely or never see their fathers again after their parents separate (Statistics Canada, 1997b). And these trends continue.

THE AFTERMATH OF DIVORCE: FEMALE SINGLE PARENTS ON WELFARE

Between 1991 and 1996, the number of female-single-parent families increased faster (by 20 percent) than the number of male-single-parent families (Statistics Canada, 1997b). By 2001, 1 311 190 Canadian children (15.7 percent) were living in single-parent families; of these children, the majority (81 percent) were living with female parents (Statistics Canada, 2003c). Female single parents have the combined responsibility of caring for their children and providing financial support in an age when most families face the necessity of two incomes. As a result, half of female single parents with their children are at risk of applying for welfare, many of these in the aftermath of marital separation and divorce.

Social policy and programme changes continue to reaffirm the individual-responsibility model, which assumes that low-income female single parents are in that position as a result of individual choice and should be able to alter it as a result of individual action. This section outlines findings from a longitudinal study of single mothers on social assistance, offering a picture over time of the experiences of low-income female single parents, including some of the options, constraints, and paths they have confronted and addressed.[2] Although the findings are based on the activities of individuals, the need for social responsibility when developing social policy to assist this family group is implicit.

"Single mother on welfare" is a phrase that evokes different images for different people. For some, the notions of dignity, struggle, and injustice are invoked. For others, hopelessness, immorality, and incompetence are suggested. It is important to understand who single mothers on social assistance are, and how they are responding to changes in their individual and family lives. From the longitudinal study of female lone parents, three themes emerged: the social diversity that exists among single mothers, the prevalence of change in their lives, and the nature of the constraints they face that affect their choice of path.

Social welfare policies directed at low-income parents are complex and contradictory. From the deterrence principle inherent in low social-assistance rates, to the inter- and intra-regional inequities in the delivery of welfare to work programmes, to the monitoring of recipients, the governing principles of legislation and their contradictory effects on women are apparent. In addition to deterrence, social welfare policies have tended to view this population as predictably, yet helplessly, yielding to overwhelming external constraints, unable to do anything to change their situation and their responses to it. When active, their response to poverty is often characterized as delinquent, deviant, or criminal, and judged ineffective and destructive for society, others, and themselves. Missing from most of this discussion is an image of the low-income female single parent as a competent actor or agent for social change. Also missing is the acknowledgement that a single parent may refuse to surrender passively to her environment, or that even "bad" environments frequently contain enabling, as well as constraining, elements.

What emerges from this longitudinal study of low-income female single parents is a portrait that stresses their persistent willingness and ability to deal with their circumstances in a positive, active, and determined manner. This does not minimize the difficulties, barriers, and problems confronting them and their children, nor does it suggest a "do-nothing" social policy response to these families. Rather, the "voices" of women interviewed reveal their competencies, their resiliency, and their determination. It is these voices that are glaringly absent from discussions of divorce and the economic vulnerability of women and their children. And it is these voices from which models of social responsibility should be drawn.

SOCIAL DIVERSITY AMONG FEMALE LONE PARENTS

Popular opinion and policy statements gloss over the diversities among single mothers, focusing instead on their presumed similarities. Low-income mothers in particular are often viewed in this manner. Many myths persist. For one, female single parents on welfare are often viewed as young, never married, and with a number of children. Young single parents are not in the majority, as only 3 percent (under age 20) are receiving welfare (National Council of Welfare, 1998). Data from the longitudinal study also challenge these stereotypes: the average age of single mothers is 32 (the range is 19 to 56), and they have one or two children living at home (the range is one to six). These figures are comparable to national data trends (National Council of Welfare, 1998). Clearly, the reason for applying for social assistance as a single parent coincides with child-bearing years for women as welfare requests drop after age 40 (National Council of Welfare, 1998).

Another myth holds that female single parents continue having more children in order to remain on social assistance. As the average number of children per family suggests, this is not the case. One single mother from the study noted: "It is mind-boggling to think that there are people that think that being on welfare is so terrific that we would want to have more children to stay on."

For most female single parents and their children, time on social assistance is short, not lengthy, as the myth suggests. National data indicated that those with a disability, followed by single parents, were most represented in the 25+ month category. National databases have not provided an accessible tracing of "time on welfare" and less clear are the rates of welfare recidivism for single-parent families. Frenette and Picot (2003) used longitudinal tax data to study changes in family income of those exiting welfare in the 1990s, observing that divorced women consistently saw their income decline more than married women and men, and more than divorced men leaving welfare. Complicating factors in this post-welfare period is the introduction of welfare to work programmes with different jurisdictional eligibility and programme criteria (Gorlick, 2002). Welfare exiting data appear to show significant numbers leaving welfare; less clear is where they are going. Explanations offered include that many female single parents are obtaining employment. Yet consistent information on the duration, benefits, and type of this employment is not available. If, as some have suggested, these jobs are entry-level and marginal in nature, what are the implications for reapplication? Furthermore, opportunities for welfare reapplication may not be limitless. Another explanation for welfare exiting numbers is the significant narrowing of welfare eligibility requirements. Also within the context of the welfare "push off" element of welfare to work programmes, female single parents moving to employment will depend on their own social capital such as education level and past employment.

It is perceived that female single parents on welfare have low levels of education. Many of the single parents in the study are fairly well educated. At the study's outset, more than half had some postsecondary education, with a quarter of them being graduates of either community college or university. On the other hand, at least a quarter of the single mothers did not graduate from secondary school. Many were upgrading their education during the 10-year study period. In the final interview round, 41 percent had earned a college diploma or university degree, 17 percent had some postsecondary education, 25 percent had graduated from secondary school, and 11 percent had not graduated from high school.

Finally, it is inappropriate to assume that single parents on welfare are all alike, or that they have similar values and attitudes, common parenting styles, or comparable hopes and expectations. Yet this assumption prevails; for example, welfare to work policy has in most jurisdictions eliminated the possibility of pursuing postsecondary education for low-income female single parent students, as there is limited or no access to both student loans and social assistance. This has occurred as a result of a post-welfare policy focus that promotes "the fastest route possible to a job" and the ongoing perception that all female single parents have insurmountable student loan debts. Some single parents have the resources and opportunities to exit welfare earlier than others. This is also true for other social assistance family groups, yet there is less tendency to attach a common label to them. This picture of single mothers on welfare is further limited because it dismisses or ignores the significance of time and change in their lives.

The Prevalence of Change in the Lives of Single Mothers

Clearly, for this group of female single parents and their children, financial uncertainty accompanies the emotional upheaval of marital separation. Sixty-six percent of women in the study said they sought spousal support soon after separation. Of those, 60 percent received the support. For many, though, the payments became erratic, unpredictable, and insufficient to sustain a family, in turn assuring women's reliance on social assistance. For the majority of single mothers, their former husband's earnings had been the primary contribution to family income before separation, even though 76 percent of the single mothers had been employed. The majority were employed full-time, with 66 percent of them in the service and clerical sectors. Immediately after separation, 54 percent were employed, primarily part-time in the service and clerical settings. Inadequate income and minimal benefits combined with child-care difficulties led many single parents to apply for social assistance.

From the initial interviews, information was collected concerning the reasons for separation and its effects. The primary reason cited for separation was mental and/or physical abuse. Sixty-six percent indicated that separation was their idea; for 13 percent, the idea came from their former husbands; and, for 21 percent, separation was a mutual decision. Eighty-four percent said the separation was final. Whatever the reason for marital separation, the beginning of the process set this family on a journey of profound and far-reaching downward mobility. The perceived speed and intensity of changes in the lives of these women and children are structural as well as personal or individual.

Monthly Income Decline   About 75 percent of the single mothers experienced a drop in their monthly income as a result of marital separation. In some instances, the drop was quite dramatic: between $1667 and $3333 each month. Between the first and second interviews, 62 percent noted that their monthly income had risen slightly through increases in employment or social assistance; 11 percent reported a decrease. Some of the single mothers experienced a decrease when they obtained full-time employment. In spite of this income decrease and the loss of certain benefits provided by welfare, they were determined to leave social-assistance programmes. The inadequacy of social assistance and the growing demand for food banks are continuous reminders of the severity of this situation. Mother–child relationships are altered, with each sometimes trying to protect the other. As one child noted, "I don't feel poor. My mum puts me ahead of herself so I can get what I need" (Cheryl, 15 years old, in Gorlick, 1995, p. 292).

Residential Changes   Eighty-six percent of the female single parents changed residences after they were separated. Also, 45 percent changed residences between the first and second interviews. Reasons given for moving include wanting a better residence, leaving a high-crime area, avoiding problems with superintendents, being evicted, wanting to be closer to school or work, and needing a different size of accommodation. Single parents suggested that these residential changes were particularly difficult for their children, who found themselves frequently adapting to different schools and new friends. Contrary to expectations, the majority of the single-parent families were not in public housing, but rather in the private rental market. National data support this, with 77 percent of single-parent families on welfare renting, 11 percent in subsidized housing, 6 percent owning their own home, and 6 percent in other or unknown housing (National Council of Welfare, 1998). Although the majority of single mothers were not living in co-operative housing, it appeared to be the most favoured. Those living in co-operative housing indicated that it was a satisfactory and a continuous alternative.

Changes in Marital Status, Family Composition, and Health   Twenty-two percent of the female single parents changed their marital status between the first and second interviews, usually because of divorce finalization, although a small number remarried. During this period, in 18 percent of the families, at least one child left home, to live either with the father or alone. Family composition continued to change over the 10-year period, although very few remarried, and fewer still had more children.

Change also has an impact on single parents' perceived health. Mothers felt that their health worsened with discontinuing social assistance, residential changes, and obtaining full-time employment. As one mother explained, "I am going off Family Benefits soon, because I have a job. But I am scared— really scared—that I may be taking too much of a chance for myself and the kids, because I'm not sure what the future will hold" (Cathy, Interview 3, in Gorlick, 1995, p. 294).

Changing Network of Friends and Relatives   In the aftermath of separation, female single parents enter a social world consisting primarily of female friends and their children. Friends, children, and relatives do not promote marital reconciliation; the majority agree with the separation or do not voice an opinion. Single mothers perceive that most of their social support comes from other females: female rather than male friends, their mothers rather than fathers, and female rather than male relatives. The one exception is that single mothers feel their sons provide as much close and self-esteem support as their daughters do. Between interviews, increased social support was the trend, although for some there was a decrease, and others felt the levels of support remained constant. Most of the single mothers did not interact with former spouses, although some maintained a relationship with their in-laws.

Invariably, relationships altered, in both positive and negative ways. One single mother commented:

> It was hard enough when my former husband would show up at Christmas with expensive gifts for the kids, when he didn't take much notice of them the rest of the year. I got used to that. But when my [married] sister would insist that her kids open up their more expensive gifts while my kids looked on, well, that hurt (Sharon, Interview 3, in Gorlick, 1995, p. 290).

In sum, the importance of female friends and their own children in the lives of single mothers is consistent and strong. Furthermore, female single parents in this study are very satisfied with the social support they continue to receive.

Changes Perceived by Children   Children identified residential, school, friendship, and family changes (Gorlick, 1995). Ninety percent of children said they have moved residence (50 percent of whom moved four to seven times); 79 percent changed schools (27 percent more than four times); and 65 percent said their friends changed. Some children (21 percent) remembered frequent changes in child-care arrangements. For many children, interaction with fathers had been infrequent and periodic, although 63 percent of the children had some contact with fathers. Seventy-three percent were 4 years of age or younger when their parents separated, with 10 percent born to never-married mothers. Throughout these constant changes, the children viewed their mother as the most important and consistent adult in their lives.

THE NATURE OF STRAINS CONFRONTING SINGLE MOTHERS, AND PATHS CHOSEN

As previously noted, the prominent strain for female single parents is lack of money, which, for the women in the study, is accompanied by the stigma of welfare. A variety of negative attitudes are perceived by low-income single mothers and are reinforced by particular policies and programmes. Another strain comes from the experience of single-parenting. Strains exist both for those female single parents on social assistance and for those who are employed. While 80 percent of single mothers on social assistance indicate a greater companionship with their children after separating, they also recognize conflict in these relationships (Gorlick and Pomfret, 1993). For both employed and unemployed single mothers, the prevalence of conflict is the same with daughters and sons. But significant gender differences emerge in the type of conflict. Most mothers report that their primary conflict with daughters occurs around their daughters' assertion of independence. With sons, mothers tend to cite their anger with separation, hyperactive behaviour, personality conflict, and stubbornness, and say that the male children were "going through a stage."

Gender differences also appear in the ways mothers prefer to deal with the conflict. With both sons and daughters, mothers prefer to deal with the conflict through communication (slightly more so with daughters). Providing a good parenting role is the second most preferred method for dealing with conflict with daughters. With sons, the second most preferred method is to do nothing.

Overall, children act simultaneously as constraints and enablers in their mothers' lives. It should not be forgotten, however, that a lack of financial resources combined with a child's request for, say, sports equipment or money for school trips or clothing, frequently augments the strains of single parenting.

Single mothers, whether on social assistance or not, have high educational aspirations for their daughters and sons. About 80 percent of both groups want their children to have some type of postsecondary education. They also have high aspirations for themselves. Single mothers convey that they are not letting the circumstances of their lives—the number of children they have, whether they have preschool children, the length of time they are on social assistance, their age or educational level—have an overwhelmingly negative impact. Age, for example, was not a factor in parental participation in educational upgrading or training. Thus, it is never too late or too early to support single mothers opting to engage in these programmes. Most of us think that the more children the single mother has, the less likely she is to enroll in a training programme or postsecondary studies, or to undertake full- or part-time employment. Contrary to expectations, however, parents with more children are slightly more likely than those with fewer children to undertake educational upgrading, such as completing secondary school.

Time on social assistance, time to initiate and engage an exit strategy, time to enter/re-enter the labour market are all aspects of low-income familial time. The manner in which individuals define time influences responses to perceived choices. For some, the embarrassment of a lengthy welfare dependency emerged with the aging of their child/ren, and for others it came at the end of educational upgrading and the frustrating search for a job. There is a negative correlation between time on social assistance and self-esteem, hopes for the future, and anticipation of future income. The longer single mothers were on social assistance, the more likely they were to believe their futures would remain the same or get worse. Self-esteem showed little measurable drop until after six years on social assistance (Gorlick, 1995).

There appears to have been a perceived period of grace, after which decline in mothers' self-esteem was apparent. Being on social assistance while the children were young appeared more socially acceptable. As children aged, mothers perceived that they were re-categorized from full-time caregiver to labour market entrants, and pressures to successfully obtain full-time paid employment became significant. In sum, single mothers did not want to remain on social assistance for long periods of time; there were, however, differing perceptions of labour market entry timing, defined by changing child-care needs, aspirations, health status, and familial readiness, as well as employment preparedness. Nevertheless, training and educational programmes are bridges to nowhere without significant labour market changes. As one single mother put it, "Retraining was unrealistic because there are no jobs. I bought into the dream that was not based on reality and now I owe $5400 and all I have is a boost to my ego" (Elaine, Interview 3, in Gorlick, 1995, p. 293).

CONCLUSION

The preceeding discussion has articulated some of the myths and realities surrounding divorce. Frequently, divorce is viewed as an ending, rather than as a starting point for realignments and changes within and outside the family. Frequently, divorce is seen as a negative experience or a positive and constructive outcome, rather than as a contradictory process involving elements of both. Too often divorced families are presented as "on hold," waiting to form another nuclear family.

While change is a predominant feature of the lives of separated/divorced female single parents, the extent to which they and their children are subjected to it varies considerably. For some, income increases. For others, it decreases. For still others, it remains the same. And a similar pattern repeats itself for place of residence, marital status, and other social and personal indicators. These changes, in turn, may reinforce or modify the strains these women confront. It is misleading and unfair to characterize female single parents as a dispirited group who have given up on themselves and their children, expecting society to take care of them. Despite the uncertainty, the unpredictability, and the strains and stresses in their lives, these women are actively resisting any temptation to simply hand over responsibility for living their lives to others. While no doubt constrained and affected by the circumstances of their lives, they are not passive, and are exerting their ability to act upon the conditions of their lives, rather than merely responding to them.

Constraint-oriented social and legal policy premised on misleading assumptions about the nature of female single parents should be replaced by approaches facilitating, fostering, and supporting choices they have already made. Will proposed divorce reforms incorporate these more constructive approaches? Will the "best interests of the child" expanded criteria enhance the parent–child relationship in custody and access decisions? Will changing the language of custody and access to "parental responsibilities," "shared parenting," and "parenting orders" lead to a decrease in the adversarial nature of divorce? Will focusing on the child's best interests and not their own decrease parents' bitterness? Are divorce policies moving toward a social responsibility approach? Do these new divorce proposals lead to an egalitarian model of divorce not only in legal interventions but also in the aftermath when families must interpret and integrate these decisions into their daily lives?

The complexity and contradictory nature of the divorce process should forewarn us of the misleading direction of an either/or analysis, the indifference to time and process, and the sometimes simplistic assumptions about divorce found in policy articulation and development.

Summary

- Divorce initiates an interactive process of individual and social realignments, strains, hopes, and expectations combined with perceptions of available options, institutional and individual constraints, and paths chosen. Divorce is also a process in which gender inequities persist and are sustained.

- It is misleading to emphasize either greater personal-growth opportunities or negative and pathologizing divorce outcomes, for each places the onus for adaptability or change solely on the individual.

- Comparisons are drawn between "intact" families—the preferred, normative, and "necessary family structure"—and "not intact" families. The divorced family presumably becomes "intact" again if divorced spouses remarry and form another nuclear family, sometimes referred to as blended, step-, reconstituted, or bi-nuclear.

- What makes this a difficult period for some children and not others is not the divorce itself, but myriad influences from family relationships, income decline, and residential changes combined with the child's age and sex.

- Changes to the Divorce Act, intended to address the win–lose orientation of custody and support decisions, have expanded the best interests of the child criteria, altered the language to promote active parental responsibility, introduced clarity to situations of family violence, and reaffirmed the role of the child advocate lawyer.

- "Single mother on welfare" is a phrase that evokes different images for different people. For some, the notions of dignity, struggle, and injustice are invoked. For others, hopelessness, immorality, and incompetence are suggested. It is important to understand who low-income female single parents are and how they are responding to changes in their individual and family lives.

Notes

1. These data were initially released by Statistics Canada as 56 percent of single-parent families having children with a least one health problem, and 9 percent of two-parent families in the same circumstance (Statistics Canada, 1992b). This information was repeated in many newspapers across Canada. It was a couple of days before Statistics Canada noticed that, in fact, the appropriate statistic was not 9 percent, but 49 percent.

Significant here is that this statistical bias went unchallenged. Perhaps one may speculate that this error supports common negative perceptions of single-parent families.

2. The study "Economic Stress, Social Support, and Female Single Parents," conducted by Carolyne Gorlick, consisted of four sets of interviews between 1986 and 1997 with the original sample of 150 single mothers receiving welfare. Close to 51 percent of the female single parents (who had at least one child under 16 living at home) in the first interviews were separated, 31.3 percent divorced, 4 percent widowed, and 14 percent never married. At the time of the first interview in 1986, 60 percent had separated in the past three years; more than half had separated during the preceding year. Approximately two years later, in 1988, 85 percent of the original sample was re-interviewed. The third round of interviews, with 80 percent of the original sample, was completed in 1993. Interviews with the children of the original group occurred in 1994. A final round of interviews was completed in 1997. Findings are included to generalize where possible to the larger provincial or national single-parent populations and offer additional insights from a smaller sample.

Critical Thinking Questions

1. Undertake a content analysis of several academic journals focusing on divorce. What theoretical approaches emerge? What themes of divorce as a social problem are present? What feminist interpretations appear? Are there, for example, illustrations of the significance of "mother presence" as well as "father absence" in the divorce literature?

2. Female single parents and their children experience downward social mobility and economic stress in the aftermath of marital separation. Identify and discuss the key policy and structural changes that might alleviate these negative experiences.

Websites

School Net
http://www.acjnet.org/youthfaq/divlaw.html
A very user-friendly website for all ages, this website offers clear, concise information about divorce. Part of Canada's School Net, this section responds to the questions children of divorce might ask such as: My parents are getting a divorce. I am 14. Are there laws about divorce? Can I read this law for myself? Can I stop my parents from getting a divorce?

Poverty Network
http://www.povnet.org/index.htm

An excellent resource for advocates, people on welfare, and community groups and individuals involved in anti-poverty work. It provides up-to-date information about welfare and housing laws and resources in Canada.

West Coast Legal Education and Action Fund
http://www.westcoastleaf.org/index.php
West Coast Legal Education and Action Fund's website promotes women's full equality by offering public legal education programmes, law reform advocacy, and equality rights litigation. It is a significant resource to the divorce policy and outcomes debate.

Department of Justice
http://laws.justice.gc.ca/en/D-3.4/index.html
A complete version of Canada's Divorce Act.

Divorce Law
http://www.international-divorce.com/canadadivorcelaw/
A shorter version of Canada's Divorce Act.

Suggested Reading

Silvia Bernardini and Jennifer Jenkins. 2002. *An Overview of the Risks and Protectors for Children of Separation and Divorce.* Ottawa: Department of Justice. http://canada.justice.gc.ca/en/ps/pad/reports/2002-fcy-2.html
From the Department of Justice Canada Research Reports, this informative overview of not just the risks for children dealing with divorce but also the protective factors and resiliency effects. The authors offer this review by focusing on the absence of non-resident parents, troubled parent-child relationships, economic disadvantage, and parental conflict.

Rhonda Bessner. 2002. *The Voice of the Child in Divorce, Custody and Access Proceedings.* Ottawa: Department of Justice. http://canada.justice.gc.ca/en/ps/pad/reports/2002-fcy-1.html
From the Department of Justice Canada Research Reports, this comprehensive paper examines the participation of children in divorce, custody, and access proceedings. A thorough examination of the Canadian family law system's response to hearing the voice of the child.

Simon Duncan and Rosalind Edwards. 1997. *Single Mothers in an International Context: Mothers or Workers?* London: UCL Press.
This book challenges the debate that stereotypes female single parents as either a threat or a passive victim, by focusing on the interplay between single motherhood, state policies, labour market structures, and neighbourhood/community supports and constraints.

L. Greaves, C. Varcoe, N. Poole, M. Morrow, J. Johnson, A. Pederson, and L. Irwin. 2002. *A Motherhood Issue: Discourses on Mothering Under Duress*. Ottawa: Status Of Women Canada. *http://www.swc-cfc.gc.ca/pubs/0662326791/index_e.html*

A very important contribution to the divorce policy debate. Drawing from a comprehensive analysis of policy documents, media portrayals and qualitative interviews, the authors have challenged us to remember mothers under duress in the articulation and implementation of divorce policy. With the focus on the best interests of the child and the increasing political strength of father's rights movements, it appears that mother's rights are less visible, particularly for this group of women dealing with substance abuse, mental health issues, and family violence.

References

Ahrons, C.R., and R. Rogers. 1987. *Divorced Families; A Multi-Disciplinary Developmental View*. New York: W.W. Norton.

Amato, Paul, and Alan Booth. 1997. *A Generation at Risk: Growing Up in an Era of Family Upheaval*. Cambridge: Harvard University Press.

Amato, P., and J. Gilbreth. 1999. "Non-Resident Fathers and Children's Well Being: A Meta-Analysis." *Journal of Marriage and the Family*, 61: 557–73.

Ambert, A. 1989. *A Study of Relationships*. Greenwich: JAI Press.

Arendell, T. 1986. *Mothers and Divorce: Legal, Economic and Social Dilemmas*. Los Angeles: University of California Press.

Bernardini, Sylvia, and Jennifer Jenkins. 2002. *An Overview of the Risks and Protectors for Children of Separation and Divorce*. Research Report for Department of Justice Canada, (2002-FCY-2E). *http://canada.justice.gc.ca/en/ps/pad/reports/2002-fcy-2.html*

Bessner, Rhonda. 2002. *The Voice of the Child in Divorce, Custody, Access and Child Support*. Research Report for Department of Justice Canada, (2002-FCY-1E). *http://canada.justice.gc.ca/en/ps/pad/reports/2002-fcy-1.html*

Birnbaum, Rachel. In press. "Rendering Children Invisible: The Forces at Play During Separation and Divorce in the Context of Family Violence." In R. Alaggia and C. Vine, eds., *Cruel but not Unusual: Violence in Canadian Families*. Wilfrid Laurier University Press.

Canadian Council on Social Development. 2002. *The Progress of Canada's Children*. Ottawa: Canadian Council on Social Development. *http://www.ccsd.ca/pubs/pubcat/pcc02.htm*

Cheal, D. 1996. *Growing Up in Canada*. National Longitudinal Survey of Children and Youth, no. 1. Ottawa: Statistics Canada and Human Resources Development Canada.

Chic, Jacquie. 2003. *Legal Challenges; The Attorney General Of Canada v. Kelly Lesiuk*. Income Security Advocacy Centre. *http://www.incomesecurity.org*

Deadbeat Dad a "Myth," MP Says. 1998, March 9. *London Free Press*, p. 1.

Edwards, Harriet. 1989. *How Could You? Mothers Without Custody of Their Children*. Freedom: Crossing Press.

Eichler, Margrit. 1993. "Lone-Parent Families: An Unstable Category in Search of Stable Policies." In B. Galaway and J. Hudson, eds., *Single-Parent Families in Canada*. Toronto: Thompson Educational.

———. 1997. *Family Shifts: Families, Policies and Gender Equality*. Toronto: Oxford University Press.

Family Justice Newsletter, vol. 1 Spring 2003. Department of Justice Canada, pages 1–4. http://canada.justice.gc.ca/en/ps/pad/news/052003.html

Ferri, Elsa, and Kate Smith. 1998. *Step-parenting in the 1990s*. Family and Parenthood: Policy and Practice Series. London: Family Policy Studies Centre.

Frenette, Marc, and Garnett Picot. 2003. *Life After Welfare: The Economic Well being of Welfare Leavers in Canada in the 1990s*. Ottawa: Statistics Canada. http://www.statcan.ca/english/IPS/Data/11F0019MIE2003192.htm

Gorlick, Carolyne. 1995. "Listening to Low Income Children and Single Mothers: Policy Implications Related to Child Welfare." In Joe Hudson and Burt Galaway, eds., *Child Welfare in Canada*. Toronto: Thompson Educational.

———. 2002. *Welfare to Work in Canada: Policy Intentions and Program Realities*. Final Report submitted to Human Resources Development Canada. The University of Western Ontario, London, Ontario.

Gorlick, Carolyne, and Guy Brethour. 1998. *National Welfare to Work Programs: From New Mandates to Exiting Bureaucracies to Individual and Program Accountability*. Ottawa: Canadian Council on Social Development.

Gorlick, Carolyne, and A. Pomfret. 1993. "Hope and Circumstance: Single Mothers Exiting Social Assistance." In B. Galaway and J. Hudson, eds., *Single-Parent Families in Canada*. Toronto: Thompson Educational.

L. Greaves, C. Varcoe, N. Poole, M. Morrow, J. Johnson, A. Pederson, and L. Irwin. 2002. *A Motherhood Issue: Discourses on Mothering Under Duress*. Ottawa: Status Of Women Canada. http://www.swc-cfc.gc.ca/pubs/0662326791/index_e.html

Lipman, E., David Offord, and Martin Dooley. 1996. "What Do We Know about Children from Single Mother Families?" In Human Resources Development Canada, *Growing Up in Canada*. National Longitudinal Survey of Children and Youth, no. 1. Ottawa: Statistics Canada and Human Resources Development Canada.

MacLean, Mavis. 1991. "Surviving Divorce: Women's Resources after Separation." In Jo Campling, ed., *Women in Society: A Feminist List*. London: Macmillan.

National Council of Welfare. 1998. *Profiles of Welfare: Myths and Realities*. Ottawa: Department of Supplies and Services.

Ontario Ombudsmen Report 2002–2003, Ombudman Ontario. *http://www.ombudsman.on.ca/english.asp*

Smith, Beverley. 2003. *Recent Research on Caregiving: Legal and Political Developments.* *http://canadiansocialresearch.net/caregiving.htm*

Statistics Canada. 1992a. *Marriage and Conjugal Relationships in Canada.* Ottawa: Minister of Supply and Services.

————. 1992b. *The Daily,* December.

————. 1997a. *1996 Census: Marital Status, Common-Law Unions and Families.* (October 14).

————. 1997b. "Canadian Children in the 1990s." *Canadian Social Trends* (Spring).

————. 2003a. "Marriages." *The Daily,* February 6, 2003. *http://www.statcan.ca/Daily/English/030206/d030206c.htm*

————. 2003b. "Divorces." *The Daily,* December 2, 2002. *http://www.statcan.ca/Daily/English/021202/d021202f.htm*

————. 2003c. "Profile of Canadian Families and Households: Diversification Continues." 2001 Census Analysis Series. *http://www.statcan.ca/english/IPS/Data/96F0030XIE2001003.htm*

Strauss, M.B. 1988. "Divorced Mothers." In B. Birns and D. Hay, eds., *The Different Faces of Motherhood.* New York: Plenum Press.

————. 1980. *Surviving the Break-Up.* New York: Basic Books.

Weiss, R.S. 1975. *Marital Separation.* New York: Basic Books.

Weitzman, L. 1985. *The Divorce Revolution.* New York: Free Press.

Part 3

Confronting Challenges and Change

Chapter 9

Family Poverty and Economic Struggles

Lesley D. Harman

LEARNING OBJECTIVES

In this chapter, you will learn that:

1. there are a number of myths about family life that need to be dispelled in order to understand family poverty in Canada;

2. far from being carefree and blissful pockets of love and security, families, for many Canadians, are experienced as requiring a constant effort to keep the wolf from the door;

3. Canada is a stratified society in which certain groups are less equal than others and tend to be more vulnerable to poverty; particularly disadvantaged are women, children, persons with disabilities, and Aboriginal people;

4. structural factors such as social reproduction and discrimination within a system of capitalism and patriarchy are the general causes of poverty in Canada today;

5. economic hardship affects all social classes, including the middle class and the "working poor," primarily as a consequence of economic downturn;

6. family poverty is deep and widespread in Canada today.

INTRODUCTION

The goal of this chapter is to discuss some of the sociological definitions, causes, and consequences of family poverty.[1] If you have ever heard someone say, "I can't afford to have children" or "I can't afford to work," you have witnessed an expression of the perpetual struggle that many people living in families today experience just to make ends meet. It is not unusual to hear people talk in economic terms about living in families, having children, and working. For those of you reading this book who have homes and children of your own, and all of the expenses that they may entail, this may not be news. For others of you who have had relatively few economic worries, it may come as quite a surprise that family poverty is a pressing concern today in Canadian society.

Perhaps the most enduring myth of family life is the belief that, once married with children, one will live happily ever after. Rarely discussed are the economic hardships, stresses, and pressures of family life. Far from being care-free and blissful pockets of love and security, families, for many Canadians, are experienced as requiring a constant effort to keep the wolf from the door. There are a number of myths about poverty that we will seek to dispel in this chapter. The first such myth is that poor people are social "failures" who bring poverty on themselves. The second is that, if one works hard enough, one can be successful and avoid poverty. The third is that family poverty is not very extensive today in Canada. The fourth is that poverty is a new phenomenon in Canada.

In this chapter, it will be argued that Canada is a stratified society in which certain groups are less equal than others and tend to be more vulnerable to poverty. Structural factors such as **social reproduction** and discrimination are the general causes of poverty in Canada today. It will also be demonstrated that economic hardship affects all social classes, including the middle class and the "**working poor**," primarily as a consequence of economic downturn. Finally, it will be shown that family poverty is deep and widespread in Canada today. Particularly disadvantaged groups include women, children, persons with disabilities, and Aboriginal people.

WHAT IS POVERTY?

Canada is a very affluent society, and our standard of living is generally so much higher than that of those societies in which the majority of the earth's population live that it is sometimes hard to speak of poverty in absolute or objective terms and really be expressing anything meaningful. Indeed, defining poverty is difficult at the best of times.

Relative and Absolute Poverty

One useful distinction is between *relative* and *absolute* poverty. By **relative poverty**, we mean that what is considered poor is relative to what the contemporary social standards are for "normal" and "wealthy." These standards change with economic fluctuations, technological developments, and changing definitions of the "good life." **Absolute poverty**, on the other hand, refers to a condition of mere physical survival. As Ross, Shillington, and Lochhead (1994, p. 4) point out, even the effort to determine absolute poverty is problematic, influenced as it is by contemporary societal norms, conditions, and services:

> The strictest application of this approach results in a standard of living sufficient only to keep the human body together…whose components are food provided by a charitable

group or food bank, shelter provided by a community hostel, second-hand clothing and access to basic remedial health care. The poverty line implied by such a budget would be very low; an annual income of $2,000 per person would probably cover it.

Objective and Subjective Poverty

Another useful distinction is between *objective* and *subjective* definitions of poverty. By **objective poverty** is meant the prevailing definitions used by bodies whose purpose it is to collect, compile, and report data on poverty within the Canadian population, such as Statistics Canada and the Canadian Council on Social Development. In the simplest case, this involves setting an income level below which a family of four would be defined as living "in poverty." Roughly translated, this means that a family that spends more than 55 percent of its income on food, clothing, and shelter is considered to be poor (Bird, 2002). In recent years, objective measures of poverty have become more sophisticated, taking into consideration such variables as the fact that the cost of living will vary between and within regions, and between types of family arrangement. The MBM (Market Basket Measure) is the most recent approach to calculating poverty. Introduced by Statistics Canada in 2003, this determines the cost of a "basket" of goods and services that are deemed essential to meet a family's needs. This basket includes allowances for food, clothing, footwear, shelter, transportation, as well as personal needs, household expenses, furniture, telephone, and entertainment (National Council of Welfare, 2003). The biggest concern in the debate around the MBM is, "Who defines what is essential to keep a family out of poverty?" This is an example of how even attempts to measure poverty objectively rely on attitudes and perceptions of "the good life" and "deservingness," pointing to the fact that what is really being measured is relative poverty (Jackson, 2000). So the definition of poverty is complex, even in objective terms, as illustrated by the Statistics Canada low-income cutoffs (see Table 9.1).

By **subjective poverty**, we refer to the way people feel about their standard of living. One may feel rich or poor entirely independently of Statistics Canada measures. For example, a full-time student living on a fixed allowance may run out of spending money early in the academic year and have to make do on $100. She might "feel" poor, even if her father is a millionaire and she stands to inherit a fortune. In this case, we would say that objectively she is rich (belonging to a wealthy family), but subjectively she feels poor. On the other hand, a homeless woman without a penny to her name might find a $100 bill in the park and feel like an heiress, if only for a day. In this case, we would say that objectively she is poor (because her annual income is virtually nothing), but subjectively she feels rich. The subjective definitions are important because we live in a society in which people tend to compare themselves with others; in which mass-media images of the "good life" are strong and compelling; in which children learn to demand consumer goods and feel inadequate, poor, and disadvantaged compared with other children if they do not have them. How we feel relative to others and relative to our perception of how we should feel also weighs heavily in our enjoyment of life and our experience of "hardship." Added to these qualifications, figure in both the depth and duration of poverty. By **depth of poverty** we refer to how far below the poverty line a family's income is, the difference being called the **poverty gap** (Ross, Scott, and Smith, 2000, p. 34). By **duration of poverty** is meant the length of time that a household lives in poverty (Ross et al., 2000, p. 35).

Both objective and subjective measures of poverty seem to take as their standard middle-class values of the "good life," which render problematic much of the sociological discussion of poverty. If it is a middle-class value system that defines what it means to be poor, then it is also the same value system that evaluates those poor people and attempts to explain why they have "failed." Indeed, poverty is rarely thought of as a virtue, but rather as a failing. It would not be an exaggeration to say that, in our culture, poverty is regularly associated with evil, and those living in poverty are thought of as somehow less worthy than those who are not. Even our language reveals that one's "worth" or "value" is expressed in monetary rather than in other social terms. With these qualifications in mind, let us examine some of the figures on poverty in Canada today.

The data on objective family poverty are striking. In 1999, almost five million Canadians were defined as living in poverty (Canadian Council on Social Development, 2002). Until the effects of the recession of the early 1990s began to be felt, it appeared as if family poverty was on the decline. By 1990, 15.3 percent of Canadians were living in poverty, a marked decrease from 16.8 percent in 1984 (Ross, 1992, p. 60). However, as Table 9.2 indi-

Table 9.1   FACT SHEET: POVERTY LINES 2002
National Council of Welfare Estimates of Statistics Canada's Before-Tax Low-Income Cutoffs (1992 Base) for 2002

Family Size	Community Size				
	Cities of 500,000+	100,000–499,999	30,000–99,999	Less than 30,000	Rural Areas
1	$19,261	$16,521	$16,407	$15,267	$13,311
2	$24,077	$20,651	$20,508	$19,083	$16,639
3	$29,944	$25,684	$25,505	$23,732	$20,694
4	$36,247	$31,090	$30,875	$28,729	$25,050
5	$40,518	$34,754	$34,512	$32,113	$28,002
6	$44,789	$38,418	$38,150	$35,498	$30,954
7+	$49,060	$42,082	$41,788	$38,882	$33,907

For more statistics on poverty, see Statistics Canada's annual publication *Poverty Profile 1999*.

Source: National Council of Welfare's Fact Sheet at *http://www.ncwcnbes.net/htmdocument/principales/povertyline.htm*. Ottawa: National Council of Welfare. Last updated in December 2003. Reproduced with the permission of the Minister of Public Works and Government Services Canada, 2004.

cates, by 1999 the rate increased to 16.2 percent, with 12.4 percent of Canadian families living in poverty (Canadian Council on Social Development, 2002).[2] Particularly striking are the figures of 55.8 percent for lone-parent families headed by females and 85.4 percent for young families headed by females 24 years or younger (National Council of Welfare, 2000). In the decade that was supposed to be dedicated to the eradication of child poverty in Canada, 18.5 percent of children living in families were defined as living in poverty. The only promising sign from the data is the substantial drop in poverty—27.1 to 23.5 percent—among the elderly.

THE WORKING POOR AND THE NEAR POOR

Often rendered invisible is a category called the "working poor." These are families in which the main earner worked 49 weeks during the year or more, but who remained poor. In 1991, 28.6 percent of all non-elderly poor households fell into this category, and 60 percent of these families had dependent children (Ross et al., 1994, pp. 76–79). By 1998, the number of working poor families with children had climbed by 20 percent (National Council of Welfare, 2000, p. 86). In addition, the "**near poor**" are those "whose standard of living closely resembles that of the poor and is much different from that of typical (or middle-income) households" (Ross and Shillington, 1990, p. 64). This category is important to include because the low-income cutoffs tend to be arbitrary and it is misguided to believe that those who fall immediately above these lines are not experiencing economic hardship. Ross and Shillington found in examining the incomes of households sitting at 110 percent

Table 9.2   **PERCENTAGE AND NUMBER OF PERSONS IN LOW INCOME/POVERTY, BY AGE, SEX AND FAMILY CHARACTERISTICS, CANADA, 1990 and 1999**

	1990	1999
	Percentage (%) of persons in low income/poverty	
All persons	15.3	16.2
Under 18 years of age	17.6	18.5
18 to 64	13.4	15.0
65 and over	21.3	17.7
Males	13.3	14.6
In two-parent families	11.0	12.1
In female lone-parent families	62.8	55.8

Note: This table uses before-tax-and-transfer income to determine poverty status. Reading this table: For example, 15 percent of all persons in Canada were living in poverty in 1990. By 1999, the proportion of persons in Canada had increased to 16.2 percent. There were an estimated 4 886 000 persons living in poverty in 1999; of these, 1 298 000 were children under the age of 18.

Source: http://www.ccsd.ca/factsheets/fs_pov9909.htm. Adapted from Canadian Council on Social Development, using Statistics Canada, Catalogue no. 75-202-XIE. Reprinted with permission.

of the poverty line (in other words, earning an income 10 percent higher than the poverty line) that the additional family income amounted to only the equivalent of a daily bus or metro fare for each member of the household. They concluded that this was "not enough to permit a change in the way households live. For all practical purposes, households in this income range are just as poor as households that are classed as poor under the Statistics Canada definition of poverty" (1990, p. 65). Accordingly, 12 percent of female lone-parent households, 15 percent of elderly couples, 15 percent of no-income households, 8 percent of single-income households, and 4 percent of dual-income households would be classified as living near poverty.

Because the objective measures of poverty are arbitrary and subject to revision at any time, it is important to consider those Canadians who live close to poverty and to realize that they are exempt only from the measure and the label "poor," not from the experience of economic difficulty. Indeed, so much of the effect of poverty stems from the subjective experiences of those undergoing it that the objective measures give us only a very partial picture at best. Nevertheless, what the figures do tell us is that there is deep and extensive family poverty in Canadian society today and that the situation seems to be getting worse, not better (see Figure 9.1).

Figure 9.1 **PERCEPTIONS OF POVERTY OVER TIME**

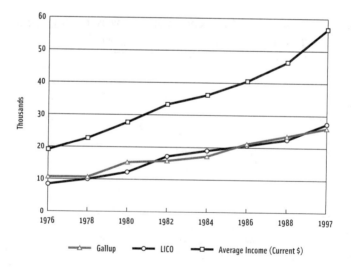

Source: David Ross, Child Poverty in Canada: Recasting the Issue. (Speaking Notes). Ottawa: Canadian Council on Social Development, 1998. Reprinted with permission.

THE HISTORY OF POVERTY IN CANADA

For many born in the post–baby boom generations, it would seem that the recent economic recession in Canada has brought about new and dreadful poverty for the first time. A glance at the pages of history, however, tells us that poverty has been a constant feature of life in Canada.

Recent Quintiles

One graphic indication of the consistency in income distribution in Canada is the Statistics Canada breakdown of national income into **quintiles**. The population is divided into fifths on the basis of wealth, and the percentage of total national income shared by that fifth is indicated. In Table 9.3, it is striking to note that, consistently between 1951 and 1987, the bottom fifth of the population has shared approximately 4 percent of the total national income, while the top fifth has shared between 42 and 43 percent. Beyond the quintile figures, Ryan notes, the figures for wealth indicate even greater inequality than income. In 1980, the top 1 percent of the population owned 18.8 percent of the national wealth, while the top 10 percent of the population owned 57.1 percent (Ryan, 1990, p. 49). The Canadian Council on Social Development has complied another way of looking at this inequality by further breaking down average Canadian incomes in 2000 by deciles (see Figure 9.2). The conclusions to be drawn from these figures are fairly straightforward. Social inequality is a real, enduring, and consistent feature of life in Canadian society (Morissette, Zhang, and Drolet, 2002). The figures defy the myths that poverty is a new phenomenon and that the situation of the poor is dramatically improved by social spending.

Table 9.3   **PERCENTAGE OF TOTAL BEFORE-TAX INCOME GOING TO FAMILIES AND UNATTACHED INDIVIDUALS 1951 to 2000**

Income Quintile	1951	1961	1971	1981	1985	1995	2000*
Lowest	4.4	4.2	3.6	4.6	4.7	3.5	5.2*
Second	11.2	11.9	10.6	10.9	10.4	10.5	11.3*
Middle	18.3	18.3	17.6	17.6	17.0	17.6	16.7*
Fourth	23.3	24.5	24.9	25.2	25.0	25.2	23.3*
Highest	42.8	41.4	43.3	41.8	43.0	43.2	43.6*
Rate of Inequality Between Lowest And Highest Quintiles**	10.3	10.2	8.3	11.0	10.9	8.1	11.9

*Figures for 2000 reflect average income (before tax) of all census families rather than including unattached individuals—derived from source: Statistics Canada 2003, *2001 Census: Analysis Series: Income of Canadian Families*. Catalogue no. 96F0030XIE2001014. p. 30.

**In other words, for every dollar received by the lowest quintile in 1951, the highest earned $10.3 and so on.

Source: Derived from information in A. A. Hunter, 1988, "The Changing Distribution of Income," pp. 86–101 in J. Curtis, E. Grabb, N. Guppy, S. Gilbert, eds., *Social Inequality in Canada: Patterns, Problems, Policies*, Scarborough, Ontario: Prentice-Hall Canada, Inc., p. 88 and Mel Hurtig, 1999, *Pay the Rent or Feed the Kids: The Tragedy and Disgrace of Poverty In Canada*, Toronto: McClelland and Stewart Limited, p. 90.

Figure 9.2   **DISTRIBUTION OF 2000 AVERAGE CANADIAN FAMILY INCOME BY DECILE, CENSUS 2001**

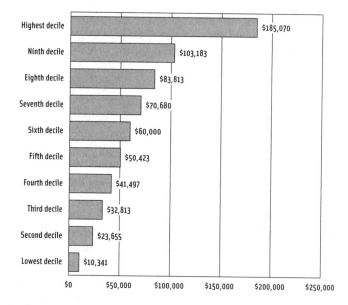

Source: *http://www.ccsd.ca/pr/2003/censusincome.htm.* Reprinted with permission.

The Great Depression

During the last century, Canada experienced a catastrophic blow to its economy that became known as "the Great Depression." Lasting from 1929 to 1939, the period has been referred to as Canada's "ten lost years" (Broadfoot, 1973). Following the collapse of the New York Stock Exchange in 1929, Canada's fledgling economy crumbled. Broadfoot summarizes the events:

> Canada's markets began to collapse. The U.S., to protect its own, erected high tariff walls, shutting out Canadian goods. The prairie wheat economy tottered as the $1.60 a bushel price of 1929 skidded to 38 cents in 2 1/2 years. By that time, even the weather had turned against us: the drought was destroying the West, and Canada like the rest of the world was deep into the worst depression in history.

> As the West and wheat went, so did the rest of Canada. Farmers stopped buying. Eastern factories closed, or laid off hundreds. Construction virtually stopped. Banks no longer lent money; instead, they called in loans. Less and less money was put into circulation and fewer and fewer goods were produced and more and more factories were shut down and the rolls of the poor grew longer and longer and the gloom and despair deepened.

> Depression is a downward spiral and there was nothing to halt it. At times, the spiral was slowed, but it was never halted. When the upturn began around 1937 or 1938, it was a long, long struggle. (p. vii)

Broadfoot's book is a collection of interviews with people who survived the Great Depression. Their stories reveal difficulties of the age that seem almost unimaginable today. For millions of Canadians, life became a matter of sheer survival. They were living in "absolute" poverty. In 1932, it was estimated that an Ontario family of five would need $6 to $7 a week to eat nutritiously (Grayson and Bliss, 1971, p. xiv). Many were required to survive on $10 or less per month (Broadfoot, 1973). Government relief was received by about 20 percent of the population in the worst year of the Depression (Grayson and Bliss, 1971, p. x). But as Grayson and Bliss point out, "These figures ignore the tens of thousands who were too proud to fall back on 'charity' and the millions whose standards of living fell but not quite far enough to force them onto relief" (p. x). One account puts the unemployment and social-assistance situation into perspective:[3]

> Lethbridge in '32, and I'm sure, quite sure of that date, had about 20 percent unemployed. That doesn't mean what it does today. It meant 20 percent of the men who had worked were on the dole. Men on the bricks. It didn't mean wives who might have wanted to work, or had once worked because, you see, not many women worked. Waitressing, five and ten, a few banks, secretaries.... And it didn't mean young people who had come out of high school or school and couldn't get a job. There were no jobs for them, and they were not listed as employables.
>
> ...The 20 percent of 1932 was only the men, the heads of families. It meant one father of a family in five had no work and so his wife and their five kids were on the relief too. Total all that up and it makes a terrible high total.
>
> Another way. One family in five was out of work. Two families were not on relief but so deep in debt and so far into poverty that they would have taken relief if they could have. The fourth family was just getting by, and the fifth family, the merchants, the lawyers, all the professional men, the grain people and the retired people living in town, they were doing very well. Very well indeed. (p. 68)

Few were spared. However, as the following story of a young immigrant shows, the wealthy seemed to profit from the misfortunes of others:

> There was this fellow, Steve Metarski. He'd come over from Poland, the Ukraine, over there, as a kid of 14 or so and worked building railroad and became a subcontractor, and when he married my cousin he was about 45. He was what you would call The Solid Citizen.... His first wife had died and he had this lovely house in a good part of Hamilton....
>
> About 1930...construction just went crash and Steve lost his business in six months. Apparently it was just plain murder. Assets didn't cover debts at the bankruptcy auction so they—and who they are, I just don't know—but they took his house and he got his lawyer to work something out so he'd still have possession and ownership as long as he made the payments. Monthly. But man, he'd bought the house in, say, the mid-twenties, and he had a big chunk of a house left to pay, and it was a hell of a house, and interest

was about 8 or 9 percent. We think 9 percent high today? Think what it was then. I'm in the business and I would say it would be crushing.

…Here was Steve, no business, no job, no cash buried in the backyard and with some screwy deal between the bank and his creditors and where was his out? There was none.

Sally said he never made more than two payments, and had to sell furniture to do that. Then the house was swiped out from under him and sold at about a quarter of actual worth to some guy in Burlington. The guy moved in with his wife and kids and let Steve and Sally live in the basement, and Sally was the maid and Steve did work around the yard, stoked the furnace and was the guy's chauffeur. A chauffeur, for Christ sakes!

Look at it this way. Say, on July 1, 1930, Steve still had a business and a fine house and a nice wife. By January 1, 1931, six months later, he's zilch. Living in the basement in his own house and his wife is the maid upstairs, and the cook. (pp. 8–9)

In another story, a survivor recounts how, during the Depression, poverty was considered a crime:

I never so much as stole a dime, a loaf of bread, a gallon of gas, but in those days I was treated like a criminal. By the twist in some men's minds, men in high places, it became a criminal act just to be poor, and this percolated down through the whole structure until it reached the town cop or the railway bull and if you were without a job, on the roads, wandering, you automatically became a criminal. It was the temper of the times.

I was, you could say, a wanderer. One of the unfortunates. A victim of the economic system? Perhaps. Certainly, most certainly a casualty in the battle between ignorant men who were running this country. There are two places in Ontario, in the fair city of Toronto and down at the even fairer city of London, where ancient records will show that I am a criminal. A criminal in that I violated the Criminal Code of Canada and thereby gained a criminal record for begging. Jail.

If you were poor but had a house and sent your kids to Sunday school, if you had no money and nothing for food, then you were unfortunate and people looked after you. If you left home, like I did, so my brothers and sisters would have more food and more room to sleep, then you became a criminal. You did not have to commit a criminal act. Mr. [R.B.] Bennett saw to that. You just had to be you, without money. Throw the guy in jail. Get him out of town. Lay the stick to his backside. Hustle him along. There's no more soup and bread and there won't be tomorrow so you guys get the hell out of here, see? How many times have I heard these things. (pp. 19–20)

One survivor speaks of finding the family's papers after the death of her father in 1968. The receipts told the tale of how her father had paid for the land:

You know what that old man had done? He had been paying off that land at two dollars a month, five dollars, sometimes ten, sometimes the receipt would read that instead of money, Connor, the owner, had taken a steer as payment. The things made me just break down and cry. Every month, he never missed a month, Dad made some sort of payment. Just the interest sometimes; and a big deal for him was a bottle of whisky at Christmas and sometimes a package of Picobac for his pipe.

He scraped and scraped and scraped and scraped some more and he kept us, Mother, me, my cousin from Calgary who was an orphan, he kept us on that farm. In those days a man would hang on to his land as if it was life itself. I guess it was. Those old and faded receipts. Two dollars, four. His life's blood. (p. 63)

Another survivor questions the official government statement that no one in Canada was starving, with the following tale:

R.B. Bennett said nobody in Canada was dying of starvation and if he meant like Biafra, kids with big bloated bellies, no, not that kind of starvation. But I know one family which lost three children from hunger. Lack of food, malnutrition, then diarrhea which they couldn't fight because they were so weak—and that to me is dying of starvation. They were my sister's kids.... (pp. 91–92)

It was a dreadful period in Canadian history, but it was not so long ago. At its worst, the Depression saw whole families lose their homes, their life savings, and all of their belongings. Many went hungry. The government set up "relief camps," where it is estimated that more than 200 000 single homeless men were "interned" between 1933 and 1936, ostensibly to offset a revolution, and paid 20 cents a day (Grayson and Bliss, 1971, p. xv). The memories are bitter, but many wonder, "Could it happen again?"

The "New" Poverty

With the economic hardships brought about by the recession of the early 1990s, politicians, planners, scholars, and citizens have wondered if we have entered a period of "new" poverty. While most tiptoe around the word "depression," perhaps for fear of causing things to get even worse, there would seem to be a growing resignation among the population that the current economic slump will be with us for some time. For Dean and Taylor-Gooby (1992), looking at Britain, this "new" poverty has been brought about primarily by the rise in unemployment. With long-term unemployment has come a general increase in the welfare rolls and the growth of the segment of society dependent on government support (see Table 9.4 on page 253). Accompanying unemployment as a factor in the new poverty has been the dramatic increase in lone-parent households, primarily headed by women. The general vulnerability to poverty of women who are not supported by men is known as the "**feminization of poverty**." Together, unemployment and the feminization of poverty are the forces at work in the "new" poverty.

CAUSES OF FAMILY POVERTY

Why do some families become poor? Sociologists have debated this question for decades. In the short space allowed, we can only highlight some of the issues.

The "Culture of Poverty" Argument

For many Canadians who have grown up in poverty, the likelihood of having a better life in their adulthood is remote. Some sociologists have attributed this to what they call the **"culture of poverty"** (Lewis, 1966). By this they mean that poor families tend to develop fatalistic values and attitudes about their lot in life, devaluing education, career aspirations, and the usual middle-class definitions of success. They develop a sense of hopelessness of ever getting out of their situation and live with a type of survival mentality. This, in turn, becomes a self-fulfilling prophecy in which failure is inevitable and poverty is seen to cause more poverty. This orientation is contrasted sharply with that of families who share a more middle-class orientation to success, career advancement, and an ever-brighter future.

Since families are the context for the most lasting socialization, these attitudes and values developed in early childhood prove to be important in the subsequent orientation of the child. Within the culture of poverty, it is argued, parents look forward impatiently to their children being able to contribute to the family's income. Prolonged school attendance will take away from the more immediate gratification offered by dropping out and getting a job. For the child as well, the prospect of having spending money to buy a car or stereo equipment, things that cash-strapped parents cannot afford, may draw them away from school work and career aspirations.

Thus, the poor do not always share the value placed on higher education by middle-class families. Not only is university or college education costly, but also it is often derided as not being "real work." As Willis (1981) found in his study of working-class youths in Britain, the prevalent attitude was that schooling is a waste of time because poor children will probably fail anyway, so what's the use of trying? In contrast, the middle-class orientation toward education is one that seeks more and better education for children, in recognition of the fact that occupations and incomes in Canadian society tend to be positively correlated with the amount of education attained. In turn, the likelihood that a high-school drop-out will get a well-paying job is very slim indeed (Canadian Council on Social Development, 1991). In addition to a lack of encouragement, poor children often have school problems because of poor diet and health care, and limited time and space at home to study (Ross, 1998). Because of all of these factors, children from poor families simply do not have the resources to compete successfully and tend to do more poorly in school than children from wealthy families. Families, schools, and governments alike often take this as evidence that they shouldn't be there in the first place.

The "Social Reproduction" Argument

The "culture of poverty" concept has been roundly criticized (Leacock, 1971). Most significantly, it has been indicted for being invented by middle-class social scientists who tend to divide the world into "us" and "them." As we have shown,

Table 9.4 FACT SHEET: WELFARE RECIPIENTS
Estimated Number of People on Welfare by Province and Territory

Province/Territory	March 31, 1993	March 31, 1994	March 31, 1995	March 31, 1996	March 31, 1997	March 31, 1998	March 31, 1999	March 31, 2000	March 31, 2001	March 31, 2002
Newfoundland	68,100	67,400	71,300	72,000	71,900	64,600	59,900	59,400	54,400	52,100
Prince Edward Island	12,600	13,100	12,400	11,700	11,100	10,900	9,800	8,400	7,900	7,500
Nova Scotia	98,700	104,100	104,000	103,100	93,700	85,500	80,900	73,700	66,800	61,500
New Brunswick	78,100	73,500	67,400	67,100	70,600	67,100	61,800	56,300	52,900	50,700
Quebec	741,400	787,200	802,200	813,200	793,300	725,700	661,300	618,900	576,600	560,800
Ontario*	1,287,000	1,379,300	1,344,600	1,214,600	1,149,600	1,091,300	910,100	802,000	709,200	687,600
Manitoba	88,000	89,300	85,200	85,800	79,100	72,700	68,700	63,300	60,500	60,100
Saskatchewan	68,200	81,000	82,200	80,600	79,700	72,500	66,500	63,800	60,900	56,100
Alberta**	196,000	138,500	113,200	105,600	89,800	77,000	71,900	64,800	58,000	53,800
British Columbia	323,300	353,500	374,300	369,900	321,300	297,400	275,200	262,400	252,900	241,200
Yukon	2,500	2,400	2,100	1,700	2,000	2,100	1,700	1,400	1,300	1,000
Northwest Territories	11,100	11,000	12,000	11,800	12,800	10,700	11,300	3,400	2,200	2,100
Nunavut								7,300e	7,300e	8,100
CANADA	2,975,000	3,100,300	3,070,900	2,937,100	2,774,900	2,577,500	2,279,100	2,085,100	1,910,900	1,842,600

* Excludes 16 450 Assistance for Children with Severe Disabilities cases (December 2001).

** Excludes Child Financial Support (CFS) programme, approximately 1500 cases. Effective May 1, 2001. Alberta Human Resources and Employment is no longer responsible for these cases. All figures are estimates.

For information on welfare rates, see *Welfare Incomes 2002*.

For more detailed statistics, see *Profiles of Welfare: Myths and Realities*.

Source: National Council of Welfare Estimated Number of People on Welfare By Province and Territory. Reproduced with the permission of the Minister of Public Works and Government Services Canada, 2004.

they assumed that the reason for poverty and its perpetuation is that poor people share values and attitudes that render them incapable of competing in the dominant culture defined by middle-class standards of success. It follows that, to eliminate poverty, one should begin by changing the values and attitudes of the poor to make them coincide with those of the dominant culture.

It is precisely this solution to poverty that is problematic, because it ignores the structural basis of poverty—that wealth in Canadian society is concentrated in the hands of a few elite groups. Lone-parent families, the aged, the unemployed, Aboriginal people, and persons with disabilities cannot singlehandedly, by altering their attitudes and values, change this rigid and enduring economic structure, or their place in it. To assume that they can takes all responsibility for poverty away from the rich and the state and allows for "**blaming the victim**" (Ryan, 1971). Critics of the culture of poverty approach admit that the values and attitudes of the poor differ from those of successful middle-class people, but they see these as the result of poverty, not its cause. Focusing exclusively on changing poor people's attitudes is thus blaming them for their problems.

Blaming the victim is as popular a pastime when discussing poverty today as it was more than 35 years ago, when Ryan (1971) brought the term into the sociological vocabulary. He was accusing social scientists who used the "culture of poverty" concept of merely engaging in a more sophisticated version of victim-blaming than that frequently engaged in by the general public. Often we tend to dismiss the troubles of others as a consequence of their own failings, rather than looking for larger structural reasons for social injustice.

Such victim-blaming is rooted in the belief that success and achievement in North American society are attributable to the hard work and ability of the individual. This is equivalent to thinking of our society as a **meritocracy**—that all have an equal chance of success and those at the top are those with the most merit. Attitudes such as "the poor are poor because they deserve it," or "people on welfare are lazy bums who don't want to work," or "anyone can make it if they really want to" reflect an unrealistic view of the current economic system and hold poor people responsible for their own misfortune. As Dean and Taylor-Gooby (1992) point out, attitudes toward the poor basically contain a dual concern with "delinquency" and "dependency." They argue that both are the source of general fear, for, to quote Elliot Liebow, "the one threatens the property, peace and good order of society at large; the other drains its purse" (1967, p. 6).

Meritocracy as a principle that explains poverty is contrasted with the "social reproduction" approach. Critics of the culture of poverty concept, such as Leacock (1971) and Ryan (1971), argue that we have to look at the structural reasons for why the rich get richer and the poor get poorer in capitalist society. Why is it that the distribution of income between classes has been so remarkably intransigent over the past 50 years, as seen earlier in

Table 9.3? We must recognize that there are important class differences in our society, and members of the well-to-do classes enjoy opportunities and privileges simply because of their class positions.

One useful tool for this is the concept of "**cultural capital**," or the cultural and financial resources that support a middle-class lifestyle. According to the social-reproduction point of view, success in capitalist society is more likely if one has cultural capital (Lipset, 1972). Cultural capital includes everything, from the financial backing to attend university and have all of the resources to educate one into the middle-class values and culture system, to "connections" in the business world that ease a child's entry into the job market, to more subtle indications like language. Bernstein (1973) argued that middle-class children learn "elaborated" codes that provide an entry into the middle-class world, while children without cultural capital tend to learn "restricted" codes that do not provide access to upward mobility. Thus, the concept of cultural capital helps us to understand the barriers that children from disadvantaged groups may experience, through no fault of their own, because their families have not had the means to provide them with the tools necessary to compete in a middle-class world. There is, then, a tendency for the social reproduction of class membership. Middle-class families not only have the means to provide their children with higher education, but also the orientation that encourages this. The tendency for families with cultural capital is to pass this on to their children (Bourdieu and Passeron, 1977) (see Figure 9.3).

Figure 9.3   POVERTY RATES BY HIGHEST LEVEL OF EDUCATION COMPLETED, 1998

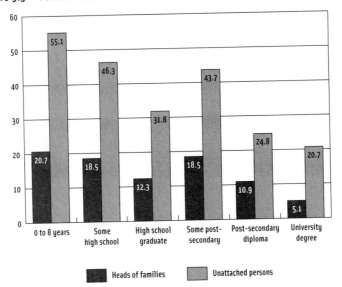

Source: National Council of Welfare (2000). *Poverty Profile 1998*. Ottawa: National Council of Welfare. Reproduced with the permission of the Minister of Public Works and Government Services Canada, 2004.

What do children need in order to get out of the cycle of poverty? Ross (1998) argues that we must look beyond the simple provision of food, clothing, and shelter. "They need economic resources; adequate shelter; access to health care, including dental; secure and attentive parenting; quality child care; schooling, with its growing list of costly items such as computers; recreational and cultural opportunities; physical safety—pollution, traffic safety, crime; concerned and nurturing communities." Many of these aspects of cultural capital are not routinely figured into "essential" basket items. There is now evidence that children from low-income families tend to have poorer health, higher levels of hyperactivity, more limited vocabularies, poorer math skills, more friends in trouble, lower sports participation, and a higher rate of unemployment when not in school than more affluent children. Bluntly put, he states, "As family incomes rise, children's chances for success increase" (Ross, 1998).

Causes of Middle-Class Poverty

Economic struggles can affect families from any class, and this has been increasingly apparent during the recent recession. Children from poor backgrounds regularly encounter a **glass ceiling**, confirming what they already know: you can't get out of the class you were born into. For middle-class families, however, it may come as a shock to realize that the future may hold the real possibility of economic hardship. **Vertical intergenerational mobility** refers to the tendency of children to be upwardly or downwardly mobile relative to their parents' status. Although it is the goal of many middle-class parents to give their children what they did not have, including childhood experiences as well as opportunities for advancement when they are adults, the likelihood of achieving upward mobility is becoming increasingly rare. There are not many ways that the child of a doctor and a lawyer can surpass her parents. Thus, we often encounter a net *downward* intergenerational mobility in the higher-income groups, producing relative poverty for these children (Porter, 1979).

For most Canadian homeowners, the single-family dwelling is the most substantial investment they will make during their lives. And while there are those wealthy citizens who do not need to work to earn a living, who live in homes that are debt-free, 89 percent of Canadians are work-dependent, which means that they must work in the paid labour force or have another source of regular income in order to cover their cost of living (Rinehart, 1987; Morissette, 2002). Mortgage payments or rent payments must be made every month. Children must be fed and clothed, and their many needs somehow provided for. Other expenses related to living up to the middle-class lifestyle, including one or more cars, holidays, and a variety of consumer goods might be affordable only through bank loans or credit card debts, which will have to be reduced through regular payments. A middle-class family may find that a variety of unexpected changes in their situation will make them experience economic hardship. Even though they have steady jobs, a sudden dramatic increase in interest rates may send a family's mortgage payments sky-high. Unexpected repairs on a house or car may entail major financial outlays. Any economic downturn may result in fewer hours, fewer sales, or fewer contracts for workers, thus reducing their net income. When the connection with the paid workforce is severed, through unemployment, illness, or death of a worker, the household unit may find it quickly imperilled, on the brink of financial disaster. Disability or lengthy illness of a breadwinner may mean little or no income, and possible job loss. The birth of a child may mean a reduction in the net family income while one parent stays at home with the baby or continues to work while paying for childcare. Clearly, in our current economic times, many families cannot count on a predictable source of income and a predictable set of expenses. This may help to explain why one outcome of the recession of the 1990s has been a severe self-imposed restriction on consumer spending.

Because it is getting more and more expensive to live up to the standards set by and for middle-class society, and because fewer and fewer jobs have long-term security attached to them, more and more families find it necessary to have two incomes in order to make ends meet. Indeed, the dual-income family is now the norm. By 1987, a full 70 percent of married Canadian women under 65 were employed, with 36 percent employed full-time all year, and 34 percent employed less than full-time all year (National Council of Welfare, 1990, p. 21). By 1991, two-thirds of mothers with children at home were in the paid labour force. However, "regardless of age, mothers working full-time…earn less than women without children at home" (Logan and Belliveau, 1995, p. 28).

One of the greatest stresses on family life is the financial strain introduced by a new baby. Joy at the arrival of this tiny new life may be tempered by the prospect of having another mouth to feed. Particularly when there have been no previous children and no hand-me-downs, there is an initial outlay of a lot of money for furniture and clothing. The weekly grocery bill may soar when the costs of formula, baby food, and diapers are added on. A parent who stays home has lost a substantial part of her income during the initial period of maternity leave, followed by a total absence of income once the maternity-leave period is up. Many families find themselves financially strapped, and women in particular experience a great deal of conflict over whether to return to work. The availability of affordable childcare, the income of the parent, and the flexibility of the occupation often shape the dilemma. To return to work after the birth of a baby means that the family will most likely have to employ a caregiver to look after the child, unless there are relatives who would do it for free (rare in this day and age).

Although the cost of childcare varies regionally and with the type of service provided, it is reasonably safe to assume that an earner would have to be making a considerable amount more than the minimum wage to justify paying for childcare. In addition, a worker requires an appropriate wardrobe and transportation, and often must pay more money for meals than she would spend at home. After taxes, it is not unusual to hear a woman say, "I can't afford to work." What this means is that it would end up costing her more to work and hire someone to look after her child than to stay at home and forfeit her income. While it may be the case that men can't afford to work in some situations, the current wage structure is gender-biased in such a way that, by 2000, women made only 81 percent of the salaries that men did. Women who are on a career track may delay childbearing for several years, being aware of the costs to their career, as well as to their financial situation, of having a child. Thus, it is not unusual to hear a woman say, "I can't afford to have children."

So, clearly, economic struggles for families are produced by and produce conflicts around work and home. These struggles are seen to be primarily women's problems, as women have been the caregivers in our society—not only for children, but also for the elderly. In fact, much of the care of the old and the sick is done within the voluntary sector, through the unpaid domestic labour of full-time homemakers (Hooyman and Ryan, 1987; Frederick and Fast, 1999). And just as it is taken for granted that women will care for children without pay or recognition, so it is taken for granted that women will care for the old and the sick. For the full-time homemaker to return to work may present "eldercare" as well as child-care dilemmas. Care of the elderly is expensive and, as aging is often associated with poverty in our society, may not be affordable without significant strain on the household budget. Unlike the daycare solution, however, care of the elderly often involves a relatively permanent assignment to an institution. Similar to the guilt experienced by parents who place their children in daycare centres, the guilt experienced in placing one's parents in a "home" suggests just how strong the social pressures are to take care of them within family settings.

The new millennium has brought us into the uneasy realization that the entire definition of work is being questioned, hurried along by the dramatic rise in unemployment across all occupations and all social classes. As Burman (1988) has noted, unemployment can deal an enormous blow to one's self-esteem, as well as placing a family in economic difficulty. In cases of long-term unemployment of a sole breadwinner, families may experience considerable stress. Stress, low self-esteem, diminished hope for future employment, substance abuse, strained family relationships, and social stigma within the community can all be consequences of long-term unemployment. As well, lengthy financial dependency on the state may mean net downward mobility for family members, having long-term consequences for the life chances of children. As more and more Canadians experience unemployment first-hand, it is imperative that as a society we begin to lift the social stigma placed on individuals and families when the economy does not favour them, and begin to look at larger structural reasons for their individual hardship. The days in which it was safe and smug to blame the victim are fading fast as we begin to realize that few are truly secure in their jobs.

DISADVANTAGED GROUPS

In Canadian society today, certain groups of people are systematically disadvantaged. Of particular interest are women, children, persons with disabilities, and Aboriginal people. When people belong to more than one of these categories, for example, Aboriginal children or disabled women, their susceptibility to poverty tends to increase.

BOX 9.1   CENSUS SHOWS GROWING POLARIZATION OF INCOME IN CANADA

The 2001 Census figures on income, released on Tuesday May 13, are telling us two very important stories. The first is that Canadian society is becoming increasingly polarized. The richest 10 percent of our population has seen its income grow by a whopping 14 percent while the bottom 10 percent has seen only a slight increase of less than 1 percent. Moreover the income of many working families has actually declined!

The second story is that we have been unable, as a nation, to tackle poverty in any meaningful way. The economic boom of the last part of the decade has clearly not benefited most Canadians, and it has failed to put any real dent in Canadian child poverty rates—despite the 1989 resolution, unanimously adopted by the House of Commons, to eradicate child poverty by the year 2000.

While we could have expected bad news during the first part of the last decade, we should have seen substantial improvements in the latter part given the economic boom. We cannot help but conclude that Canada is doing a less than impressive job in most social policy areas. In one of the richest countries on the planet, our lack of attention to social policy is hard to justify and an increasing source of embarrassment.

It is time that we start to pay careful attention to social policy and social programmes. A few years ago we began to realize that our healthcare system was in real trouble, so government conducted numerous studies, launched provincial and royal commissions, and made substantial new investments. What the Census results are telling us is that we need to start doing the same thing for social policy in this country.

We need to be harnessing all of our collective efforts and energies towards turning the tide. Let's move beyond federal/provincial jurisdictional battles, let's recognize the role of cities and communities in strengthening our social fabric, and let's support our voluntary sector across the country so that we can truly begin to address the issues that the recent Census has made so evident.

Source: *http://www.ccsd.ca/pr/2003/censusincome.htm*

Women

It has been argued so far in this chapter that the myths of family life have concealed widespread family poverty and economic struggles in Canadian society. What has become increasingly evident is that women's economic dependency within patriarchal society has made poverty very likely for them if they live alone. Lone-parent families headed by females are the most likely families to be poor. This is symptomatic of a larger trend known as "the feminization of poverty."

The term "feminization of poverty" means that, without the support of a man, a woman is likely to be poor. This problem is widespread in Canadian society. According to the National Council of Welfare (1990, p. 15), 84 percent of all women will spend at least part of their adult lives without husbands, having to support themselves and their children. In 1998, 54.2 percent of never-married female lone parents, 39.4 percent of unattached women over 65, and 41.9 percent of unattached women under 65 were living in poverty in Canada (National Council of Welfare, 2000, p. 38). At every stage of their lives, women are more prone to poverty than men, and more likely to be trapped, and eventually die, in a life of poverty (Harman, 1992).

The Working Poor   Changes in women's work both in and out of the home have paralleled changes in the nature of the household as an economic unit. The interdependency between the private and the public realms necessitates that most families engage in both social and biological reproduction in the private realm and productive labour (earning an income) in the public realm, as demonstrated in Figure 9.4.

The gendered division of labour has ensured that women occupy the private realm and men occupy the public realm. Women's work has been restricted to the "double ghetto" of unpaid domestic labour in the home and poorly paid, low-status pink-collar jobs in the paid labour force (Armstrong and Armstrong, 1978). Men's work, on the other hand, has been compartmentalized into the highly paid, high-status white-collar sector and the traditionally physical blue-collar sectors. Both arenas of "men's work" have been

Figure 9.4   THE HOUSEHOLD AS AN ECONOMIC UNIT

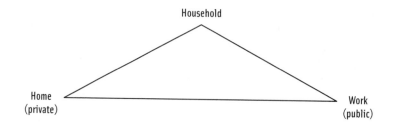

Source: Created by Leslie Harman. Reprinted with the permission of the author.

seen to reflect men's greater suitability for the hard, cold, aggressive, competitive marketplace that is the public realm, while both arenas of "women's work" have been seen to reflect women's greater suitability for the soft, emotional, passive, and nurturant roles of wife, mother, and overall caregiver. Although in recent years more and more women are being employed in nontraditional occupations, a substantial majority of women continue to be employed in the traditional pink-collar sectors (clerical, teaching, nursing, social work, and domestic activities). In 1988, 76 percent of women in the paid labour force worked in these traditional female jobs (National Council of Welfare, 1990, p. 21). And while it is also true that more and more men are doing unpaid domestic labour in the home, women continue to do the bulk of the housework. When they also work in the paid labour force, they are often forced to work a "double day"—to do a full day's work outside of the home during the day, followed by the equivalent amount of time doing the domestic labour required to keep the household operating (Luxton, Rosenberg, and Arat-Koc, 1990).

Significant shifts in the paid labour force in recent years, particularly the dramatic rise in unemployment during the recession of the 1990s, are important in understanding family poverty. Women's participation in the paid labour force has steadily increased, from 28 percent of all workers in 1961 to 44 percent in 1988 (National Council of Welfare, 1990, p. 20). By 1989, 58 percent of Canadian women were in the paid labour force (Parliament, 1990, p. 18).

According to Pat Armstrong (1984), while women have progressively been moving into the workforce, it is a fallacy to assume that they have been "taking jobs away from men." Rather, there are several forces at work. First, because of economic downturn, many previously single-income families have experienced economic difficulties, and women have been "pushed" out of the home into the labour force. They have also been "pulled" out by the opening up of low-paying, typically pink-collar jobs as the state has expanded dramatically since the last war, to the point of being the largest employer in Canada. Technological changes such as the computer revolution, through which desktop computers have become standard office fare and data processing has become an industry in its own right, have opened up vast opportunities for work in a traditionally female-dominated field, at the same time dramatically changing the skills and job requirements associated with clerical work. For example, "filing"—manually sorting and storing paper documents, once occupying armies of poorly educated and poorly paid women—has taken on a totally new meaning over the past 20 years. Now the mountains of paper have been reduced to electromagnetic fields stored on computer memory, and the physical act of filing to the pushing of a button. Computer innovations have also been responsible for job losses in some blue-collar areas, typically the arena of "men's work." The worker composition of the automobile industry, for example, has been significantly altered by the introduction of robots to perform work that men once did. Unemployment in blue-collar areas has also served to push women into the workforce, in some cases to become the sole breadwinner in families.

The reasons for women's increased labour-force participation are rooted in the larger structural relations of patriarchal, capitalist society. The triangulation between home, work, and household (see Figure 9.4) means that women are often caught between realms when they strive to "have it all." It is difficult for women to thrive financially without being dependent on a male breadwinner. As the biological reproducers of the species, women have been socially cast into roles that place priority on motherhood. When women work for an income they tend to be discriminated against, as it is assumed that their paid labour is less significant than that of men's. Women's paid labour can become a poverty trap, with a catch-22: many women cannot make enough money in the paid labour force to pay someone else to look after their children, therefore ensuring that they will stay home, thus disadvantaging themselves when they do seek re-entry into the labour force. Financial independence becomes increasingly difficult. If women live without men, either by choice or by necessity, they are often forced to become dependent on the state through family benefits payments.

Lone Parents

In 1991, **lone-parent families** made up 13 percent of all Canadian families (Oderkirk and Lochhead, 1992, p. 27). This figure is not much different from that in 1941, when just over 12 percent of all Canadian families were lone-parent families (1992, p. 27). The major demographic differences, however, are that in 1941 death of a spouse was the most frequent cause of lone parenting, whereas today lone-parent families tend to be more the result of separation, divorce, and widowhood (79 percent), or never-married women raising their children alone (16 percent) (1992, p. 28).

Throughout the life cycle, living in a potentially pregnant body means that reproduction will significantly affect women's material existence. Teenage pregnancy frequently leads to early and long-term poverty. Along with high rates of separation, divorce, and widowhood, these life events result in 82 percent of lone-parent families being headed by women (1992, p. 27).

A study of gender differences in lone-parent families reveals that, as with other disadvantaged groups, lone parents are doubly disadvantaged when they are women. In general, female lone parents tend to be younger, less well educated, and more likely to live in poverty than male lone parents. In 1991, lone mothers with dependent children constituted 30 percent of all poor families, compared with 24 percent in 1981, indicating that female-headed lone-parent families are making up an increasing proportion of Canada's poor (Ross et al., 1994, p. 63). In 1998, a shocking 85.4 percent of female lone parents under the age of 25 were raising their children in poverty. Poverty is at its highest when children are young, and increases with the number of pre-school children (National Council of Welfare, 2000, p. 47). Seventy-six per-cent of these families with children under 7 were poor, while 81 percent of never-married mothers were raising their children in poverty (Ross, Scott, and Kelly, 1996, p. 3).

As we saw in Chapter 8, the prospects for getting out of a life of poverty are often bleak for female lone parents, who often become dependent on the state and face systemic blocks to their opportunities to "get off the system." Early pregnancy, whether in a marriage or not, virtually excludes the possi-bility of women getting enough education and training to develop a career that might eventually lead to economic independence. And as women age, their job prospects are not always very favourable. In old age, women usually outlive their male partners and may find themselves impoverished, living on a fixed income and all alone. Increasingly, we are witnessing the ultimate tragedy of the feminization of poverty in the growing visibility of homeless women.

Children

In 1989, it was brought to the attention of the Canadian public that more than one million Canadian children under the age of 16 were growing up in poverty (Barter, 1992, p. 11). The House of Commons passed a motion stating a goal of eliminating poverty among children by the year 2000 (Kitchen et al., 1991). The 1990s were to be the decade in which child poverty was redressed in this country. However, child poverty is on the rise. Between 1989 and 1998, child poverty increased by 42 percent (National Council of Welfare, 2000, p. 87). By 2000, 1.3 million, or one in five, Canadian children were living in poverty (Bird, 2002, p. 30).

Children are particularly vulnerable to poverty. Living in families means that they are dependent, economically as well as emotionally, on the family unit. If the family is poor, so are the children. And as the lessons of the Great Depression should tell us, the "lost years" spent in childhood poverty have long-term consequences for the life chances of children.

Poverty can affect the life chances of a child even before she is born. Kitchen and colleagues (1991) report that low-income expectant mothers tend to have poorer diets, probably a result of inadequate nutritional educa-tion and insufficient funds to purchase adequate or healthier food. Poor maternal diet "increases the likelihood of prenatal and neonatal mortality or prematurity" (1991, p. 5). Indeed, the figures on infant mortality show a sig-nificant class difference. In 1986, the rate of infant mortality was 10 per 1000 for the lowest-income quintile, while it was 5 per 1000 for the highest-income quintile (Canadian Institute of Child Health, 1989, p. 98).

For the children who do survive birth, a life of poverty means that they will very likely not have adequate nutrition to develop to their full physical and mental potential. It is also a fairly strong predictor of stress and even violence in the home. As we have already seen, poor children do not have the cultural capital or the opportunities to strive for middle-class goals, and will likely have their opportunities for getting out of the class they were born into severely curtailed. Children living in poverty have twice the likelihood of developing chronic illness, physical disability, or emotional difficulties; poor academic attainment; dropping out of high school; living in unsafe housing; and smoking. The social reproduction of poverty is most striking when it is shown that, in 1990, 18 percent of poor female teenagers became pregnant, compared with 4 percent of teenagers from higher-income homes (Ross et al., 1996).

Persons with Disabilities

"Disability" is defined by the World Health Organization as "any restriction or lack (resulting from an impairment) of ability to perform an activity in the manner or within the range considered normal for a human being" (Statistics Canada, 1989, p. xxi). The definition contains the essence of the experience of being in a disabled body: that the world of work, family, and life in general is the privileged sphere of non-disabled people, the "normals." It was not so long ago that individuals who did not strictly conform to the category of "normal" were considered freaks, unentitled to work in the public sphere, or to have love, happiness, and family in the private sphere (Goffman, 1963). This has meant systematic blocks to opportunities for advancement, in formal education and in the workplace, and almost certain poverty and dependency for the disabled.

There has been increasing awareness in recent years that persons with disabilities are routinely discriminated against in the job market, and they now constitute one of the recognized "target groups" of visible minorities in efforts to promote diversity in the workplace. Nevertheless, years of disadvantage at the hands of a discriminatory labour market have left disabled persons as a group more vulnerable to poverty.

Adults with disabilities tend to have lower incomes than non-disabled Canadians. In 1986, 40 percent of Canadians with disabilities aged 15 to 64 were employed, while 70 percent of non-disabled adults were employed (Nessner, 1990, p. 5). But these figures should be interpreted carefully, as 51 percent of adults with disabilities defined themselves as not in the workforce, and hence not "unemployed." Many persons with disabilities who are not in the workforce depend on various forms of state support, such as disability pensions, to get by. Such incomes tend to be low and geared at providing a subsistence level of survival. Consequently, adults with disabilities tend overall to have significantly lower incomes than other Canadians. In 1985, the median income for adult men with disabilities was $13 000, while it was

$20 900 for non-disabled males (Nessner, 1990, p. 5). In 1995, 36.1 percent of people with disabilities were poor, compared to 23.1 percent of those without disabilities (Lee, 2000, p. 40).

When gender and disability are combined, we find that women with disabilities are doubly disadvantaged. If non-disabled women are more prone to poverty than men, and systematically make less money in the labour market, then one might expect that women with disabilities would be even more vulnerable to poverty. Statistics seem to bear this out. According to Barile (1992, p. 32), 66.1 percent of women with disabilities working in regulated industries earned less than $20 000, while only 14.6 percent of men with disabilities did. At the other end of the wage scale, 2.7 percent of women with disabilities made over $40 000, while the figure climbed to 20.6 percent for males with disabilities.

Aboriginal People

To be an Aboriginal person in Canada today is to face a strong likelihood of poverty, disease, and a short lifespan. As we saw in Chapter 4, Aboriginal people have faced a history of hatred and discrimination in Canadian society at the hands of a violent and imperialistic state. The injustices done to this group are only beginning to be appreciated; however, the scars are deeply felt in a community in which an Aboriginal person will die, on average, 10 years sooner than other Canadians, and in which an Aboriginal person is three times more likely to end up in jail than in a high-school graduating class (Comeau and Santin, 1990, p. 2). Urban Aboriginals are more than twice as likely to live in poverty than non-Aboriginals, which translated to 55.6 percent in 1995. While making up only 1.5 percent of the population, Aboriginals constituted 3.4 percent of the urban poor (Lee, 2000, p. 38).

Demographics indicate that, as a group, Aboriginal people have been structurally maintained in a situation of poverty. According to Frideres (1998), the average Aboriginal income is 70 percent of a non-Aboriginal income; unemployment ranges between 17 percent among off-reserve Aboriginal people to 57 percent among those on-reserve, compared with the national average of 10 to 11 percent; and the high-school completion rate is two-thirds the national rate. The dependency ratio—the proportion of the population not in the workforce (the young and the old) relative to the population in the workforce—is twice as high among Aboriginal people as in the general population.

As a rule, Aboriginal culture has not shared the dominant middle-class values, so higher education—with the value placed on competition—and paid employment—with the value placed on consumerism—have not typically been viewed with the same importance. Coupled with **systemic discrimination** and racism at the hands of schools and employers, Aboriginal people have occupied a distinct and certainly disadvantaged social position within Canada.

CONSEQUENCES OF POVERTY

While we may debate the definitions and causes of poverty, for poor Canadians it has very real and bleak consequences. Poverty means having little money to get through the month and buy even life's necessities: shelter, food, and clothing.

Poor-Quality Food and Health

Poor families may find that they have to buy the cheapest food in order to get through the month, and go hungry when that has run out. You may have noticed that, for much food there is a negative correlation between its price and its nutritional value. Additives and high fat content are common in low-priced foods. If consumed in large quantities, such foods may be cancer-causing. Certainly the links between fat and chronic disease such as cancer and heart problems have now been established, as has the link between such chronic disease and poverty (Antonovsky, 1967; Hay, 1988). Lack of education may keep the poor unaware of how their own life expectancy may be diminished by their poor diet. Clothing, particularly winter clothes to protect against the harsh Canadian climate, is expensive and may be simply unafford-able, increasing the likelihood of illness.

The increased use of food banks, emergency shelters, and other charitable organizations providing life's necessities gives us a clue as to how desperate many Canadians now are. The number of food banks in Canada has mush-roomed from one, in Edmonton, in 1981, to 292 by October 1991. Food-bank use is most common in Ontario, where 28 of every 1000 people are recipients of monthly aid. More than 40 percent of the recipients in Canada are children, and families with children received two-thirds of the food relief in 1990. Most of the people who make use of food banks are on welfare (Oderkirk, 1992, p. 7).

As an indication that poverty does not just strike the uneducated mem-bers of society, Toronto's Daily Bread Food Bank records show that the educa-tion level of food-bank recipients is going up. In 1991, 9 percent had graduated from college or university (compared with 4 percent in 1987), 9 percent had some college or university (4 percent in 1987), and 22 percent had graduated from high school (5 percent in 1987) (Oderkirk, 1992, p. 12). In total, 40 percent of those who used this food bank had a high-school diploma or more.

Welfare

Welfare may be the last resort for those who are able to work but whose Employment Insurance benefits have run out, or for those who are unable to work because of illness, physical disability, or having to raise preschool chil-dren. Welfare payments across Canada fall miserably below the low-income cutoffs, keeping recipients destitute and often in such misery that they become unable to extricate themselves from this state. In 1990, there were 1.93 million welfare recipients in Canada, with families constituting the majority, at 63 percent (Oderkirk, 1992, p. 11).

Homelessness

Thousands of Canadian men, women, and children face homelessness today. Although members of all social classes can experience economic struggles, the experience of being homeless is perhaps the closest one can come to the absolute poverty that Ross and Shillington describe (1990, p. 236). For here, the fragile connections between public and private realms have been severed. There is no private realm, there is no household, and there is no steady work.[4]

Homelessness is a general category for those who have no fixed address. It is telling to focus on the language we use, and to realize that within the label "homeless" is contained a world of meaning. "Homelessness" denotes deficiency; there is something very important missing, and that is "home." As we have seen above, the connections between home, household, work, and family are so strong in our society that they form a web that contains us within the class system. When the web is broken, the swift and steady descent to homelessness takes one out of the class system altogether to the nether regions of the "underclass."

No one knows how many homeless people there are, and this is primarily because the homeless are not part of the larger system of control through which the state monitors the lives and activities of its citizens. Although efforts have been made to count and keep track of the homeless, the problem is that they are not locatable according to the same criteria as are the "homeful." Those who are connected in the web of relations between home and work are locatable through an array of codes and numbers. A fixed address locates one, as does a telephone number. Paid employment locates one, as does a social insurance number, bank account, credit card, driver's licence, and health insurance number. The myriad ways in which the homeful are accountable also enable the state to exercise control over them.

Not so for the homeless, whose descent to the underclass puts them so "low" as to be outside and below the entire system of membership of our society, disentitling them from even the most basic of rights and privileges, such as enumeration for voting. Indeed, it is not unusual to hear the homeless referred to as "less than human," belonging "in the gutter." Such talk reveals the bitter truth that what is really valued in our society, which is seen to give us our humanity, is "homefulness" and property ownership. In this sense, not much has changed in attitudes toward the homeless since the Great Depression.

The experience of homelessness is to lose claim to the private realm altogether. As much as we idealize the home as the place where one can "be oneself," the realization that simple, taken-for-granted daily routines such as bathing and sleeping cannot be performed in private suggests the bleak reality of homelessness. Imagine for a moment what you would do if you did not have a place to go to sleep, eat, rest, keep your things, and have some privacy. Perhaps you have found yourself in a strange city with no money and nowhere to go. Chances are, however, that help was just at the other end of the phone: the bank, your parents or friends, some source of support to tie you into the world of the homeful. For the homeless, there are no such ties. Soup kitchens, food banks, emergency shelters, and handouts provide the necessities of life. Public washrooms, public transportation, public libraries, and all-night doughnut shops become "home," and the daily routines of life are practised there for the entire world to see.

When I was interviewing women for my study on homeless women (Harman, 1989), one woman told me "the city is a great place...if you have money." Her experience of the abject poverty of homelessness was to see another side to the city, the underside, with its filth, violence, hunger, cold, and despair. Living on the street means being basically exposed to the elements—the winter cold, the rain, and the blazing heat of summer. Inadequate food, shelter, and clothing increase susceptibility to disease. Women in particular are targets of violence: rape, theft, and the day-to-day degradation of being treated as less than human. Fear of violence may make women reluctant to fall asleep at night, wandering about in search of a quiet, safe place.

The visibly homeless are only a part of the picture, however. In fact, there are many different stages and shapes that homelessness may take. Women's economic dependency means that they are more vulnerable to becoming homeless. Watson and Austerberry (1986) distinguish between **concealed homelessness** and **potential homelessness** as two categories that are applicable to women. By "concealed homelessness," they mean the condition of living temporarily with friends or family. While appearing to be homeful, the individual may in fact be relying on the goodwill of others for a roof over her head. By "potential homelessness," they mean those, particularly women, who could be homeless at any time or who will be soon. Here we see that by virtue of their dependency on male breadwinners whose paid labour provides a roof over their heads, these women are not yet homeless. However, if they leave the situation, or the male breadwinner becomes unable to work for any reason, the interconnections between home and work cannot be maintained, and the entire family, or just the women and children, might quickly become homeless.

Homelessness might be temporary, as in the case of an abused woman who leaves her husband and takes her children to stay at a shelter until she gets on her feet. Although many such women do not have adequate job skills or support in the community to survive economically, some are able to become self-supporting. Sadly, many of the women in this situation find themselves chronically dependent on emergency shelters. For many such clients, the "hostel becomes a home" (Harman, 1989). Here, a substitute for the shelter of the homeful is provided. Food, clothing, and structured domestic activities such as cooking and cleaning serve to reproduce the domestic roles familiar to many once-homeful women. In this way, women's dependency on the male breadwinner is replaced by dependency on providers of social services. Unfortunately, the alternatives to this kind of life are limited, as there is not sufficient affordable housing or community support to give these women the kind of opportunities required for them to be independent. Those who avoid the hostel route, for example, teenage runaways, may find themselves doomed to a life on the street, working as prostitutes, addicted to drugs, and involved in petty crime.

CONCLUSION

Family poverty and economic struggles affect men, women, and children in Canada today who are all struggling to make ends meet and maintain some kind of a lifestyle in the face of economic uncertainty. We have seen that the definitions and meanings of poverty are problematic, influenced as they are by middle-class values of the "good life." We have distinguished between relative and absolute poverty and objective and subjective definitions of poverty. We have seen that there is disagreement as to the causes of poverty, with some sociologists tending to blame the victim in identifying a culture of poverty and others recognizing that poverty is an inevitable outcome for some within a stratified system in which the rich tend to get richer. Certain groups, such as women, children, persons with disabilities, and Aboriginal people, are more susceptible to poverty than those who occupy positions of privilege.

The consequences of poverty mean that life is a constant struggle. Long-term unemployment can be stressful on family relations as well as affect the opportunities available to children. The contemporary living arrangements of most Canadians necessitate some kind of balance between the public and the private realms; losing that balance may mean severe economic struggle. For 1.9 million Canadians, living on welfare has meant relying on the safety net of the state to meagerly support them. The homeless live the closest to absolute poverty in Canadian society today, with many homeless or potentially homeless women being concealed through the charity of friends, community, or the state.

Our discussion of family poverty began with a list of four poverty myths: that poor people are social "failures" who bring poverty on themselves; that if one works hard enough, one can be successful and avoid poverty; that family poverty is not very extensive today in Canada; and that poverty is a new phenomenon in Canada. In contrast to these myths, we have learned that poverty is most often a consequence of factors beyond an individual's control; that poverty strikes even those who are well educated, from affluent families, and working full-time; that family poverty is a deep and widespread reality for millions of Canadians; and that social inequality has been a persistent fact of life in Canada during this century, with the most devastating experience being that of the Great Depression.

It would be wrong to offer false hope in times of economic uncertainty. Nevertheless, one can hope that, by revealing the poverty myths through a sociological perspective on poverty, we might all gain a more realistic understanding of the problem. The task of the future would seem to be to avoid blaming the victim and to begin examining how we can work collectively to improve the life chances of all Canadians.

Summary

- There are different meanings and definitions of poverty, including relative versus absolute poverty, and objective versus subjective poverty.
- People living near poverty, such as the working poor and the near poor, experience economic hardship.
- Unemployment and the feminization of poverty are the forces at work in the "new poverty."
- The "culture of poverty" argument tends to blame the victim.
- The "social reproduction" argument finds that social classes tend to reproduce themselves intergenerationally.
- The most economically disadvantaged groups in Canada today are women, children, persons with disabilities, and Aboriginal people.
- Consequences of poverty include poor-quality food and health, welfare dependency, and homelessness.

Notes

1. The author gratefully acknowledges the valuable insights offered by Bernard Hammond during the preparation of this chapter. This chapter is dedicated to my children—Matthew, Daniel, and Beth.

2. Of the objective measures of poverty, the Statistics Canada figures tend to be the more conservative, with the Canadian Council on Social Development (CCSD) determining higher low-income cutoffs, and therefore higher rates of poverty. As with all attempts to use statistical calculations to measure the social world, the "operationalization of variables" determines what one finds.

3. Extracts from Grayson and Bliss (1971) are reprinted with permission by the University of Toronto Press.

4. An understudied population among the homeless are the working poor, who have paid employment but still cannot find affordable housing and are forced onto the street or into charitable shelters. This discussion focuses on those who are without steady paid employment.

Critical Thinking Questions

1. Reflect on times when you might have experienced "subjective" poverty and compare those experiences with a state of "objective" poverty. What does living in poverty mean to you? How difficult is it to define poverty?

2. Compare and contrast the "culture of poverty" argument with the "social reproduction" argument. Why do you think it is so easy and so popular to blame the victim?

3. Why do you think it has been so easy to blame unemployment on women, when the facts point to economic, technological, and policy reasons for this state of affairs?

4. Identify some ways to minimize child poverty in Canada.

5. Empty your wallet and examine the variety of codes and numbers that are in some way identified with your name. Imagine your life without these connections, and you will have made the first step in imagining what it might be like to be homeless.

6. Play "The Poverty Game" in your class. This board game was created by a group of single mothers in British Columbia. The game enables participants to experience vicariously many of the challenges of trying to get through the month on a fixed income while raising children.

Websites

The Canadian Fact Book on Poverty
http://www.canadiansocialresearch.net/poverty.htm
This website links to information about the measurement of poverty in Canada.

Maple Leaf
http://www.mapleleafweb.com/features/general/poverty
An in-depth article outlining the various issues surrounding poverty in Canada and around the world.

Suggested Reading

Sheila Baxter. 1988. *No Way to Live: Poor Women Speak Out.* Vancouver: New Star.
Poor women talk about their lives in poverty.

Barry Broadfoot. 1973. *Ten Lost Years 1929–1939: Memories of Canadians Who Survived the Depression.* Toronto: Doubleday.
First-hand accounts of life in Canada during the Great Depression.

Lesley D. Harman. 1989. *When a Hostel Becomes a Home: Experiences of Women.* Toronto: Garamond.

A participant observation study of homeless women in Toronto in the mid-1980s.

———. 1992. "The Feminization of Poverty: An Old Problem with a New Name." *Canadian Woman Studies* (Summer): 6–9.

An overview of the ways in which women are more likely than men to live in poverty at all stages of their lives.

Brigitte Kitchen, Andrew Mitchell, Peter Blutterbuck, and Marvyn Novick. 1991. *Unequal Futures: The Legacies of Child Poverty in Canada*. Toronto: Child Poverty Action Group and Social Planning Council of Metropolitan Toronto.

A discussion of the causes and consequences of child poverty in Canada today.

References

Antonovsky, Anton. 1967. "Social Class, Life Expectancy, and Overall Mortality." *Millbank Memorial Fund Quarterly* 45: 31–73.

Armstrong, Pat. 1984. *Labour Pains: Women's Work in Crisis*. Toronto: Women's Press.

Armstrong, Pat, and Hugh Armstrong. 1978. *The Double Ghetto: Canadian Women and Their Segregated Work*. Toronto: McClelland & Stewart.

Barile, Maria. 1992. "Disabled Women: An Exploited Underclass." *Canadian Woman Studies* 12/4: 32–33.

Barter, Kenneth A. 1992. "The Social Work Profession and Public Welfare." *Perception: Canada's Social Development Magazine* 16(2/3): 11–14.

Bernstein, Basil. 1973. *Class, Codes and Control*, vol. 1. London: Routledge and Kegan Paul.

Bird, John. 2002. "Young, Poor, and Canadian." *The Observer* February 2002: 28–33.

Bourdieu, Pierre, and Jean-Claude Passeron. 1977. *Reproduction in Education, Society and Culture*. Beverly Hills, CA: Sage.

Broadfoot, Barry. 1973. *Ten Lost Years, 1929–1939: Memories of Canadians Who Survived the Depression*. Toronto: Doubleday.

Burman, Patrick. 1988. *Killing Time, Losing Ground: Experiences of Unemployment*. Toronto: Thompson Educational.

Canadian Council on Social Development. 1991. "Tackling Canada's High Drop-Out Rate." *Social Development Overview* 1 (Fall): 7–8.

———. 2002. "Fact Sheet: Poverty Statistics." Ottawa: Canadian Council on Social Development (*www.ccsd.ca*).

Canadian Institute of Child Health. 1989. *The Health of Canada's Children: A CICH Profile*. Ottawa: Canadian Institute of Child Health.

Comeau, Pauline, and Aldo Santin. 1990. *The First Canadians: A Profile of Canada's Native People Today*. Toronto: James Lorimer.

Dean, Hartley, and Peter Taylor-Gooby. 1992. *Dependency Culture: The Explosion of a Myth*. New York: Harvester Wheatsheaf.

Frederick, Judith A., and Janet E. Fast. 1999. "Eldercare in Canada: Who Does How Much?" *Canadian Social Trends* 54 (Autumn): 26–30.

Frideres, James S. 1998. *Aboriginal Peoples in Canada: Contemporary Conflicts*, 5th ed. Scarborough: Prentice-Hall.

Goffman, Erving. 1963. *Stigma: Notes on the Management of Spoiled Identity*. New York: Simon and Schuster.

Grayson, L.M., and Michael Bliss. 1971. *The Wretched of Canada: Letters to R.B. Bennett, 1930–1935*. Toronto: University of Toronto Press.

Harman, Lesley D. 1989. *When a Hostel Becomes a Home: Experiences of Women*. Toronto: Garamond.

———. 1992. "The Feminization of Poverty: An Old Problem with a New Name." *Canadian Woman Studies* (Summer): 6–9.

Hay, David A. 1988. "Mortality and Health Status Trends in Canada." In B. Singh Bolaria and Harley D. Dickinson, eds., *Sociology of Health Care in Canada*. Toronto: Harcourt Brace Jovanovich.

Hooyman, Nancy R., and Rosemary Ryan. 1987. "Women as Caregivers of the Elderly: Catch-22 Dilemmas." In Josefina Figueria-McDonough and Rosemary Sarri, eds., *The Trapped Woman: Catch-22 in Deviance and Control*. Beverly Hills: Sage.

Jackson, Andrew. 2000. "Defining and Redefining Poverty." *Perception: Canada's Social Development Magazine* 25 (2): 3–6.

Kitchen, Brigitte, Andrew Mitchell, Peter Blutterbuck, and Marvyn Novick. 1991. *Unequal Futures: The Legacies of Child Poverty in Canada*. Toronto: Child Poverty Action Group and the Social Planning Council of Metropolitan Toronto.

Leacock, Eleanor Burke, ed. 1971. *The Culture of Poverty: A Critique*. New York: Simon and Schuster.

Lee, Kevin K. 2000. *Urban Poverty in Canada: A Statistical Profile*. Ottawa: Canadian Council on Social Development.

Lewis, Oscar. 1966. "The Culture of Poverty." *Scientific American* 215/16: 19–25.

Liebow, Elliot. 1967. *Tally's Corner: A Study of Negro Streetcorner Men*. London: Routledge and Kegan Paul.

Lipset, Seymour M. 1972. "Social Mobility and Equal Opportunity." *The Public Interest* 29: 90–108.

Logan, Ron, and Jo-Anne Belliveau. 1995. "Working Mothers." *Canadian Social Trends* 36 (Spring): 24–28.

Luxton, Meg, Harriet Rosenberg, and Sedef Arat-Koc. 1990. *Through the Kitchen Window: The Politics of Home and Family*, 2nd ed. Toronto: Garamond.

Morisette, Rene. 2002. "Families on the Financial Edge." *Perspectives on Labour and Income* 14 (3): 20.

Morisette, Rene, Xuelin Zhang and Marie Drolet. 2002. "Are Families Getting Richer?" *Canadian Social Trends*. 66 (Summer): 15–19.

National Council of Welfare. 1990. *Women and Poverty Revisited*. Ottawa. Ministry of Supply and Services.

———. 2000. *Poverty Profile 1998*. Ottawa: National Council of Welfare.

———. 2003. "Fact Sheet: Definitions of the Most Common Poverty Lines used in Canada—June 2003." Ottawa: National Council of Welfare (*www.ncwcnbes.net*).

Nessner, Katherine. 1990. "Profile of Canadians with Disabilities." *Canadian Social Trends* 18 (Autumn): 2–5.

Oderkirk, Jillian. 1992. "Food Banks." *Canadian Social Trends* 24 (Spring): 6–14.

Oderkirk, Jillian, and Clarence Lochhead. 1992. "Single Parenthood: Gender Differences." *Perception: Canada's Social Development Magazine* 16(2/3): 27–32.

Parliament, Jo-Anne B. 1990. "Labour Force Trends: Two Decades in Review." *Canadian Social Trends* (Autumn): 16–19.

Porter, John. 1979. *The Measure of Canadian Society: Education, Equality, and Opportunity*. Toronto: Gage.

Rinehart, James. 1987. *The Tyranny of Work*. Toronto: Harcourt Brace Jovanovich.

Ross, David. 1992. "Current and Proposed Measures of Poverty, 1992." *Perception: Canada's Social Development Magazine* 15(4)/16(1): 60–63.

———. 1998. "Child Poverty in Canada: Recasting the Issue." Speaking Notes. Ottawa: Canadian Council on Social Development, April 1998 (*www.ccsd.ca*).

Ross, David P., Katherine Scott, and Mark Kelly. 1996. *Child Poverty: What Are the Consequences?* Ottawa: Canadian Council on Social Development.

Ross, David, Katherine J. Scott, and Peter J. Smith. 2000. *Canadian Fact Book on Poverty—2000*. Ottawa: Canadian Council on Social Development

Ross, David P., and Richard Shillington. 1990. *The Canadian Fact Book on Poverty, 1989*. Ottawa: Canadian Council on Social Development.

Ross, David P., E. Richard Shillington, and Clarence Lochhead. 1994. *The Canadian Fact Book on Poverty, 1994*. Ottawa: Canadian Council on Social Development.

Ryan, Michael T. 1990. *Solidarity: Christian Social Teaching and Canadian Society*, 2nd ed. London: Guided Study Programs in the Catholic Faith.

Ryan, William. 1971. *Blaming the Victim*. New York: Pantheon.

Statistics Canada. 1989. *Health and Activity Limitation Survey: Subprovincial Data for Ontario*. Ottawa: Statistics Canada.

Watson, Sophie, and Helen Austerberry. 1986. *Housing and Homelessness: A Feminist Perspective*. London: Routledge and Kegan Paul.

Willis, Paul E. 1981. *Learning to Labor: How Working-Class Kids Get Working-Class Jobs*. New York: Columbia University Press.

Chapter 10

"Politicizing the Personal": Feminism, Law, and Public Policy

Dorothy E. Chunn

LEARNING OBJECTIVES

In this chapter, you will learn that:

1. historically, feminists in Canada and elsewhere have placed great emphasis on the role of sociolegal reforms in achieving equality for women;

2. despite many changes over the years, family law and policy have always privileged the **nuclear family** form;

3. sociolegal reforms related to families always have differential impacts on women that are linked to class, race, ethnicity, (dis)ability, and sexual orientation;

4. sociolegal reform is a necessary but insufficient basis for achieving equality for all women.

INTRODUCTION

Increasingly, many scholars, activists, and policymakers have embraced the revisionist view that societal institutions are social constructs created within the constraints of particular structures at particular times (Foucault, 1980; Garland, 1985; Weeks, 1986). Thus, state, law, and family are not always and everywhere the same in a specific society or in societies with similar histories. In Canada, for example, it is possible to identify three major periods of social transformation since 1840: the development of industrial capitalism and a laissez-faire state, corporate capitalism and a welfare state, and transnational capitalism and a neoliberal form of state (Brodie, 1995; Chunn, 1992; Denis, 1995; Evans and Wekerle, 1997; Moscovitch and Albert, 1987; Ursel 1992).

These changes in forms of capitalist organization and social relations were accompanied by analogous transformations in forms of **patriarchal** relations; albeit the gender order in liberal states always has privileged a nuclear family model that is based on heterosexual marriage, the sexual division of labour, and the **"public/private split"** (Barrett and McIntosh, 1982; Zaretsky, 1976). Although long dominant in Canadian law and social policy related to the so-called private sphere, however, this model of "the **family**" has faced increasing challenges in the developing neoliberal state that may signal the emergence of a "new gender order" (Cossman and Fudge, 2002; see also Boyd, 1997a; Brodie, 1996; Eichler, 1997; Luxton, 1997; Pulkingham and Ternowetsky, 1996).

Revisionist analyses of sociolegal reform in capitalist, patriarchal societies also reveal that reform is an inherently contradictory phenomenon (Chunn, 1992; Donzelot, 1980; Foucault, 1980; Garland, 1985). As the product of political struggle and negotiation, reforms invariably generate positive as well as negative effects, which, in turn, are mediated by gender, race, class, sexual orientation, age, and (dis)ability. On the one hand, then, law and public policy help maintain the status quo by buttressing particular forms of social and family organization. On the other hand, individuals and groups seeking to (re)form the status quo can sometimes exert considerable influence on law and public policy (Boyd, 1997a; Gavigan, 1993, 1999; Smart, 1984, 1986).

Since the late nineteenth century, feminists and the organized women's movements in Canada have played a prominent role in campaigning for legal and policy reforms and thus in the transformations outlined above (Adamson, Briskin, and McPhail, 1988; Bacchi, 1983; Ross, 1995; Strong-Boag, 1976).[1] Like their counterparts in other Western market societies (Brophy and Smart, 1985; Zaretsky, 1982), they were instrumental both in constructing the foundations of the welfare state and in reordering it.[2] First-wave feminism helped to promote reforms that collectively shaped welfare-state structures in order to regulate the "private" sphere of the family, or reproduction; second-wave feminism played a major role in bringing about reforms that have reshaped those structures since the 1960s.[3] Therefore, while often unhappy with the unanticipated outcomes of the reforms they promote, women cannot be viewed simply as passive victims of a "male" state (Andrew, 1984; Bacchi, 1983; Baines, Evans, and Neysmith, 1998; Gordon, 1988, 1990; McCormack, 1991; Zaretsky, 1982).

This chapter examines the historical and contemporary role of women, especially feminists, in constructing and reordering the Canadian welfare state through their successful advocacy of legislation and policies governing the "private" sphere of the family. The discussion centres on four topics: (1) feminist theoretical perspectives on family, law, and the state that historically have guided reform demands; (2) selected reforms in the areas of **family law** and public policy that were inspired and/or supported by first-wave and second-wave feminists in Canada; (3) the differential and contradictory impact of those reforms on women; and (4) concluding comments on future directions and strategies for feminists concerned with law and social policy.

FEMINIST THEORETICAL PERSPECTIVES ON STATE, LAW, AND FAMILY

The history of **feminism** is a history of diversity (Bacchi, 1991; Barrett and Hamilton, 1986). While feminists begin with the assumption that the majority of women in most societies occupy a subordinate position vis-à-vis men and that feminists must concentrate on altering the dynamics of power to achieve true equality for women, they often diverge in their explanations of why and how women are subordinated, and on the best means of bringing about change. Thus, all feminist perspectives on law and social policy operate with particular conceptions of the state, law, and family that, in turn, shape the legislation and policies promoted by adherents of the various theories.

The following discussion outlines theoretical perspectives on state, law, and family that have guided Canadian feminists and the implications of each for legislative and policy reforms to improve women's position in both the public and the private spheres.

First-Wave Feminists and Reforms

Although first-wave feminism in Canada followed a somewhat different developmental trajectory than it did elsewhere,[4] the catalyst for the emergence of an organized women's movement was the same as in other Western market societies—the legal invisibility of women, particularly married women, during the nineteenth century. Governed by laws based on the unity doctrine,[5] a wife was viewed as a mere extension of her husband and had the "status…of an infant or institutionalized incompetent" (Kieran, 1986, p. 41; see also Backhouse, 1991, Ch. 6). Single women had more rights than their married sisters, but the rise of organized feminism was clearly linked to a desire to end the legal subordination of all women—more specifically, of white, middle-class women.

First-wave feminists were activists and did not articulate formal theories, but their "commonsense" theoretical perspectives on state, law, and family can be abstracted from writings and speeches of prominent feminist leaders. In Canada, maternal feminism was the dominant perspective associated with the first wave (Bacchi, 1983; Roberts, 1979). Maternal feminists were not revolutionaries—they initially accepted the nineteenth-century liberal conception of the non-interventionist state as a neutral arbiter of the common good. Only after some experience dealing with the laissez-faire state did they adopt the more liberal welfarist view that, to safeguard the common good, the state might have to intervene on behalf of the disadvantaged (e.g., women) and help them to improve their position vis-à-vis more powerful individuals and groups (e.g., men). As Nellie McClung put it: "More and more the idea is growing upon us that certain services are best rendered by the state, and not left to depend on the caprice, inclination, or inability of the individual" (1976, p. 322; see also Bacchi, 1983).

For first-wave feminists, law was a positive instrument of social engineering and reform that could be used to end women's devalued status relative to men. Legislation and policies that recognized their special needs and distinct qualities could assist and empower women. Thus, maternal feminists strongly believed that, while not inherently inferior, women are different from men by virtue of their unique ability to mother and perform other domestic tasks (McClung, 1976). At the same time, they assumed that women could, and should, work with men to obtain legislation and policies that would enhance the status of wives and mothers in "their proper sphere" (Ibid.).

The maternal-feminist assumptions, which assert that nurturing and caregiving are "feminine" qualities and providing and protecting are "masculine" traits, reflected an uncritical belief in the normality of the nuclear family based on a heterosexual marriage relationship in which each member of the nuclear unit has a specific role. The sexual division of labour leaves husband and wife in charge of separate but equal spheres of activity. He is predisposed to enter the public arena and to act as provider/protector, while she is similarly inclined to manage the private realm of the family as caregiver/housekeeper. Children exist in a "natural" state of dependency on parents and must not be allowed to act like adults; they must attend school, eschew paid employment, and be supervised in their leisure activities (Chunn, 1990; Mandell, 1988).

Second-Wave Feminists and Reforms

The second-wave women's movement was initially associated with liberal feminism that re-emerged in the 1960s (Adamson et al., 1988). Liberal feminists replicated the failure of first-wave feminists to overtly challenge assumptions about the sexual division of labour and the public/private split and thus their conceptions of state, law, and family differed little from those of their first-wave (liberal) sisters. They, too, viewed the state as a mediator or neutral arbiter, primarily in the "public sphere." Thus it was assumed that once women obtained the same access to and opportunity to compete in the public sphere as men, the state would not treat their interests any differently from those of men. Like their historical counterparts, then, liberal feminists of the 1960s believed that discrimination against women could be removed through the implementation of reforms and without any fundamental restructuring of societal institutions (Adamson et al., 1988; Andrew and Rodgers, 1997; Boyd and Sheehy, 1986; Chunn, 1999; Chunn and Lacombe, 2000).

Similarly, second-wave liberal feminists continued to emphasize law as the route to women's equality. Like first-wave feminists, they assumed that women could work cooperatively with men in pursuit of equality and that, indeed, such alliances were crucial to achieve it (Boyd and Sheehy, 1986; Williams, 1990).

During the 1960s, however, liberal feminists no longer had to concentrate all their energies on the fight to attain legal personhood and political rights for women. As a result, they were able to shift their attention to the development of legal strategies for eliminating sex discrimination and implementing equality more generally in all societal institutions, including the family.

Unlike maternal feminists, however, liberal feminists of the 1960s conceptualized women and men in terms of sameness rather than difference and they made a direct link between liberation and economic independence. Paid employment was viewed as the route to equality for (married) women (Friedan, 1963). Thus, although liberal feminists did not develop an overt critique of the (nuclear) family, they implicitly challenged the sexual division of labour by arguing for the movement of married women *en masse* into the public realm. The stage was set for the "grassroots" radical and **socialist feminists** who mounted an explicit critique of the nuclear family model, encapsulated in the slogan "*the personal is political*," and began to exert an important influence on campaigns around law and social policy during the 1970s and early 1980s (Adamson et al., 1988; Boyd and Sheehy, 1986; Chunn and Lacombe, 2000; see also Barrett, 1988).

Although both groups came out of the "new left" Marxist-influenced political movements of the time, they formulated very different analyses of women's subordination (Ibid.). Echoing maternal feminists, radical feminists operate on the assumption of gender difference. Unlike their first-wave precursors, however, radical feminists argue that women and men constitute two gender classes with diametrically opposed and irreconcilable interests that exist under patriarchy—men's dominance over women. A transhistorical phenomenon, patriarchy is based on male control over women's sexuality and reproduction (Ibid.).

For radical feminists, the patriarchal, nuclear family is a major site of women's oppression. In "politicizing the personal" by demonstrating the "public" nature of supposedly "private" troubles (e.g., violence), they have emphasized the need for women to avoid the enslavement that results from "**compulsory heterosexuality**," as exemplified by heterosexual marriage (Rich, 1980). Women's liberation, however, cannot be achieved within patriarchal structures where the state and law are simply "male protection rackets" (MacKinnon, 1987, p. 31) and therefore not amenable to any sort of social-engineering or piecemeal reform. To regain control over their sexuality and reproductive decisions, women will have to liberate themselves through consciousness-raising and the creation of alternative structures (MacKinnon, 1987).

While radical feminists exploded the ideology of "separate spheres" with a critique of "compulsory heterosexuality" and marriage, socialist feminists were launching a different project that led them in the same direction—namely, the reformulation of orthodox Marxist theory, which is gender-blind and offers virtually no analysis of the "private" sphere.[6] In contrast to radical feminists, socialist feminists reject a transhistorical conception of patriarchy; that is, the idea that women's oppression is everywhere and always the same. Rather, they argue that patriarchal relations assume different forms as changes in social organization occur and analyses of women's subordination must be historically and culturally specific (Barrett, 1988; Burstyn and Smith, 1985).

Socialist feminists link women's secondary status in capitalist societies to the undervalued work that they perform inside and outside the family. Most women straddle, and are subordinate in, both the public and private spheres because their work is unpaid domestic labour and/or underpaid, non-standard employment. Thus, any analysis of women's inequality must focus on the family, or more specifically, on how women are psychologically, economically, and/or physically subordinated through heterosexual marriage (Barrett and McIntosh, 1982; Luxton, Rosenberg, and Arat-Koc, 1990).

Given this focus, socialist feminists conceptualize the state and law very differently from both liberal and radical feminists. The precise ways in which law and social policy reproduce women's subordination change over time in different forms of state. In laissez-faire states, law was a direct instrument of gender oppression; in welfare and neoliberal democratic states, the ideological influence of law is much more important in maintaining women's inequality. That is to say, law (and social policy) incorporates certain assumptions about men, women, and the relations between them that are accepted uncritically by most of the people who make, administer, or are subject to it (Barrett and McIntosh, 1982; Gavigan, 1988, 1993).

Among various ideologies affecting law and social policy, socialist feminists consider **familial ideology** crucial to the perpetuation of women's inequality historically in Canada and other liberal democracies (Ibid.). Only a minority of people in these societies has actually lived in the ideal-type, nuclear family with a wife/mother homemaker and husband/father breadwinner. Yet even in the late twentieth century, polls and research revealed a continuing belief among young women that they would marry for life and be full-time homemakers, at least when their children were young (Luxton et al., 1990). These assumptions about marriage and the "normal" family also have strongly influenced the drafters and implementers of legislation and social policy.

Moreover, law is an ideological mechanism that helps perpetuate class as well as gender inequalities. Thus, gender and class relations are intertwined, generating both intra-gender and inter-gender differences and similarities. For instance, women (and men) have gender but not necessarily class in common. Unlike their radical counterparts, then, socialist feminists view law as a means of working toward women's equality in capitalist liberal democracies like Canada. Law is not an "absolute good" in the liberal-feminist sense, but women themselves, or women and men together, can sometimes achieve legal and social-policy reforms that raise political consciousness and further their collective struggles against class and/or gender inequalities (Adamson et al., 1988; Boyd and Sheehy, 1986). While a reform such as a national daycare programme might be most directly beneficial to working-class and/or single mothers in the labour force, for example, it would also help some middle-class mothers and fathers in paid employment.

Since the late 1980s, the three theoretical perspectives associated with second-wave feminism in Canada have been extensively critiqued because they speak primarily to the experiences of white, able-bodied, and/or heterosexual women. Aboriginal and racialized women documented the absence of an analysis of race and ethnicity in these feminist frameworks (Bannerji, 1993; Herbert, 1989; Kirkness, 1988; Monture, 1989; Monture-Angus, 1995; Ng, 1988; Razack, 1992, 1998; Williams, 1990). Lesbian feminists noted a similar theoretical silence on the issue of sexual orientation (Herman, 1990, 1994; Robson, 1992, 1994). Likewise, the failure of feminist theory to address women with disabilities has been underscored (Mosoff, 1997; Wendell, 1996). These critiques, as well as anti-feminist "backlash" (Cossman and Fudge, 2002), have stimulated a rethinking of the ways in which feminists conceptualize state, law, and family (Boyd, 1997a, 2003; Gavigan, 1993, 1999; Mossman and MacLean, 1997; see also Smart and Neale, 1999).

We turn now to an examination of how Canadian feminists have "politicized the personal," both historically and in the contemporary context, through the advocacy of legal and policy reforms related to social reproduction.[7]

FEMINIST REFORMERS AND SOCIAL REPRODUCTION: HISTORICAL SHIFTS IN FAMILY LAW AND PUBLIC POLICY

In retrospect, it is clear that first- and second-wave feminists exercised an important influence on law and social policy in Canada. During both periods, feminists worked under the umbrella of national women's organizations and, often, in concert with men. The National Council of Women of Canada, formed in 1893, brought feminist and non-feminist women together in a common goal to protect and uphold the family (Strong-Boag, 1976). Almost 80 years later, the National Action Committee on the Status of Women was established in 1972 to represent women's interests and concerns and to press for the implementation of the numerous recommendations of the 1970 Royal Commission on the Status of Women. Since the 1970s, status-of-women councils—federal and provincial—have also exerted a strong influence on law and social policy related to the family.

Upgrading Women's Status in the Family

Historically, both England and Canada have created a two-tiered system of family law: one related primarily to the propertied classes, and the other focused mainly on the underclasses of society (Chunn, 1992; Mossman and MacLean,

1986, 1997). First-wave feminists helped to reshape this dual system in the emergent welfare state. Although maternal feminists did not challenge the sexual division of labour, they did "politicize the personal" because of a desire to upgrade women's status in their "proper sphere" of the family. From the 1880s onward, the maternal feminist focus on making the "separate but equal" doctrine a reality led to the promotion of numerous laws and policies aimed at regulating both biological (McLaren and McLaren, 1998; McLaren, 1990) and social reproduction (Strong-Boag, 1976; Ursel, 1992).

Maternal feminists particularly wanted to reinforce women in their motherhood role and to keep mother-led families together in the midst of the "social disorganization" generated by the rapid industrialization and urbanization of Canada between 1880 and 1940 (Ursel, 1992; see also Strong-Boag, 1976). As well as promoting educational initiatives aimed at preparing women for marriage and a domestic "career" (Strong-Boag, 1976, 1988), they joined in campaigns for the implementation of legislation and policies that gave mothers and wives some rights if a marriage failed. On the one hand, maternal feminists fought for reforms in divorce, custody, and property law that would benefit middle- and upper-class women who could afford legal counsel. On the other hand, they promoted child- and family-welfare laws related to guardianship, maintenance, and support that would assist women in marginal families (Chunn, 1992; Snell, 1991).

In the area of custody and guardianship, we find that, although nineteenth-century law was not static, few judges exercised their "increasing discretionary power" to give mothers legal custody of their children (Boyd, 2003, p. 34; see also Backhouse, 1991, Ch. 7). By the beginning of the twentieth century, however, feminists and other reformers had obtained some legal recognition of the importance of women's motherhood role. For example, in 1897, British Columbia laid the foundations of the "tender years" doctrine by authorizing judges to award custody of children under the age of seven to non-adulterous mothers who were deemed "fit" parents (Backhouse, 1991, p. 204). By the 1950s, the principle that "all other things being equal, a young child should be with its natural mother" (Weeks v. Weeks, 1955) was beginning to erode the historical legacy of automatic paternal rights to the custody of children (Boyd, 2003, p. 71).

Married women also gained new rights to property during the nineteenth century. Under the unity doctrine, a wife was legally obliged to hand over to her husband everything she had—land, furniture, money, including wages, and even the clothes on her back. However, three successive reform "waves" culminated with the implementation of separate property regimes in some provinces by 1900 (Backhouse, 1992). In Ontario, for instance, a series of legal reforms dating from 1859 ultimately was consolidated and expanded with the enactment of the Married Women's Property Act in 1884, which gave husbands and wives control over their own property, whether it was acquired before or during the marriage (Kieran, 1986; Morton, 1988). Other provinces followed suit. Subsequently, when a marriage failed, each partner kept what was his or hers.

With regard to financial support, feminists and other reformers obtained provincial legislation during the late nineteenth and early twentieth centuries that imposed a legal obligation on husbands and fathers to support their wives and children upon marital breakdown or their children in cases of unmarried parenthood. Previously, men could abandon their dependants and leave them destitute while retaining legal control over wives and/or children (Kieran, 1986, p. 49). However, rapid industrialization and urbanization from the 1880s onward brought disproportionate numbers of women and children to the growing cities and left increasing numbers of mother-led families living in destitution when male breadwinners did not join them. This **"feminization of poverty"** was one reason behind the enactment of desertion statutes, which allowed non-adulterous wives and mothers to obtain maintenance orders from the courts that compelled the male deserter to pay support or face sanctions, including a jail term. In 1888, Ontario enacted the first Deserted Wives' Maintenance Act, with other provinces following (Chunn, 1992).

In cases when a deserter could not be located or when the male protector/breadwinner was absent from the family because of death or mental or physical incapacity, the state sometimes assumed the financial role of husband and father through the payment of mothers' pensions or allowances. "A broad spectrum of articulate, middle-class Canadians" (Strong-Boag, 1979, p. 25) had promoted such an income-support policy from the turn of the twentieth century without success until an increase in mother-led families during World War I generated fears that "the family" was in crisis. After the war, many provinces implemented mothers' pensions to help "deserving" women fulfill their "natural" homemaker role by enabling them either to work part time rather than full time outside the home or to earn money at home through self-employment. Thus, recipients of mothers' pensions or allowances were considered state employees who were expected to supplement their government salaries with other earnings (Strong-Boag, 1979, p. 27; Little, 1998).

Clearly, first-wave feminists were major players in the reform of legislation and policy governing the private sphere of reproduction in the emergent Canadian welfare state. Together with other reformers, they created a system of family and welfare law that remained intact until the 1960s and 1970s, when another generation of feminist reformers came of age.

Solving the "Problem with No Name"

Second-wave feminism developed in the general context of the civil rights movements that characterized Canada and other liberal democracies during the 1960s. Women, the poor, racial and ethnic minorities, and gay men and lesbians, among others, began to enter the political arena in an effort to temper, if not eradicate, discrimination based on gender, race, class, and sexual orientation; that is, to implement the principle of formal legal equality in every social institution.

In Canada, feminist agitation ultimately helped persuade the federal government to establish the Royal Commission on the Status of Women. Like first-wave feminists, the commissioners placed great faith in law as a vehicle of incremental social change and their 1970 report set the second-wave reform agenda for the next two decades (Andrew and Rodgers, 1997). However, their emphasis on rights and formal legal equality contributed, first, to a complete overhaul of the family law and social policy that maternal feminists had worked so hard to achieve and, second, more generally to a restructuring of the Canadian welfare state.

Whereas maternal feminists had "politicized the personal" to enhance the position of women within the family, their second-wave liberal feminist successors were determined to create the conditions that would facilitate flexibility and interchangeability of roles for men and women in both the public and the private spheres. Since 1968, then, Canada's family law system has been reordered extensively along liberal egalitarian lines. The federal divorce law and provincial legislation governing marriage and separation are no longer sex-specific or predicated on "fault." Rather, they are gender-neutral and based on the principle of **formal equality** between spouses—with no rights to property, custody, and maintenance, and no familial roles based on sex (Eichler, 1997).

Custody   Currently, family law is based on the assumptions that women are no more predisposed than men to assume child-care responsibilities and that fathers and mothers are equally capable of parenting. Thus, the "tender years" doctrine that worked in favour of women who were deemed "fit" mothers has been displaced by the gender-neutral "best interests of the child" principle— the presumption that when a marriage ends, children should live with the parent who can best serve their interests (Boyd, 2003, Ch. 5). In 1998, the federal government initiated another custody law reform process. Proposed new legislation (Bill C-22), which would have replaced the language of "custody and access" with that of "parenting orders" and "contact" while retaining the gender-neutral "best interests" principle, passed second reading in the House of Commons in February 2003 (Douglas, 2003). However, Bill C-22 died when the House of Commons prorogued before the Bill had received third (and final) reading.

The notion of equal parenting also underlies the parental-leave programme, implemented in 1990 through an amendment of the federal Unemployment Insurance Act (now the Employment Insurance Act). In addition to the 15 weeks of maternity benefit that an employed, pregnant woman could claim, the reform allowed either parent to take 10 weeks of partially paid leave following the birth or adoption of a child. The rationale for parental leave is the reduction of work–family conflict and the potential for changing the gendered division of labour both at home and in the workplace (Evans and Pupo, 1993; Iyer, 1997). Amendments to the EI Act in 2001 extended parental leave "significantly" by enabling mothers and/or fathers to take up to 35 weeks of partially paid leave to care for their young children (Madsen, 2002, p. 12).

Marital Property   Both federal and provincial family laws now stipulate that the division of marital property will be governed by the principle of equalization incorporated in a deferred-community-property regime. That is to say, as a general rule, separate property rights exist so long as the marriage is intact, but if the relationship dissolves, all family assets are to be shared equitably, although not necessarily equally, between the spouses (Steel, 1985). Moreover, the concept of property has been greatly expanded to cover "virtually anything of which one could conceive" (Morton, 1988, p. 260). Since 1986, for example, the Ontario Family Law Act has included not only the usual assets such as land, but also deferred profit sharing plans, pensions, and interests in estates or trusts (Morton, 1988).

Spousal and Child Support   Contemporary Canadian family law is based on the principles of spousal self-sufficiency and equal parental responsibility for child support. It applies both to marriages and to opposite-sex and same-sex cohabitation relationships (Holland, 2000, p. 141). Gone are the sex-specific clauses that characterized the divorce, desertion, and other family-related legislation promoted by first-wave feminists, obliging men to maintain their dependants and requiring women to be non-adulterous to qualify for support. Today, the courts assume that in most cases of relationship breakdown, each spouse can attain economic independence and/or contribute financially to the upkeep of their children. Therefore, spousal-support orders usually are short-term with the sole purpose of allowing a dependent partner to become self-supporting (Mossman and MacLean, 1997).

Since the early 1980s, however, concern about the increasing number of people, primarily women and children, who become state dependants following a relationship breakdown has generated a focus on "dead-beat dads" (Mandell, 2001) and has led to court decisions and public policies aimed at ensuring that families take care of their own. Several Supreme Court of Canada judgments (e.g., *Moge v. Moge*) have recognized the relevance of factors that impact on the ability of a spouse to attain self-sufficiency and independence upon separation and divorce to the determination of spousal-support orders (Bailey and Melamed, 1999). Similarly, the federal **child-support guidelines** implemented in 1997 attempt to link child-support awards to both the costs of raising children and the income of the payer.

Legislation has also addressed the enforcement of support orders. When the historical pattern of default on support orders continued after new family-relations laws were implemented during the 1970s and 1980s, several provinces, including Manitoba, Ontario, and British Columbia, established maintenance-enforcement programmes to reduce the astronomical rate of non-compliance (Mandell, 2001, pp. 44–48). The programmes essentially are state-sanctioned collection agents on behalf of the persons who are not receiving the support ordered by the courts. For example, an individual who consistently fails to pay maintenance without good reason may have his or her wages garnisheed.

Family welfare law has also been reformed. In the social-assistance legis-lation of every province, the "man in the house" rule is now the gender-neutral "spouse in the house" rule (Gavigan, 1993, 1999; Mossman and MacLean, 1997). The increasing neoliberal emphasis on self-sufficiency and independence through the 1990s sparked major reforms aimed at removing people, including "welfare moms," from provincial welfare rolls—dramatic cuts to social assistance benefits, particularly in Ontario, Alberta, and British Columbia, implementation of compulsory welfare-to-work programmes, and crackdowns on welfare fraud (Chunn and Gavigan, 2003).

THE CONTRADICTORY AND DIFFERENTIAL EFFECTS OF FAMILY LAW AND SOCIAL POLICY

Even a cursory analysis reveals the contradictory and differential effects of the family-law and social-policy reforms promoted by first- and second-wave femi-nists. Beginning with first-wave reforms, we can see a number of positive con-sequences in practice. First, the legal recognition of the work performed by women in their role as mothers and, to a lesser degree, wives was a concrete acknowledgement that the "private" sphere of reproduction was important and should be taken into account when a marriage ended. Clearly, the "tender years" doctrine assisted some women in their attempts to gain custody or guardianship of their children. Similarly, desertion legislation and enforcement mechanisms, such as family courts, helped some women to obtain financial support for them-selves and their children. The early family courts in Ontario collected substantial sums on behalf of women and children, as did the superintendent of child wel-fare, who dealt with unmarried mothers' cases (Chunn, 1992).

Second, reforms such as mothers' pensions represented some recognition of social or state responsibility at the provincial level to directly oversee the well-being of disadvantaged individuals and if necessary to contribute materially to their subsistence rather than simply leaving the burden to families and charities in the "private" sector or to local governments. During the interwar years, increasing numbers of women received "state salaries for mothers," as provinces began to assume some responsibility for aid to mother-led families. In British Columbia, for example, the number of mothers or foster mothers receiving allowances rose from 636 in 1919–20 to 1751 in 1938–39, and the amount expended by the province increased from $612 645 in 1927–28 to $790 101 in 1938–39 (Strong-Boag, 1979, pp. 26, 28–30).

Third, although statistics are lacking, it seems likely that feminist-supported legislation and policies to shore up the nuclear family left some poor, white women and children without male breadwinners at least marginally better off in the urban, industrial context than they might have been otherwise. Similarly, the federal liberalization of divorce in the 1920s meant that middle- and upper-class women could now obtain a divorce on the same grounds as their husbands, while the implementation of separate property regimes saved some women from the destitution that previously befell many wives who were divorced or deserted by their spouses (Backhouse, 1992; Kieran, 1986, Ch. 7; Snell, 1991).

Negative Effects of First-Wave Reforms

With hindsight, negative consequences of family-related legislation and policies supported by maternal feminists also are readily apparent. First, these reforms entrenched the ideology of separate spheres and helped to perpetuate the structured dependency of women within marriage by sanctifying the nuclear-family model and the sexual division of labour. Married women acquired more power within the family not so much in their own right as women, but because of their role in social reproduction, particularly as mothers (Brophy and Smart, 1985, Ch. 1; Chunn, 1992). The failure of maternal feminists to attack the economic dependency of women within marriage was ultimately underlined by cases like *Murdoch v. Murdoch* (see Box 10.1), which revealed a basic weakness of the separate-property regime.

Second, the family-related reforms promoted by maternal feminists were all premised on, and therefore reinforced, the sexual double standard. Women who applied for custody, maintenance, or mothers' allowances were routinely scrutinized for moral fitness. "Uncondoned adultery" by a wife and/or mother automatically barred her from obtaining spousal maintenance upon marital

BOX 10.1 *MURDOCH v. MURDOCH*

The Murdochs were Alberta ranchers who separated in 1968 after 25 years of marriage, during which time Irene Murdoch had worked alongside her husband to the extent that he did not have to hire a hand. However, when she sued for half-interest in their property, cattle, and other assets, the Alberta courts and, ultimately, the Supreme Court of Canada decided that Mrs. Murdoch was entitled to alimony but had no claim on the value of the property because she had not made "a direct financial contribution" to the ranch; the work she had carried out for 25 years was "the work done by any ranch wife." In short, Mr. Murdoch held the title to the property, and Irene Murdoch "was expected to hoe, mow, dehorn, brand (and cook, clean, and bear and raise children)" with no hope of a share of it when the marriage ended (Kieran, 1986, p. 142; see also Morton, 1988).

breakdown and led to the rescinding of existing support orders if the husband provided proof of her immoral conduct to the court. Similarly, a woman who received public assistance because her male breadwinner had absconded or who drew a mothers' pension was subject to the discriminatory "man in the house" rule. If she resided with a man, authorities assumed that he must be supporting her and she became ineligible for state benefits, but the same rule did not apply to men. Indeed, women have been charged with fraud for collecting public assistance at the same time that they shared living quarters with a man, and some were actually jailed.[8] Thus, only the morally "deserving" received state assistance; the "undeserving" were punished through loss of their children, denial of financial support, and even criminal prosecution.

Third, for the most part, maternal feminists supported legislation and policies that emphasized the responsibility of individual men for maintaining their dependants—wives, children, and parents. They sought and achieved the use of state power to enforce "private" responsibility for the costs of social reproduction; that is, men's continuing duty to maintain women in their "natural" role as caregivers and housekeepers when the male breadwinner was no longer part of the family unit. Although state agencies such as family courts collected and distributed considerable sums of money to women and children, the majority of men defaulted on or were chronically in arrears with their support payments (Chunn, 1992). Moreover, even when the state assumed some direct financial responsibility for social reproduction (e.g., mothers' pensions), women were encouraged to find another male breadwinner and remarry (Little, 1998, p. 60).

Finally, the differential impact of the legislation and policies supported by first-wave feminists must be underscored. White, middle-class, heterosexual women, and to a lesser extent their counterparts in the "respectable" working classes, did benefit from family-law reforms related to custody, property, and support. However, white women in the ranks of the working and dependent poor, particularly single mothers, had to trade off the assistance they received from the paternalistic state against increased surveillance and scrutiny of their family life (Chunn, 1992; Little, 1998). Lesbians and racialized and Aboriginal women were invisible in the statutes and public policies outlined above. Indeed, First Nations women (and men) and members of many racial and ethnic minorities did not even have voting rights until the 1940s and 1950s (Kirkness, 1988; Williams, 1990). Moreover, most Aboriginal women living on-reserve did not live in nuclear-family units and were governed entirely by the federal Indian Act. Thus, provincial legislation and policies related to marriage, matrimonial property, maintenance, and other family matters were irrelevant to their lives (Turpel, 1991). Similarly, First Nations women have been embroiled more often in guardianship battles with the state than with the fathers of their children (Monture, 1989).[9]

Positive Effects of Second-Wave Reforms

The effects of sociolegal reforms achieved, in part, by second-wave feminists since the 1960s have been just as contradictory as those of their first-wave precursors. On the positive side, the implementation of formal legal equality in family law ended the blatant sexual discrimination and policing of morals that characterized federal divorce law and provincial desertion and mothers' allowances legislation. Gender-neutral family law and policy meant that women were no longer held accountable to a sexual double standard in the form of adultery clauses; maternal conduct was eliminated as a ground for denying women custody and/or spousal support.

Similarly, the gender-neutral parental-leave policy reinforces the feminist critique of the sexual division of labour. By facilitating the assumption of child-care responsibilities by fathers, the policy helps to undercut the widespread belief that women are more naturally predisposed toward, and better at, nurturing than men. Moreover, the policy can potentially improve women's position in the paid workforce by enabling them to remain attached to the labour force on "leave" while they stay home to care for a child, rather than "leaving" the ranks of the employed altogether (Evans and Pupo, 1993; Iyer, 1997).

Another positive result of second-wave family law reform has been the increased recognition of women's financial contribution to marriage through the implementation of deferred-community-property regimes for the division of family assets upon marital breakdown. Redefining assets to include social benefits (such as pensions) and intangible assets (such as university degrees) has improved the lot of women who, like Irene Murdoch (see Box 10.1), had never been part of the paid workforce when divorce ended a long-time marriage and of women who left the labour force and/or worked part time to accommodate child-care responsibilities (Keet, 1990; Steel, 1985).

Third, the implementation of gender-neutral legal and social-policy reforms advocated by second-wave feminists has facilitated, to some degree, a recognition of the "functional similarit[y]" between cohabitation and marriage that has benefited some (women) cohabitants when a relationship ends (Holland, 2000, p. 129). With the decision in M. v. H (see Box 10.2), for instance, the maintenance sections of all provincial family relations acts now apply to same-sex as well as to opposite-sex cohabitants and married couples who separate.

While family law on the division of property still privileges marriage, recent court decisions in Ontario (*Halpern*, 2003) and British Columbia (*Barbeau*, 2003) broadened the definition of marriage to include same-sex couples. Moreover, both opposite-sex and same-sex cohabitants can sometimes successfully invoke the "principle of unjust enrichment" when dividing property at the end of a relationship. In *Anderson v. Luoma* (1986), for example, the B.C. Supreme Court applied this principle to the facts of the case and imposed the remedy of constructive trust. Title to houses and property the two women had acquired and/or lived in together during their 10-year

BOX 10.2   *M. v. H.*

M. and H. lived together in a same-sex relationship beginning in 1982. When the relationship deteriorated, M. moved out of the common house in 1992 and claimed spousal support from H., her financially better-off former partner. M.'s claim raised a constitutional challenge to the definition of "spouse" under section 29 of the Ontario Family Relations Act (OFRA), which applied only to married and to cohabiting opposite-sex couples who had lived together "continuously" for at least three years. M. argued successfully in the Ontario courts that the Act discriminated on the basis of sexual orientation because it did not apply to same-sex partners, one of whom was dependent upon the other when the relationship ended. On appeal, the Supreme Court of Canada upheld the lower court's decision that legislation that includes opposite-sex but not same-sex cohabitants is unconstitutional; thereby defining same-sex cohabitants as "spouses" in family-law provisions that govern support (Holland, 2000, pp. 35–39).

relationship was mainly in the name of the "substantively better-off Luoma," but the B.C.S.C. concluded that fairness required Luoma to share the property with Anderson (Gavigan, 1995, pp. 110, 116–17).

Family Law and Women's Inequality

Although few regret the repeal of legislation and policies rooted in paternalism, feminists have been confronted with some negative, unintended consequences of the gender-neutral family law and policy they struggled so hard to achieve (Andrew and Rodgers, 1997; Busby, Fainstein, and Penner, 1990; Fineman, 1991). Clearly, the implementation of formal equality in family law and social welfare has not only failed to end women's structured inequality but also exacerbated it in some instances when a relationship ends. So we have to ask: "How does gender-neutral law continue to help perpetuate women's inequality?"

The short answer is that strict adherence to the principle of formal equality in the absence of **substantive equality** leads to inequality because treating those who are not alike in the same way simply reproduces differences. More specifically, we need to examine the ways in which pervasive, often competing, ideologies and discourses about family and equality influence how judges interpret and administer gender-neutral legislation. When legal rules change, "old" assumptions and beliefs do not automatically disappear (Gavigan, 1988).

The New Politics of Child Custody

Since attaining legal rights, mothers have assumed sole legal and physical custody of children in the vast majority of cases by agreement with fathers—a pattern that reflects women's disproportionate responsibility for childcare prior to separation or divorce. Analyses of custody and access outcomes in contested cases after the implementation of gender-neutral law suggest, however, that overall the reform has increased the power of fathers to lay claim to their children (Bourque, 1995; Boyd, 2003). The percentage of cases where mothers obtain sole custody of children through informal negotiation with fathers has dropped and, in contested cases, men have a good chance of "winning" either sole or joint custody (Bertoia and Drakich, 1993; Bertoia, 1998; Boyd, 2003, pp. 103–05). Moreover, from the late 1980s, judicial decisions in cases involving disputes over access of non-custodial fathers to their children seem to have expanded fathers' rights at the expense of mothers' (Bourque, 1995; Boyd, 2003, Ch. 6; Taylor, Barnsley, and Goldsmith, 1996).

This new "politics of custody" places feminists in a quandary. They have long advocated equal parenting, but formal legal equality seems to advantage fathers over mothers. For the most part, however, this trend is not the result of overt discrimination against mothers but rather reflects the ways in which ideologies and discourses related to family, motherhood, fatherhood, and equality influence judicial interpretation of that most malleable concept, "the best interests of the child" (Boyd, 1989, 2003; Drakich, 1989).

Despite the implementation of gender-neutral custody law, some judges have continued to interpret "the best interests of the child" principle in terms of maternal conduct, which disadvantages women who do not adhere to the norms of the "good" mother—white, middle-class, heterosexual, and married. A review of outcomes in contested cases involving young children during the 1980s revealed that, regardless of her parenting abilities, a lesbian mother almost always lost custody to a (heterosexual) father unless she hid her sexual orientation and appeared to fit the norm (Arnup, 1989). In *Elliott v. Elliott* (Sage, 1987), Mr. Justice MacKinnon of the B.C. Supreme Court explicitly stated that he was granting Mr. Elliott custody of his 7-year-old daughter because Ms. Elliott had violated a previous custody order by establishing a live-in relationship with a lesbian partner: "Whatever one might accept or privately practise, I cannot conclude that indulging in homosexuality is something for the edification of young children" (Sage, 1987, pp. 1, 8). During the 1990s, the sanctioning of lesbian mothers became more implicit. Judges no longer cited a live-in homosexual relationship as the sole ground for denying a parent custody; rather, they began to consider the effects of a parent's "lifestyle" on children (Boyd, 2003, pp. 111–12).

In some cases, the application of the "best interests of the child" principle still is influenced by sex-specific ideas about parental roles, encapsulated in the (male) breadwinner/(female) homemaker model of family, that seem to disadvantage mothers more than fathers. Regardless of sexual orientation, a mother who engages in full-time or part-time employment to support her children can lose custody to a husband who has a new homemaker-wife, a housekeeper, or some other surrogate mother to look after the children, even if he earns less money than she (Boyd, 1997b, 2003). Similarly, a full-time mother, especially one who lives at or close to the poverty line, can lose custody to a more economically secure father because, in the view of the court, he can provide a better standard of living for the children (Boyd, 2003).

Since the 1980s, judges assessing "the best interests of the child" have also been swayed by the ideologies of equal parenting and the "new" fatherhood incorporated in the demands of **fathers' rights** groups (Boyd, 2003, Chs. 5, 6; Drakich, 1989). In Canada and elsewhere, judicial judgments about custody and access increasingly reflect assumptions that children must have a father in their lives and that contemporary men are equally involved in parenting their children. Such decisions not only privilege the nuclear-family form, they also ignore research that shows most fathers do not contribute equally to the care of their children prior to divorce and that the benefits of contact for children are "contingent on lack of conflict between the parents" (Boyd, 2003, pp. 132, 168–69; see also Bourque, 1995; Taylor et al., 1996). Moreover, studies of participants in fathers' rights groups indicate that they are demanding neither sole responsibility for children nor an equal division of childcare and responsibility. They want equal status as legal parents, which really is a demand "to continue the practice of inequality in postdivorce parenting but now with a legal sanction" (Bertoia and Drakich, 1993, p. 612).

The success of fathers' rights advocates can be seen in the rise of court-ordered joint custody awards and the growing emphasis on maternal responsibility to ensure fathers' access to children. While Canadian law contains no presumption in favour of **joint custody**, the number of such awards "rose significantly" during the 1990s, sometimes in the absence of parental agreement and/or evidence of parental ability to cooperate (Boyd, 2003, p. 130).[10] Moreover, the so-called "friendly parent" or "maximum contact" provision in the federal Divorce Act, which directs courts to operate on the principle that children should have as much contact with each parent as is in their "best interests," places the onus on some women to accept a joint-custody arrangement and facilitate access of fathers who have been physically or sexually abusive to their children. A mother who resists may lose custody altogether because she is perceived as being uncooperative and/or as putting her own interests before those of the children (Bourque, 1995; Boyd, 2003, pp. 125–27; Rosnes, 1997). Thus, judges prioritize paternal access and seem unwilling to accept mothers' allegations of abuse despite evidence indicating that "calculated falsifications" by parents are rare and more likely to come from fathers (Boyd, 2003, p.195; see also Bala, 1999).

Clearly, then, judicial determinations of custody, based on notions of equal parenting and justified by the "best interests" principle, work to the disadvantage of many mothers by rendering invisible their disproportionate work as primary caregivers (Boyd, 2003). The impact of gender-neutral law governing spousal and child support has been similar. Liberal feminists, who strongly critiqued the old paternalistic divorce and desertion statutes and pressed hard for family law based on formal legal equality, never anticipated such an outcome. They believed that once women entered paid employment, they would achieve economic independence from men and gender equality would follow (Friedan, 1963).

Marital Breakdown and Economic Inequalities

The implications of the liberal-feminist failure to adequately theorize women's work at home as well as in the labour force were realized only over time. Simply moving married women into paid employment did not produce liberation because most often they found themselves trying to cope with a "double day" comprised of low-paid service or clerical work in the "pink ghetto" and unpaid domestic labour to service their families (Evans, 1998; Morton, 1988, 1993). The significance of the devalued nature of women's work in both the public and the private spheres was painfully revealed when the Canadian divorce rate spiralled upward after the introduction of some **"no-fault"** grounds for divorce in 1968 and again following the 1985 divorce reform that removed "fault" as a ground for divorce altogether.[11]

Although women have always been disproportionately vulnerable to poverty, the unprecedented rate of marital breakdown since the 1970s has greatly exacerbated women's poverty (Evans, 1998). Middle- and upper-class women began to join the ranks of the poor after separation or divorce and the percentage of impoverished, mother-led families increased substantially during the 1990s (Ibid.). Why? Partly because in applying family law based on the principle of formal legal equality, the courts have assumed that when a relationship ends women are as capable of achieving self-sufficiency as men, despite the evidence that in most cases they are substantially less able to be self-supporting (Morton, 1988; Mossman and MacLean, 1986, 1997).

In adjudicating spousal support and property claims, courts often have failed to consider, first, the value of women's unpaid contributions to family or social reproduction and, second, the impact of non-standard employment on women's ability to achieve economic independence (Bailey, 1989, p. 628; Keet, 1990; Morton, 1988, 1993). For instance, leaving the labour force for years at a time to take care of young children has a significant negative effect on women's opportunities and advancement in paid work. Similarly, more women than men are engaged in low-paid and/or temporary/part-time employment and even women in full-time, full-year jobs make less money on average than do their male counterparts. The gender–wage gap narrowed during the 1990s but only because a "feminization" of the labour market caused a deterioration in men's wages and employment conditions (Fudge and Cossman, 2002, p. 26).

In sum, judicial determinations about spousal and child support and property that are based on formal equality often fail to address the substantive inequality in the economic situations of men and women upon marital breakdown. Courts have tended to interpret self-sufficiency not in terms of previous standards of living, but in terms of earning any sort of living at all (Bailey, 1989; Keet, 1990; Morton, 1988, 1993). Increasingly, however, judges have confronted the issue of an ex-spouse who has not achieved even minimal self-sufficiency.

The courts have adopted contradictory positions on the question of who is responsible for supporting a former spouse when she or (occasionally) he does not become self-sufficient after separation or divorce. During the 1980s, judicial decisions about support tended to emphasize the idea of a "clean break" between ex-spouses. A "trilogy" of cases (*Caron v. Caron, Pelech v. Pelech, Richardson v. Richardson*) decided by the Supreme Court of Canada (S.C.C.) in 1987 established what became known as the "causal connection test": if a spouse who applies for maintenance or an increase in existing maintenance demonstrates "that he or she has suffered a radical change in circumstances flowing from an economic pattern of dependency engendered by the marriage," the court may "exercise its relieving power." The main argument put to the S.C.C. in the "trilogy" was that, after signing a separation agreement that set limits on her ex-husband's financial responsibilities, each of the three ex-wives found that her financial position changed for the worse and only further support from her former spouse would enable her to get off social assistance. However, the S.C.C. found no relationship between the changed economic situation of the three women and their previous marital relationships. Therefore, the state, and not their ex-husbands, was deemed to be responsible for their maintenance (Bailey, 1989).

During the 1990s, governments' determination to reduce social expenditures, including social assistance, intensified the responsibility of families to look after their members even after a separation or divorce (Fudge and Cossman, 2002). Some court decisions indirectly supported this state emphasis on fiscal restraint. For instance, the 1992 Supreme Court of Canada decision in *Moge v. Moge* supported the claim of the ex-wife that her former husband, who had not lived with her for many years, should continue to pay spousal support. The S.C.C. was persuaded by the argument that women's unpaid contributions to a marriage, such as domestic labour and childcare, were typically undervalued in spousal-support awards, and this undervaluing is linked to the rise in women living in poverty as divorce and separation increase. Therefore, "the responsibility for women's poverty should rest wherever possible with a man with whom they have had a recognized relationship" (Boyd, 1996, pp. 176–77; see also Bailey and Melamed, 1999). Significantly, the judgment addressed the issue of substantive (in)equality, but advocated an individual, non-state solution.

This trend to reduce social responsibility for poverty is even clearer in the area of welfare law. The administration of ostensibly gender-neutral welfare legislation and policy still reflects sex-specific assumptions about morality and the family unit (Gavigan, 1993, 1999; Mossman and MacLean, 1997). Although the "man in the house" rule is now the "spouse in the house" rule in the social assistance legislation of every province, it is almost always applied to women who live with men rather than the reverse (Carruthers, 1995; Martin, 1992). Moreover, the 1990s welfare reforms have left virtually no one "deserving" of state assistance. Even mothers of young children are expected

to achieve self-sufficiency and independence through welfare to work programmes or, alternatively, to obtain support from non-state sources such as
ex-spouses and other family members or through the establishment of
another spousal relationship (Chunn and Gavigan, 2003).

Overall, the family-law and policy reforms implemented since the 1960s
have intensified the historical emphasis on familial responsibility for the costs
of reproduction. Second-wave feminists sought to "politicize the personal,"
but the neoliberal emphasis on ensuring that individual men and individual
women assume responsibility for themselves and for their dependent children
actually "personalizes the political" and has produced some unintended and
negative consequences.

Reform and the "Personalization of the Political"

First, reforms based on the assumption of individual responsibility for social
reproduction make poverty a personal problem and, as discussed earlier, have
contributed to increased poverty, primarily among women and children. For
example, although the federal child-support guidelines have established minimum levels of support and the maintenance-enforcement programmes implemented in some provinces have reduced the default rate on support payments,
neither policy can eliminate or even substantially ameliorate poverty since both
spousal- and child-support awards are generally so low (Eichler, 1991; Mandell,
2001; Pulkingham, 1994). Similarly, property laws based on formal equality do
not guarantee a 50–50 split of all assets between spouses. In some provinces,
property owned by one spouse for strictly business purposes is excluded; legal
marriage contracts can override an equal division of assets; and upon application from one of the spouses, the courts have discretion to order an unequal
division of property if judges determine that it would not be just or fair to
enforce the equalization principle (Keet, 1990; Morton, 1988). Because courts
often do not consider unpaid contributions to the accumulation of property, the
division of property tends to disadvantage women, who usually do the majority
of unpaid work during a marriage and who are less likely than men to be economically independent at the point of separation or divorce.

Second, the intensified focus on familial responsibility for reproduction
has preempted the creation of new social programmes. For example, using tax
exemptions and/or credits for child-care expenses incurred by parents, rather
than creating a national child-care programme, reinforces the idea that social
reproduction is a personal rather than a public issue (Ferguson, 1998).
Moreover, unless the "financial rewards" for child-care work are increased, it
will remain overwhelmingly "women's work" because men have no incentive
to participate (Ibid., p. 207). Thus, individualized approaches to caregiving
simply perpetuate the sexual division of labour (Teghtsoonian, 1997).

Finally, we need to consider the differential effects of legislative and
policy reforms based on formal equality that tend to "personalize the polit-

ical." In retrospect, the lack of focus on class, race, and sexual orientation in many second-wave feminist campaigns for sociolegal change is obvious. As with first-wave reforms, white, middle-class, heterosexual women, and to a lesser extent their counterparts in the more affluent sectors of the working class, have gained the most from the reordering of family law since the 1960s. But many couples have no property to split when their relationship dissolves. Or, if common property exists, it is most often a house with a mortgage, so there is nothing to divide except mutual debt. Similarly, as low as they are, child- and spousal-support obligations imposed on the working poor may mean that two families are impoverished rather than one or that child support is not paid (Mandell, 2001). Moreover, the legal recognition of different forms of family—same-sex marriage and same-sex/opposite-sex cohabitation—seems to be correlated with the extent to which they resemble traditional, heterosexual marriages and is more reflective of neoliberal concerns to enforce familial responsibility for reproduction (i.e., keep people off welfare) than of any democratization or abandonment of familial ideology.

The same disparities are generated by individualized child-care policies. During the 1980s, only slightly more than 50 percent of pregnant women in paid employment claimed maternity benefits under the Unemployment Insurance Act, probably because the benefit was so low (60 percent of average insurable earnings). The situation is even worse under the current Employment Insurance Act because the benefit for both maternity and parental leave is lower (55 percent of average insurable earnings); eligibility now is based on hours rather than weeks worked (600 hours of insurable work in the previous 52 weeks); and the maximum weekly payment has been reduced (Iyer, 1997, p. 187; Madsen, 2002, pp. 40–43). Thus, it is primarily more affluent women and couples who can take advantage of these programmes (Evans, 1998, pp. 196–97). The poorest women, who are often racialized and ethnic minority women and women with disabilities, are "effectively excluded from maternity and parental leave" (Madsen, 2002, p. 47). Likewise, tax credits and exemptions for childcare are most helpful to women and couples who can afford to hire a nanny or to support a stay-at-home mother (Macklin, 1992). Moreover, the reliance of many affluent families on poor, racialized women to provide childcare has created conflicts among feminists about the exploitation of some women by other, more privileged women (Arat-Koc, 1990; Macklin, 1992; Ng, 1988).

Overall, feminist support for individualized solutions to the problems of child and spousal support, childcare, and social reproduction generally has clearly helped some women. However, it has also had the unintended effect of contributing to the depoliticization of these issues and made it less likely that in the near future the state will implement comprehensive social programmes that would benefit the majority of Canadian families. In retrospect, it is painfully apparent that Aboriginal women, immigrant women, racialized women, and women with disabilities face difficulties that were simply not part of the picture of women painted by the 1970 Royal Commission on the Status of Women (Abner, Mossman, and Pickett, 1991; Arat-Koc, 1990; Williams, 1990).[12]

CONCLUSION

Although feminists soon recognized the limitations of sociolegal reforms based on formal equality, they have had meagre success in their efforts to obtain legislation and policies that address substantive inequality among women and between women and men (Cossman and Fudge, 2002). Moreover, since the late 1980s, the mixed and often negative effects of feminist-inspired legislation and social policies have helped to fuel a "backlash" against feminism (Ibid.; see also Bala, 1999). On the one hand, a neoconservative, pro-family movement, exemplified by REAL Women of Canada and fathers' rights groups, blames feminists for undermining fatherhood and causing the demise of "the family" (Bertoia and Drakich, 1993). Women are exhorted to "Blow Feminism, Girls, Find Mr. Right" (*Vancouver Sun*, 1991, p. A5). On the other hand, the decontextualized, neoliberal focus on formal equality and gender neutrality undermines the legitimacy of feminism as a social movement. Since "we are all equal now," there is no need for "special interest" groups such as feminism.

Debate among feminists about women's position in families and disillusionment with the process of sociolegal reform has also diluted, and even erased, the feminist impact on contemporary law and policy (Cossman and Fudge, 2002; Peters, 1997; Smart 1989). Nonetheless, many feminists continue to see law and the state as critical sites of struggle (Cossman and Fudge, 2002; Gavigan, 1993; Razack, 1991). In the current context, feminists cannot simply abandon the legal and policy arenas to either the neoconservative proponents of "family values" (Peters, 1997, p. 49) or the neoliberal advocates of equal (i.e., identical) treatment for everyone. However, it also is clear that sociolegal reforms per se cannot end women's inequality. Thus, feminists must think carefully about the unintended as well as the intended consequences of the family-related reforms they advocate, and strategize about how they can reinject feminist perspectives on family law and policy into the political and public cultures (Boyd, 1997a; Cossman and Fudge, 2002; Luxton, 1997).

Summary

- Historically, feminist movements in Canada and elsewhere have been dominated by theoretical perspectives that place primary emphasis on using law to achieve equality for women with men. First-wave, maternal feminism promoted sociolegal reforms that would guarantee women's "separate but equal" status in the family, while second-wave, liberal feminism advocated family-related legislation and policies based on formal equality and gender neutrality.

- Neither maternal nor liberal feminists explicitly challenged the idea that the "normal" family is a nuclear unit based on a heterosexual, marriage relationship, a sexual division of labour, and the public/private split. Consequently, family-related sociolegal reforms consistently have privileged the nuclear-family model regardless of whether they were promoted by feminists or by non-feminists.

- Nonetheless, feminist-inspired reforms related to families clearly have "politicized the personal" and contributed to greater equality for some women vis-à-vis men over time. Historically, maternal feminists helped make women legally visible in their roles as mothers and wives through the implementation of legislation and policies giving them rights to custody, financial support, and property. Contemporary liberal feminists helped to entrench formal legal equality for women with men in the family through the implementation of gender-neutral legislation and policies governing custody, maintenance, and property.

- However, the negative and differential impact of family-related reforms reveals the weaknesses of both maternal and liberal feminism and demonstrates that feminists cannot litigate their way to equality. Through their belief in "separate but equal spheres," first-wave, maternal feminists achieved reforms that entrenched women's dependency on marriage and a male breadwinner. Likewise, second-wave, liberal feminists secured reforms that asserted women's formal equality with men but ignored the substantive inequality with men that most women experience. Moreover, neither maternal nor liberal feminists factored differences among women into their reform proposals. Thus, the main beneficiaries of family-related reforms historically have been the most privileged women in society (i.e., white, middle-class, and respectable working-class women).

- Despite the contradictory and differential effects of sociolegal reforms, feminists can use law in conjunction with initiatives in other arenas, such as the media and politics, to work toward the achievement of full equality for all women in Canada. Above all, feminists must promote legislation and policies that recognize the differences as well as the commonalities among women and between women and men—that treat those who are not alike differently—in order to move beyond simple formal equality toward substantive equality. They need to think about both employment and pay equity; about extended, single-parent, and same-sex families as well as heterosexual, nuclear ones; and about the complex ways in which race, class, sexual orientation, and (dis)ability intersect with gender to reproduce structured inequalities. In short, feminists have to focus on moving the women at the bottom up to effect any fundamental change in society.

Notes

1. This chapter focuses primarily on feminist reform activities in Anglo-Canada, where provincial family law is derived from English precedents.

2. In this chapter, the welfare state is conceptualized as a set of services and ideas that operates at two levels: the "male stream," where aid (e.g., Employment Insurance) is a right or entitlement; and the "female stream," where assistance (e.g., mothers' allowance) is charity meted out to the "deserving" (Gordon, 1988).

3. The terms "first-wave" and "second-wave" feminism denote the organized feminist movements that emerged in Canada and elsewhere during the late nineteenth and early twentieth centuries and during the 1960s, respectively.

4. In the United States and England, for example, liberal feminism predated maternal feminism and exercised a strong influence on feminist activism from the 1850s onward, whereas, in Canada, the two perspectives emerged almost simultaneously during the late nineteenth century. Moreover, first-wave feminism had a less distinct presence in Canada than elsewhere because feminist activists tended to be subsumed within larger social, moral, and urban reform movements in Anglo-Canada from the 1880s to the 1920s and in the aftermath of those movements between the wars (Bacchi, 1983, 1991; Roberts, 1979).

5. The most succinct statement of the unity doctrine is attributed to Sir William Blackstone, the English legal commentator: "In law husband and wife are one person, and the husband is that person" (Kieran, 1986, p. 41). Blackstone was writing about Anglo, white married couples, but Canadian authorities also expended great effort to force the First Nations to conform to this patriarchal, authoritarian marriage law (Backhouse, 1991, Ch. 1).

6. Radical and socialist second-wave feminists critiqued the three major assumptions underlying the nuclear-family model: first, that the nuclear family is the natural, inevitable, and highest family form; second, that there is a sexual division of labour; and third, that there is a public/private distinction.

7. There are two interrelated forms of reproduction: biological reproduction of the species is linked to the physical processes of conception, pregnancy, and birthing; social reproduction of the species is linked to the unpaid work that (primarily) women perform to maintain the physical and emotional health of individual family members, and hence of the society as a whole (Luxton et al., 1990, pp. 58–61). For reasons of space, this discussion focuses on law and social policy related to social reproduction.

8. In a 1982 Ontario case, for example, a 50-year-old woman received a three-month jail term for a $19 373 welfare fraud even though her lover did not provide financial support for her or her children and he also had another woman friend. The judge said the courts must punish women who "are prepared to allow themselves to be used in that fashion" (Porter and Gullen, 1984, p. 215).

9. Historically, the First Nations were shockingly overrepresented among children in care and adopted children (Monture, 1989, p. 2). More recently, First Nations have asserted control over child welfare, but government cuts to welfare funding in Canada may erode this control (Kline, 1997).

10. Indeed, both legislators and the judiciary have demonstrated some support for proposals to implement mandatory joint custody, or "co-parenting," as a way of acknowledging the presumed increase in men's involvement in parenting. Yet in jurisdictions where it has been implemented, fathers are benefiting at the expense of mothers because women often remain the primary caregiver (physical custody), but men have equal say in the decision-making about the children (legal custody) and thereby continue to exercise control over their ex-wives. Men can also be required to pay reduced child support because they are supposedly caring for the children half of the time.

11. Although the Canadian divorce rate fell in the late 1980s, it remains significantly higher than prior to the 1968 law reform: in 1951, one in every 24 marriages ended in divorce; in 1990, one couple divorced for every 2.4 who married (Mossman and MacLean, 1997, p. 119).

12. The commissioners did not even address the situation of Aboriginal women who lost their Indian status if they married non-Indian men. Such women had to leave their reserves, could neither inherit nor hold property on the reserve, and were denied recognition as Indians, as were their children (Kirkness, 1988; Turpel, 1991).

Critical Thinking Questions

1. Discuss the similarities and differences between first-wave, maternal feminists and second-wave, liberal feminists with respect to their views on family, law, and social policy.

2. Compare and evaluate the relative strengths and weaknesses of radical and socialist feminist approaches to "politicizing the personal."

3. Outline and assess the argument that feminist movements in Canada and other Western countries have reflected the experience of and improved the position of a select group of women in those societies.

4. Explain the "two-tiered system" of family law in Canada and discuss the feasibility of creating one system of family law that will reflect the reality of, and apply equally to, very different types of family.

5. Given the contradictory effects of family-related legislation and social policies, discuss the pros and cons of using law as a feminist strategy to achieve substantive equality for women.

Websites

Canadian Council on Social Development
http://www.ccsd.ca
> The Canadian Council on Social Development's website provides information about research and publications in the areas of economic security and poverty, employment and labour market issues, and social policies and programmes.

Department of Justice Canada
http://canada.justice.gc.ca/en/
> The Department of Justice Canada's website provides information about Canadians and the law and links to resources including information on legal life events (divorce, childbirth, and so on), family law issues (such as family violence), specific family-related legislation such as National Child Benefit, and a list of relevant videos.

Ontario Attorney General
http://www.attorneygeneral.jus.gov.on.ca/english/family/
> The Ontario Attorney General's website on family justice issues includes information on child support, family violence, and family courts in Canada. This website also provides a list of relevant online publications.

Suggested Reading

Abigail B. Bakan and Daiva Stasiulis, eds. 1997. *Not One of the Family: Foreign Domestic Workers in Canada*. Toronto: University of Toronto Press.
> This book documents the institutionalized unequal treatment of immigrant domestic workers in Canada. Since the 1940s, the number of women recruited from the "South" to work in Canadian homes has increased markedly, while the rights of citizenship for such workers have declined.

Susan B. Boyd. 2003. *Child Custody, Law, and Women's Work*. Toronto: Oxford University Press.
> This book places Canadian child-custody legislation and its application by the courts in a socioeconomic context from the nineteenth through the

twenty-first century. The author considers the extent to which child-custody law reform per se can lead to the social transformation of parenting.

Brenda Cossman and Judy Fudge, eds. 2002. *Privatization, Law, and the Challenge to Feminism.* Toronto: University of Toronto Press.

This text addresses the reordering of relations among the state, the market, and the family in Canada. Assuming that "privatization" marks a transition from a welfare to a neoliberal state, the authors examine the role of law in this process and its impact on gender and social relations.

Martha A. Fineman and Isabel Karpin, eds. 1995. *Mothers in Law: Feminist Theory and the Legal Regulation of Motherhood.* New York: Columbia University Press.

In this book, feminist theorists examine the legal issues surrounding motherhood. They show how law defines the ideal and the deviant mother, often without reference to the actual practices of motherhood.

Carol Smart and Bren Neale. 1999. *Family Fragments?* Cambridge: Polity Press.

The authors draw on a qualitative study of parents in the process of separating to examine the diverse and fluid patterns of parenthood that are negotiated and renegotiated following separation. They show that the quality of pre- and post-separation parental relationships strongly affects the nature of parenting after divorce.

References

Abner, Erika, Mary Jane Mossman, and Elizabeth Pickett. 1991. "'No More Than Simple Justice': Assessing the Royal Commission Report on Women, Poverty and the Family." *Ottawa Law Review* 22/3: 573–606.

Adamson, Nancy, Linda Briskin, and Margaret McPhail. 1988. *Feminist Organizing for Change: The Contemporary Women's Movement in Canada.* Toronto: Oxford University Press.

Andrew, Caroline. 1984. "Women and the Welfare State." *Canadian Journal of Political Science* 17 (December): 667–81.

Andrew, Caroline, and Sandra Rodgers. 1997. *Women and the Canadian State.* Montreal: McGill-Queen's University Press.

Arat-Koc, Sedef. 1990. "Importing Housewives: Non-Citizen Domestic Workers and the Crisis of the Domestic Sphere in Canada." In M. Luxton, H. Rosenberg, and S. Arat-Koc, eds., *Through the Kitchen Window: The Politics of Home and Family,* 2nd ed. Toronto: Garamond.

Arnup, Katherine. 1989. "'Mothers Just Like Others': Lesbians, Divorce and Child Custody in Canada." *Canadian Journal of Women and the Law* 3: 18–32.

Bacchi, Carol Lee. 1983. *Liberation Deferred? The Ideas of the English-Canadian Suffragists, 1877–1918.* Toronto: University of Toronto Press.

————. 1991. *Same Difference: Feminism and Sexual Difference.* Sydney: Allen and Unwin.

Backhouse, Constance. 1991. *Petticoats and Prejudice: Women and the Law in Nineteenth-Century Canada.* Toronto: The Osgoode Society.

————. 1992. "Married Women's Property Law in Nineteenth-Century Canada." In Bettina Bradbury, ed., *Canadian Family History: Selected Readings.* Toronto: Copp Clark Pitman.

Bailey, Martha J. 1989. "*Pelech, Caron,* and *Richardson.*" *Canadian Journal of Women and the Law* 3/2: 615–33.

Bailey, Martha J., and Daniel S. Melamed. 1999. "Separation Agreements Post-*Moge, Willick* and *L.G. v. G.B.*: A New Trilogy?" *Canadian Journal of Family Law* 16/1: 51–135.

Baines, Carol, Patricia Evans, and Sheila Neysmith, eds. 1998. *Women's Caring: Feminist Perspectives on Social Welfare,* 2nd ed. Toronto: McClelland & Stewart.

Bala, Nicholas. 1999. "A Report from Canada's 'Gender War Zone': Reforming the Child Related Provisions of the *Divorce Act.*" *Canadian Journal of Family Law* 16/2: 163–227.

Bannerji, Himani, ed. 1993. *Returning the Gaze: Essays on Racism, Feminism and Politics.* Toronto: Sister Vision Press.

Barrett, Michele. 1988. *Women's Oppression Today: The Marxist Feminist Encounter,* revised edition. London: New Left Books.

Barrett, Michele, and Roberta Hamilton, eds. 1986. *The Politics of Diversity.* London: Verso.

Barrett, Michele, and Mary McIntosh. 1982. *The Anti-Social Family.* London: Verso.

Bertoia, Carl. 1998. "An Interpretative Analysis of the Mediation Rhetoric of Fathers' Rightists: Privatization Versus Personalization." *Mediation Quarterly* 16/1: 15–32.

Bertoia, Carl, and Janice Drakich. 1993. "The Fathers' Rights Movement: Contradictions in Rhetoric and Practice." *Journal of Family Issues* 14/4: 592–615.

Bourque, Dawn. 1995. "'Reconstructing' the Patriarchal Nuclear Family: Recent Developments in Child Custody and Access in Canada." *Canadian Journal of Law and Society* 10/1: 1–24.

Boyd, Susan B. 1989. "Child Custody, Ideologies and Employment." *Canadian Journal of Women and the Law* 3/1: 111–33.

————. 1996. "Can Law Challenge the Public/Private Divide? Women, Work and Family." *Windsor Yearbook of Access to Justice* 15: 161–85.

————, ed. 1997a. *Challenging the Public/Private Divide: Feminism, Law, and Public Policy.* Toronto: University of Toronto Press.

————. 1997b. "Looking Beyond Tyabji: Employed Mothers, Lifestyles, and Child Custody Law." In S.B. Boyd, ed., *Challenging the Public/Private Divide: Feminism, Law, and Public Policy.* Toronto: University of Toronto Press.

————. 2003. *Child Custody, Law, and Women's Work.* Toronto: Oxford University Press.

Boyd, Susan B., and Elizabeth A. Sheehy. 1986. "Feminist Perspectives on Law." *Canadian Journal of Women and the Law* 2/1: 1–51.

Brodie, Janine. 1995. *Politics on the Margins: Restructuring and the Canadian Women's Movement.* Halifax: Fernwood.

————, ed. 1996. *Women and Canadian Public Policy.* Toronto: Harcourt Brace & Company, Canada.

Brophy, Julia, and Carol Smart. 1985. *Women-in-Law.* London: Routledge and Kegan Paul.

Burstyn, Varda, and Dorothy E. Smith. 1985. *Women, Class, Family and the State.* Toronto: Garamond.

Busby, Karen, Lisa Fainstein, and Holly Penner, eds. 1990. *Equality Issues in Family Law.* Winnipeg: Legal Research Institute of the University of Manitoba.

Carruthers, Errlee. 1995. "Prosecuting Women for Welfare Fraud in Ontario: Implications for Equality." *Journal of Law and Social Policy* 11: 241–62.

Chunn, Dorothy E. 1990. "Boys Will Be Men, Girls Will Be Mothers: The Regulation of Childhood in Vancouver and Toronto." *Sociological Studies in Childhood Development* 3: 87–110.

————. 1992. *From Punishment to Doing Good: Family Courts and Socialized Justice in Ontario, 1880–1940.* Toronto: University of Toronto Press.

————. 1999. "Feminism, Law, and 'the Family': Assessing the Reform Legacy." In Elizabeth Comack, ed., *Locating Law: Race/Class/Gender Connections.* Halifax: Fernwood.

Chunn, Dorothy E., and Shelley A.M. Gavigan. 2003. "Welfare Law, Welfare Fraud, and the Moral Regulation of the 'Never Deserving' Poor." Paper presented at the Canadian Law and Society Association Annual Meeting, Halifax, N.S., June.

Chunn, Dorothy E., and Dany Lacombe. 2000. "Introduction." In D.E. Chunn and D. Lacombe, eds., *Law as a Gendering Practice.* Toronto: Oxford University Press.

Cossman, Brenda, and Judy Fudge, eds. 2002. *Privatization, Law, and the Challenge to Feminism.* Toronto: University of Toronto Press.

Denis, Claude. 1995. "'Government Can Do Whatever It Wants': Moral Regulation in Ralph Klein's Alberta." *Canadian Review of Sociology and Anthropology* 32/3: 365–83.

Donzelot, Jacques. 1980. *The Policing of Families.* New York: Pantheon.

Douglas, Kristen. 2003. *Bill C-22: An Act to Amend the Divorce Act, the Family Orders and Agreements Enforcement Act, the Garnishment, Attachment and Pension Diversion Act and the Judges Act and to Amend Other Acts in Consequence: Legislative Summary.* Ottawa: Parliamentary Research Branch.

Drakich, Janice. 1989. "In Search of the Better Parent: The Social Construction of Ideologies of Fatherhood." *Canadian Journal of Women and the Law* 3/1: 63–87.

Eichler, Margrit. 1991. "The Limits of Family Law Reform, or the Privatization of Female and Child Poverty." *Canadian Family Law Quarterly* 7: 59–83.

———. 1997. *Family Shifts: Families, Policies, and Gender Equality.* Toronto: Oxford University Press.

Evans, Patricia M. 1998. "Gender, Poverty, and Women's Caring." In C. Baines, P.M. Evans, and S. Neysmith, eds., *Women's Caring: Feminist Perspectives on Social Welfare,* 2nd ed. Toronto: McClelland & Stewart.

Evans, Patricia, and Norene Pupo. 1993. "Parental Leave: Assessing Women's Interests." *Canadian Journal of Women and the Law* 6/2: 402–18.

Evans, Patricia M., and Gerda R. Wekerle, eds. 1997. *Women and the Canadian Welfare State: Challenges and Change.* Toronto: University of Toronto Press.

Ferguson, Evelyn. 1998. "The Child-Care Debate: Fading Hopes and Shifting Sands." In C. Baines, P.M. Evans, and S. Neysmith, eds., *Women's Caring: Feminist Perspectives on Social Welfare,* 2nd ed. Toronto: McClelland & Stewart.

Fineman, Martha. 1991. *The Illusion of Equality: The Rhetoric and Reality of Divorce Reform.* Chicago: University of Chicago Press.

Foucault, Michel. 1980. *The History of Sexuality,* vol. 1. New York: Vintage.

Friedan, Betty. 1963. *The Feminine Mystique.* New York: Dell.

Fudge, Judy, and Brenda Cossman. 2002. "Introduction: Privatization, Law, and the Challenge to Feminism." In Brenda Cossman and Judy Fudge, eds., *Privatization, Law, and the Challenge to Feminism.* Toronto: University of Toronto Press.

Garland, David. 1985. *Punishment and Welfare.* Brookfield: Gower.

Gavigan, Shelley A.M. 1988. "Law, Gender and Ideology." In Anne F. Bayefsky, ed., *Legal Theory Meets Legal Practice.* Edmonton: Academic Printers and Publishing.

———. 1993. "Paradise Lost, Paradox Revisited: The Implications of Familial Ideology for Feminist, Lesbian, and Gay Engagement to Law." *Osgoode Hall Law Journal* 31/3: 589–624.

———. 1995. "A Parent(ly) Knot: Can Heather Have Two Mommies?" In Didi Herman and Carl Stychin, eds., *Legal Inversions: Lesbians, Gay Men and the Politics of Law.* Philadelphia: Temple University Press.

———. 1999. "Legal Forms, Family Forms, Gendered Norms: What Is a Spouse?" *Canadian Journal of Law and Society* 14/1: 127–57.

Gordon, Linda. 1988. "What Does Welfare Regulate?" *Social Research* 55/4: 609–29.

———, ed. 1990. *Women, the State and Welfare.* Madison: University of Wisconsin Press.

Herbert, Jacinth. 1989. "'Otherness' and the Black Woman." *Canadian Journal of Women and the Law* 3/1: 269–79.

Herman, Didi. 1990. "Are We Family? Lesbian Rights and Women's Liberation." *Osgoode Hall Law Journal* 28: 789–815.

———. 1994. *Rights of Passage: Struggles for Lesbian and Gay Legal Equality.* Toronto: University of Toronto Press.

Holland, Winifred. 2000. "Intimate Relationships in the New Millennium: The Assimilation of Marriage and Cohabitation?" *Canadian Journal of Family Law* 17/1: 114–69.

Iyer, Nitya. 1997. "Some Mothers Are Better Than Others: A Re-examination of Maternity Benefits." In S.B. Boyd, ed., *Challenging the Public/Private Divide.* Toronto: University of Toronto Press.

Keet, Jean. 1990. "The Law Reform Process, Matrimonial Property, and Farm Women: A Case Study of Saskatchewan, 1980–1986." *Canadian Journal of Women and the Law* 4(1): 166–89.

Kieran, Sheila. 1986. *The Family Matters: Two Centuries of Family Law and Life in Ontario.* Toronto: Key Porter.

Kirkness, Verna. 1988. "Emerging Native Women." *Canadian Journal of Women and the Law* 2/2: 408–15.

Kline, Marlee. 1997. "Blue Meanies in Alberta: Tory Tactics and the Privatization of Child Welfare." In S.B. Boyd, ed., *Challenging the Public/Private Divide.* Toronto: University of Toronto Press.

Little, Margaret. 1998. *"No Car, No Radio, No Liquor Permit": The Moral Regulation of Single Mothers in Ontario, 1920–1997.* Toronto: Oxford University Press.

Luxton, Meg, ed. 1997. *Feminism and Families: Critical Policies and Changing Practices.* Halifax: Fernwood.

Luxton, Meg, Harriet Rosenberg, and Sedef Arat-Koc, eds. 1990. *Through the Kitchen Window: The Politics of Home and Family,* 2nd ed. Toronto: Garamond.

MacKinnon, Catherine. 1987. *Feminism Unmodified: Discourses on Life and Law.* Cambridge: Harvard University Press.

Macklin, Audrey. 1992. *"Symes v. M.N.R.*: Where Sex Meets Class." *Canadian Journal of Women and the Law* 5/2: 498–517.

Madsen, Lene. 2002. "Citizen, Worker, Mother: Canadian Women's Claims to Parental Leave and Childcare." *Canadian Journal of Family Law* 19/1: 11–74.

Mandell, Deena. 2001. *'Deadbeat Dads': Subjectivity and Social Construction.* Toronto: University of Toronto Press.

Mandell, Nancy. 1988. "The Child Question: Links Between Women and Children in the Family." In Nancy Mandell and Ann Duffy, eds., *Reconstructing the Canadian Family: Feminist Perspectives.* Toronto: Butterworths.

Martin, Dianne L. 1992. "Passing the Buck: Prosecution of Welfare Fraud; Preservation of Stereotypes." *Windsor Yearbook of Access to Justice* 12: 52–97.

McClung, Nellie. 1976. "What Will They Do With It?" In Ramsay Cook and Wendy Mitchinson, eds., *The Proper Sphere.* Toronto: University of Toronto Press.

McCormack, Thelma. 1991. *Politics and the Hidden Injuries of Gender: Feminism and the Making of the Welfare State.* CRIAW Papers no. 28. Ottawa: Canadian Research Institute for the Advancement of Women.

McLaren, Angus. 1990. *Our Own Master Race: Eugenics in Canada, 1885–1945.* Toronto: McClelland & Stewart.

McLaren, Angus, and Arlene Tigar McLaren. 1998. *The Bedroom and the State: The Changing Practices and Politics of Contraception and Abortion in Canada, 1880–1980,* 2nd ed. Toronto: McClelland & Stewart.

Monture, Patricia A. 1989. "A Vicious Circle: Child Welfare and the First Nations." *Canadian Journal of Women and the Law* 3/1: 1–17.

Monture-Angus, Patricia. 1995. *Thunder in My Soul: A Mohawk Woman Speaks.* Halifax: Fernwood.

Morton, Mary E. 1988. "Dividing the Wealth, Sharing the Poverty: The (Re)formation of 'Family' in Law in Ontario." *Canadian Review of Sociology and Anthropology* 25/2: 254–75.

———. 1993. "The Cost of Sharing, the Price of Caring: Problems in the Determination of 'Equity' in Family Maintenance and Support." In J. Brockman and D.E. Chunn, eds., *Investigating Gender Bias in Law: Socio-Legal Perspectives.* Toronto: Thompson Educational.

Moscovitch, Allan, and Jim Albert, eds. 1987. *The "Benevolent" State: The Growth of Welfare in Canada.* Toronto: Garamond.

Mosoff, Judith. 1997. "'A Jury Dressed in Medical White and Judicial Black': Mothers with Mental Health Histories in Child Welfare and Custody." In S.B. Boyd, ed., *Challenging the Public/Private Divide.* Toronto: University of Toronto Press.

Mossman, Mary Jane, and Morag MacLean. 1986. "Family Law and Social Welfare: Toward a New Equality." *Canadian Journal of Family Law* 5: 79–110.

———. 1997. "Family Law and Social Assistance Programs: Rethinking Equality." In P.M. Evans and G.R. Wekerle, eds., *Women and the Canadian Welfare State.* Toronto: University of Toronto Press.

Ng, Roxana. 1988. "Immigrant Women and Institutionalized Racism." In S. Burt, L. Code, and L. Dorney, eds., *Changing Patterns: Women in Canada.* Toronto: McClelland & Stewart.

Parton, Nicole. 1991. "Blow Feminism, Girls, Find Mr. Right." *Vancouver Sun,* November 9, p. A5.

Peters, Suzanne. 1997. "Feminist Strategies for Policy and Research: the Economic and Social Dynamics of Families." In M. Luxton, ed., *Feminism and Families.* Halifax: Fernwood.

Porter, Marion, and Joan Gullen. 1984. "Sexism in Policy Relating to Welfare Fraud." In J.M. Vickers, ed., *Taking Sex into Account.* Ottawa: Carleton University Press.

Pulkingham, Jane, 1994. "Private Troubles, Private Solutions: Poverty among Divorced Women and the Politics of Support Enforcement and Child Custody Determination." *Canadian Journal of Law and Society* 9/2: 73–97.

Pulkingham, Jane, and Gordon Ternowetsky, eds. 1996. *Child and Family Policies: Struggles, Strategies and Options.* Halifax: Fernwood.

Razack, Sherene. 1991. *Canadian Feminism and the Law: The Women's Legal Education and Action Fund and the Pursuit of Equality.* Toronto: Second Story.

———. 1992. "Using Law for Social Change: Historical Perspectives." *Queen's Law Journal* 17/1: 31–53.

———. 1998. *Looking White People in the Eye: Gender, Race, and Culture in Courtrooms and Classrooms.* Toronto: University of Toronto Press.

Rich, Adrienne. 1980. "Compulsory Heterosexual and Lesbian Existence." *Signs: Journal of Women in Culture and Society* 5/4: 631–60.

Roberts, Wayne. 1979. "'Rocking the Cradle for the World': The New Woman and Maternal Feminism, Toronto, 1877–1914." In L. Kealey, ed., *A Not Unreasonable Claim.* Toronto: Women's Press.

Robson, Ruthann. 1992. *Lesbian (Out)Law: Survival under the Rule of Law.* Ithaca: Firebrand Books.

———. 1994. "Resisting the Family: Repositioning Lesbians in Legal Theory." *Signs: Journal of Women in Culture and Society* 19/4: 975–96.

Rosnes, Melanie. 1997. "The Invisibility of Male Violence in Canadian Child Custody and Access Decision-Making." *Canadian Journal of Family Law* 14/1: 31–60.

Ross, Becki L. 1995. *The House That Jill Built: A Lesbian Nation in Formation.* Toronto: University of Toronto Press.

Sage, Barbara. 1987. "B.C. Lesbian Mother Denied Custody of Daughter." *The Lawyers' Weekly* 6/38: 1, 8.

Smart, Carol. 1984. *The Ties That Bind.* London: Routledge and Kegan Paul.

———. 1986. "Feminism and Law: Some Problems of Analysis and Strategy." *International Journal of the Sociology of Law* 14: 109–23.

———. 1989. *Feminism and the Power of Law.* London: Routledge.

Smart, Carol, and Bren Neale. 1999. *Family Fragments?* Cambridge: Polity Press.

Snell, James G. 1991. *In the Shadow of the Law: Divorce in Canada, 1900–1939.* Toronto: University of Toronto Press.

Steel, Freda M. 1985. "The Ideal Marital Property Regime—What Would It Be?" In Elizabeth Sloss, ed., *Family Law in Canada: New Directions.* Ottawa: Advisory Council on the Status of Women.

Strong-Boag, Veronica. 1976. *The Parliament of Women: The National Council of Women of Canada, 1893–1920.* Ottawa: Museum of Man.

————. 1979. "'Wages for Housework': Mothers' Allowances and the Beginnings of Social Security in Canada." *Journal of Canadian Studies* 14/1: 24–34.

————. 1988. *The New Day Recalled: Lives of Girls and Women in English Canada, 1891–1939.* Toronto: Copp Clark Pitman.

Taylor, Georgina, Jan Barnsley, and Penny Goldsmith. 1996. *Women and Children Last: Custody Disputes and the Family Justice System.* Vancouver: Vancouver Custody and Access Support and Advocacy Association.

Teghtsoonian, Katherine. 1997. "Who Pays for Caring for Children? Public Policy and the Devaluation of Women's Work." In S.B. Boyd, ed., *Challenging the Public/Private Divide.* Toronto: University of Toronto Press.

Turpel, Mary Ellen. 1991. "Home/Land." *Canadian Journal of Family Law* 10/1: 17–40.

Ursel, Jane. 1992. *Private Lives, Public Policy: 100 Years of State Intervention in the Family.* Toronto: Women's Press.

Weeks, Jeffrey. 1986. *Sexuality.* London: Tavistock.

Wendell, Susan. 1996. *Rejected Body: Feminist Philosophical Reflections on Disability.* New York: Routledge.

Williams, Toni. 1990. "Re-forming 'Women's' Truth: A Critique of the Report of the Royal Commission on the Status of Women in Canada." *Ottawa Law Review* 22/3: 725–59.

Zaretsky, Eli. 1976. *Capitalism, the Family and Personal Life.* New York: Harper and Row.

————. 1982. "The Place of the Family in the Origins of the Welfare State." In Barrie Thorne and Marilyn Yalom, eds., *Rethinking the Family.* New York: Longman.

Cases Cited

Anderson v. Luoma, [1986] 50 R.F.L. (2d) 127 (B.C.S.C.)

Barbeau v. British Columbia (Attorney General) (2003), B.C.C.A. 406

Caron v. Caron, [1987] 7 R.F.L. (3d) 274 (S.C.C.)

Elliott v. Elliott, [1987] B.C.J. No. 43 (Q.L.) (S.C).

Halpern et al. v. Attorney General of Canada et al. (2003), O.C.A.

M. v. H., [1999] 2 S.C.R. 3, 46 R.F.L. (4th) 32 (S.C.C.)

Moge v. Moge, [1992] 3 S.C.R. 813 (S.C.C.)

Murdoch v. Murdoch, [1973] 41 D.L.R. (3d) 367 (S.C.C.)

Pelech v. Pelech, [1987] 7 R.F.L. (3d) 225 (S.C.C.)

Richardson v. Richardson, [1987] (3d) 304 (S.C.C.)

Weeks v. Weeks (1955), 3 D.L.R. 704 (B.C.C.A.)

Chapter 11

Aging and Families: Ties Over Time and Across Generations

Anne Martin-Matthews

LEARNING OBJECTIVES

In this chapter, you will learn that:

1. a main source of variability between women and men in later life is that whereas most men live out their old age as married persons, most women spend their last years as widows;

2. most of the care and assistance provided to elderly persons is provided by other old people, usually women. Although daughters provide most of the care to elderly persons by their children, sons are increasingly involved in providing care and assistance across the generations to elderly family members and friends;

3. the popular notion of the **"sandwich" generation** caught between responsibilities for their children and their elderly parents is largely a myth; very few families in Canada face competing intergenerational demands simultaneously;

4. Canada's changing health-care system has significant impact on elderly persons and their families, because reductions in medical and hospital-based services have not been matched by the further development of community-based care;

5. immigration policies promoting family reunification have contributed to the ethnic diversity of Canada's elderly population, a substantial minority of which speaks neither English nor French.

INTRODUCTION

The aging of the population is one of many factors contributing to the increasing diversity and change in Canada's families. The rise in the number of elderly people and the increased longevity of both women and men are associated with structural changes in the size and composition of families. These changes in turn have an impact on the roles that family members play, the dynamics of these roles and relationships, the emergence of new issues in the negotiation of **intergenerational relations**, and increasing diversity in terms of what "family" actually means throughout the life course.

The heterogeneity and broad diversity of the population of older persons living in Canada is often glossed over in general references to "the elderly." Elders in Canada represent a wide diversity of people. For example, Canada's elderly population is more ethnically diverse than is the Canadian population as a whole. While 17 percent of the total Canadian population is foreign-born, 27 percent of residents aged 65 years and over were born outside Canada (Chappell, Gee, McDonald, and Stones 2003). Also, our language often does not reflect the many ways in which the experiences of aging in families are gendered, and are influenced by socioeconomic status, by location in particular sociocultural contexts, and by geographic and regional differences in the access people have to supportive policies and services. These factors all contribute to the diversity of Canada's elderly population.

This chapter examines change and continuity in the context of aging and families in Canada. It considers a number of factors that reflect the diversity of family ties over time and across generations. This analysis begins with the changing demographic context of family ties in later life, including marital-status patterns, socioeconomic status, and family structures over the life course. We also examine the dynamics of intergenerational and **intragenerational relations** in later life, such as those between individuals in couple relationships, among adult children and their elderly parents, sibling relationships, and grandparent–grandchild relationships. We challenge the predominance of the "caregiving" paradigm in framing analyses of intergenerational relations and we explore the myth of the sandwich generation, the ways in which changing health and social policies impact older people and their families, the balance of work and family responsibilities, the issue of family payment for care of elderly kin, and statutory obligations across **generations** within families. Throughout, the diversity of aging Canadian families is emphasized, with particular focus on gender, ethnicity, and geographical and regional location.

THE CHANGING DEMOGRAPHIC CONTEXT OF FAMILIES IN LATER LIFE: ELDERLY PEOPLE IN CANADA

In order to set the context for considering aging and families, it is necessary to understand the basic characteristics of **population aging** in Canada. In 2002, 13 percent of Canada's population of just over 31 million people was over the age of 65 (Statistics Canada, 2003). Age 65 is typically used as the criterion for defining the "elderly" population, because this has historically been the age at which people become eligible for pension and income-security benefits (although some people now receive these benefits at younger ages). Age 65 has also long been associated with retirement from the paid labour force. However, many Canadians now leave full-time employment before age 65; about one-third of "retired" people are under 60 years of age (Statistics Canada, 1997). This transition has become blurred because many "retired" people continue involvement in the labour force in a part-time, contract, or seasonal capacity. Nevertheless, the age of 65 remains, somewhat arbitrarily, as the point at which individuals are defined as having reached "old age."

Canada's population is much "older" than it was at the turn of the century, although it is still considered young in comparison with many countries in the industrialized world. A century ago only 6 percent of the population of Canada was over the age of 65. With increases in **life expectancy** and the aging of what is commonly known as the "baby boom generation," the proportion of the population over the age of 65 will increase even further, to approximately 25 percent by the year 2031. This trend will begin to accelerate around 2011, when the oldest baby boomers, born in 1946, reach age 65.

Although people often think of the population over the age of 65 as one homogeneous group, this is not the case. In fact, many people over the age of 65 also have at least one child who is also over the age of 65. In an attempt to reflect the heterogeneity of old age, some people distinguish between the "young old" (often those between 65 and 80 years of age) and the "old old" (usually those aged 80 or 85 and older). This "old old" population has been the fastest growing age group in Canada over the past decade. The number of Canadians over the age of 80 "soared by 41 percent" between 1991 and 2001, and by 2011 will include an estimated 1.3 million people! Not only are increasing numbers of people reaching age 65, individuals are living longer in old age. At age 65, women can expect to live another 20 years and men another 16 years (Chappell et al., 2003).

Reflecting Diversity: Geography and Location

There is wide variability across Canada in the prevalence and concentration of elderly people. Manitoba and Saskatchewan are the "oldest" provinces, each having 15 percent of their population over the age of 65. Alberta, the "youngest" province, has 10 percent of its population over age 65, while the Territories have substantially lower proportions (Yukon, 6 percent and Nunavut, 2 percent) (Statistics Canada, 2003). Another source of diversity in Canadian families is geographical and regional location. Just as the relative proportion of the elderly population varies across Canada, so too does the proportion of the young-adult generation in each of these provinces and regions. Together, these patterns affect not only the opportunity for intergenerational family contact and support, but also the population of employed persons contributing to the resource base upon which services are built and from which public pensions are drawn.

As an illustration, Denton and Spencer (1997) document dramatic changes in the profile of population aging in the province of Newfoundland and Labrador. Population aging is the result of both fertility and migration patterns. Newfoundland and Labrador currently has the lowest birth rate and the highest rate of out-migration of young adults in all of Canada. It is projected that out-migration will result in the loss of one-fifth of the province's population over the next 20 years. Most of these emigrants will be young people, with the percentage of the province's population under 20 dropping by almost half by 2021. As a result, over the next 20 years the proportion of persons over the age of 65 in Newfoundland and Labrador will more than double from 11.4 per cent to 25.8 per cent (Lilley and Campbell, 1999; Wideman, 2003).

These changes will produce a "top-heavy" population structure, quite unlike that of any other province, in terms of the very high proportion of elderly persons in the population. The implications for family life and social policy will be profound in terms of the availability of a wage-earning population base to support the costs of care, as well as the availability of informal supports for the aged population.

Another source of diversity for Canadian families is location in a rural or an urban environment. Close to 30 percent of all elderly Canadians reside in the three largest cities in the country: Toronto, Montreal, and Vancouver (Moore and Rosenberg, 1997). However, fully a quarter of all elderly Canadians live in rural areas, defined as areas with fewer than 1000 inhabitants. The highest percentage live in communities of 10 000 or fewer residents. Rural elders typically have limited access to a range of formal support services, despite the fact that rural and small-town Canada has a disproportionate share of our elderly population (Joseph and Martin Matthews, 1994). In many small communities, fully 25 to 30 percent of the population is over the age of 65 years; in some, over 5 percent of the population is over the age of 80 years! Rural environments present particular challenges in later life, in terms of the lack of variety of supportive housing options, the limited range of health and social services, and transportation difficulties.

Reflecting Diversity: Ethnicity and Cultural Issues

Canada has had an immigration policy of family reunification in recent decades, and this has resulted in many elderly family members from ethno-cultural minorities, as noted earlier.

It is important to consider the impact of cultural norms involving **filial obligation** and also expectations of family members about appropriate family roles and responsibilities, on the lives of elderly persons who are members of "minority" ethnic groups. For example, in a study of second and third generation Japanese families, Kobayashi (2000) found that although most (64%) of the adult children believed in the concept of filial piety, only about one-half reported feelings of ethnic identification with being "Japanese."

As Canada's aged population becomes increasingly ethnically diverse, we will need to re-examine many of our old assumptions about family life and family ties. For example, in the case of elderly widowed women, we have assumed (and research has confirmed) that daughters are a strong and supportive tie. However, "it is rather ethnocentric for [North] Americans to assume that the mother–daughter tie is inevitably the closest one, since that is not the case for so many societies" (Lopata, 1995, pp. 121–22). For example, throughout much of Asia and the Middle East (countries whose residents increasingly immigrate to Canada), it is a son, and not a daughter, who has the closest relationship with an elderly mother.

Bengtson, Rosenthal, and Burton (1996) point out that, in many cases, elderly members of minority ethnic groups may be embedded in large supportive networks. However, we know little about how pervasive these networks are, both within and across minority groups; the extent to which comparable networks exist for non-ethnic minority elders; and the exact nature of the burdens as well as the benefits of membership in extended kin networks. We do not know the extent to which economic need overrides cultural choice in terms of levels of kin network involvement and living arrangements. For example, we do not fully understand whether cultural preference and/or economic need contribute to multi-family homes among immigrant populations (Chappell et al., 2003).

Further, members of ethnocultural minorities may find that language barriers, religious and cultural differences, and economic dependency reduce their access to community-based health and social services. Structural factors such as living arrangements, gender, and age are often stronger predictors of the level of assistance provided across generations than are culturally relevant expectations of filial obligation and ethnic-group identification (Keefe, Rosenthal, and Béland, 2000). These findings suggest important avenues for further exploration of issues of ethnicity and care of older persons by family members.

Reflecting Diversity: Issues of Gender

Since women live approximately seven years longer than men, the world of elderly people is largely a world of women. However, this is changing as the gap between male and female mortality rates has narrowed somewhat in the last few decades. Hence our discussions of the patterns and dynamics of families and aging will largely be of elderly women. Wherever possible, comparisons and contrasts between the family lives of elderly men and women are considered. It is important to keep in mind that men's involvement in family life in old age is often overlooked and is by no means negligible (Creedon, 1995; Phillips and Bernard, 1995).

Men and women are almost equally likely to provide instrumental assistance to elderly relatives, such as shopping and transportation. However, men are only half as likely as women (7 versus 14 percent) to be involved in providing such personal care as bathing, feeding, toileting, and dressing (Martin-Matthews and Campbell, 1995). Some suggest that the predominance of women in providing care reflects the fact that women also predominate as receivers of intergenerational care. Certainly, mothers or mothers-in-law account for about three-quarters of older people receiving intergenerational assistance (Martin-Matthews and Rosenthal, 1993). Although Box 11.1 depicts the personal care provided by a son, John Daniel, to his mother, there are strong cross-gender taboos concerning the provision of such care by men to women, even when they are related as parent and adult child.

Canadian research has examined the involvement of sons in filial care (that is, care to elderly parents) (Campbell and Martin-Matthews, 2000a, 2000b, 2003). Men's help to elderly parents was categorized in terms of activities often thought of as "traditionally male" tasks (e.g., yard maintenance), more gender-neutral tasks (e.g., transportation), and typically "non-traditional" tasks for men (e.g., personal care). Factors such as distance and

BOX 11.1 CAREGIVING

I never looked forward to helping my mother with her shower. She wasn't the least self-conscious about baring her body in my presence, but something in me shrank from it. To be with her in her nakedness seemed too intimate for a grown son. And some other part of me, the child who wants always to be cared for and never burdened with responsibility, felt put upon and put out. Why was I having to do this? It seemed an indignity, and it touched an open wound...

...In her own mind, the mind I believe she inhabited most of the time, she was perfectly capable of taking a shower by herself if she wanted to. In this mind she was still the woman she had been five years ago, a woman who came and went and drove a car, a woman who lived on her own...and was only temporarily exiled in a distant place.... But in her present mind she knew, ...just how incapable she had become. She knew, and she hated it. How could she not have hated it? And if she had to bear it, she didn't want me... or anyone else to have to help her bear it. She wanted to carry herself on her own stooped shoulders....

She would let me stop rinsing only when she could rub a bit of her hair between finger and thumb and make it squeak. Then I would steady her out of the shower stall, her two hands in mine. It felt at moments like a kind of dance, a dance that maybe I knew how to do and needed to do.

...No matter how hard she might have resisted the idea, a bath or shower always seemed to renew her: ...the old woman came forth cleaner of spirit...

...I guess I came out of the bathroom cleaner of spirit myself...whatever the tenor of our conversation, I appreciate now what a privilege it was to help my mother with her shower. I wish I'd seen it more clearly at the time.

Source: John Daniel. 2001. "Looking After: A Son's Memoir." In Alexis J. Walker, Margaret Manoogian-O'Dell, Lori A. McGraw, and Diana L.G. White, eds., *Families in Later Life: Connections and Transitions.* Pp. 107–09. Thousand Oaks, Ca.: Pine Forge Press (a Sage Publications Company).

sibling-network composition (whether the son is an "only" child, or has sibling networks of brothers only, or sisters) predicted men's filial care, independent of the type of task. However, the gendered nature of the task was important in determining how other factors—such as filial obligation, and parent status, education, and income—influence the care men provide (Campbell and Martin-Matthews, 2003).

The concept of "legitimate excuses" has been employed in discussions of family obligation (Finch, 1989) and negotiating family responsibilities (Finch and Mason, 1993). Although the term "excuses" may imply "a kind of illicit avoidance of obligation," it is used to reflect a range of accounts, explanations, and justifications that are constructed when individuals negotiate family obligations and care relationships. Research suggests that "gendered biographies can mean that women—unlike men—*are seen as being* in a position which makes them able to juggle various commitments simultaneously without the need to prioritise one over another" (Finch and Mason, 1993, p. 124). Women's biographies, and not men's, put them in positions where the "legitimacy" of other commitments and constraints may hold less weight than the commitments and constraints on men; this situation can contribute to the tendency for men to have their excuses accepted as "legitimate" *more* readily than are women's.

Research on the gendered nature of intergenerational relations has focused primarily on the gender of the adult child. What about the gender of the older parent? Comparatively little is known about older men's family roles and family relationships, especially among older unmarried men. Some researchers suggest that, in old age, men may be even more at risk than are women, because family relationships based on parenthood and marriage become more important in later life (Goldscheider, 1990, p. 553). As illustration, Canadian adult children report that they are somewhat less likely to keep in touch with a widowed father than with a widowed mother (Smith and Dumas, 1994).

While most studies of families and aging do not find broad patterns of disadvantage among older men, it is important that the study of diversity and change in intragenerational and intergenerational roles and relationships includes both men and women in our research and analyses. Accounts of men's "caring roles," such as John Bayley's (1999) depiction of his care for his wife, the noted writer Iris Murdoch, as she suffered the progressive effects of Alzheimer's disease, give voice to a neglected area within the study of families and aging. This "lack of visibility of men" in aging families (Bengtson, Rosenthal, and Burton, 1996, p. 267) is often due to the fact that in many studies, sample sizes are simply not large enough to provide enough males for meaningful analyses of gender differences, controlling for kin relationships. But systemic biases in research populations notwithstanding, it is important to realize the extent to which the experience of later life, and especially of advanced old age, is a largely female experience.

MARITAL STATUS PATTERNS IN LATER LIFE

Table 11.1 provides time, age, and gender comparisons for four marital status categories: married or cohabiting, widowed, divorced, and single. Data from two census periods are provided. Among some age groups, marital status patterns have remained fairly constant over the 20-year interval (for example, the percentages of women aged 85 and over who are divorced, or who have never married). For other marital statuses, however, there has been considerable change. For example, while 25 percent of men aged 85 and older were married in 1981, by 2001 over half of all men in that age group were married. Over a 20-year period, the percentage of widowed women aged 55–64 has dropped from 17 percent to 11 percent. These changes have significant implications for men and women in old age. Other changes depicted in Table 11.1 are equally dramatic, although their implications for aging families and later life is difficult as yet to predict; for example, while 9 percent of men aged 35–44 were single in 1981, two decades later fully 28 percent of men in that age group have never married.

We will now focus specifically on several of these marital status patterns. While the family roles of older persons involve a number of marital statuses, the most typical marital status for women in later life is widowhood. We know that widowhood is both age-related and sex-selective (Martin Matthews, 1991). Table 11.1 illustrates how the percentages of the population who are widowed increase with advancing age. In the 2001 data, for example, fully 56 percent of women aged 75–84 years are widowed, compared with 29 percent of women aged 65–74.

These data also reflect the sex-selective nature of widowhood. In Canada, widows outnumber widowers by a factor of five to one. While half of all marriages end with the death of the husband, only one in five ends with the death of the wife. The data in Table 11.1 illustrate this trend very clearly, especially from age 50 onwards. For example, while only 3 percent of men aged 55–64 years are widowed, 11 percent of women in the same age **cohort** are widowed.

There are several reasons for the sex-selective nature of widowhood. These include differences in life expectancy between men and women (today, life expectancy at birth for women is about 81 years, while it is 75 years for men); the fact that women marry men who are on average two or three years older than they are; and also the differences between men and women in their rates of remarriage. Men are not only far less likely to become widowed, but also less likely than are women to remain widowed. Approximately 14 percent of widowers and 5 percent of widows remarry. Among the population aged 70 years and older, widowers are nine times more likely than are widows to remarry.

However, the likelihood of remarriage for widows and widowers has declined in recent years in Canada. This is due to societal norms that increasingly favour cohabitation without marriage, as well as economic disincentives to remarriage. These disincentives often involve private pension plans and

Table 11.1   PERCENTAGE DISTRIBUTIONS OF MARITAL STATUS BY GENDER AND AGE: CANADA, 1981 and 2001

Age	Married/Cohabiting				Widowed				Divorced				Single (Never Married)			
	Men		Women		Men		Women		Men		Women		Men		Women	
	1981	2001	1981	2001	1981	2001	1981	2001	1981	2001	1981	2001	1981	2001	1981	2001
25–34	69	58	76	66	<1	<1	<1	<1	—	3	—	4	26	39	16	27
35–44	87	64	86	67	<1	<1	2	<1	4	8	6	11	9	28	7	21
45–54	87	72	83	70	1	1	6	3	—	13	5	16	8	14	6	11
55–64	86	78	73	69	3	3	17	11	3	12	4	14	8	8	7	7
65–74	81	79	52	57	8	8	37	29	2	7	2	8	8	7	9	6
75–84	69	73	26	34	21	18	63	56	1	4	1	4	9	6	10	6
85+	25	51	7	10	66	37	83	78	<1	2	<1	2	9	7	9	10

Source: Adapted from Statistics Canada, *Census of Canada*, 1981, 2001.

survivor benefits that some people receive when they are widowed; remarriage is discouraged because these people are financially "punished" by having these benefits discontinue upon remarriage. Recent analyses of remarriage patterns following the removal of marriage penalties from the surviving spouse pensions of the Canadian public pension system in the 1980s confirm that marriage penalties can have large and persistent effects on marriage decisions in later life (Baker, Hanna, and Kantarevic, 2003).

Rates of remarriage are also influenced by the attitudes and reactions of family members to the formalizing of a new partner relationship in later life. Research also suggests that older widows, many of whom had very traditional marriages, often express reluctance to give up their independence, at the risk of subsequently having to provide care to their new partner in case of illness and/or to risk losing another partner through death. "I am enjoying my freedom too much now. I brought up my children, and I looked after my husband to the best of my ability. I cared for my parents until they died, and it was a joy and I liked it, but I am enjoying the freedom now of not having to account to anybody for what I do" (Connidis, 2001, p. 109).

The data in Table 11.1 also indicate that the likelihood of widowhood in later life is decreasing. Reductions in mortality rates of men and the increase in divorce among older people both explain this trend. This does not reflect the rate at which elderly persons are terminating their marriages, but rather the fact that an increasing number of individuals are entering old age as divorced persons. This rate of divorce, in turn, has major implications for patterns of widowhood in later life.

The projections are that, with continuing low rates of marriage and remarriage, about half of all women entering old age in 2025 will not be in any marriage (Martin-Matthews, 1991, 1999b). Table 11.1 illustrates the exceptionally high rates of singlehood amongst the population aged 25–34, and the magnitude of change between 1981 and 2001. The issue is whether many of these individuals will in fact ever marry or enter into a long-term cohabitation relationship. It is entirely possible that as cohorts of younger women grow older and move into old age, widowhood will no longer be the normative marital status in later life.

Some studies of the relative impact of various life events suggest that widowhood is one of the most stressful life events, surpassed only by the death of a child in its impact. Widowhood is best understood not only as an event involving the loss of a spouse who in most cases has been a long-time partner, but also as a process of transition over time. This transition begins with the illness of the spouse and proceeds through a period of bereavement, and typically to adaptation and resolution. It is not uncommon, however, for the period of bereavement to be characterized by intense feelings of grief, feelings of meaninglessness, disorganization of one's social world, and identity confusion. But these feelings may not characterize the experience for some.

The experience of grief and bereavement is highly diverse, depending on such factors as the nature and duration of the spouse's final illness, the sociocultural context within which the couple lived, their socioeconomic status, the nature and extent of the social supports available to the bereaved family members, and the nature of the marital relationship or partnership prior to the death.

The issue of marital status has been considered at length because of the major impact it has on life experiences and family dynamics in later life. As discussed below, marital status also significantly affects access to socioeconomic resources as individuals age.

ACCESS TO RESOURCES AND SOCIOECONOMIC STATUS IN LATER LIFE

Although the economic circumstances of many elderly persons in Canada are comparatively better today than they were before the introduction of old-age security and related pension benefits, there is considerable disparity in the level of economic security of old people. Two of the primary factors that produce this inequality of access to economic resources are gender and marital status. Here we discuss how these two factors intersect in relation to the incomes of older persons.

As discussed in Chapter 9, Canada does not have an official measure of "poverty." Instead, analysts often use Statistics Canada's low-income cutoffs as indicators of economic need. Of those elderly persons who fall below Statistics Canada's low-income cutoffs,[1] the majority are elderly women who are "unattached." These women are on their own either because they have remained single throughout their lives or, more typically, because they have become widowed or divorced (McDonald, 1997). Despite some improvements in the economic circumstances of older women in Canada, even today most women remain "one man away from poverty" (McDonald, 1997). While poverty is often tied to women's transition to "unattached" status in later life, it is important to note that poverty in later life is not exclusive to them. Among men, levels of poverty in later life are also highest among those who have never married.

Of the many life changes that accompany the transition to being an "unattached" person in later life, the transition to poverty, even temporarily, occurs for many women. "The transition from spouse to survivor still holds substantial economic peril" (Burkhauser, Butler, and Holden, 1991, p. 504). For many widowed women who had never been poor as a member of a couple, bereavement is often associated with the experience of poverty (Hurd and Wise, 1987).

Using data from Statistics Canada's *Survey of Aging and Independence* and from in-depth interviews with 40 retired widows, researchers compared retired widows with married, separated/divorced, and ever-single women (McDonald, Donahue, and Moore, 2000). They found that retired widows had the lowest income of all four groups, with "an alarming 49 percent of retired widows" living below the low-income cutoffs (Ibid., p. 330).

Not only were these widows less likely than women in all other marital status groups to plan for retirement (by gathering information, contributing to an RRSP, or making investments), the majority did not plan for widowhood either. Some underestimated their chances for joint survival, and the death of the husband was totally unexpected. Some simply had no resources with which they could plan. And others had not wanted "to acknowledge emotionally the impending deaths of their husbands that planning implied" (McDonald et al., 2000, p. 339).

Overall, middle-income women appeared to be hit the hardest by widowhood, while for some of the poorest women, their economic situation actually improved as a result of becoming widowed. "The combination of lower education, discontinuous work histories, wage discrimination in the labour market, and their marital and family responsibilities have placed today's widows uncomfortably close to financial distress" (McDonald et al., 2000, p. 342).

Based on these analyses and considering the labour force patterns of women today, McDonald and colleagues conclude that the next generation of widows will probably fare only slightly better economically. In another study, based on analyses of four cohorts of women, including the baby boomer generation, Canadian researchers tracked cohort trends in family-related intermittent work, savings patterns, and other socioeconomic behaviours (Rosenthal, Martin-Matthews, Denton, and French, 2000). They similarly concluded that "most of tomorrow's older women, like today's will not be financially secure in later life unless they are married" (Rosenthal et al., 2000, p. 108).

These data illustrate the financial penalties women incur for periods outside paid employment, as in taking time for child rearing. As well, the rise in "non-standard" work—part-time, seasonal, contractual, low-paying—has particularly affected women and typically provides few or no workplace-based financial benefits, such as sick leave or pension benefits. Other factors include the low availability of employer-sponsored pension plans in Canada, and the even lower availability of survivor benefits for women who have lost a spouse (Schellenberg, 1994). Thus women's lower wages, their typical pattern of interrupted labour-force attachment, and the often marginal nature of their paid employment combine to contribute to the poverty that "unattached women," in particular, experience in later life.

However, not all widowed individuals experience the transition to poverty. Here again diversity is a characteristic of the experience of socioeconomic change associated with marital status transition in later life. Thus, while elderly persons in Canada overall are far less likely today to live in poverty than they did several decades ago, structural factors do increase or decrease their chances of being poor. Several of these structural factors reflect the intersection of gender and marital status. For example, elderly women living alone are seven times more likely to be poor than are men living with spouses in their old age. Being male, living as a couple, and having a history of continuous full-time employment all reduce the likelihood of poverty in later life (Moore and Rosenberg, 1997).

FAMILY STRUCTURES OVER THE LIFE COURSE

Increased longevity and the overall aging of the Canadian population have also changed the structure of family ties. For example, new roles (such as great-grandparenthood) and responsibilities (such as being an elderly "child" aged 65 years or older and having a very aged parent still alive) have developed in recent decades.

Increased longevity has also meant a substantial increase in the duration of family ties across generations. It is now common for parents and children to share 50 or even 60 years together. When persons born in 1910 reached their fiftieth birthday in 1960, only 16 percent of them had at least one of their parents still alive. By comparison, when persons born in 1930 reached their fiftieth birthday in 1980, 49 percent of them had at least one of their parents still alive. Projections suggest that when persons born in 1960 reach their fiftieth birthday in 2010, fully 60 percent of them will have at least one of their parents still alive to celebrate the event with them (Gee, 1990).

Not only are family roles more enduring; in some cases they have assumed different responsibilities as well. For example, because of the increase in the rate of divorce and the poverty of children, among other factors, grandparents now may find themselves in situations requiring that they "parent" their grandchildren, through either ongoing or intermittent custodial relationships (Jendrek, 1993, 1994). Others find their rights of access to grandchildren or great-grandchildren diminished by separation and divorce in succeeding generations (Kruk, 1995).

Another result of increased longevity, and also of declines in fertility (Gee, 2000), is the trend toward what has been called the "verticalization" of the family or the development of the "bean-pole family." As McPherson (1998, p. 197) describes it, this trend represents a shift from "the traditional 'pyramid' shape (four to five siblings in a two-to-three-generation family) that prevailed early in the century, to a 'beanpole' shape (four to five generations with zero to two siblings per generation)." Although some sociologists contend that bean-pole families are not as prevalent as is currently supposed (Connidis, 1994; Rosenthal, 1998; Uhlenberg, 1993), these demographic shifts are important and reflect the need to view changes in fertility rates (and their implications for aging families) in historical perspective. Some analysts suggest that more vertical structures will deplete the numbers of family members available to nurture and provide care to long-lived elderly kin. Others, however, argue that the increased duration of ties "combined with less restrictive definitions of what constitutes family membership, makes family relations more complex and could actually widen the net of family carers, despite times of lower fertility" (Connidis 2001, p. 10).

Another structural change in family ties across generations involves the acceleration of rates of "generational turnover" (Hagestad, 1981). This refers to the length of time between the birth of the first and the birth of the last child in families. In the past, when larger families were prevalent, childbearing often extended over 20 or more years of a woman's life. Today, generational turnover is much more rapid, with the duration of childbearing often covering only a few years. For example, in my father's family, the spread of 16 years separating the oldest child from the youngest meant that the eldest and youngest siblings grew up with few common experiences and network ties outside the immediate family. By comparison, my two children are typical of many families today, in that they are less than two years apart in age; therefore, virtually all of their childhood and social experiences even outside the family—such as school activities and neighbourhood contacts—are experienced in common. That commonality of experience[2] becomes yet one more feature of their ties as siblings.

At the same time, in some families today there is a trend toward what has been called an "age-gapped" structure, with increasing numbers of years between the birth of one generation in a family and the birth of the next (McPherson, 1998). The interval between generations is usually measured in terms of the age of the mother at the birth of her first child. This calculation is the primary method for classifying intergenerational family structure as either "age-condensed" or "age-gapped." Early fertility results in small age distances between generations; that is, not only a young mother, but also young grandparents and, perhaps, young great-grandparents. In age-condensed families, boundaries between generations are likely to blur because of the narrow age gap between them (Bengtson, Rosenthal, and Burton, 1990). In contrast, an age-gapped family structure (where, for example, the first child is born when the mother is age 30 or older) may hinder the development of affective bonds and value congruence across generations (Bengtson et al., 1990).

In studies I have conducted with individuals in mid- and later-life who have responsibilities for care of one or more elderly parent(s), this issue of the age-gap between generations has arisen: "I wish our parents were younger when we were born. I feel I am in a sandwich position, squished in the middle between my family and my parents. If they were younger, they would be healthier now" (Martin-Matthews and Matthews, 2001).

Taken together, these structural characteristics—duration of ties, verticalization of families, acceleration of generational turnover, and age-condensed/age-gapped structures—contribute to the diversity of families in different historical time periods, with different social and structural influences. In this way, the structures of families have an impact on the nature of the roles and responsibilities of multiple generations of the family over the life course.

FAMILY TIES IN LATER LIFE

Many different types of ties connect family members together over the life course. Only a few of these can be examined here. An important point to remember is the extent to which the decisions made or circumstances experienced by one member of the family impact on the lives of other family members and create change for them. For example, marriage in one generation creates in-laws in another (Hagestad, 1981). Parenthood creates grandparenthood and great-grandparenthood. Divorce creates "ex" or "former" relationships that require negotiation. Bereavement creates not only widowhood, but also the loss of a parent or grandparent. The poverty of a single-parent daughter may precipitate her return to her parent's home. Geographic relocation changes the patterns of contact across multiple generations.

Couple Relationships

Among Canadians aged 65 years and over, over half (56 percent) are married. In studies of later-life marriage, researchers have been primarily interested in how marital roles and marital quality change over time. Especially today, with increasing levels of labour-force participation among older women, and the trend to earlier retirement among older men, couple relationships in later life are increasingly diverse. The recent legalization of same-sex marriages in Canada will contribute even further to this diversity of later-life couple relationships. Currently there is very little literature on same-sex partnerships, especially those in later life. How couples—both gay and straight—negotiate the transition to retirement is an important indicator of the level of satisfaction of their later years as a couple. In many cases, retirement from paid employment brings a couple into greater day-to-day contact than they may have had for many years—a transition that requires adaptability on the part of both members of the couple.

Earlier research suggested a curvilinear pattern in marital satisfaction, with a drop following the birth of children and an increase once children were launched into the world. While this portrayal is considered inaccurate today, it does seem that "on balance, older couples appear to be more satisfied with their marriages than their younger counterparts" (Connidis, 2001, p. 57). A number of factors could account for this pattern: a process of selectivity with only "better" marriages lasting a long time, a stage in the family life cycle, or a cohort-specific commitment to marriage.

Certainly, the accounts of couples provide a range of perspectives. One 68-year-old woman referred to her husband's pivotal role in enabling her to care for her 97-year-old mother: "It helps immeasurably that I have been married for 45 years to the most wonderful man. He is so supportive and understanding, my rock and my strength. I look at our life together and I cannot believe my good fortune in having him as my life mate."

However, the protagonist in Ethan Canin's *We are Emperors of the Air* (as cited in Cole and Winkler, 1994) provides a different image of his marriage of 46 years to Francine: "Time has made torments of our small differences and tolerance of our passions" (p. 236).

While the vast majority of elderly persons, especially those less than 80 years of age, enjoy relatively good health and have comparatively little need for what are called "formal" supports provided by health and social-service agencies, advancing age does bring changes in functional health status and increasing frailty in one or both members of a couple. As a result, the nature of the couple relationship inevitably changes toward the end of the life of at least one of the partners. While much of the literature on "caregiving" focuses on the care of elderly persons by their adult children, in reality most of the assistance provided to elderly persons is provided intragenerationally; that is, by someone of the same generation, usually a spouse. Because, at the end of life, most women are widowed but most men are married, it is very typical for elderly married women to spend their last years of marriage caring for an increasingly frail spouse.

While providing this care, women may themselves experience health problems (Gee and Kimball 1987, p. 31). They are, in fact, more likely than men to report chronic, ongoing health problems such as high blood pressure and arthritis, and to experience physical limitations. Cognitive impairment in very old age can result from a number of factors, including strokes or drug interactions. More permanent impairment may be associated with dementia, which results from chronic brain damage caused by circulatory problems such as hardening of the cerebrovascular arteries or to disease states in the brain. The most well known form of dementia is Alzheimer's disease. Symptoms may include memory loss, disorientation, and loss of emotional abilities (McPherson, 1998). While about 8 percent of Canadians aged 65 and over meet the criteria for a diagnosis of dementia (Chappell et al., 2003), its incidence increases with age, from 2 percent of those aged 65–74 years, to 11 percent of those aged 75–84 years, to 35 percent of those aged 85 years and older (Canadian Study of Health and Aging, 1994).

Among elderly couples, then, there are many women caring for a very ill partner whose personal characteristics are quite unlike those present before the onset of dementia (O'Connor, 1999). In some cases, illness progresses to the point where one partner can no longer provide the needed care, and one member of the couple is institutionalized (Gladstone, 1995). As a result, some elderly spouses (usually women) continue to live independently in the community while their partners permanently reside in a long-term-care facility, a situation that has been described as "**quasi widowhood**" (Rosenthal and Dawson, 1991; Ross, Rosenthal, and Dawson, 1997) or "married widowhood" (McPherson, 1998). These circumstances represent significant marital status "ambiguity" for those who experience them (Martin-Matthews, 1999b).

Adult Child–Older Parent Relationships

Although adult child–older parent relationships have in recent years come to be characterized very much in terms of the "care" the younger generation provides to the older generation (Martin-Matthews, 2000), there is considerable evidence of typically supportive bonds between most older persons and their adult children throughout the life course. Approximately 80 percent of Canadians aged 65 and older have at least one living child; indeed, more than 10 percent of those aged 65 and over have a child who is also over the age of 65 (Rosenthal and Gladstone, 1994). This latter fact highlights the complexity of intergenerational ties and the fallacy of equating family roles (such as being a grandparent or being someone's adult "child") with membership in particular age cohorts.

The vignettes in Box 11.2 provide two examples of parent–child ties characterized by strong family bonds and the flow of assistance across households and generations, and what appear to be emotionally close and emotionally reciprocal relationships. Both vignettes depict intergenerational linkages and dynamics as described by social scientists: attachment, filial piety and obligation,

BOX 11.2   PARENT–CHILD TIES

Maureen is 45 years old and employed part-time as a physiotherapist. She and Mike have one child, a daughter Erin, aged 22, who is in second-year university about a two-hour drive from her parent's home. Mother and daughter are especially close. Erin phones her mother at least every second day, and they talk at length about concerns they both have, but most especially about Erin's social life and how she is doing in her courses. Maureen regularly sends money to Erin. Because Erin has chronic asthma problems, Maureen occasionally travels the two hours to help care for her daughter if she has a particularly bad attack, or if she is too unwell to travel home on her own. Helping Erin in this way helps Maureen through the periods of "feeling blue" that have plagued her all her life.

Janet is a 32-year-old part-time art teacher and freelance artist. Recently married, she lives about a five-minute walk from the home of her parents, Martin and Thelma, both in their early 70s. A sister lives nearby and a brother in a city about three hours drive away. Janet, the youngest child in the family, is close to both her parents, especially so since their recent health problems. Thelma has severe arthritis and suffered a mild heart attack about three years ago. In the past two years, Martin has suffered a series of mild strokes. Martin and Thelma are limited in their mobility, and Janet helps out, running errands for them, especially in the winter when the driving is treacherous, taking them to lunch regularly to help get them out of the house, even augmenting their meagre pensions whenever she gets extra cash from an art sale. Her brother also helps his parents financially and, when he visits, with house and yard maintenance. Janet and her parents exchange telephone calls almost daily. In appreciation for Janet's help, Thelma sews items, like draperies and quilts, to decorate the newlywed's home.

Source: Anne Martin-Matthews. 2000. "Intergenerational Caregiving: How Apocalyptic and Dominant Demographies Frame the Questions and Shape the Answers." In E. M. Gee and G. M. Gutman, eds., *The Overselling of Population Aging: Apocalyptic Demography, Intergenerational Challenges and Social Policy.* Pp. 64–79. Toronto: Oxford University Press.

and various forms of solidarity, including affective and normative (Bengtson, Cutler, Mangen, and Marshall, 1985). However, in recent years researchers have described these relationships solely in terms of caregiving.

The word "caregiving" has come to dominate the study of intergenerational relations involving adult (especially mid-life) children and their aging or elderly parents. Originally, the term was used specifically to refer to family members attending to the needs of relatives with extremely heavy physical care needs, often those with Alzheimer's disease and other dementias. In fact, its use in describing not only paid but also unpaid (often call "informal") care by family members was originally intended by many researchers as a way to acknowledge and reinforce the important labour of women in providing care to elderly family members. Today, however, its use is far more widespread and encompasses almost any helping behaviour within, and especially across, the generations. In its most reductionist form, relationships between elderly kin and adult family members are couched in terms of "eldercare," a pejorative term implying that the care of an elderly person is parallel to "childcare" (Martin-Matthews, 1996).

Today, researchers in aging have begun to acknowledge the implications of the "caregiving" bias in their research. Several recent books provide a welcome counterpoint to the overwhelming caregiving focus of research on aging families and intergenerational relations. Researchers are now critiquing the tendency to focus on the dyadic relationship between one individual who occupies the role of "primary caregiver" and another who occupies the role of "elderly care recipient" (Matthews, 2002). Instead, families are understood as "networks whose members take one another into account to accomplish the family labour of meeting the needs of old parents" (Matthews, 2002). From this perspective, families are conceptualized "as relationships rather than roles" and this leads to better understanding of life in older families. A vivid image of the power of these parent–child relationships, transcending death, is provided in Box 11.3, in Linda Pastan's poetic notes to her mother.

"Caregiving" ignores the prevalence of reciprocal exchanges between elderly people and members of their kin and friendship networks. In fact, many studies document that the flow of aid between generations is predominantly "down" rather than "up" the generations; the assistance provided by older persons to their adult children typically includes help with childcare, financial assistance, and advice. However, this reciprocal exchange of aid across the generations is ignored in studies that depict older people as passive "recipients" of "care."

Participants in several of my own research projects frequently provided unsolicited descriptions of the assistance they received from their elderly kin, and they provided this detail in spite (or perhaps because) of the fact that the study itself was quite specifically focused on the nature of the assistance they provide to their elderly family members. These individuals constantly

BOX 11.3   NOTES TO MY MOTHER

Your letters to me

Are forwarded to my dreams

Where you appear in snatches

Of the past...

And since your gravestone

Is shaped like the front

Of our old mailbox,

I'll try to leave my messages

of flowers there.

...

I'm still homesick eight years after

You left me in my life for good:

...

Though I learned to love

the woman you became

after the stroke,

I never quite forgave her

for hiding my real mother—you,

somewhere

in the drifted snows beyond

that unscalable

widow's peak.

...

You taught me always

to write thank you notes, though

I never thanked you properly,

Not even when you were dying. But

I thought our inarticulateness

in the face of love was as elemental

as the silence on stones

in the same streambed. I thought

you wanted it that way.

As I grow older, I try

to draw the world in close

as if it were a shawl you had crocheted for me

from small indulgences—morning coffee

from the same cracked cup,

a stroll downhill past empty mailboxes...

So in the last moments of wakefulness

I recreate that lost world

whose textures are like Braille

beneath my fingertips: the enamel

of the 40s stove where you taught me

to cook; the floral wallpaper you chose

whose roses had no thorns...

And here sleep comes

with all its complicated gifts

and treacheries to gather me

in its arms.

reminded us of what they received from their elderly relatives in return for their "care." This reciprocity may be a current feature of the relationship, as when an elderly woman, receiving several hours of help each week from her daughter, reciprocates by having the grandchildren come to her apartment after school one or more days a week. In other circumstances, the reciprocal nature of the relationship lies in the perception of the current "giver" of care of how much she has, in the past, received from her elderly relative who is now the care "receiver." This has been referred to as having a "support bank" or "reciprocal credentials" (Martin-Matthews, 2000b) from the past. Such statements as "She gave me a wonderful childhood and this is the least I can do for her now"; "She always was a loving mother who did everything she could for her children. Whatever we do for her now is really no more than what she gave to us when she was able to" illustrate this concept. Such comments evoke both reciprocity and attachment as foundational elements of family ties across generations.

The image of "caregiving" adult children providing support for needy aging parents is also embedded in notions of the sandwich generation. According to this concept, many family members, and particularly women, find themselves trapped between the demands of their adolescent children and their aging parents. However, the belief about the widespread prevalence of the sandwich generation is largely a myth (Rosenthal, Martin-Matthews, and Matthews, 1996). Typically, caregiving evolves through the life span with responsibilities following one another rather than overlapping (Centre on Aging and the Caregivers Association of British Columbia, 1995, pp. 17–18).

Sibling Relationships

Most older people have at least one living sibling. In many respects, the sibling relationship is unique among later-life family ties because of both its long duration and what it represents in terms of shared early-childhood family experiences (Connidis, 1989). Several Canadian studies suggest that sibling ties, frequently having waned throughout young adulthood and midlife, often become quite salient in later life, especially among sisters, and particularly when both are widowed (Connidis, 1989, 1992; Connidis and Davies, 1990; Martin Matthews, 1991). There is as yet no evidence of a comparable pattern amongst divorced older persons.

One aspect of family life that we expect to be different for elderly persons in the future is the number of sibling ties. Those who will enter old age in the next 15–25 years (the "baby boomers") will, as a result of the high fertility rates in the 1950s, have a substantial number of brothers and sisters. In this respect they differ from both the elderly population of today, and younger adults of today. Canadians now in their 50s have more living siblings than do those in their 30s because large families were more common in the 1950s than in the late 1960s and early 1970s (Smith and Dumas, 1994). What does this mean for aging and family life? First, there will, potentially at least, be more kin available to contribute to the care of elderly relatives than is currently the case. Second, the sibling tie is the longest in duration of all family relationships. Given the acceleration of "generational turnover" noted previously, siblings today and in the future will be more likely to share the same historical events and life experiences than has been the case in previous generations.

Grandparent–Grandchild Relationships

The vast majority of older people who have children also have one or more grandchildren. Despite its association with old age, the transition to grandparenthood typically occurs in midlife. Research findings suggest that regular interaction with grandparents usually leaves children with fewer prejudices about old people (McPherson, 1998). For the most part, the grandparent role is seen as one "with minimal rights and obligations" (Rosenthal and Gladstone, 1994), although typically it has a symbolic function in the lineage and dynamics of the family. It primarily involves emotional rather than tangible support. Of the family ties discussed in this chapter, the grandparent–grandchild tie is rather unique in terms of its contingent and mediated nature. Becoming a grandparent is a "contingent transition," dependent upon the behaviour of one's children (Connidis, 2001). At the same time, the tie is mediated by the person(s) who connect these two generations (those in the middle generation) and is, as a result, vulnerable to disruption, particularly in cases of breakdown of the marriage or partnership of the parents (Chappell et al., 2003).

As an example, the increase in the rate of divorce among Canadian families and in the number of children affected by divorce has seen the emergence of "grandparent rights" groups across the country. Kruk (1995) has identified four circumstances primarily associated with loss of contact between grandparents and grandchildren. These include parental divorce, conflict with both parents, death of adult child, and stepparent adoption following remarriage. Kruk found that grandparents whose child was the noncustodial parent (usually paternal grandparents) are at high risk for contact loss, and adult children-in-law appear to be the primary mediators in the ongoing grandparent–grandchild relationship.

Perhaps because of recent increases in the number of baby boomers becoming grandparents, grandparent–grandchild relationships have begun to receive more research attention of late. Research is needed that captures the diversity of this intergenerational tie; while much of the previous research focused on older grandparents and younger grandchildren, relationship patterns are in fact considerably more diverse, often involving midlife grandparents with younger grandchildren, older grandparents with adolescent and young-adult grandchildren, and, for the most part, very old great-grandparents with young great-grandchildren (Connidis, 2001).

Other "Family" Relationships in Later Life

The kinds of family relationships described above are only a few of the relationships to be found among the diverse forms of Canadian families. For example, among the 8 percent of elderly Canadians who have remained single throughout their lives, ties to a broad range of kin (including nieces, nephews, aunts, uncles, and cousins) are common; in addition, many have an extensive network of very close friends, often referred to as fictive kin (Connidis, 2001; MacRae, 1992). And, with the increasing numbers of ever-single women now having children, future generations of seniors will not equate being single with childlessness (Rosenthal 1998, p. 10).[3]

Fictive kin ties in later life are by no means restricted to those who have remained single throughout their lives. My research on the family ties and social supports of widowed and non-widowed elderly persons in Ontario found that fully 4 percent of non-widowed and 8 percent of widowed people included at least one friend in their descriptions of their "family" (Martin Matthews, 1991). In similar research in a small Nova Scotia community, MacRae (1992) found that a majority of elderly persons identified at least one person as "fictive kin," with many of these being lifelong friends, and many playing other roles in the family, such as "godparent" to children. Other such ties come later in life, and are founded on a shared life circumstance. "Mother is fortunate in that her block has a dozen or more elderly widows in residence who help each other frequently and provide local, mutual, emotional support. Two of them in particular are like sisters to her."

One way in which the current cohorts of very elderly persons—the "oldest old"—differ from the cohort now entering old age is in their high rate of childlessness. Canadian women born in the first two decades of the twentieth century had unusually high rates of childlessness and low rates of fertility (Gee and Kimball, 1987). Especially for those women whose one child was a son, many have outlived their only child. As a consequence, substantial proportions of very old people do not have any living children. In fact, my research on caregivers to frail elderly persons receiving home-help services (Martin Matthews, 1993) found that fully 56 percent of the elderly persons interviewed (predominantly women) identified someone other than a child as the primary person providing assistance to them; 15 percent identified a non-relative as providing the most help.

While there is some evidence of higher rates of institutionalization among childless and ever-single elderly persons, overall, elderly people without children are not seen to be especially disadvantaged in later life. However, little is known about the intergenerational ties of childless persons in later life. Research on siblings suggests that childless older persons are quite likely to be involved with the children of their siblings (Connidis, 2001). One 38-year-old man caring for two elderly relatives observed that, "As my uncle's health failed, the medical needs increased and so did his general needs. He became more verbally demanding and more difficult to deal with rationally. There was a mixture of emotions on my part, that ran from pity to empathy to guilt for not being able to help sufficiently." And a woman in another family commented, "It is very hard for us now as my husband's sister is bed ridden and sleeps most of the time...."

As noted earlier in the discussion of couple relationships, a quite neglected research area within the study of families, aging, fictive kin, and "family like" ties is that of gay and lesbian relationships among elderly people. There is some indication that, for older gay men in particular, high levels of social integration into the gay community provide high levels of supportive relationships and life satisfaction (Dorfman et al., 1995). Lesbian women report similarly high levels of support; there is also some evidence that ties with parents and other family members are more likely to be maintained by lesbian women than by gay men (Dorfman et al., 1995; Dorrell, 1991). However, much of the literature on these populations is based on individuals with active links to gay and lesbian communities.

HEALTH AND SOCIAL POLICIES: CHANGING THE NATURE OF "CAREGIVING"

Already we have identified structural features of Canadian society, such as participation in the labour force and survivor benefits in pension plans, which create the conditions affecting how gender and marital status intersect in the access old people have to socioeconomic resources. Health and social policies, and changes to them, also have an impact on aging individuals and families. For example, in comparison with families in many countries of the world, Canadian families benefit enormously from our national medical insurance programme (Martin-Matthews, 1999a). Although health-care policy is changing, currently it still functions to reduce the economic and social burden to families when their members, old or young, become ill. How long this continues to be true remains to be seen. Throughout the 1990s, Canada was engaged in a thorough review of its federally and provincially funded social programmes. Health-care programmes and policies, under provincial jurisdiction, were of particular concern. Initially, health-care reforms were expected to benefit the elderly and those who care for them by channelling funds away from hospitals and institutions and to more preventative and community-based programmes (Béland and Shapiro, 1994).

However, as the federal government tackled its deficit by reducing transfer payments to provinces for health, postsecondary education, and welfare, health-care provision has changed significantly in Canada. Although there are variations amongst the provinces, most have opted for caps on payments to individual physicians, along with the removal of certain products (for example, specific medications) and procedures (such as cataract surgery) from the list of insured services.

The implications for elderly Canadians and their families are complex and as yet unclear since health care is still very much in the midst of restructuring (Chappell et al., 2003). Nevertheless, these changes in Canadian health-care policy and delivery stand to have substantial impact on Canada's elderly and those who care for them (Martin-Matthews, 1999a). Several years ago Carolyn Rosenthal, a Canadian gerontologist, observed "…governments expect families to provide more care than ever to frail elderly who, increasingly, will remain in the community where…services and programs will increasingly be under-funded or absent…. Such an assumption is clearly dangerous for everyone. Older people may be left without adequate sources of support. Or, women may leave paid employment, thereby damaging their own present and future economic situations" (1997, p. 18). These predictions have proven all too true. In a current review of the process of health reform in Canada, the researchers conclude that "the vision of health reform…has allowed for a shifting of the burden of care in old age from the public purse onto individuals and families even though this was not part of the rhetoric or the vision of health reform" (Chappell et al., 2003, pp. 432–33).

THE "COSTS" OF CARING: BALANCING WORK AND FAMILY LIFE

Many studies in social gerontology examine the issue of the "costs of caring." These "costs" may be measured in a number of ways, such as the physical and psychological "burden" of care or the economic costs of care provision, especially in terms of lost, altered, or relinquished labour-force attachment. Recently, researchers, policymakers, and human-resources personnel in both the public and private sectors have focused on the impact of family members' efforts to combine or balance their responsibilities to their employment and to their families, especially to their elderly relatives.

In examining the factors associated with employees' involvement in the provision of care to elderly family members, several Canadian studies have sought to distinguish between shorter-term job costs, longer-term career costs, and personal costs.[4] These costs have been discussed in terms of types of care (Martin Matthews and Rosenthal, 1993) and by gender (Martin Matthews and Campbell, 1995). For both women and men, the provision of assistance with bathing, feeding, toileting, and dressing of an elderly relative (personal care) is associated with a greater impact than is assistance with shopping, transportation, home and yard maintenance, laundry, and financial arrangements (instrumental care). This pattern holds for virtually all types of job, career, and personal costs.

Once again, the gendered nature of these costs is evident. Employed women are more likely than are men to use sick days in order to meet their family obligations and are more likely to miss work-related social events. Men are generally more likely than women to report interrupted workdays. A major gender difference is evident in relation to promotion or advancement within the hierarchy of the workplace, with women almost twice as likely to report lost opportunities for promotion because of providing family care. Regardless of the type of care provided, women are also significantly more likely than are men to report career costs. However, the long-term consequences associated with not seeking promotion or career advancement are particularly pronounced for women involved in the provision of personal care (Martin Matthews and Campbell, 1995). Clearly the inequalities associated with the combination of employment and care to elderly family members (personal care, in particular) "render women less able to be competitive for the best opportunities that society can offer" (McDaniel, 1993, p. 140).

PAYMENT FOR FAMILY CARE: A VIABLE OPTION?

Policy analysts have attempted to address the costs borne by caregivers. In particular, the issue of financial compensation for family members providing informal care to elderly relatives has been debated for some time in Canada and around the world. The examination of the "payment for care" issue is based on both the recognition that informal (usually family) caregivers play vital roles in caring for and supporting older persons and the acknowledgement that, with reductions in institutional care and the slow pace of development of adequate community support programmes, caregivers require special support in carrying out their roles (Keefe and Fancey, 1998). Programmes vary in terms of whether or not they involve direct or indirect approaches to financial compensation. Indirect compensation may involve tax relief, pension schemes, or social-security benefits, while direct compensation involves the transfer of money through an allowance, stipend, grant, or voucher system, payable either to the giver or to the receiver of the care (Keefe and Fancey, 1998).

One such programme in Canada is the Nova Scotia Home Life Support Program, which financially compensates family members for care of an elderly relative. Financially compensated caregivers tend to be younger females who live in non-urban areas and co-reside with the elderly care recipient. The greater proportion of financially compensated caregivers in non-urban areas is likely influenced by both the limited availability of home-help services and the high rates of unemployment and **underemployment** in these areas; these factors combine to create a surplus pool of labour that is available to provide services to elderly persons in need at very minimal costs (Keefe and Fancey, 1997).

STATUTORY OBLIGATIONS WITHIN FAMILIES

There are legal as well as financial incentives to provide care for elderly family members. Under the Family Law Act in most Canadian provinces, adult children have an obligation to support a parent who can prove need and "who has cared for or provided support for the child" (Snell, 1990; Canadian Press, 1996). While this section of the Family Law Act has existed in various forms since 1921, it has been "rarely ever used" (Carey, 1995, p. A1).

Attempts to enforce filial obligation laws have seldom been an effective means of gaining support for an elderly parent when the support is not given willingly (Snell, 1990). In the past decade, however, courts in several provinces have addressed the issue of the limits of the legal obligations between elderly parents and their adult children. A review of these cases (Parsons and Tindale, 2001) found that, in each decision rendered, certain factors were associated with the award of support from one or more adult children to their parent(s): the parent had to establish that he or she was in financial need; that the adult child(ren) had the financial capacity to provide the needed support; and that the parent had provided adequate care and support to the child when he or she was a "minor." The various judicial interpretations of these cases also reflect a "scale of priorities" that holds "an individual's obligation to support his or her immediate family to be of greater priority than responsibilities to his or her family of origin" (Parsons and Tindale, 2001).

Such cases are of interest and relevance not only in terms of the nature of the judicial decision making in relation to each, but also in terms of societal responses to them. For example, a court ruling ordering three adult children to provide monthly support to their 60-year-old mother was characterized as illustrating that "as the welfare state begins to be restructured or crumble, we may see more jurisdictions calling on these statutory obligations.... Now, the suggestion is that families must once again take on these responsibilities" (Glossop, quoted by Carey, 1995, p. A9). Thus far the pace of submissions for judicial consideration in no way demonstrates such an increase (Parsons, for example, reviewed eight cases from the 1980s and seven from the 1990s). Nevertheless, the perception exists that, as baby boomers age and governments cut back on the social safety net, "going after children could become a way of saving the public purse" (Carey, 1995, p. A1).

CONCLUSION

This chapter has addressed a broad range of issues relevant to family ties in the context of population aging in Canada today. It has documented a variety of structural changes—involving increasing longevity, the duration of intergenerational and intragenerational ties, marital-status patterns, women's labour force participation, immigration rates and trends—and their impact on aging families.

Summary

- Structural changes play out in the dynamics of increasingly diverse relationships between members of couples, between adult children and their aging parents, between generations, and among siblings. They find new expression in fictive-kin ties and the emergence and societal recognition of various "non-traditional" family forms.

- This chapter has also demonstrated the impact of policy changes, especially those involving health and social care, on elderly persons and those who care for them. Other factors that impact the relationship between elderly persons and their families have been considered, such as options involving payment for care and statutory obligations to provide care.

- And, finally, the diversity of family forms, structures, and dynamics discussed in other chapters in this book are also examined in the context of families and aging. This chapter has emphasized the extent to which the experience of aging in families varies substantially as a function of socioeconomic status, ethnocultural affiliation, geographical and regional location, and gender.

Notes

1. Statistics Canada's "low-income cutoff" defines people as living "in poverty" if they spend more than 58.5 percent of their total income on food, clothing, and shelter. The figures are adjusted annually for single individuals, for families of varying sizes, and for residence in rural and urban areas of varying sizes.

2. I use the term "generation" here to refer to lineage positions in families (such as the "parental" generation or the "child" generation), as it is used by Hagestad (1981) and others. However, "generation" is used in a variety of ways in studies of aging. Sometimes it describes age groups (people grouped according to their similar ages, usually measured at five-year intervals, e.g., 20- to 24-year-olds). Others use the term to describe age cohorts (people born at particular points in history, e.g., the "baby-boom generation"). Others use it to describe kinship lineage descent, as I have done. Bengston (1993) calls for conceptual clarity in defining "generation."

3. Rosenthal (1998) reports that among never-married women aged 55–59 in 1991, 13 percent had at least one child, compared with 5 percent of those aged 70 years or older.

4. Job costs include arriving late for work or having to depart early, having to use sick days when they personally were not sick, and using vacation time to attend to family obligations. Career costs involve declining or not seeking a promotion, experiencing difficulty with one's manager or supervisor, and missing business meetings or training sessions. Personal costs include reducing volunteer work, missing sleep, and reducing leisure activities.

Critical Thinking Questions

1. As increasing proportions of women enter later life outside of marriage, how will this change their experience of old age?

2. For most of this century, the experience of later life has been substantially different for women than for men. How are these differences compounded by being a member of a minority ethnic group, or living in a rural area or within a particular region of the country?

3. Many researchers, and certainly the popular press, emphasize the abandonment of elders by their families, on the one hand, and the burdens of the "sandwich generation," on the other. In what ways do these images provide inaccurate portrayals of aging and family dynamics? Why do these myths persist?

4. When adult children and elderly parents no longer share a household, what kinds of obligations, moral and legal, do they have in relation to one another?

5. Intergenerational relations between adult children and elderly parents are typically characterized as "caregiving" between a "primary caregiver" and a "care recipient." How is our understanding of intergenerational relations changed when we use the lens of familial relationships rather than caregiving roles in studying aging families?

Websites

Canadian Association on Gerontology
http://cagacg.ca
> This is the official website of the Canadian Association on Gerontology. The site provides information about the CAG's many publications, which offer a variety of viewpoints and disciplines to individuals interested in the field of gerontology. They help promote the professional advancement of CAG members and keep members abreast of new research and developments.

Gerontological Society of America
http://www.geron.org
> This is the official website of the Gerontological Society of America, which is a non-profit professional organization with more than 5000 members in the field of aging, primarily in the United States, but also worldwide. GSA provides researchers, educators, practitioners, and policymakers with opportunities to understand, advance, integrate, and use basic and applied research on aging to improve the quality of life as one ages.

Division of Aging and Seniors at Health Canada
http://www.hc-sc.gc.ca/seniors-aines/index_pages/whatsnew_e.htm

This is the official website of the Division of Aging and Seniors at Health Canada. This unit provides federal leadership in areas pertaining to aging and seniors. The Division works to provide advice and to support policy development; supports research and education activities; and encourages communication and dissemination of information about seniors and aging in Canada. The many publications of the Division of Aging and Seniors and the National Advisory Council on Aging are a great source of reliable information for and about Canadian seniors.

Suggested Reading

Sara Arber and Jay Ginn, eds. 1995. *Connecting Gender and Ageing: Sociological Reflections*. Buckingham: Open University Press.

> This book highlights the different social effects of aging on women's and men's roles, relationships, and identity over the life course. The contributors use a feminist perspective to explore the impact of aging on gender roles across a wide range of situations, such as in the workplace, in retirement, and in marital and other relationships.

Ingrid Arnet Connidis. 2001. *Family Ties and Aging*. Thousand Oaks: Sage Publications.

> This book examines diversity within family ties in later life, focusing on Canadian data in international comparative context. While inter- and intragenerational relationships and sibling ties are emphasized, Connidis examines these ties with a contemporary lens often neglected in other studies. Topics include live-in partnerships not formalized by marriage, the family ties of gays and lesbians, and sociocultural and racial comparisons. Research and policy issues and implications are discussed.

Ellen M. Gee and Gloria M. Gutman, eds. 2000. *The Overselling of Population Aging: Apocalyptic Demography, Intergenerational Challenges and Social Policy*. Toronto: Oxford University Press.

> This book challenges the popular, alarmist notion that the aging of the population will necessarily place a massive burden on Canada's pension, welfare, social, and health-care systems. Chapters on social policy, hospital usage, aging families, caregiving, intergenerational dynamics, retirement, and women's pensions not only challenge popular myths and negative stereotypes of old age and later life, but argue for recognition of the contributions made by older to younger generations.

Sarah H. Matthews. 2002. *Sisters and Brothers/Daughters and Sons: Meeting the Needs of Old Parents*. Bloomington: Unlimited Publishing.

> This book provides a counterpoint to the caregiving focus of much research on aging families and intergenerational relations. Based on qualitative analyses of the verbatim accounts of two adult siblings in each of

149 families with at least one parent over the age of 75, Matthews examines the ways in which these brothers and sisters, their siblings and their elderly parents interact as members of older families. It provides a dynamic portrayal of the personal meanings that siblings attach to behaviours within and across of families .

Sheila M. Neysmith, ed. 1999. *Critical Issues for Future Social Work Practice with Aging Persons*, New York: Columbia University Press.

This book brings a critical feminist analysis to the study of older women. It challenges readers to move beyond traditional frameworks in understanding the social conditions within which people age and the organizational contexts within which services are delivered to them. Chapters focus on such topics as dominant images of ability and the social construction of dependency, challenge our understanding of such concepts as agency and autonomy, and force a consideration of readers' understandings of frailty and the meanings and implications of ethnocultural diversity.

References

Baker, M., E. Hanna and J. Kantarevic. 2003. "The Married Widow: Marriage Penalties Matter!" NBER Working Paper No. W9782. New York: National Bureau of Economic Research.

Bayley, John. 1999. *Elegy for Iris*. New York: St. Martin's Press.

Béland, F., and E. Shapiro. 1994. "Ten Provinces in Search of a Long Term Care Policy." In V. W. Marshall and B. D. McPherson, eds., *Aging: Canadian Perspectives*. Peterborough: Broadview.

Bengtson, V. L. 1993. "Is the 'Contract Across Generations' Changing? Effects of Population Aging on Obligations and Expectations across Age Groups." In V. L. Bengtson and A. Achenbaum, eds., *The Changing Contract across Generations*. New York: Aldine de Gruyter.

Bengtson, Vern L., Neal E. Cutler, David J. Mangen, and Victor W. Marshall. 1985. "Generations, Cohorts and Relations beween Age Groups." In Robert H. Binstock and Ethel Shanas, eds., *Handbook of Aging and the Social Sciences*, 2nd ed. New York: Van Nostrand Reinhold.

Bengtson, Vern L., C. J. Rosenthal and Linda Burton. 1990. "Families and Aging: Diversity and Heterogeneity." In R. H. Binstock and L. K. George (eds.), *Handbook of Aging and the Social Sciences*, 3rd ed. New York: Academic Press.

———. 1996. "Paradoxes of Families and Aging." In Robert H. Binstock and Linda K. George, eds., *Handbook of Aging and the Social Sciences*, 4th ed. San Diego: Academic Press.

Burkhauser, R.V., J.S. Butler, and K.C. Holden. 1991. "How the Death of a Spouse Affects Economic Well-Being after Retirement: A Hazard Model Approach." *Social Science Quarterly* 72/3: 504–19.

Campbell, L. D., and A. Martin-Matthews. 2000a. "Caring Sons: Exploring Men's Involvement in Filial Care." *Canadian Journal on Aging* 19/1: 57–79.

————. 2000b. "Primary and Proximate: Implications of Distance and Relationship in Men's Caring Roles." *Journal of Family Issues*, 21/8: 1007–031.

————. 2003. "The Gendered Nature Of Men's Filial Care." *Journal of Gerontology: Social Sciences.* 58B/5: In press.

Canadian Press. 1996. "Mother Wins Court Fight for Adult Children to Support Her." *Vancouver Sun*, January 24, p. A5.

Canadian Study of Health and Aging. 1994. "Patterns of Caring for Persons with Dementia in Canada." *Canadian Journal on Aging* 13/4: 470–87.

Carey, E. 1995. "Can Kids Be Forced to Support Parents?" *Toronto Star*, September 17, pp. A1, A9.

Centre on Aging and the Caregivers Association of British Columbia. 1995. *Informal Caregivers to Adults in British Columbia: Joint Report.* Victoria: University of Victoria.

Chappell, N.L., E. M. Gee, L. McDonald, and M. Stones, eds. 2003. *Aging in Contemporary Canada.* Toronto: Prentice Hall.

Cole, T. R., and M. G. Winkler, eds. 1994. *The Oxford Book of Aging: Reflections on the Journey of Life.* Oxford: Oxford University Press.

Connidis, I.A. 1989. *Family Ties and Aging.* Toronto: Butterworths/Harcourt Brace.

————. 1992. "Life Transitions and the Adult Sibling Tie: A Qualitative Study." *Journal of Marriage and the Family* 54/4: 972–82.

————. 1994. "Growing Up and Old Together: Some Observations on Families in Later Life." In V. W. Marshall and B.D. McPherson, eds., *Aging: Canadian Perspectives.* Peterborough: Broadview.

————. 2001. *Family Ties and Aging.* Thousand Oaks: Sage Publications.

Connidis, I.A., and L. Davies. 1990. "Confidants and Companions in Later Life: The Place of Family and Friends." *Journal of Gerontology: Social Sciences* 45/4: S141–S149.

Creedon, Michael A. 1995. "Eldercare and Work Research in the United States." In Judith Phillips, ed., *Working Carers: International Perspectives on Working and Caring for Older People.* Aldershot: Avebury.

Denton, Frank T., and Byron G. Spencer. 1997. "Population Aging and the Maintenance of Social Support Systems." *Canadian Journal on Aging* 16/3: 485–98.

Dorfman, R., K. Walters, P. Burke, L. Hardin, T. Karanik, J. Raphael, and E. Silverstein. 1995. "Old, Sad and Alone: The Myth of the Aging Homosexual." *Journal of Gerontological Social Work* 24(1–2): 29–44.

Dorrell, B. 1991. "Being There: A Support Network of Lesbian Women." *Journal of Homosexuality* 20(3–4): 89–98.

Finch, J. 1989. *Family Obligations and Social Change.* Cambridge: Polity Press and Basil Blackwell.

Finch, J., and J. Mason. 1993. *Negotiating Family Responsibilities.* London: Routledge.

Gee, Ellen M. 1990. "Demographic Change and Intergenerational Relations in Canadian Families: Findings and Social Policy Implications." *Canadian Public Policy* 16: 191–99.

———. 2000. "Voodoo Demography, Population Aging and Canadian Social Policy." Pp. 5–25 in E. M. Gee and G. M. Gutman, eds., *The Overselling of Population Aging: Apocalyptic Demography, Intergenerational Challenges and Social Policy.* Toronto: Oxford University Press.

Gee, Ellen M., and Meredith M. Kimball. 1987. *Women and Aging.* Toronto: Butterworths/Harcourt Brace.

Gladstone, J. 1995. "The Marital Perceptions of Elderly Persons Living or Having a Spouse Living in a Long-Term Care Institution in Canada." *The Gerontologist* 35/1: 52–60.

Goldscheider, F. 1990. "The Aging of the Gender Revolution." *Research on Aging* 12: 531–45.

Hagestad, G.O. 1981. "Problems and Promises in the Social Psychology of Intergenerational Relations." In R. W. Fogel, E. Hatfield, S. B. Kiesler, and E. Shanas, eds., *Aging: Stability and Change in the Family.* New York: Academic Press.

Hurd, M., and D. Wise. 1987. *The Wealth and Poverty of Widows: Assets Before and After the Husband's Death.* Washington, D.C.: National Bureau of Economic Research Working Paper. #2325. Washington D.C.

Jendrek, Margaret. 1993. "Grandparents Who Parent Their Grandchildren: Effects on Lifestyle." *Journal of Marriage and the Family* 55/3: 609–21.

———. 1994. "Grandparents Who Parent Their Grandchildren: Circumstances and Decisions." *The Gerontologist* 34/2: 206–18.

Joseph, A. E., and A. Martin Matthews. 1994. "Growing Old in Aging Communities." In Victor Marshall and Barry McPherson, eds., *Aging: Canadian Perspectives.* Peterborough: Broadview.

Keefe, J. M., and P. Fancey. 1997. "Financial Compensation or Home Help Services: Examining Differences among Program Recipients." *Canadian Journal on Aging* 1/2: 254–78.

———. 1998. *Financial Compensation versus Community Supports: An Analysis of the Effects on Caregivers and Care Receivers: Final Report.* Ottawa: Health Canada.

Keefe, J. M., C. J. Rosenthal, and F. Béland. 2000. "The Impact of Ethnicity on Helping for Older Relatives: Findings from a Sample of Employed Canadians." *Canadian Journal on Aging* 19/3: 317–42.

Kobayashi, K. M. 2000. "The Nature of Support from Adult Children to Older Parents in Japanese Canadian Families." *Journal of Cross Cultural Gerontology,* 15(3):185–205.

Kruk, E. 1995. "Grandparent–Grandchild Contact Loss: Findings from a Study of 'Grandparent Rights' Members." *Canadian Journal on Aging* 14/4: 737–54.

Lilley, S., and J. Campbell. 1999. *Shifting Sands: The Changing Shape of Atlantic Canada. Economic and Demographic Trends and their Impacts on Seniors.* Health Promotion and Programs Branch, Atlantic Regional Office, Health Canada.

Lopata, H. Z. 1995. "Feminist Perspectives on Social Gerontology." In Rosemary Bleiszner and Victoria H. Bedford, eds., *Handbook of Aging and the Family.* Westport: Greenwood Press.

MacRae, H. 1992. "Fictive Kin as a Component of the Social Networks of Older People." *Research on Aging* 14/2: 226–47.

Mandell, Nancy, and Ann Duffy, eds. 1995. *Canadian Families: Diversity, Conflict and Change.* Toronto: Harcourt Brace.

Martin Matthews, A. 1988. "Aging in Rural Canada." In Eloise Rathbone-McCuan and Betty Havens, eds., *North American Elders: United States and Canada,* Westport: Greenwood Press.

————. 1991. *Widowhood in Later Life.* Toronto: Butterworths/Harcourt Brace.

————. 1993. "Issues in the Examination of the Caregiving Relationship." In Steven H. Zarit, Leonard I. Pearlin, and K. Warner Schaie, eds., *Caregiving Systems: Formal and Informal Helpers.* New York: Lawrence Erlbaum Associates.

Martin-Matthews, A. 1996. "Why I Dislike the Term 'Eldercare.'" *Transition* 26/3: 16.

————. 1999a. "Canada and the Changing Profile of Health and Social Services: Implications for Employment and Caregiving." In V.M. Lechner and M.B. Neal (eds.), *Work and Caring for the Elderly: International Perspectives.* Pp. 11–27. Washington: Taylor & Francis.

————. 1999b. "Widowhood: Dominant Renditions, Changing Demography and Variable Meaning." In S. M. Neysmith, ed., *Critical Issues for Future Social Work Practice with Aging Persons.* New York: Columbia University Press.

————. 2000. "Intergenerational Caregiving: How Apocalyptic and Dominant Demographies Frame the Questions and Shape the Answers". In E. M. Gee and G. M. Gutman, eds., *The Overselling of Population Aging: Apocalyptic Demography, Intergenerational Challenges and Social Policy.* Toronto: Oxford University Press.

Martin-Matthews, A., and L. D. Campbell. 1995. "Gender Roles, Employment and Informal Care." In S. Arber and J. Ginn, eds., *Connecting Gender and Ageing: Sociological Reflections.* Buckingham: Open University Press.

Martin-Matthews, A., and R. Matthews. 2001. "Living in Time: Multiple Timetables in Couples' Experiences of Infertility and its Treatment." In K. J. Daly, ed., *Minding the Time in Family Experience: Emerging Perspectives and Issues.* Pp. 111–34. Oxford: Elsevier Science.

Martin-Matthews, A., and C. J. Rosenthal. 1993. "Balancing Work and Family in an Aging Society: The Canadian Experience." In G. L. Maddox and M. P. Lawton, eds.,

Annual Review of Gerontology and Geriatrics: Focus on Kinship, Aging and Social Change. New York: Springer.

Matthews, S. H. 2002. *Sisters and Brothers/Daughters and Sons: Meeting the Needs of Old Parents.* Bloomington: Unlimited Publishing.

McDaniel, S. A. 1993. "Caring and Sharing: Demographic Aging, Family and the State." In J. Hendricks and C. J. Rosenthal, eds., *The Remainder of Their Days: Domestic Policy and Older Families in the United States and Canada.* New York: Garland.

McDonald, L. P. 1997. *Transitions into Retirement: A Time for Retirement.* Final report, National Welfare Grants Program, prepared for Human Resources Development Canada.

McDonald, L., P. Donahue, and B. Moore (2000). "The Poverty of Retired Widows." In F. T. Denton, D. Fretz, and B. G. Spencer, eds., *The Independence and Economic Security of the Elderly.* Pp. 328–45. Vancouver: The University of British Columbia Press.

McPherson, B. D. 1998. *Aging as a Social Process,* 3rd ed. Toronto: Harcourt Brace.

Moore, Eric, and Mark Rosenberg. 1997. *Growing Old in Canada: Demographic and Geographic Perspectives.* Ottawa: Statistics Canada.

O'Connor, Deborah. 1999. "Living with a Memory Impaired Spouse: (Re)cognizing the Experience." *Canadian Journal on Aging,* 18/2: 211–35.

Parsons, J., and J. Tindale 2001. "Parents Who Sue Their Children for Support: An Examination of Decisions by Canadian Court Judges." *Canadian Journal on Aging* 20/x: 451–70.

Phillips, Judith, and Miriam Bernard. 1995. "Perspectives on Caring." In Judith Phillips, ed., *Working Carers: International Perspectives on Working and Caring for Older People.* Aldershot: Avebury.

Rosenthal, Carolyn J. 1997. "Family Care in Canada in the Context of Social and Demographic Change." *Ageing International* 24/1: 13–31.

Rosenthal, Carolyn J., and Pamela Dawson. 1991. "Wives of Institutionalized Elderly Men: The First Stage of the Transition to Quasi-Widowhood." *Journal of Aging and Health* 3/3: 315–34.

Rosenthal, Carolyn J., and James Gladstone. 1994. "Family Relationships and Support in Later Life." Pp. 158–74 in V. Marshall and B. McPherson (eds.), *Aging: Canadian Perspectives.* Peterborough: Broadview Press.

Rosenthal, C.J., A. Martin-Matthews, M.A. Denton, and S. E. French. 2000. "Changes in Work and Family over the Life Course: Implications for Economic Security of Today's and Tomorrow's Seniors." In F. T. Denton, D. Fretz, and B. G. Spencer, eds., *The Independence and Economic Security of the Elderly.* Pp. 85–111. Vancouver: The University of British Columbia Press.

Rosenthal, C. J., A. Martin-Matthews, and S. H. Matthews. 1996. "Caught in the Middle? Occupancy in Multiple Roles and Help to Parents in a National Probability Sample of Canadian Adults." *Journal of Gerontology: Social Sciences* 51 B: S274–83.

Ross, Margaret M., Carolyn J. Rosenthal, and Pamela G. Dawson. 1997. "Spousal Caregiving in the Institutional Setting: Task Performance." *Canadian Journal on Aging* 16/1: 51–69.

Schellenberg, Grant. 1994. *The Road to Retirement: Demographic and Economic Changes in the 90s.* Ottawa: Canada Council on Social Development, Centre for International Statistics.

Smith, G., and J. Dumas. 1994. "The Sandwich Generation: Myths and Reality." In J. Dumas and A. Belanger, eds., *Report on the Demographic Situation in Canada 1994.* Ottawa: Statistics Canada.

Snell, James G. 1990. "Filial Responsibility Laws in Canada: An Historical Study." *Canadian Journal on Aging* 9/3: 268–77.

Statistics Canada. 1997. "Measuring the Age of Retirement." *The Daily,* June 6.

———. 2003. "Population by sex and age group." http://www.statcan.ca/english/Pgdb/demo31d.htm

Uhlenberg, Peter. 1993. "Demographic Change and Kin Relationships in Later Life." In George L. Maddox and M. Powell Lawton, eds., *Annual Review of Gerontology and Geriatrics: Focus on Kinship, Aging and Social Change.* New York: Springer.

Wideman, G. 2003. "The Impact of Out-Migration on the Lives of Older Persons in Newfoundland and Labrador." Presentation at the International Conference on Rural Human Services, Halifax, N.S.

Chapter 12

Families at Work: Making a Living

Meg Luxton and June Corman

LEARNING OBJECTIVES

In this chapter, you will learn that:

1. family survival depends on two labours, but income-generating work and domestic labour are contradictory;

2. women's and men's responsibilities for income-generating and domestic labour change, often setting couples against one another;

3. in countries with a capitalist democracy, such as Canada, the conflicts caused by work–family conflicts are also the responsibility of the state and employers;

4. appropriate state-based policies include: quality, affordable childcare and eldercare; more statutory holidays; and longer and better-paid parental leaves;

5. family-friendly work arrangements include flex-time, topping up parental leave payments, and leaves associated with emergencies, compassion, and illness.

INTRODUCTION[1]

In 1953, the school superintendent walked up to Rita Tagseth as she hung diapers on the line. He offered her a teaching position. Rita was excited because her husband's income was barely enough to provide for a family of four. Yet, she was already busy looking after two children. She knew the offer was unusual. Few married women, much less mothers, had employment in the 1950s. Managing both jobs would be a challenge (Study 1, 1985).

By 2003, mothers who had paid employment still faced many of the challenges confronted by Rita Tagseth and her family. Maternity and parental leaves gave some relief after giving birth but the absence of a nationwide, quality, affordable child-care programme left many parents scrambling. Evenings and weekends were filled with cooking, cleaning, and household maintenance.

346

Families depend for their survival on two kinds of labour—the activities involved in making a living, such as running a business, farming, fishing, or earning a wage or salary, and the activities involved in running the home and caring for the people who live there. While the two labours sustain individual families, they also are key aspects of **social reproduction**—the activities required to ensure the day-to-day and generational reproduction of the population. In contemporary capitalist societies like Canada, the organization of **income-generating work** on the one hand and **domestic labour**, and especially caregiving, on the other, has resulted in a situation where the demands of one are contradictory to the demands of the other. The state partially regulates the conflicts between the two spheres (for example, through the provision of education and health care) while also shaping the context in which both operate. As a result, throughout the past century, the problems posed by those contradictions have led to struggles between, for example, women and men, employees and employers, and citizens and their governments—struggles that have generated profound social changes in the way families work.

Here we examine families at work, arguing that, while every family is unique, and while families make a living in a wide variety of ways, there are some key trends that have been common to the way most families work in Canada since the late nineteenth century. We illustrate our argument with examples from three case studies: 1. The Saskatchewan Rural School Teachers Project; 2. The Hamilton Steelworkers Project; and 3. The Caregiving Among Family, Friends, Neighbours, and Community Project (see Appendix A at the end of this chapter for details).[2] Together, these studies look at families between the years 1910 and 2000, in rural farming communities, in an industrial city, and in economically diverse Toronto.

At the start of the twentieth century, most families were **heterosexual** and **nuclear** and based on a sharp **sex/gender division of labour**. Men of all classes, as husbands and fathers, typically engaged in income-generating work, either by producing for the market (for example, by farming or fishing), by running businesses, or by working for wages. Most women, as wives and mothers, devoted themselves to running their homes and caring for their families. The higher and more secure the man's income relative to household costs, the easier it was for the family to conform to that idealized sex/gender division of labour. Where family incomes were more precarious, women were under pressure to take up income-generating work. At the same time, that division of labour left married women vulnerable to economic dependence on their husbands and restricted their capacities to participate in social, political, and economic life.

Throughout the twentieth century, this family form and its division of labour were sites of contestation in a struggle that undermined the dominance of the heterosexual nuclear family form and challenged the sex/gender division of labour. By the early twenty-first century, as gays and lesbians fought for legal recognition of same-sex marriage, a variety of family forms had proliferated and women and men engaged in a much wider range of occupations.

Other struggles over the extent to which the well-being of individuals is a private family matter or a collective social responsibility have generated changing patterns of state and workplace provision of social services. For example, when governments wanted married women in the paid labour force during the 1939–1945 war, they provided child-care services and produced propaganda insisting that childcare was good for children. In an effort to get married women out of the labour force in the post-war period, they closed the nurseries and produced propaganda claiming maternal care was best for children (Prentice et al., 1988, pp. 298–99, 305–06). Continuing debates about whether the provision of social services is best done by governments, by the not-for-profit sector, or through the market have significantly altered the legal and policy contexts in both governments and workplaces. However, by the start of the twenty-first century, families still depend on income-generating work and domestic labour and they still face the challenges of trying to resolve the tensions between the two.

INCOME-GENERATING WORK

Men's Work

Men as husbands and fathers have typically assumed primary responsibility for earning the income that supports their families. The type of job they can get, its earnings and benefits, its hours and vacations, the flexibilities it permits workers, and the way it energizes or exhausts them, all affect not only the kind of living men can provide for their families but also the ways in which they can participate in family life. Wealthy men can obviously provide high standards of living for their families. The systemic discriminations working-class men, men of colour, Aboriginal men, immigrant men, and men with disabilities confront in the labour force have profound effects, limiting the livelihoods they can provide and the family life possible for them, sometimes even making family life impossible.

The expectation that men are responsible for family financial security imposes a compulsion on those men who are, or want to be, husbands and fathers to find and keep a source of income and job security, tying them to the job even when it is personally unrewarding, detrimental to their health, or demeaning. Ironically, this economic imperative to support their families reduces the possibility of their active involvement in domestic labour. Whether they run businesses, farm or fish, or work for pay, the occupations typically available to men have been organized on the assumption that while men are on the job they are freed from their domestic responsibilities and most families organize their domestic divisions of labour to accommodate the demands of men's jobs. Their financial contribution discharges their major obligation to their family, simultaneously justifying their lack of involvement in domestic labour and entitling them to its benefits.

Women's Work

Women have increasingly become involved in earning an income in ways that have taken them away from the home, particularly through participation in the labour force. In 1901, only 14 percent of all women were in the formal labour force, making up just 13 percent of the total labour force. All women, and particularly married women, increasingly moved into the paid labour force so that by 2002, 61 percent of women between 15 and 65 years old (compared to 73 percent of men) were in the formal labour force, making up almost half of the total labour force (Statistics Canada, 2002a).

These overall patterns obscure the significant differences among women, especially the ways in which race and class privilege and discrimination differentiate women's lives. Bourgeois women, most of whom also enjoy race privilege as whites, command sufficient wealth to hire other people to do their domestic labour, including paying nannies or boarding schools for childcare (Duffy, 1986).

The work patterns of women in other classes and minority groups reveal the centrality of the competing demands of paid employment and domestic labour. In the early twentieth century, women's attachment to the labour force was largely precluded by marriage, and labour force limitations strongly reinforced prevailing sexual divisions of labour by creating economic incentives for women to marry. Women were limited to specific occupations that typically reflected the kinds of work that women were expected to do in the home. A woman who "chose" to teach explained: "Another reason for choosing teaching was the fact that when I completed High School in 1939–40, there were not many choices career wise for women: teacher, nurse, or housewife" (Study 1, 1985).

Women's wages were typically much lower than men's, rarely high enough to support a woman on her own and inadequate to support children (Fox, 1980). Women of racial and ethnic groups faced racial discrimination, a fundamental component of Canadian Aboriginal and immigration policies, and of labour force employment practices. Racism meant that both family formation and income security were more precarious. Aboriginal women had few opportunities for paid work even as their access to the land and its resources was restricted (Campbell, 1973). Black and immigrant women were forced into the lowest-paid and least secure jobs and typically had higher than average rates of labour force participation, making it harder for them to devote time to domestic activities and caregiving for their families (Brand, 1983; Bristow et al., 1994). Sometimes legal restrictions prohibited some immigrants, such as domestic workers, from having families (Bakan and Stasiulis, 1997).

Married women who were not in the formal labour force developed various strategies to contribute to their families' economies. In family enterprises—from farms to corner stores—wives often worked alongside their husbands, but such activities were seen as part of their commitment to the marriage, rather than a career choice. Some contributed additional income by extending their domestic labour in their own homes—taking in boarders, or doing laundry or sewing, for example (Bradbury, 1985).

As households increasingly needed more cash, particularly with the dramatic increase in the costs associated with property taxes, housing, and heating, it became harder for people to meet their needs by intensifying their labour at home. Changing standards of living meant that many basic household goods and services such as heating had to be purchased (Connelly, 1978, p. 54). Increasingly, items such as clothing or baked goods that had formerly been produced at home could be bought as finished goods more cheaply than the raw materials for home production. As compulsory schooling kept children out of paid labour, their capacity to contribute to household earnings declined and their prolonged economic dependency increased their parents' expenses. As a result, the importance of women's income steadily increased throughout the twentieth century for both urban and rural women. A woman who taught off and on for 25 years between 1946 and 1983 commented, "I don't think I intended a lifetime career of teaching. It was generally understood that your teaching career ended with marriage. In fact, prior to 1951, I never met any married women teachers. I started teaching in 1946, married in 1953 and stayed home for 5 years. Economic pressures plus poor living accommodations prompted a return to teaching in 1958 for 25 years" (Study 1, 1985).

Many women also wanted paid employment; both to secure their own financial independence from their husbands and to provide them with the interest and status accorded paid work. A career teacher explained: "I planned a life-long career, but did stop for about 11 years to raise three children until the youngest was of school age. Even then, when there was not a teacher available I filled in for weeks or months at a time. I enjoyed teaching and found it

BOX 12.1   FARM FAMILIES MAKE THE TRANSITION

Driving around the grain fields gave 75-year-old Eddie lots of time to reflect. His son certainly works a lot different than he had. When Eddie was 35, he had spent the summer bumping up and down on the tractor seat, exposed to the sun, cultivating the fields day in and day out. When he finished for the day, he was too hot and tired to do much of anything but put his feet up and watch television. In contrast, his son, Ted, drives a large air-conditioned tractor that seems to finish the work in no time. Ted's not so beat at the end of the day. Good thing too because his wife often can't be home. Ted cooks meals, vacuums, and minds the kids.

Eddie had never had the time or energy for those jobs. But of course, his wife had worked on the farm too. She had minded the children while she grew vegetables, made preserves, canned chickens, sewed the clothes, cooked the meals, and cleaned the house. Ted's wife doesn't have time for a garden, chickens, and sewing. With her paycheque she can buy all those goods and more. Her paycheque is pretty handy now that grain prices are so low. Besides, she enjoys socializing at the office and truth be known, Ted really enjoys his time with the children.

rewarding and challenging" (Study 1, 1985). As individuals, through women's organizations, and through the labour movement, women organized and fought for access to education, to jobs, and to better pay and working conditions. However, the growing involvement of married women in the paid labour force generated considerable opposition and created problems for women and their families.

The belief that men should be income earners making a "**family wage**" sufficient to support a wife and children was so deeply entrenched in the early twentieth century that even when employers preferred to hire women, they often felt compelled to defend their practices (Parr, 1990). Employed women were subject to discrimination that was justified in terms of nuclear family male income earner ideologies (Sangster, 1995, p. 107). The assumption that women would be **homemakers** permeated socialization practices and educational systems, with the consequences that, until recently, women were discouraged from obtaining the educational or training credentials that would enable them to qualify for many jobs (Gaskell, McLaren, and Novogrodsky, 1989).

Women's difficulties both in obtaining the education and training necessary to apply for paid work and in getting hired kept married women out of the paid labour force in large numbers. This position was reinforced by hiring practices that prevented married women from holding paid work and by state regulations that either explicitly prevented them from holding civil service jobs or more generally made such employment difficult. For example, as late as 1946, many urban school boards, including those in Saskatoon and Winnipeg, refused to hire married women as teachers, only changing their policies when the severe shortage of male teachers forced the issue (Corman, 2002, pp. 78–79). The assumption that women should and would have husbands to support them was used to justify both the limited range of occupations open to them and their lower wages.

Despite such barriers, during the second half of the twentieth century there was an increasing trend for married women to combine responsibility for domestic labour with paid employment (Duffy and Pupo, 1989). The proportion of women with young children in the labour force increased rapidly. By 2001, nearly two-thirds (62 percent) of mothers whose youngest child was under three years were employed; three quarters of mothers whose youngest child was six to 15 were employed (Statistics Canada, 2002b). Women gradually expanded the range of occupations open to them and challenged existing pay differentials. But in 2001, even when women were working for pay full-time and full-year, they only earned 71.6 percent of what men earned. And the real gap was much greater because so many women, especially wives and mothers, had part-time or part-year employment. Married women earned only 65.3 percent of what married men earned (Statistics Canada, 2003a). Aboriginal and visible minority women earned even less than white women. As a result, it continues to be difficult for most women to support themselves and their children without a partner. There remains an economic compulsion for women to marry.

Family Finances

By the early twenty-first century, while some families continued to rely on farming, fishing, or other family businesses, the majority of adults depended on paid employment: among people aged 25 to 65 years, 85 percent of men and 73 percent of women were employed (Statistics Canada, 2002a, p. 118). The majority of two-parent families depended on the earnings of both adults. By 1992, on average, families needed at least 77 weeks of paid employment to meet the basic standard of living for the year. If a man was earning for 52 weeks, someone had to work for pay for at least an additional 25 weeks over the year (Vanier Institute of the Family, 1997). In 1999, 19 percent of families raising children with one income were low income; only 3 percent of dual-earner families with children were low income. If these women had not been employed, this number would have increased to 16 percent (Statistics Canada, 2001).

At the same time, as more and more families depended on both adults participating in the labour force, paid employment for most workers became less compatible with family life (Duffy, Mandell, and Pupo, 1989). The relative decline in earnings that had pushed more married women into the labour force was accompanied by a growing insecurity as many workers faced layoffs, more and more jobs became precarious, access to social security provisions such as Employment Insurance was increasingly restricted, and more jobs demanded shift work, irregular hours, or longer hours from their employees. The demands of paid employment were eroding workers' time and energy for family life without providing any significant financial recompense.

DOMESTIC LABOUR

Unlike paid employment, domestic labour is unregulated, unpaid, and often so taken for granted that, despite its vital importance in reproducing daily life, it is often not recognized as work. As the awkward term "domestic labour" indicates, there is no everyday word for unpaid work in the home. In the 1990s, in response to feminist demands that it be recognized as an important economic contribution, various statistical and economic agencies began to explore ways of calculating its contribution to the economy. The United Nations reported that internationally in 1995, the monetary value of unpaid labour was $16 trillion— $11 trillion produced by women (UNDP 1995, chapter 4).

As part of such initiatives, Statistics Canada conducted studies to investigate what domestic labour was done in Canadian households, who typically did the work, and how much time it took. They found that since 1960, women have continued to do about two-thirds of all unpaid work in Canada; women do more domestic labour than men, even as teenagers (Statistics Canada, 2000, p. 97). Women who were employed did more than their male partners; in fact, men living with employed women did less than men whose wives were not employed (Statistics Canada, 2000, p. 111). The 2001 Census reported that women were 2.5 times more likely than men to spend more than 30 hours a week looking after children without pay, 2.9 times more likely to spend more than 30 hours a week on unpaid housework, and 2 times more likely to spend 10 or more hours on unpaid caregiving to seniors (Statistics Canada, 2003b).

Statistics Canada evaluated the value of domestic labour performed in Canada by calculating the replacement costs, that is, how much workers in the paid labour force doing the same work are paid.[3] They concluded that in 1992 the value of household work was $285 billion, equal to 41 percent of the GDP and 60 percent of personal disposable income. Comparing women's and men's contributions, they concluded that the domestic labour done by women was worth almost $17 000 per year and that done by men worth about $13 000 (Chandler, 1994). Since then there have been no national studies to permit updates, but domestic labour continues to make a major (though still unrecognized) contribution to Canada's economy. Domestic labour not only takes up enormous amounts of time and energy and contributes extensively to the national economy, but also plays a critical role in ensuring the well-being of the population (Luxton and Corman, 2001, p. 181).

Domestic labour includes all those activities required to maintain a home and care for the people who live in it. It involves at least four distinct types of work: housework, household maintenance, managing household economics, and caregiving. In contrast to paid employment, where the divisions of labour and the hours of work are clearly (and usually contractually) known, domestic labour is task-oriented and the tasks involved can vary in the amount of time they take each time they are done and in the frequency with which they are done. The skills required for domestic labour and the amount done on a regular basis in any particular household vary enormously and have changed significantly throughout the century (Parr, 1995). They depend on a complex interaction of factors such as the number and ages of the people living in the house, the amount of time, energy, and money they have available, the size and condition of the house, the type of household machinery available such as vacuums, washing machines, dryers, and microwave ovens, the personal preferences and standards of the people who live there, and even natural events such as snowfall or how quickly the grass grows.

The caregiving aspects of domestic labour are even more complex. The assumption that family members love each other and that love is expressed through ongoing, mutual expressions of care makes it harder to see the labour aspects of caregiving because the demands of caregiving as a labour process are often obscured by discourses of romantic love, parental dedication, and family devotion. A woman trying to explain what looking after her husband and children meant to her revealed the tensions and ambiguities between loving and caring about others and looking after or caring for them: "That's what family is about; it's about caring for your husband and your kids. If you get married and have kids, then you have to care for them. After all, you love them, naturally you would look after them. And I do love them. I want to care for them." She went on to express her frustration with the demands such caring imposed on her: "I feel pulled in all directions at once. I want to be more attentive, more loving, and I want to scream" (Study 2, 1984).

Caregiving is most clearly understood as work when it involves looking after those who cannot look after themselves—especially children or those who are ill or elderly or who have special needs. But even the most loving marriage requires considerable emotional work to sustain it. The type of work, its intensity, and how the caregiver experiences it all depend on the quality of the relationship at the time: the experience of comforting someone who is vomiting is very different if the person has the flu or is drunk. Caregiving is also shaped by the degree of dependence and the nature of the care needed: raising a child involves different dynamics than nurturing an elderly person who is dying.

A man described how he came to appreciate the complexity of domestic labour and how difficult it was for him to learn how to do it well:

> Thirty years I was married and my wife did all the household stuff—cooking, cleaning, shopping. She kept our home nice and it was always so easy. There was always good food in the fridge, nice meals, a tidy house. I never gave it any thought—just took it for granted. After she left, I assumed it was all easy, what she did and that I could manage just as well as she could. Well, was I in for a shock! Nothing was easy and I had to learn everything (Study 3, 2001).

His new appreciation of the knowledge, skill, and work involved in running a home also reveals how often women's domestic labour is invisible, not only to economists estimating the value of work done in a national and international economy, but to family members who are its direct beneficiaries.

Women's Work

In the early twentieth century, the dominant assumption was that, as wives and mothers, women were responsible for running the home and caring for family members (Strong-Boag, 1986). These activities were often described as "a labour of love" and equated with "natural" feminine behaviour, obscuring the recognition that they also involved work. The assumption that domestic labour was "women's work" both justified men's resistance to doing it and posed difficulties for those men who did it. A women in her forties described her father: "He was used to my mother doing everything at home. He never did anything inside the home. When he moved in with me, it was the same thing. He would sit in his chair and call out when he wanted something, a drink, the paper, his other shoes, it didn't matter what. At the dinner table, it was the same thing. He'd announce 'More potatoes' and expect me to serve him. And he was shocked when I didn't jump" (Study 3, 2001).

The widespread claim about the importance of being a wife and mother and caring for the family encouraged many women to opt for being at home full time. While working full-time at home offered many women great satisfaction, its low status, endless demands, social isolation, and lack of pay reveal the contradiction between the rhetoric of its importance and the actual lack of social respect shown to women who do it. Similarly, the limited number of jobs available to women in the formal labour force and the lack of conveniences to meet the demands of domestic labour reinforced the tendency for women to be homemakers. Throughout the twentieth century, as more and more married women took on paid employment, and as the spread of feminist ideas undermined beliefs in fixed sex/gender divisions of labour, the easy association of domestic labour and women became more problematic. The more involved they were in paid employment, the less time and energy women had for domestic labour. At the same time, a growing acceptance of principles of gender equality forced women and men to confront existing divisions of labour and ask whether they were fair and why they should continue, especially when women were also contributing to family incomes.

While housework and other household tasks were gradually recognized as work that could be done by a variety of people without challenging fundamental family values, women as mothers, wives, and daughters continued to be providers of caregiving in general and most specifically of childcare. A woman described what this meant in her life in 2001:

My husband and [two] kids (aged 24 and 27) are great about doing their share of housework. They cook and clean. My husband made a chore chart and we all take turns and I think they do it all as well as I do. No problems there. But they still expect me to, kind of, I can't describe it. They expect me to notice what they are feeling, ask them about it, give them emotional support. And none of them ever think I need that too. Mom's the strong one who makes sure everyone else feels okay (Study 3, Take Care, 10).

As both women and men contributed an income to their families, increasing numbers of children were cared for by people other than just their parents. For example, in 1988 almost 60 percent of children under 12 years of age had some non-parental care in addition to school and almost 80 percent of children between three and five years of age had non-parental caregivers (Goelman et al., 1993). As mothers' free labour disappeared, questions about what kind of child-care arrangements were or should be available, who should bear the costs, and what arrangements were best for children, families, and society as a whole became hotly debated. Conservatives insisted that mothers must stay home to care for their own children (Richards, 1997) and that if mothers did choose to work for pay, then the individual family was responsible for finding and paying for alternative care (Teghtsoonian, 1993). The women's movement called for a national programme that would provide free, top-quality, non-profit childcare for all, arguing that collective care was ideal for children (Cameron and Pike, 1972).

Neither option is readily available. Few men earn enough to support a wife and children. Even family farms and independent fishers increasingly rely on women's earnings (Binkley, 2002, p. 151; Kubik and Moore, 2001, p. 8). Women who remain out of the labour force are vulnerable, just a death or divorce away from poverty and unlikely to have a secure income in their old age; almost half (49 percent) of single, widowed, or divorced women over 65 are poor (Statistics Canada, 2000, p. 138). On the other hand, centre-based childcare is hard to find. In 2001, due to the lack of regulated child-care centres in Canada, only 18 percent of children under six years of age had access to such centres (ECEC, 2002, p. 2). Regulated childcare was also expensive. In 1998, the average full fees in Canada for an infant (0–17 months) were $531 per month, $477 for toddlers (18–35 months), and $455 for preschoolers (3–5 years) (de Wolff, 2003, p. 10). For example, in 2003, the Rosalind Blauer Child Care Centre at Brock University in St. Catharines, Ontario, charged $175 a week for infants aged 0–17 months, $150 a week for toddlers (18–35 months), and $125 a week for children over 35 months.[4] Given the lack of spaces and the costs, most children were cared for by unlicensed providers (de Wolff, 2003, p. 10).

The contradictions posed by the dilemma related to childcare are reflected in the ambiguous (and gender-distinct) responses people gave to the 1995 General Social Survey, in which 73 percent of women and 68 percent of men agreed that both spouses should contribute to household income, and 59 percent of men and 67 percent of women said an employed mother can establish just as warm and secure a relationship with her children as a mother who does not work for pay, but 51 percent of women and 59 percent of men said a preschool child was likely to suffer if both parents were employed (Ghalam 1997, pp. 13–17). In the face of strong ideologies that insist children are best cared for in their own homes by family members, and in the absence of any widespread child-care system, individual parents make do as best they can. Even when they have excellent child-care arrangements for young children or when the children as teenagers no longer require full-time care, parenting still takes up many hours each week and requires extensive care and attention and skill. Typically women still do more of it than men.

Men's Work

While domestic labour has been overwhelmingly "women's work," men have always been involved in certain aspects such as household maintenance, car repairs, grass cutting, and snow removal. Many men have played an active role in their children's lives, even if they did not take responsibility for primary care. As women were increasingly unable to do, and more and more unwilling to accept responsibility for, all the domestic labour in their households, men were under pressure to take on greater responsibility for a wider range of household work.

Several factors impede men's participation in domestic labour. Some men resist, defending their privileges. Some women actively discourage men's involvement, claiming domestic labour as their particular sphere of control. Most men's paid jobs are organized on the assumption that men are freed from domestic responsibilities when they are at work. A man contrasted his experiences at work (as a senior partner in a large office) with his wife's (as a bank teller) as they both struggled to care for a seriously ill child: "Well her workplace is highly regulated, specified times for holidays, specific leaves, what have you. But they were terrific. Her manager said she should take whatever time she needs, keep track of the hours off and she can make them up later, any time in the next three years. I'm a partner, one of the bosses, but my partners were adamant I couldn't take time off. I did take two days and they called a meeting and chewed me out. One of them even told me: 'It's your wife's responsibility. Leave it to her'" (Study 3, 2000). A woman described how her husband's job in a major steel plant precluded his involvement in childcare even in an emergency: "Once I was in hospital and both our kids got sick. He tried to get time off work to stay with them, but his foreman said he had no time coming so if he didn't come in, he would be suspended or fired" (Study 2, 1994).

Gender ideologies about what is appropriate for women and men mean few boys learn the skills of domesticity and many men are subject to ridicule if they admit doing such work. A 26-year-old man described the first months after he and his female partner started living together: "We agreed we would do things together. That's fair. I think men should do their share of the housework. But suddenly we were having fights and I realized, I didn't know what to do. I'd never cooked or cleaned up. My mother had always done all that stuff. She taught my sisters but not me. But my girlfriend expected me to know stuff and slowly we came to see that I didn't even know what I didn't know! I had to learn everything. My girlfriend is still mad at me even though she knows I'm trying" (Study 3, 2001). Another described his family's reaction when he decided to stay home to look after their three young children: "They went nuts. The whole lot of them were up in arms, telling me I was fool to give up my job (but they never criticized my wife when she did it), that I was setting a terrible example for my son (he's three for heaven's sake). My uncle told me I was a wimp" (Study 2, 2000).

The demands of their paid work combined with the assumptions that childcare is women's work mean that many men do not know their children very well and are unsure of how to care for them. These gender differences mean that parental labour is not neutral; one parent cannot simply substitute for the other, because parents develop different levels of skill (Luxton and Corman, 2001, p. 198). As children learn that their mothers are likely to be more responsive, they themselves become active agents in reproducing gender-specific patterns of parenting. When a father of two preschoolers got laid off, he and his wife cancelled the babysitter and he stayed home with the children: "At first it was awful. They kept telling me 'mummy does it this way' and as soon she came in the door they were all over her wanting her, not me. There would be great tears at bedtime when I tried to give them a bath or read their story. They always wanted mummy. I think they are more used to me now but they still prefer her to me anytime" (Study 3, 2000).

Even when men do domestic labour, their participation is often qualified. Men are frequently described as babysitting when they do childcare, implying that they are helping out rather than fulfilling a parental obligation. A 32-year-old man, employed full-time and whose wife was also employed full-time, described his involvement with his 3-year-old son:

> I am very involved with my son. I'd say we share caring for him. Well, she stayed home with him for the first year so I didn't do much then. I'd get up at night with him if she was really exhausted but, you know, I had to go to work the next day, so most nights she took care of him. Since she went back to work, he goes to a sitter. I take him every day and pick him up every evening unless I have to work late. So I am very involved. And on weekends, I sometimes take him to the park. I really like that (Study 3, 2000).

He explained that his wife got the child up every morning and put the child to bed each night. He had never changed a diaper and had never refused to work late because he had child-care responsibilities. His wife had to be ready to pick the child up any evening he decided to work late even though the journey added an extra hour to her travel time. His insistence that he was very involved and shared caregiving was undermined by his description of his own ability to choose when he provided care, a choice predicated on his confidence that his wife would always be there if he wasn't.

However, such gender patterns are under pressure and subject to change. In 1994, a steelworker described how such attitudes had changed over two generations: "I'm thirty-five and there's quite a few guys in my age bracket, say from forty down and then, the forty above. And it's like two different species...there might be six guys around the lunch table, and for three, there's no problem changing diapers" (Study 2, 1994).

Even when men actively want to share domestic labour, the imperatives of their financial obligations are difficult to overcome. Parents of newborn babies often plan to share parenting equally but the circumstances they find themselves in make it difficult. Economically it makes sense for the lower income earner, usually the woman, to take a leave and care for the baby. The resulting drop in income puts pressure on the man to work longer hours if possible (Fox, forthcoming). Men who try to change the way their paid work is organized to make it more accommodating to domestic labour often confront ridicule and criticisms that they are not serious about their careers. In 2001, a new father described the reactions of his co-workers when he announced his plan to take parental leave: "Most of them thought I was nuts. They said I would get way behind, that I was hurting my chances for promotion. One guy got pissed off and yelled at me that he would have to do more work to cover for me and that wasn't fair. Only one guy, who has a little kid too, said he wished me well" (Study 3, 2000).

The 2001 Census indicated that men were more involved than in earlier years in both housework and caregiving. However, a wide array of studies from Canada and internationally indicate that men's involvement in domestic labour remains more discretionary and less time-consuming than women's and that the overall responsibility for its planning and execution remain largely in the hands of women (McMahon, 1999). And even if men actually do half of all domestic labour in their households, the problem remains that the demands of paid employment and unpaid domestic labour are incompatible. In that context, individual families develop a range of coping strategies.

FAMILY STRATEGIES

Most families try to manage the competing demands on them by attempting to ensure that enough domestic labour gets done, especially childcare, while at the same time, family members earn enough to provide an adequate standard of living. Few people succeed in finding jobs that pay well, with regular hours and the flexibility to take time off for family responsibilities. In fact, the trend since the 1980s has been for more and more employment to be low paid and precarious, with few benefits, irregular hours, and little recognition of workers' family responsibilities (Vosko, 2000). Constrained by the larger economy and the availability of services, individual families have a variety of options available. On the one hand, they can try to either increase their earnings so that they can buy more services or they attempt to limit their hours of paid work so they have more time available at home. On the other hand, they can try to increase the available domestic labour by increasing the involvement of men and children while also reducing the domestic labour done. All of these strategies are problematic. Even if all household members cooperate, there is not enough time available, especially for satisfactory caregiving. For the most part, women assume responsibilities for handling the tensions associated with efforts to combine paid employment with caregiving.

The higher a family's income, the more they can purchase goods and services to make their lives easier and more comfortable. Almost all the tasks involved in domestic labour can be bought, from prepared foods and dog walking to childcare and eldercare. However, people often have difficulties ensuring satisfactory care, even when they can afford it.

For people with fewer financial resources, the possibilities are more limited. The most readily available option draws men and children into domestic labour. But efforts to get men and children more involved often create tensions over what work has to be done, who should do it, and to whose standards. They also often end up making more work for women, who are often responsible for assessing options, developing strategies, and implementing them. While increased sharing of domestic labour reduces some of the work-load on women, it does so by increasing pressures on men and children, who are often already under pressure to work harder on the job and at school.

In many households women (and sometimes men) adapt their labour force participation to the demands of their household responsibilities. They take part-time employment, get jobs closer to home, work at home, or take time off to be at home. For example, in 2001, 27 percent of all women in the work force worked less than 30 hours a week at their main job as compared with just 10 percent of men. More than one in five women said they worked part-time because of personal or family reasons as compared with 2 percent of men (Statistics Canada, 2002b). The long-term economic consequences of such strate-gies have contributed to women's higher poverty rates. In some households, par-ents try to coordinate their schedules, working alternating shifts, so that one of them is at home with the children all the time. Such strategies depend on their workplaces accommodating their choice of shifts and often limit their chances for promotion or to move to a better job. While that approach assures childcare, the adults rarely have time together. Each ends up working a double shift, so nei-ther has much time left to be together or for anything else.

Another option involves cutting back on domestic labour by lowering stan-dards and leaving undone as much as possible. Up to a point such cuts may have a limited impact on standards of living. More subtle dynamics may also be at work as some men respond to the pressures on them by spending money to offset their own labour and as the economics of purchasing goods and services is made more possible by the increased income available from the woman's earnings.

However, especially when the cuts affect caregiving, the trade-offs may be costly, creating stress and anxiety. Parents with few other options may be forced to leave their children unattended, trusted to care for themselves before and after school. But even when children are clearly old enough to be on their own, parents may worry that a lack of supervision may permit the children to "get into trouble." A mother described her concerns about the impact of her absence on her 16-year-old son and 12-year-old daughter: "She is such a good girl, so reliable. I trust her completely but I worry because I think she takes on too much. She doesn't want to worry me so she would never tell me if she was scared to be alone or if anything unpleasant happened to her. She tries to protect me. My son is another story. He is such a difficult one, I worry about him all the time. I suspect he is smoking, and even drinking when I am not there, and maybe worse. I phone them every afternoon around four when they should be home. If they don't answer, I get ballistic but even when they do, I still worry. I don't think I really have my mind on work from the end of school til I get home" (Study 3, 1999).

In the absence of state support, such as childcare, after-school pro-grammes, support for people with disabilities, and eldercare, the responsibility for providing care falls to their immediate families, and typically to women, no matter what burden that imposes. But individual families do not have the capacity to absorb unlimited demands on their resources. A woman with a toddler and a seriously ill teenager and elderly mother was having difficulty coping when her father-in-law became ill. "Then the doctor phones to announce that I have to move my husband's father into our house because he needs—get this—full-time care. I lost it. I was totally hysterical." She had a nervous breakdown. Several years later she noted: "If they had just given me a little help when I first needed it, we would have been okay. Instead, all of us needed lots of help for a long time and it cost the system so much more" (Study 3, 2000).

While people may grumble about the specific way their paid work and family responsibilities conflict, and may develop strategies for coping, it is difficult for individuals to envision how things might be arranged differently and to organize for such changes. A woman who had worked as a steelworker and who had been active in the feminist movement offered this insight. She explained that in workplaces, the combination of collective action and institutional practices supported women who were trying to change sexist behaviours and offered men ways to change without humiliating them. "In the union, we could say: 'There's discrimination going on here' and there were lots of other women and some men who would agree and who would help us try to change it. And there were policies and laws and stuff. And years of the women's movement. So you could go to some guy who was being a real pain and say, 'Hey man, you can't do this and here's why.' And if he didn't change, you had lots of ways of dealing with him, like other guys would talk to him, or he could be charged or whatever. And you could always make him feel like it wasn't him that was a jerk, even if he was. You could say, 'This is how things are done here. Like it or lump it'" (Study 2, 1996).

She contrasted that with the dynamics in private family relations: "But in the home, it's his home, it's his wife. What's she going to say? She can't just say it's not OK for men to sit around while their wives do all the work because society doesn't work that way any more. She doesn't have any union to say we have policies that men have to do their share of the housework or legislation that says she has a right to pay equity in the home if she wants to go shopping. No. Instead it's like her saying, 'I don't like who you are any more.' She has to be really mad before she'll go that far. And he sure won't find that easy to hear" (Study 2, 1996). Her insight, that efforts to change things at the level of individual families easily pits women and men against each other, underscores her argument that the most effective ways to make paid employment and family responsibilities more compatible lies in collective actions aimed at improving workplace and state policies and services.

STATE AND WORKPLACE POLICIES

Unlike some European countries, none of the provinces of Canada, except for Quebec, have explicit family policy; rather, they have an array of policies and practices that affect families either directly or implicitly in at least three distinct areas: family formation, such as marriage, divorce, reproduction, adoption, custody and child support; family income, such as minimum wage and employment insurance, taxes, child and leave benefits; and family services, such as subsidized housing, family-related leaves, adult dependent care, home care and health services, childcare and child protection (Baker, 1995, p. 5). In contrast to the federal government and other provinces, since the 1980s, Quebec has focused explicitly on family policy, from massive state support for childcare to housing and labour market policies such as unpaid family-responsibility leave up to five days a year (Le Bourdais and Marcil-Gratton, 1994).

There are two distinct types of benefits available: employment-based and citizen-based. Each of these can be either universal or targeted. Where policies are universal, recipients are entitled to them and they foster greater equality among the population. In contrast, targeted policies subject recipients to bureaucratic scrutiny and foster inequalities.

Benefits based on employment include some government-legislated programmes such as Employment Insurance, Workers' Compensation, and Canada Pension Plan required for all employees covered by the legislation. Others are employer-specific as some workplaces, especially where unionized workers have won contract provisions, also have policies that complement or extend state policies such as additional paid and unpaid leaves, and various additional health, drug, and dental plans. Paid for out of payroll deductions and employer contributions, these are typically available only to full-time, long-term employees of large enterprises. While employees' spouses and children are often also covered, part-time, temporary employees rarely are and employees in small enterprises or self-employed people typically are not. According to a federal study, two-thirds of firms do not have formal policies such as part-time work options, flexible work hours and childcare or eldercare services. One-third of firms have flex-time schedules but provision of other policies is almost non-existent (Beauchesne, 2003).

Citizen-based benefits are available to those who meet the regulated criteria and, reflecting assumptions about familial self-reliance and male income earners, were typically designed to supplement family obligations and to provide minimal support when family support was not available. Paid for out of general tax revenue, these include the two major universal programmes for health care and education, as well as social assistance, child benefits, Old Age Security, and Guaranteed Income Supplements. Typically the latter offer minimal support, are often punitive in their implementation, and rarely work to help the recipients develop long-term strategies for improved standards of living (Bezanson et al., forthcoming; O'Connor, Orloff, and Shaver, 1999).

The mix of federal, provincial, and territorial policies (with their often competing allocation of powers) with the array of policies and practices in different workplaces produced a hodge-podge of policies. Maternity and parental leaves are illustrative. Such leaves are vital, so that women can have babies, and parents can look after new children without the risk of losing their jobs while being assured of a sufficient income (White, 1993). Responding to demands for better parental leaves, in 2003, federal government policy granted those eligible 17 weeks of maternity leave for a woman giving birth and 37 weeks of parental leave for parents of a newborn or adopted child. The possibility of men's involvement in domestic labour was recognized in policy when the new parental leaves permitted both men and women to stay home with a new child. However, the benefit was so low, at 55 percent of insurable earnings to a ceiling of $413 a week, that few parents could afford to take it and the eligibility criteria excluded many parents (Human Resources, 2003). Some unions won victories requiring their employer to pay "top-ups" from the government's 55 percent of insurable income to 95 percent. Only 20 percent of employees, however, received a financial top-up from their employers in 2001 (Harding, 2003).

Other workplace initiatives recognizing employees' caregiving responsibilities include a variety of alternative working arrangements such as flextime or personal and bereavement leaves (Skrypnek and Fast, 1996; de Wolff, 2003). A woman whose husband was hospitalized for three weeks said that her employer allowed her to have one week paid "emergency" leave and two weeks unpaid leave. She was deeply grateful and made full use of both: "It was so wonderful. I could just stay at the hospital and not have to even think about work. My company was really good to me" (Study 3, 2000). However, her husband's illness lasted more than the time allowed her. She had to go back to work just when he was sent home, still too ill to care for himself. Like so many

BOX 12.2   STATE SUPPORT FOR EMPLOYEES WITH FAMILY RESPONSIBILITIES

1. Quality, affordable, and available childcare and eldercare.
2. Longer and higher-paid parental leave.
3. State-legislated provisions for family-responsibility leave.
4. More paid vacations and statutory holidays and mandatory paid sick days.
5. Quality health-care programmes that provide care in the hospital and in the home.
6. National programme for extended health, pharmacare, dental, and vision insurance.
7. A well-funded education system that does not rely on parental support for children's learning or school-based fundraising.
8. Expanded definitions of families and spouses.
9. Employment equity programmes.

others in her situation, she found that existing policies are insufficient. "I was in a state of panic for weeks. It was so difficult. I went to work, but how could I concentrate? I was frantic with worry about what was happening at home" (Study 3, 2000). As her experience shows, such policies offer important, but seriously limited support. They are also only available to some workers. Most people have access to few such supports.

The absence of a cohesive national family policy is consistent with the dominant frameworks shaping both government and business policies: families are, and should be, private, self-sufficient units in which the family group assures the well-being of all its members. Government regulations and policies typically reflect that orientation while responding to pressures generated when families are not and cannot be self-reliant, and to a lesser extent, when inequalities within families make some members, particularly women and children, more vulnerable.

In the 1950s and 1960s, Canada, like many OECD countries, developed a welfare state that offered a few programmes that modified the individual responsibility model. Based on the assumption that "the well-being of the economy depends on the well-being of the people in it," governments regulated the capitalist market and taxed capital to provide some basic security and social services (Cohen, 1997, p. 5). In particular, government services provided a range of caregiving intended to supplement family care. However, the assumptions underlying the Canadian welfare state were that the prevailing and appropriate family was heterosexual, nuclear, and based on a division of labour in which men were income earners and women were full-time homemakers, and most of the government's policies reinforced such relations (McKeen and Porter, 2003, p. 110).

Since the early 1980s, governments in Canada, inspired and supported by most business organizations and pressure from the United States as a result of international trade agreements, increasingly rejected earlier orientations

BOX 12.3   EMPLOYER SUPPORT FOR EMPLOYEES WITH FAMILY RESPONSIBILITIES

1. Workplace childcare.
2. Assistance with the care of sick children.
3. Facilities for seniors or family members with disabilities.
4. Opportunities for part-time work, job-sharing, and flex-time.
5. Extended paid parental leave.
6. "Top-up" of employment benefits during parental leave.
7. Family-responsibility leaves.
8. Paid sick leave.
9. No overtime in situations where members are laid off.
10. Limited mandatory overtime.

toward a welfare state, adopting instead neoliberal policies that tend to minimize interventions in the marketplace and to reduce state spending on social services (OECD, 1981). These policies reasserted claims that individuals and families must bear more of the costs of social reproduction themselves (Allahar and Cote, 1998). The prevailing ideology of neoliberalism replaced the philosophy of the welfare state with a belief that "social and economic well-being for people is subordinate to the well-being of the corporate sector" (Cohen, 1997, p. 5). Justified by arguments about competitiveness and fiscal restraint, "efficiencies" in the public and private sectors were often actually a transfer of costs to the domestic sector where they were hidden by the invisibility of domestic labour. Increasingly, the majority of families, and particularly women, were compelled to absorb the costs of cuts to schools, hospitals, and social service agencies, or do without the caregiving and related services altogether.

CONCLUSION

The cumulative effect of changes in the way work is organized has had a profound impact on families. A small privileged elite has experienced increased wealth that reduces the constraints on their family life. For the majority of people in Canada, the demands of both paid employment and domestic labour have increased without securing greater possibilities for family life. One of the clearest indications that families aren't working well is that women are delaying childbirth and having fewer children. In 1968, the average age of women at the birth of their first child was 23 years. By 1997 it was 26.8 (Statistics Canada, 2000, p. 35). By 1996 woman on average were having only 1.8 children, fewer than is required to ensure population replacement (Dumas and Belanger, 1997, p. 41). In 1959 there were 116 births per thousand women aged 15 to 49 years. In 1970 this rate had dropped to 71 births per thousand women and by 1997 it was down to 44 births per thousand women, a decrease of 23 percent since 1990 (Statistics Canada, 2002a, p. 34).

Expressed popularly as the problem of balancing work and family, the conflicts, at one level, are problems of scheduling, of arranging alternative care for dependants, of the fatigue of the double day. But the conflicting demands of work and family are more than that. At a deeper level, family households embody the contradictions between the process of producing and sustaining people and the process of profit maximization for enterprises and shareholders. The conflict between, on the one hand, employers trying to reduce labour costs to maximize profits and governments eliminating services to cut taxes and, on the other hand, workers struggling to ensure their livelihoods through higher wages, benefits, and services, means that social reproduction for the majority is in conflict with the process of capital accumulation and profit maximization. At stake is the way the costs of social reproduction of the population as a whole are met in a **capitalist society**: to what extent are the responsibilities and costs borne by individuals and by employers or provided by the state with the costs spread across all taxpayers? The costs of social reproduction are reduced for the business sector to the extent that families and households absorb them and bear the costs themselves. Conversely, the more that working people are able to insist on collective responsibility for social reproduction, funded either by employers directly or by personal and corporate taxes, the higher their standards of living and the less profit individual capitalists can appropriate for themselves. Either side—labour or capital—can only win concessions. This contradiction, systemic to a free market economy, cannot be resolved.

Consigning the responsibility of producing and sustaining daily life to individual households has implications beyond the costs and accumulations of tensions and stress for family members. As Barrett and McIntosh (1982, p. 78) have argued, the nuclear family takes so much time and energy that participants have little left over for building and sustaining strong friendship networks or community organizations, or to organize collectively through protest movements. Wherever people have the opportunity to come together, pool information, and develop shared analyses, they have the possibility of generating strategies for change. In their workplaces and unions, in community groups and in political movements such as the women's movement, and in single-issue groups, people have formulated demands and put them on the political agenda. Women, in particular, through the labour movement and the women's movement, have called for a range of policies intended to make it easier for recipients to manage their lives and caring responsibilities (de Wolff, 2003). Both women and men need these structural supports because resolving the contractions between paid employment and family life is not a women's issue but a social issue.

Any measures that ensure greater economic security for the majority of people, such as an adequate income or decent prices for crops and fish, control over hours, improved minimum-wage legislation, employment insurance, pay equity, old-age pensions, higher pay rates and benefits, all provide the recipients with a better standard of living—the basic prerequisite for personal and family life. A range of other services such as long-term and home care for people with disabilities or chronic illnesses, or who are elderly, as well as childcare and education, directly affect the demands that domestic labour makes on individual households. The more public services available, the easier it is for individuals to manage. The more such services are universal, the greater equality is fostered. The struggle over the extent to which governments and employers will assume responsibility for resolving the tensions between paid work and family life is still a major political challenge in the twenty-first century. The ways in which those responsibilities are distributed significantly affect whether or not people can actually form families, and shape the kinds of families and the lives they lead.

Summary

- Domestic labour is often taken for granted as women's work.

- Although domestic labour, especially childcare, is said to be important, it is accorded low status.

- Family-based strategies alone cannot resolve the underlying contradictions between participating in both income-generating work and maintaining a household.

- Both the state and employers have responsibilities for addressing these conflicts.

Notes

1. We thank Bonnie Fox, Ester Reiter, Viola Bartel, Ann Duffy, and Nancy Mandell for their comments on an earlier version.

2. Whenever we have quoted from one of the three case studies, we have indicated which study (Study 1, 2, or 3 and the date of the interview).

3. For a critique of Statistics Canada's approach that argues it seriously underestimates the time involved and value of the labour, see Luxton, 1997, pp. 431–39.

4. Interview by Sara Cummings with the coordinator of the Rosalind Blauer Child Care Centre, Brock University, St. Catharines, Ontario, August 7, 2003.

Critical Thinking Questions

1. What conditions set women up as responsible for domestic labour?

2. What conditions impede men's participation in domestic labour?

3. Why are state and employer policies a more appropriate response than simply leaving individual families to cope with these tensions?

Websites

Labour Force Historic Review
http://www.chass.utoronto.ca/datalib/codebooks/dsp/lfhr2002.htm
   This website contains information on participation in the labour force for women and men over the last century from the document "Labour Force Historical Review."

York University: Gender and Work
http://www.genderwork.ca
   Drawing on statistics and published papers, this website contains valuable information on paid and unpaid labour in Canada.

Human Resources Development Canada
http://labour-travail.hrdc-drhc.gc.ca/worklife
> This website contains reports on worklife including a study of caring friendly provisions in major collective agreements in Canada.

Suggested Reading

Marion Binkely. 2002. *Set Adrift: Fishing Families.* Toronto: University of Toronto Press.
> Women married to men who work in the coastal and deep-sea fishery provide labour necessary both to support their husband's ability to earn an income and to organize their households on a daily basis.

Alice de Wolff. 2003. *Bargaining for a Better Life.* Toronto: Ontario Federation of Labour.
> This informative document outlines a workplace checklist for creating work–life balance. It proposes that employees have more control over their work, enhanced paid and unpaid leaves, and workplace services for children and seniors.

Barbara Ehrenreich. 2001. *Nickel and Dimed: On (Not) Getting By in America.* New York: Metropolitan Books.
> Drawing on her own experiences and her observations as a minimum wage worker, the author analyzed the strategies of minimum wage earners to make ends meet. The benefits of minimum wages and the associated lack of benefits and pensions to the American capitalist economy involve great sacrifices for the workers and their families.

Meg Luxton and June Corman. 2001. *Getting By in Hard Times: Gendered Labour at Home and On the Job.* Toronto: University of Toronto Press.
> Based on working-class households in Hamilton, Ontario, the book charts how families make a living by combining paid employment and unpaid domestic labour and the impact of economic restructuring on their lives.

References

Allahar, Anton, and James Cote. 1998. *Richer and Poorer: The Structure of Inequality in Canada.* Toronto: Lorimer and Co.

Bakan, Abigail, and Daiva Stasiulis. 1997. *Not One of the Family: Foreign Domestic Workers in Canada.* Toronto: University of Toronto Press.

Baker, Maureen. 1995. *Canadian Family Policies: Cross-national Comparison.* Toronto: University of Toronto Press.

Barrett, Michelle, and Mary McIntosh. 1982. *The Anti-Social Family.* London: Verso.

Beauchesne, Eric. 2003. "Many Firms Don't Help Balance Work and Family." *The Leader Post*. Regina, July 7, p. 4.

Bezanson, Kate, Anne O'Connell, and Sheila Neysmith. (forthcoming). *Telling Tales: Living the Halifax Effects of Policy Change*. Fernwood.

Binkley, Marian. 2002. *Set Adrift Fishing Families*. Toronto: University of Toronto Press.

Bradbury, Bettina. 1985. "The Home as Workplace." In Paul Craven, ed., *Labouring Lives: Work and Workers in Nineteenth Century Ontario*, Toronto: University of Toronto Press.

Brand, Dionne. 1983. "A Working Paper on Black Women Toronto: Gender, Race and Class." *Fireweed* 16: 149–55.

Bristow, Peggy, Dionne Brand, Linda Carty, Afua P. Cooper, Sylvia Hamilton, and Adrienne Shadd. 1994. *'We're Rooted Here and They Can't Pull Us Up': Essays in African Canadian Women's History*. Toronto: University of Toronto Press.

Cameron, Barbara, and Cathy Pike. 1972. "Collective Child Care in a Class Society." Discussion Collective #6. Women Unite Toronto: The Canadian Women's Educational Press.

Campbell, Maria 1973. *Halfbreed*. Toronto: McClelland and Stewart.

Chandler, William. 1994. "The Value of Household Work in Canada, 1992." *Canadian Economic Observer*. Statistics Canada. Cat. No. 11-010 (April), 3.1–3.9.

Cohen, Marjorie. 1997. "What Women Should Know About Economic Fundamentalism." *Atlantis: A Women's Studies Journal* 21/2: 4–15.

Connelly, Patricia. 1978. *Last Hired, First Fired Women and the Canadian Work Force*. Toronto: The Women's Press.

Corman, June. 2002. "Returning to the Classroom: Married Women Fill the Void for Teachers in Saskatchewan." *Atlantic: A Women's Studies Journal* 27(1): 77–86.

De Wolff, Alice. 2003. *Bargaining for Work and Life*. Toronto: Canadian Labour Congress, Ontario Coalition for Better Child Care, Ontario Federation of Labour, and the Feminist Political Economy Network, Graduate Programme in Women's Studies, York University.

Duffy, Ann. 1986. "Reformulating Power for Women." *CRSA* 23(1): 22–46.

Duffy, Ann, Nancy Mandell, and Norene Pupo. 1989. *Few Choices: Women, Work and Family*. Toronto: Garamond Press.

Duffy, Ann, and Norene Pupo. 1989. *Part-Time Paradox: Connecting Gender, Work and Family*. Toronto: McClelland and Stewart.

Dumas, Jean, and Alain Belanger. 1997. *Report on the Demographic Situation in Canada 1996*. Ottawa, Statistics Canada, cat. no. 91-209.

Early Childhood Education and Care. 2002. "Diversity or Disparity: Early Childhood Education and Care in Canada." ECEC Indicators Report. October. Found at *www.campaign2000.ca/ci/rep10*.

Fox, Bonnie. (forthcoming.) "Motherhood as a Class Act: The Various Ways in which Intensive Mothering is Entangled with Social Class." In Kate Bezanson and Meg Luxton, eds., *Rethinking Social Reproduction*.

Fox, Bonnie, ed. 1980. *Hidden in the Household: Women's Domestic Labour under Capitalism*. Toronto: Women's Educational Press.

Gaskell, Jane, Arlene McLaren, and Myra Novogrodsky. 1989. *Claiming an Education: Feminism and Canadian Society*. Toronto: Our Schools/Ourselves Education Foundation.

Ghalam, Nancy Zuckenwick. 1997. "Attitudes toward Women, Work and Family." *Canadian Social Trends* 46. Ottawa: Statistics Canada.

Goelman, Hillel, Alan Pence, Donna Lero, Lois Brockman, Ned Glick, and Jonathan Berkowitz. 1993. *Where are the Children?* Ottawa: Statistics Canada, cat. no. 89-527.

Harding, Katherine. 2003. "Few Employers are Topping Up Parental Benefits." *The Globe and Mail*. April 23, p. C3.

Human Resources Development Canada. 2003. www.hrdc-drhc.gc.ca/ae-ei/pubs.

Kubik, Wendee, and Robert J. Moore. 2001. *Women's Diverse Roles In the Farm Economy and the Consequences for their Health, Well-being and Quality of Life*. University of Regina, Campion College.

Le Bourdais, Celine, and Nicole Marcil-Gratton. 1994. "A Quebec's Pro-active Approach to Family Policy: Thinking and Acting Family." In Maureen Baker, ed., *Canada's Changing Families: Challenges to Public Policy*. Ottawa: Vanier Institute of the Family.

Luxton, Meg. 1997. "Women, The United Nations and the Politics of Unpaid Work." *Women's Studies International Forum* special issue on "The Home" 20(3): 431–39.

Luxton, Meg, and June Corman. 2001. *Getting By in Hard Times: Gendered Labour at Home and on the Job*. Toronto: University of Toronto Press.

McKeen, Wendy, and Ann Porter. 2003. "Politics and Transformation: Welfare State Restructuring in Canada." In Wallace Clement and Leah Vosko, eds., *Changing Canada Political Economy as Transformation*. Montreal and Kingston: McGill-Queens University Press, 109–34.

McMahon, Anthony. 1999. *Taking Care of Men: Sexual Politics in the Public Mind*. Cambridge: Cambridge University Press.

O'Connor, Julia, Ann Shola Orloff, and Sheila Shaver. 1999. *States, Markets, Families: Gender, Liberalism and Social Policy in Australia, Canada, Great Britain and the United States*. Cambridge: Cambridge University Press.

OECD. 1981. *The Welfare State in Crisis*. Paris: OECD.

Parr, Joy. 1990. *The Gender of Breadwinners: Women, Men and Change in Two Industrial Towns, 1880–1950*. Toronto: University of Toronto Press.

———. 1995. "Shopping for a Good Stove; A Parable about Gender, Design and the Market." Pp. 75–97. In Joy Parr, ed., *A Diversity of Women: Ontario, 1945–1980.* Toronto: University of Toronto Press.

Prentice, Alison, Paula Bourne, Gail Cuthbert Brandt, Beth Light, Wendy Mitchinson, and Naomi Black. 1988. *Canadian Women: A History.* Toronto: Harcourt, Brace.

Richards, John. 1997. *Retooling the Welfare State.* Toronto: CD Howe.

Sangster, Joan. 1995. *Earning Respect: The Lives of Working Women in Small-Town Ontario, 1920–1960.* Toronto: University of Toronto Press.

Skrypnek, Berna, and Janet Fast. 1996. "Work and Family Policy in Canada: Family Needs, Collective Solutions." *Journal of Family Issues* 17(6): 793–812.

Statistics Canada. 2000. "Women in Canada 2000: A Gender-Based Statistical Report." Ottawa: Industry Canada.

———. 2001. *The Evolution of Wealth Inequality in Canada 1984–1999.* Ottawa: Ministry of Industry, Science and Technology.

———. 2002a. *Historic Labour Force Review.* Ottawa: Ministry of Industry, Science and Technology.

———. 2002b. *Women in Canada: Work Chapter Updates.* Catalogue No. 89F0133XIE Ottawa: Ministry of Industry, Science and Technology.

———. 2003a. "Average Earnings by Sex and Work Pattern, Full-Time and Full-Year." Cansim Table 202-0102. www.statcan.ca/english/Pgdb/labour01a.

———. 2003b. *Census of Canada 2001.* Ottawa: Ministry of Industry, Science and Technology. www12.statcan.ca/english/census01/products/analytic/companion/paid/canada.cfm.

Strong-Boag, Veronica. 1986. "Pulling in Double Harness or Hauling a Double Load: Women, Work and Feminism on the Canadian Prairies." *Journal of Canadian Studies* 21(3): 35–52.

Teghtsoonian, Katherine. 1993. "A Neo-Conservative Ideology and Opposition to Federal Regulation of Child Care Services in Canada and the United States." *Canadian Journal of Political Science* 16(1): 97–122.

United Nations Development Programme. 1995. "Human Development Report." New York and Oxford: Oxford University Press, chapter 4.

Vanier Institute of the Family. 1997. *From the Kitchen Table to the Boardroom.* Ottawa: Vanier Institute of the Family.

Vosko, Leah. 2000. *Temporary Work: The Gendered Rise of a Precarious Employment Relationship.* Toronto: University of Toronto Press.

White, Julie. 1993. *Sisters and Solidarity: Women and Unions in Canada.* Toronto: Thompson Educational Publishing.

Appendix A

This chapter reports on the findings from three case studies conducted by the authors:

1. The Saskatchewan Rural School Teachers Project (June Corman)
   Based on 250 firsthand accounts, collected by Irene Poelzer and June Corman, this project explores the lives of women who began teaching in Saskatchewan between 1910 and 1955.

2. The Hamilton Steelworkers Project (June Corman, David Livingstone, Meg Luxton, and Wally Seccombe with Belinda Leach)
   Between 1983 and 1996 the project conducted four surveys, five different sets of open-ended in-depth interviews, and one time budget study. This included interviews with 196 steelworkers (2 women and 194 men) who were members of Local 1005 employed by Stelco at Hilton Works in Hamilton, Ontario; 187 people (2 men and 185 women) who were partners with one of the steelworkers interviewed; 34 (22 men and 12 women) steelworkers who had been laid off by Stelco; 26 women who were involved in the campaign to get women hired at Stelco or who were hired as a result of the campaign; and 798 randomly selected people from the Hamilton area. Subsequently, follow up interviews were conducted with a total of 103 participants. For details of this project, see Luxton and Corman, 2001, pp. 267–70 "Appendix A Data Collection Strategies."

3. The Caregiving Among Family, Friends, Neighbours, and Community Project (Meg Luxton)
   A total of 137 in-depth interviews were conducted in Toronto, Ontario between January 1999 and January 2002 with 97 women and 40 men. The interviews investigated what is involved in negotiating, informal caregiving among family, friends, neighbours, and communities.

Glossary

Numbers in parentheses refer to the chapter(s) containing the main discussion of the term.

absolute poverty

a condition of mere physical survival, most closely approximated by homelessness. (9)

"best interests of the child" approach

refers to the standard typically applied under current family law provisions in Canada and the United States in which the paramount standard in deciding custody and access is "the best interests of the child." (7)

black Loyalists

blacks who had been granted freedom in the American colonies for supporting the British. (2)

"blaming the victim"

holding those whose situation is produced by structural factors beyond their control responsible for their situation in life. (9)

blended family

a family that contains spouses who may have been divorced, widowed, or never married, and with or without children. Within this family unit are various configurations of stepparents and step-/adopted siblings, as well as stepgrandparents/ aunts/uncles/cousins. (1, 8)

capitalist society

an economy based on private ownership of productive facilities and reliant on wage labour provided by the majority of the population. Profit maximization is the primary objective of economic activity. (12)

census definition of family

the census, which is taken every five years, counts what it calls the census family; refers to a now-married couple (with or without never-married sons and/or daughters of either or both spouses), a couple living common-law (again with or without never-married sons and/or daughters of either or both partners), or a lone parent of any marital status, with at least one never-married son or daughter living in the same dwelling. (1)

Centre for Contemporary Cultural Studies

refers to an academic centre founded in the 1970s at the University of Birmingham, England, where the researchers and theorists explored the roles of hegemony and counter-hegemony in modern society. In particular, they tended to focus on the ways in which resistance to hegemony and challenges to the dominant groups were embedded in popular, youth culture. (3)

child-support guidelines

a policy implemented by the Canadian government in 1997 to standardize and improve the determination of child-support awards by linking the amount awarded to the income of the payer. (10)

civil union partners

a new status created in June 2002 when Quebec enacted Bill 84 and that is open to both unmarried opposite-sex and same-sex conjugal partners. This legal status accords almost all the same benefits and obligations as formal marriage. (7)

cohabitation

living together without legal marriage. (1)

cohort

a group of individuals born in the same year (for example, 1970) or within the same period of time (for example, a five- or 10-year period). Sometimes those cohorts whose members have experienced and reacted similarly to significant social, political, or historical events that emerged at particular points in their life cycle come to be characterized in a particular way, such as "baby boomers" or "Generation Xers." (11)

common-law couples

common-law spouses have been given many of the rights and responsibilities of married couples as to support, employment benefits, and custody and support of children. (1)

communal family

a group of families sharing financial resources, responsibilities, and living arrangements. (2)

compulsory heterosexuality

the belief that people are naturally attracted to the opposite sex and that, therefore, gay and lesbian relations are unnatural or inferior to heterosexual relations. (10)

concealed homelessness

living temporarily with friends or family. (9)

conjugal family

a form of nuclear family in which the emphasis is on the marital bond. (1)

counter-hegemony

like "hegemony," also developed by Gramsci; refers to the potential for marginal groups to fight back against the forces that oppress them—challenging and mocking powerful dominant institutions. (3)

cult of domesticity

a Victorian ideal that made women responsible for the moral and everyday affairs of the home. (2)

cultural capital

the cultural and financial resources to support a middle-class lifestyle. (9)

culture of poverty

the view that poor families tend to develop fatalistic values and attitudes about their lot in life, devaluing education, career aspirations, and the usual middle-class definitions of success. (9)

culture shock

a sense of bewilderment with a new way of life and the sense that one is a "foreigner." (4)

dead-beat dads

noncustodial fathers who are in arrears in their child-support payments. (8)

depth of poverty

a measure of poverty that refers to how far below the poverty line a family's income is. (9)

deviance model of divorce

a sociological and psychological perspective that tends to view divorce as a social problem. (8)

domestic labour

all those activities required to maintain a home and care for people who live in it. It involves at least three distinct types of work: housework, managing household economics, and caregiving. (2, 12)

donor insemination (DI)

refers to the process whereby a woman may seek to become pregnant by insemination with a donor's sperm. This is a practice that may occur in a medical context as part of the new reproductive technology, or it may be undertaken privately. This process would be an important option for lesbians who wish to become parents. (7)

duration of poverty

the amount of time that a household lives in poverty. (9)

economic immigrants

those who migrate for better opportunities for employment and income for themselves and/or their families. (4)

ethnocentrism

viewing and judging the world with one's own ethnic group as a reference point. (2)

exchange/social control theory

the theoretical perspective that approaches family violence in terms of a win–loss calculation. Victimizers employ violence because they can; that is, it achieves their desired goals and does not result in undesired costs. In particular, victimizers achieve control over family members. (6)

extended family

encompasses the nuclear family and all other relatives. (2)

failure of intimacy

primarily the concern of women when they do not achieve the emotional closeness that they desire in their romantic relationships. (5)

familial ideology

the idea that the nuclear-family unit, comprising husband, wife, and their dependent children, is the "normal" and highest form of family. (10)

familialism

the glorification of an idealized nuclear family—a family construed as consisting of a socially and legally recognized heterosexual couple. (6)

family

a social ideal, generally referring to a unit of economic cooperation, typically thought to include only those related by blood, but revised by feminists to include those forming an economically cooperative, residential unit bound by feelings of common ties and strong emotion. (1, 10)

family-based economy

a form of economic production wherein the household is a basic unit of the economy and the site for most of the production and distribution of goods, services, and income. (2)

family law

the legal rules that govern spousal and/or parent–child relationships both during and after the dissolution of a family unit, as well as the relationship between families and the state. (10)

family reunification

a governmental policy of allowing immigrants to sponsor their family members from abroad; in practice, not all family ties are recognized in the same way at all times. Canadian policy currently does not recognize, for example, the married children of immigrants or their children over 19 as being in the same class as their other children. (4)

family stress theory

a theory that approaches family violence and abuse in terms of the stressors that impact on family life. These
stressors may be personal (pregnancy,
unemployment) or institutional/
structural (military conflict). (6)

family violence

the complex array of behaviours—
physical, emotional, financial, and
sexual—that singly or in combination intentionally result in harm for
one or more members of a family
group. (6)

family wage

a wage paid to a male worker
deemed sufficient to support an
economically dependent wife and
children. (2, 12)

fathers' rights

the social movement based on the
assumption that fathers have lost
legal rights as a result of family-law
reforms, particularly regarding custody of children. (10)

feminism

a worldview based on the assumptions that, historically, women have
occupied a subordinate status relative
to men in most societies, and that
women must mobilize politically to
achieve equality with men; diverse
political theories and principles
interrogating and advocating social,
economic, cultural, and political
equality for women. (4, 10)

feminization of poverty

a marked increase in the number of
women living in poverty, particularly elderly women and sole-sup-
port mothers, that has characterized
Canadian society during the late
nineteenth and late twentieth centuries; the tendency for a woman
to be poor without the support of a
man. (9, 10)

filial obligation or piety

a felt need, duty, or moral obligation
to honour and care for one's parents
in their later years of life. (11)

les filles du roi

the poor and orphaned young
women sent from Paris in the sev-
enteenth century to become wives
of men in the colony of New
France. (2)

formal equality

the liberal principle that, regardless
of differences (e.g., gender), every
citizen is equal under the law and
is entitled to the same legal and
civil rights and opportunities. (10)

Frankfurt School of Social Research

refers to a German school of social
research that was founded in 1923
and that became best known for
critiques of modern capitalism. The
school's leading theorists, Theodor
Adorno, Max Horkheimer, and
Herbert Marcuse, fled from Nazi
Germany and played an important
part in analyzing mass culture and
control through culture in North
America. (3)

functionalist theory

describes a view of society as a
system made up of functional,
interdependent parts. (1)

gender roles

socially constructed attitudes and
behaviour, usually organized
dichotomously as masculinity and
femininity, and based on the cultural expectations associated with
gender. (2)

generation

kinship lineage positions in families (such as the "parental" generation or the "child" generation). This term is often misused to describe age groups or age cohorts. (11)

"get self-sufficient quick"

a legal-context orientation primarily directed to those women who have interrupted their employment for marriage and/or childcare. This approach assumes that in most current marriages both spouses have careers, and that wives generally have worked full time or intermittently throughout the marriage. This orientaton, reinforced by judicial indifference to gender-based wage inequalities, influences decisions regarding retraining periods for the dependent spouse. (8)

glass ceiling

a structural barrier, invisible to the naked eye, through which those beneath gaze upward at the lifestyle and opportunities of the more privileged above. (9)

hegemony

a term developed by the early twentieth century Italian revolutionary Antonio Gramsci; refers to the ways groups in power (such as upper classes) are able to maintain their privileged position by developing strategies to ensure that marginal/oppressed groups consent to their power. (3)

heteronormativity

the taken-for-granted assumption that heterosexuality is a *natural* sexual orientation. (5)

heterosexual, nuclear family

a living arrangement that includes only a woman and a man and possibly children. (12)

homemaker

a woman who has taken on responsibility for domestic labour and who is financially dependent on her spouse/partner. (12)

homophilic

a term coined by Jesse Bernard (1985) that describes nonsexual, same-sex friendships. (5)

homophobia

refers to a fear, dislike, or hatred of homosexuality and homosexuals. A distinction is made between **public homophobia**, in which this fear, dislike, or hatred is embedded in societal activities, and **private homophobia**, which refers to this fear, dislike, and hatred as it occurs on a personal level. (7)

honour killings

instances in which family members or agents of the family kill a member of the family (typically female) who is perceived by the family to have dishonoured the family by her behaviour; for example, engaging in sexual relations outside of marriage. (6)

household

refers to people who occupy the same dwelling, and can consist of one or more families, a single person, or a group of related or unrelated people; for example, brothers and sisters, a live-in nanny, or apartment mates. (2)

ideological assumptions
taken-for-granted, widely shared cultural ideas that profoundly influence our perceptions and behaviour. (5)

ideological hegemony
processes by which ruling-class ideas become dominant in society through consensus or coercion. (1)

ideology
a system of beliefs that distorts reality at the same time that it provides justification for the status quo. (2)

income-generating work
the activities involved in making a living, such as running a business, farming, fishing, or earning a wage or salary. (12)

intergenerational relations
patterns of interaction with individuals in different generations of the family lineage, either in older generations, such as parents and grandparents, aunts, and uncles, or in younger generations, such as children and grandchildren, nieces, and nephews. (11)

intergenerational transmission
See social learning. (6)

intimacy
a desirable goal for romantic relationships involving emotional and sexual closeness. (5)

Intimacy Discourse
dominant rhetoric about romantic relationships that constructs our ideas about what intimacy is, and how, where, and with whom it can be achieved. (5)

intimacy work
the efforts that people, typically women, expend with the goal of achieving emotional closeness in their romantic relations. (5)

intragenerational relations
patterns of interaction with individuals who hold similar lineage positions within the family, such as the spouse or partner, brothers and sisters, brothers- and sisters-in-law, and cousins. (11)

joint custody
a legal concept based on the assumption that, when parents separate or divorce, they should share legal and/or custodial responsibility for their children. Regardless of residence, both parents have legal rights in decision-making regarding the child's welfare, including education and religious upbringing. (10)

lesbian baby boom
refers to the recent upsurge in the number of lesbians becoming mothers through a variety of processes including adoption, surrogacy, and donor insemination. (7)

lesbigays
abbreviation for lesbians and gay males. (1)

life expectancy
the average number of years of life remaining at a given age (e.g., at birth, or at age 65). (11)

lone-parent family
a household in which one parent resides with his or her children. (1, 9)

marriage
an institution which has, so far, been legally and socially defined as a union between a man and a woman. (1)

materialist theory

a view of society that sees how an individual satisfies his or her economic needs for food, clothing, and security as conditioning or determining their social, cultural, and political relationships. (1)

matrilineal

based on ancestry and inheritance traced through the mother. (1, 2, 4)

matrilocal/patrilocal

the practice of living with bride's/ groom's family after marriage. (2)

meritocracy

the belief that all have an equal chance of success and that those at the top are those with the most merit. (9)

metanarratives

the definitive, grand, or incontrovertible accounts of a series of events. (1)

monogamy

marriage to one person at a time; this practice is upheld in Canadian society in our customs, laws, and religious beliefs. (2)

multigenerational households

households with at least three generations including grandparents, parents, and grandchildren (used to be called "extended families"). (1)

near poor

families whose standard of living is very close to that of the poor. (9)

neolocal

describes the practice of living with neither the bride nor the groom's family after marriage. (1)

nexus approach

refers to the approach taken by judges in Canada and many American states by which they do not assume that homosexuality by itself (the *per se* approach) means a parent is unfit but rather seek to determine what effect, if any, the parent's sexual orientation will have on the well-being of the child. (7)

"no-fault" divorce

a legal concept based on the assumption that terminating a marriage relationship should not be contingent upon one or both spouses each demonstrating that the other was to blame for the marital breakdown because of adultery, mental or physical cruelty, and so on. (8, 10)

nonbiological lesbian mothers

refers to the lesbian partner who does not give birth to the lesbian couple's child but who provides contributions in terms of childcare, financial support, and so on. These co-parents have typically been denied legal rights (for example, visitation rights, custody rights) by the courts. (7)

nuclear family

usually regarded as married parents and their children. Nuclear families come in two forms: families of origin or orientation (those we are born into and raised in) and families of procreation (those we form through marriage and in which we raise our children). (2, 10, 12)

objective poverty

the prevailing definitions used by bodies whose purpose it is to collect, compile, and report data on poverty within the Canadian population, such as Statistics Canada and the Canadian Council on Social Development. (9)

patriarchal family (theory)
a theoretical viewpoint that sees the male breadwinner/female domestic labourer model as natural, universal, and essential. (1, 6, 10)

patrilineal
based on kinship traced through the father's line. (1, 4)

patrilocal
See matrilocal. (2)

pedophilia
refers to a psychological disorder in which the afflicted individual is sexually attracted (sometimes exclusively) to young children or adolescents (of the same or opposite sex). This disorder is falsely associated with homosexuality. (7)

PLUR
an acronym referring to the philosophy of peace, love, unity, and respect, which is embraced by some youth in the rave culture. (3)

polygamy
the practice of one person being married to several others of the opposite sex. (1)

population aging
a demographic phenomenon in which, because of decreased fertility and increased life expectancy, an increasing percentage of the population is made up of older people. (11)

post-familial family
a phrase coined by Elizabeth Beck-Gernsheim (1999) to signal the way in which people are able to choose their family relationships more now than in the past. (5)

postmodernism
in the social sciences, modernism is usually contrasted with postmodernism, which designates a new social condition that contemporary advanced industrial societies are alleged to have reached and that questions some of the fundamental assumptions of the Enlightenment tradition in the West including: belief in rational progress; universal standards and values; singular truth; and objective standards of truth. (1)

potential homelessness
living on the verge of homelessness. (9)

poverty gap
the amount relative to the poverty line that would have to be transferred to poor families to bring their incomes up to the poverty line, which is an income level considered minimally sufficient to sustain a family in terms of food, housing, clothing, medical needs, and so on. (9)

production
the act or process of bringing or making; the creation of utility: the making of goods available for human wants. (1)

public/private split
the notion that the world of the family is private, and therefore separate from and uninfluenced by the public world of work and other social institutions. (10)

"quasi widowhood"
the situation in which one partner in a couple resides permanently in a long-term-care institution while the other continues to reside in the community. Also known as "married widowhood." (11)

quintile
one of the groups produced when the population is divided into fifths on the basis of wealth. (9)

racialized

a term that indicates the reality that some groups of people, due to their physical appearance and frequently because of the way they live, are categorized by a powerful or dominant group as being qualitatively different from it; so different, in fact, that they are held to belong to separate classes of beings (usually inferior), or "races." (4)

racism

a bias against other groups besides your own, especially when it is a systematic bias; can be applied to both cultural and racial groups (see Isajiw, 1999, p. 144). (4)

rave

a culture of youth whose members are renowned for their interest in computer-generated techno music, the use of amphetamine drugs, and attendance at all-night parties known as raves. (3)

refugee claimants or asylum seekers

people who have not yet been adjudged to be refugees but who come to Canada and claim refugee status at the border or within the country. (4)

refugees

people with a well-grounded fear of persecution or danger on grounds specified by the United Nations Convention on Refugees (such as ethnicity, race, religion, gender, and political affiliation). (4)

relative poverty

poverty as measured against contemporary standards for "normal" and "wealthy." (9)

reproduction

the act or process of reproducing; the act of forming, creating, or bringing into existence again. (1)

resource theory

a theoretical approach that considers the availability of resources as a critical element in the etiology of family violence. Families that lack financial, emotional, or other resources (poverty, isolation) are understood as being at increased risk of abuse and violence. (6)

romantic love

idealized or sentimental love. (2, 5)

same-sex couple

partners of the same sex who share a relationship; such couples have recently gained standing as common-law partners. (1)

sandwich generation

individuals, usually in midlife, who are "caught" between the simultaneous demands of dependent children and elderly parents or other relatives. (11)

second parent adoption

a legal step that allows the nonbiological parent to assume rights and responsibilities as a parent without requiring the original parent to forfeit his or her parenting status. Lesbian and gay parents have increasingly sought this option to protect their rights and describe their responsibilities. (7)

serial monogamy

refers to sequential marriage patterns of marriage, divorce, marriage. (1)

sex/gender division of labour

a situation in which typically, men would engage in income-generating work and women would have responsibility for domestic labour. (12)

shared household

refers to grandparents and grandchildren living in the same home, which may be either a multigenerational (including the middle generation), or a skip-generation (no middle generation present) household. (1)

single mother on welfare

refers to women who, through marital/common-law separation (or the birth of a child to a never-married woman), find themselves applying for and receiving social assistance, and the negative myths that accompany them. (8)

skip-generations

grandparents who live with only grandchildren and no middle generation. (1)

social capital

refers to social networks, norms, and trust that facilitate coordination for mutual benefits. Individuals generally draw upon actual resources (economic, human, or cultural capital) or networks of resources. (1)

social interaction vantage point

the mid-level vantage point in theorizing that seeks to transcend purely individual (psychological) explanations but not address societal/structural concerns; for example, addressing child abuse in terms of the specifics of the mother–child or father–child relationship and patterns of interaction reflects this social interaction approach. Socialization is a prominent example of this approach. (6)

socialist feminism/feminists

feminism that links the liberation of women with the liberation of the working classes. (10)

socialization

refers to the process whereby individuals learn how to think and behave according to the norms of their society and/or of their subgroup. This concept generally refers to children, but the process is lifelong. (1)

socialization literature

the wealth of research and theory that has examined the processes by which each individual is socially constructed. In particular, through the early years of life, the family, peers, media, and educational system (and related institutions) along with other social agents directly and indirectly inform the individual's beliefs, values, attitudes, and emotions. (6)

social learning/intergenerational transmission

the theoretical perspective in the sociology of family violence that calls attention to the ways in which children growing up in a violent family learn violent roles and, subsequently, may play out the roles of victim or victimizer in their adult families. (6)

social reproduction

the view that social class is reproduced intergenerationally as a result of structural factors such as capitalism and patriarchy; the activities required to ensure the day-to-day and generational reproduction of the population. (9, 12)

sodomy laws

laws that ban specific consensual as well as nonconsensual sexual activities; notably, oral copulation and anal intercourse. (7)

spouse

any two persons who live together in a "marriage-like" relationship for at least two years. (1)

subjective poverty

how people feel about their standard of poverty. (9)

substantive equality

the principle that, regardless of differences (e.g., gender), every member of a society is entitled to equality or equal outcomes under law and policy. (10)

surrogacy

refers to the process whereby a woman agrees in a formal or informal contract to become pregnant and give birth and then turn over all or most rights to that child to another individual or couple. There are two types of surrogacy: **traditional** surrogacy, in which a surrogate mother is artificially inseminated either with sperm from the intended father or from an anonymous donor and carries the baby to term, and **gestational** surrogacy, in which an egg is removed from the mother and fertilized with the sperm of the intended father or anonymous donor. The fertilized egg is then implanted in the womb of the surrogate mother, who carries the baby to term. For example, in a lesbian couple, one woman might donate the fertilized ovum and her partner might carry the resultant baby to term. (7)

symbolic interactionism

a theoretical perspective frequently employed in the socialization literature. The emphasis here is on the ways in which symbols (ranging from language to clothing to gesture) are learned through the process of socialization and in the process become key to understanding the ways in which members of society communicate (or fail to) with one another when they interact. (6)

systemic discrimination

standard policies, procedures, and practices that result in the disadvantaging of a disempowered group. (9)

traditional family

generally refers to the patriarchal family (*see* patriarchal family). (1)

underemployment

being employed below one's level of education/training. (11)

vertical intergenerational mobility

the tendency for children to be upwardly or downwardly mobile vis-à-vis their parents. (9)

visible minorities

people who state that they are not white and not Caucasian but who are not Aboriginal in their descent. (4)

working poor

families in which the main breadwinner works at least 49 weeks of the year but that remain poor. (9)

youth culture

refers to the historical emergence of a set of beliefs, values, attitudes, norms, styles, and tastes associated with the younger (teen) segment of the Canadian population. (3)

Name Index

Subject Index